For Another E

A Class Analysis of European Economic Integration

GUGLIELMO CARCHEDI

V

VERSO

London • New York

First published by Verso 2001
© Guglielmo Carchedi 2001
All rights reserved

Verso
UK: 6 Meard Street, London W1F 0EG
USA: 180 Varick Street, New York, NY 10014–4606

Verso is the imprint of New Left Books
www.versobooks.com

ISBN 1–85984–610–6 (hbk)
ISBN 1–85984–319–0 (pbk)

British Library Cataloguing in Publication Data
A catalogue record for this book is available from the British Library

Library of Congress Cataloging-in-Publication Data
Carchedi, Guglielmo.
    For another Europe: a class analysis of European economic integration / Guglielmo Carchedi.
    p. cm.
    Includes bibliographical references and index.
    ISBN 1-85984-319-0 (pbk.) — ISBN 1-85984-610-6 (cloth)
    1. Europe—Economic integration. 2. Social classes—Europe. 3. Capitalism—Europe. 4.
Europe—Economic conditions—1945—Regional disparities. 5. European Union
countries—Economic policy. 6. European Union countries—Social policy. 7. European
federation. 8. Marxian economics. I. Title.
HC241.C366 2001
337.1'42—dc21   00-069676

Typeset in 9½/11pt ITC New Baskerville by
SetSystems Ltd, Saffron Walden, Essex
Printed by Biddles Ltd, Guildford and King's Lynn

Contents

List of Tables and Figures

Tables

Figures

Introduction

Books on the economics of the European Union abound. Yet almost all of them share the same theoretical matrices: they are inspired either by neo-classical or by Keynesian economics. This book argues that neither of these two approaches can provide a satisfactory account of the origin and development of the European Union. Only a work based on the production and distribution of value as the economy's bedrock, and thus on social classes as the basic unit of social life, can throw light on those internal contradictions which are the real source and motor of the process of European economic integration. Two specific features emerge from this approach. On the one hand, those topics usually dealt with in textbooks on the European Union (competition and social policies, the Economic and Monetary Union, the Common Agricultural Policy, etc.) are treated in what follows in a manner that challenges the received view. On the other, subject matters ignored in those textbooks (development and underdevelopment, the economics of the Common Defence Policy, the role of interest groups in the Union's decision-making process, etc.) are shown to be of fundamental importance for a complete analysis and understanding of the economics of the European Union. As a result, this book is not only an introduction to, but also a radical critique of, European economic integration.

The theme around which this work revolves is that the European Union is not, or at least is not only, a heterogeneous collection of states with widely divergent economic and political power. But neither is it a homogeneous economic and political entity. The degree of economic, political, social and cultural heterogeneity among its fifteen member states is undoubtedly greater than that of its two major rivals (the United States and Japan). This is certainly one of the major causes of the Union's weakness in terms of that grand project which is the construction of a new super-power. However, in the course of the past four decades, the European Union has emerged as an entity of its own; it has been forging features which cannot be reduced to the simple summation or combination of those of its member states. It is on these distinctive aspects that this work focuses, rather than on what demarcates the member states. The basic thesis is that three coordinates both delimit and inform Europe's economic integration and thus unification process.

First, this process has been fuelled by European oligopolies under the leadership of German oligopolies. As a result, the European Union has reproduced within itself some of the features of both old and new imperialism. Second, the same process has resulted in the emergence of a new powerful economic bloc with its own imperialist ambitions towards non-member countries. This will necessarily lead to increasing confrontations with the other two economic leaders, the US and Japan. However, as matters stand now, the Union is still a 'weak superpower' due to its internal political and cultural heterogeneity and its almost total dependence upon US military might. Third, the European working class has been locked out as much as possible from the construction of the European Union. But this does not mean that its presence has not been felt. On the contrary, the whole project has been shaped by the need either to appease it (see the Common Agricultural Policy) or to make it pay for the process of integration (see the Economic and Monetary Union). Moreover, certain phases of this process have been stalled by European labour, as in the case of the first attempt to launch the Economic and Monetary Union in 1969–74. European economic integration is the outcome of the interplay among these three interrelated forces.

A few words on the organization of the book are in order. Chapter 1 ('History, Institutions and Enlargements') carries the message that, from the very beginning, the EU project had two interrelated aspects. On the one hand, it was conceived as an economic power (possibly to result in a unified, federalist, European state) able to compete with the world hegemony of the US. On the other, it bore the imprint of an anti-socialist project. This in a double sense. A united Europe was meant to contain and to destroy the Soviet bloc. At the same time, the same project was part and parcel of the post-war fight against the growing influence of European communist parties and social movements.

Europe has thus been from the very beginning capital's Europe. It has been said that in the conscious construction of European integration, labour has been always there, as the enemy to be reckoned with and neutralized. As a result, the European institutions – including the Commission, the Parliament and the Council of Ministers – could not but contain and express these anti-democratic, anti-socialist features. Chapter 1 introduces the major European institutions as well as their transformation through the years, and thus at the same time it introduces the class content of these institutions and thus of the construction of a unified Europe. It provides the framework within which to analyse (in the following chapters) the specificity of the imperialist nature and class content of the different aspects of European economic integration.

But chapter 1 has also another, equally important, function. European decision-making institutions not only express but also mediate between different and often contradictory interests. Even though the focus of this book is on the economic aspects, a proper understanding of these aspects requires at least an acquaintance with the institutional setting emanating from those economic policies. For these reasons, chapter 1 is basic for a proper understanding of the EU.

Chapter 2 ('The Ideology of Economic Integration') would seem to fall without a narrowly defined work on European economic integration. Yet it is of vital importance. One of the book's key themes is that mainstream economics cannot explain the process of European unification. This chapter's task is that of proving this point. More specifically, texts on European economic integration not only deal with more or less the same topics but also do so from the same perspective, mainstream neo-classical or Keynesian economics. The aim of this book is that of providing (a) an introduction to the same topics (as well as to other themes) from a Marxist perspective and (b) at the same time a topic-by-topic critique and refutation of the mainstream approach. The ideal reader will compare approaches, and the explanatory validity, for each of the topics dealt with. This holds also for the usual chapter on the 'pure' theory of economic integration that opens standard texts. To refute this theory, the reader is asked to take on the basics of mainstream economics. However, the task is facilitated by the fact that no concepts are taken for granted and that they are explained as the need arises. By debunking the neo-classical approach to economic integration, chapter 2 opens the way to an alternative, Marxist, approach.

Chapters 3 and 4 inquire into the relationship between different levels of technological development, the appropriation of international value, the formation of international prices, international trade, and the crystallization of the world economy into two major economic blocs. Chapter 3 ('A Value Theory of European Economic Integration') starts with a Marxist theory of capitalist production, based on the production of value and surplus value. This is the basis upon which both a theory of economic crises and cycles and a theory of international prices are built. Particularly important is a theory of exchange rates which stresses that exchange rates, far from being only a technical arrangement for the conversion of different currencies, are a mechanism rewarding the technological leaders and punishing the technological laggards. From the point of view of value appropriation, devaluations and revaluations have not only (un)favourable effects on importers and exporters. They also make possible international streams (appropriation) of value from the technological laggards to the technological leaders. This appropriation of value is one of the basic laws of movement of the capitalist system. This all provides the framework within which to analyse stock exchange and international monetary crises. Economic integration is placed against this background. It is shown that its motive force has nothing to do with the achievement of comparative advantages. Rather, it is the need for capitals to realize the highest rate of profit (if need be abroad) which propels both international trade and economic integration.

Chapter 4 ('The Economic and Monetary Union') is the logical sequel of the previous chapter. It argues for the primary importance of technological competitiveness and for the advantages deriving from it to the European Union as one of the major economic blocs. The EMU is seen as the first real threat posed by the EU to the United States and thus as the first real threat posed by EU imperialism to US imperialism. This calls for a discussion of different types of imperialism, on the specificity of EU imperialism, and on the level of competitiveness of the EU. Oligopolies and oligopolistic competition are defined and the EU competition policy analysed and shown to favour Europe's oligopolies. The EMU is shown to be functional for the interests of Europe's advanced (i.e. oligopolistic) capital under the leadership of Germany's oligopolies. The costs of the EMU are shown to be borne by Europe's labour and an assessment is made of the reasons why the weaker capitals and countries have joined this project. The conditions for the Euro to become a real challenger of the US dollar are also examined.

Chapter 5 ('The Geo-politics of the Euro') continues the analysis of the EMU, but by placing it now in a geo-political context. The central theme is the appropriation of value through international seigniorage. After a clarification of national and international seigniorage, full dollarization is analysed, with particular reference to Latin America, and the conclusion is reached that dollarization is one of the strategies the US is deploying in order to counter the rise of the Euro as a competitor of the dollar.

The next chapter ('Trade, Development and Wars') reviews those international trade organizations and agreements which masquerade the search for maximum profits by commercial capital in the most powerful countries as if they were aimed at facilitating the attainment of universal comparative advantages through generalized free trade. Further, it builds upon this analysis and considers how the power relations between the EU on the one side and two specific groups of countries on the other promote either lack of (capitalist) development or dependent development in those countries. Finally, it evaluates the military arm of the EU (the Western European Union) as a means to impose its trade and (under)development policies on other countries. It concludes that the EU, in spite of its economic might, lacks not only the political homogeneity but also the military power needed for the Euro to replace the US dollar. For the foreseeable feature, the Euro can be at most a rival of the dollar.

The seventh chapter ('The Common Agricultural Policy') deals with that area of the EU that accounts for about 50 per cent – thus a highly significant proportion – of the EU budget. The chapter starts by reviewing the several periods of the CAP and analyses the changes in the green rates from the point of view of the appropriation of value within the EU. Further, it inquires into the question as to who loses and who wins from the process of capital concentration and centralization fostered by the CAP. It then analyses the relation between the formation of international food prices and world hunger and relates this analysis to a value theory of European agricultural protectionism. It concludes by examining the relationship between the CAP and the environment.

The next area the book deals with is EU social policies. This is the theme of chapter 8. If the focus is on those indicators that are important for labour, like unemployment, social degradation, income and regional inequalities, environmental destruction and resurgent racial conflicts, the EU record is poor indeed. It is argued that social policy has traditionally been of secondary importance for the Union, with the exception of the great season of workers' militancy and egalitarian movements. More specifically, this chapter focuses on policies concerned with redistribution, employment, the regions and immigration. The Schengen System is given due attention. Its two major features, social control and the criminalization of foreign labour, are emphasized. The thesis is developed that, rather than accepting xenophobic and racists' social values, Europe's labour should press for greater representative and participatory power for 'foreign' labour as a means for labour as a whole to achieve greater representative and participatory power.

Finally, chapter 9 concludes this work. It argues that a different Europe should be built upon social relations based on solidarity, egalitarianism and self-determination, and that only economic and social policies inspired by these principles can propel Europe's labour beyond purely defensive visions and policies. It also argues that these policies are perfectly feasible, that, yes, they are a utopia but a realizable one. Another Europe is possible, a Europe based not on increasing but on diminishing social and economic polarization; not on the strengthening but on the reduction and abolition of Europe's imperialist relations with the dominated countries of the world; not on the multiplication of legislative and executive bureaucratic institutions but on really democratic organs of self-determination; ultimately not on the egoism secreted by capitalist relations and the market but on solidarity.

As the process of European unification develops, its effects are increasingly felt by the European masses. A project which for decades has (rightly) met with popular indifference (and sometimes resistance) is now being increasingly questioned by those who pay for it in terms of deteriorating living and working conditions. Ultimately, this work's success will depend upon whether and in what measure it will have shown not only that this Europe should be rejected and that another Europe is possible, but also upon whether and in what measure it will have contributed to the emergence of an alternative consciousness, to the strengthening of movements resisting capital's Europe and fighting for labour's Europe.

History, Institutions and Enlargements

1.1 Three Perspectives on European Integration

The emergence of the European Union (EU) through its different phases can be interpreted through different theoretical perspectives. The most influential, nowadays, are the (neo-)institutionalist and the intergovermentalist. The former explains integration basically as the result of a structural necessity: once an institution has been formed, its effects spill over to other areas of integration. The 'spill-over' is the basic dynamic factor. New forms of institutionalism have abandoned the automatism implied in the spill-over effect and recognize the possibility of setbacks in the process of integration, that is, the 'spill-backs', due to, for example, political factors. The intergovermentalist approach, on the other hand, stresses the different states' interests as the principal dynamic factor. Within this approach, integration advances when the interests of the major European states in it are mutually compatible.[1]

A third option, based on class analysis, while potentially much more fruitful, has been expelled, for obvious ideological reasons, from official academic discourse. This is, nevertheless, the perspective to be adopted in this work. Very schematically, the essence (or structure) of society is seen as being its social relations. If they are, as they are under capitalism, contradictory, they can be the condition either of their own reproduction or of their own supersession. This contradictory functionality is their social content. In order to reproduce (or supersede) themselves, social relations must determine their own conditions of reproduction or supersession. Particularly important for the purposes of this work are institutions. The way social relations and institutions interrelate can be seen as follows.

Social relations determine institutions because the former are the conditions of existence of the latter in the sense that social relations transfer their contradictory social content (i.e. the functionality for their own reproduction or supersession) to institutions. But this is not sufficient for social relations to be their own condition of reproduction or of supersession. To this end, they must take a concrete form. Institutions are one of the many forms of appearance of relations. At the same time, institutions are determined by social relations because the former are the conditions of reproduction or possibly of supersession of the latter in the sense that, owing to the contradictory nature of the social content they got from those social relations, some institutions become conditions of existence and others become conditions of supersession of social relations. Institutions fulfil the task of being conditions of reproduction or of supersession of social relations by interacting with each other. The changing form taken by institutions is the result of this interaction, as well as of the interaction each institution has with all other forms of appearance of social relations.

More specifically, within a capitalist system, national states are seen as the result of containing, shaping and directing the conflicts among and within the different classes, fractions of classes, and other social groups (i.e. the manifestations of the capitalist social relations) constituting that system. Given the international nature of capitalism, and thus of the classes constituting it, a national state is the expression of social, and ultimately of class, strife on a global as well as on a national level. Moreover, contradictory class relations give rise to a whole series of other institutions, besides national states, some national and some international. Of the latter, some represent the interests of only a few member states while others aim at representing the general interests of the greatest possible number of states and thus of the dominant classes in those states, even if through a very mediated and contradictory process. It is this constant interrelation among all the forms of manifestation of class relations which shapes concrete local, national and supranational institutions, but it is these latter's determination by classes and their struggle which gives them their specific class content.

Class analysis differs from the (neo-)institutionalist approach in that supranational institutions are seen as concretizations of the interests of (perhaps nascent) social classes, or fractions of classes, or interclass social groups. From this angle, the spill-over or spill-back effects are the result of the conscious action by these social groups (classes) in fostering the conditions of their own reproduction or in checking them, neutralizing them or possibly transforming them into their opposite, that is, in the conditions of their own supersession.[2] As for the intergovermentalist approach, class analysis differs from it in that it stresses both the centrality and the international nature of classes. Therefore, it sees the so-called 'international community' as a complex structure of international organizations (like the UN, the IMF, the World Bank, the WTO), of regional organizations (like the EU, NATO, the ASEA, Mercosur, the OSCE), of NGOs, and of national states as being the expression of, and thus as fostering, opposing interests grounded in the last analysis in social classes both within nations and on a global scale.

Let us consider now how these different frames of reference produce different perspectives of the process of European integration. When the story is told, both the intergovermentalist and the (neo-)institutionalist approaches place emphasis on the following factors:

- the realization that European nations were no longer large enough to hold their own in world markets;
- the desire to avoid economic protectionism, which had characterized

inter-war Europe and which was widely thought to have been one of the causes of the Second World War;

- the desire to contain the expansion of the Soviet Union and of the European communist parties;[3] and
- the desire, especially by France, to contain a possible resurgence of German expansionism by integrating the German economy in a European context.[4]

These four points highlight the motives behind the birth of the EU (at that time, the European Economic Community).[5] They represent the view of European capital, that is, its preoccupation with economic and political competitors, both from other capitalist and from non-capitalist countries. However, this view, while illuminating some real reasons, is also at the same time ideological. It suggests that capitalist integration is based upon, and reinforces, European capital's common interests (*vis-à-vis* both non-European capital and non-capitalist nations). From the perspective of class analysis, however, given the imperialist past and nature of the countries founding the European Economic Community, the body emerging from their integration could not but contain the same seeds and develop into the same weed. It is hard to believe that colonial (imperialist) nations could join into a supranational body of a different nature. From this point of view, capitalist integration arises from, and reinforces, capital's internal contradictions (*vis-à-vis* both non-European capital and non-capitalist nations). Thus,

- the argument concerning the relatively small size and uncompetitiveness of European nations, that is, of European firms especially relative to US companies, while reflecting a real situation (see Mandel, 1970), conceals the expansionist nature of the European project after de-colonization (in the post-war period) reduced Europe's international weight[6] and after the weight of the dominant nation, Germany, had been further reduced through its splitting into West and East Germany;
- the thesis concerning the desire to avoid protectionism carefully avoids mentioning the EEC's own protectionism *vis-à-vis* non-EEC (including Third World) countries, especially in the Common Agricultural Policy;
- the view stressing the urge to contain the ex-Soviet Union reveals the desire to destroy it not only for ideological and political reasons but especially for reasons of economic expansionism; and
- the claim that France wished to contain German expansionism barely disguises France's own expansionist project, a project which (owing to France's insufficient economic weight) could be realized only within a new context of 'cooperation' with other ex-colonial powers, that is, within a united Europe. This project was facilitated by the 'Cold War context, in which the United States and the USSR effectively checked German ambitions, and which empowered France to act as an arbitrator of European integration' (Hollman and van der Pijl, 1996, p. 71).

These are so many facets, to be examined in detail in this and the following chapters, of a process moved by the interests of (inter)national capital[7] in which, not by chance, popular participation (not to speak of real democratic decision-making power) has been remarkably absent. To understand this process, that is, the rise, development and nature of the EU, we must first survey some of its most important signposts. These are the European Economic Community (1958), the European Community (1965) and the European Union (1992). It should be stressed that these are different phases of the same, evolving, complex of institutions.

1.1.1 The European Economic Community

The origins of the European Union go back to the post-World War years. In 1947 the Economic Commission for Europe was established as a regional organization of the United Nations. Its aim was to facilitate the economic reconstruction of Europe by fostering cooperation between all states of Europe. However, by the time it began to operate, the Cold War had emerged and the Eastern European countries had become integrated into the Soviet-led Council for Mutual Economic Assistance (CMEA). From that point onwards the Economic Commission for Europe directed its efforts towards Western European integration. The same year, 1947, saw the creation of the General Agreement on Tariffs and Trade (GATT) (see chapter 6). Its aim was to liberalize international trade through tariff reductions. The Marshall Plan was also announced that year. This was aimed at helping the economic reconstruction of Western Europe, basically in order to help contain the influence of the Soviet Union and of the growth of the European communist parties. The organization in charge of implementing the Marshall Plan was the Organization for European Economic Cooperation (OEEC), which was superseded by the Organization for Economic Cooperation and Development (OECD) in 1961.

The United States, besides being the provider of the Marshall Plan aid, had a position of preeminence both in the United Nations and in GATT. Moreover, the economic reconstruction of Europe took place under the military shield of NATO, which was formed in 1949, and in which the US played a predominant role too. Also, already in 1944, the Bretton Woods agreement had established the post-war principles of international monetary cooperation. These were to be carried out by the International Monetary Fund and the World Bank. The Bretton Woods agreement too derived from, and was functional for, the economic and thus monetary supremacy of the US (see chapter 4). In short, the framework within which the first steps towards European economic integration were taken was strongly influenced by the international supremacy and interests of the US. Thus, the process of European economic integration, while responding principally to the European drive towards an increased economic and political weight in world affairs, was conditioned by the economic and military might of the US. This process was welcomed by both the US and Europe because it satisfied interests common to the ruling elites of these countries (like the reconstruction of Europe and the containment of the influence of the Soviet Union). However, as we shall see, powerful conflicts of interest between the US and Europe were implicit in this drive and were bound to emerge later on.

The first concrete step towards a European entity was the establishment in 1948 of the Benelux, a customs union between the Netherlands, Belgium and Luxembourg. A customs union goes further than a free trade area. The latter abolishes all customs duties and quotas on trade among member states but each member state is free to determine the customs duties on imports from outside the area. A customs union, on the other hand, applies also a common external tariff on imports from third countries. The Benelux was followed in 1951 by the Treaty of Paris, which instituted the European Coal and Steel Community (ECSC). This too was to be not just a free trade area but a customs union, albeit limited to coal, steel and related sectors. But its importance was much greater than its limited scope because these were some of the most strategic sectors of the European economy.

The reasons for forming the ECSC were basically economic and political. On the one hand, France wanted to avoid the resurgence of German expansionism. The ECSC was to provide a framework for Franco-German reconciliation as well as the bedrock for cooperation between the two countries in some vital sectors. On the other hand, the ECSC was to ensure the security of supplies, the modernization of those sectors, and the managing of serious shortages or gluts. In this sense, it can be said that the Treaty of Paris was the founding moment of what was to become the EU. It brought France, Germany, Italy and the Benelux countries under a High Authority (the equivalent of the Commission of the EC). The High Authority was staffed by independent civil servants and headed by nine members appointed by the members states. It also instituted an Assembly, composed of sixty-eight delegates from the six national parliaments, with the power to dismiss it. Other institutions were the Council of Ministers (comprising representatives of the member states), the Consultative Committee (made up of representatives of the employers, trade unions, and consumers concerned with the activities of the ECSC) and the European Court of Justice. This institutional model was adopted by the European Economic Community.

The next step was the Rome Treaty of 1958, which provided for the creation of the European Atomic Agency Community (Euratom) and the European Economic Community (EEC). Now there were three supranational European institutions, the ECSC, Euratom and the EEC. The EEC was a common market. A common market goes a step further than the customs union in that it adds the free movement of the factors of production, labour and capital, within the area. The EEC instituted the Commissions (one for the EEC, one for Euratom and one for the ECSC), the European Parliament and the Council of Ministers. In order to facilitate the free movement of goods, services and the factors of production, the Treaty provided for the harmonization of the member states' laws and for the institution of a system which would ensure that competition would not be distorted (however, as chapter 3 will show, competition was implicitly understood in a very specific sense). Common policies were to be established in agriculture and transport. To improve the standard of living of the populations and the development of the less developed regions (this too, as we shall see later on, within very strict limits), the Treaty called for the establishment of the European Social Fund (ESF) and of the European Investment Bank (EIB). Also, a common policy *vis-à-vis* the rest of the world was to be developed and special trade and development arrangements had to be made for the colonial and ex-colonial dependencies (see chapter 6).

The Rome Treaty also recognized that the greater the degree of economic integration, the greater would be the impact of national macroeconomic policies on the other member states. This would be particularly the case when a member state took action to rectify a balance of payments deficit (see chapter 4). The Treaty called for cooperation and coordination rather than the unification and centralization which would be required in an economic and monetary union. An economic and monetary union is a common market in which the monetary and fiscal policy has been unified. There is a common currency which is controlled by a central authority and in effect the member states become regions within the union.

1.1.2 The European Community

In 1965 the ECSC, Euratom and the EEC were merged into the European Community (EC) (see Figure 1.1). The Merger Treaty was signed in 1965 but did not come into effect until 1967. In 1973 Denmark, Ireland and the UK joined the European Community. Further accessions were those of Greece in 1981 and of Spain and Portugal in 1986. In the latter year, the first comprehensive revision of the Rome Treaty, the Single European Act (SEA), was signed. The SEA came into effect on 1 July 1987. The motivations behind the SEA were basically economic. The period encompassing the early 1970s up to the early 1980s was one of economic stagnation. The European states reacted to it by resorting to 'a range of instruments like subsidies, socialization of private losses, and public contracting' (Hollman and van der Pijl, 1996, p. 62) which were consonant with the then prevalent Keynesian economic policy orientations. This step backwards in the process of economic integration could hardly be checked by the Community because it lacked the proper legal means. The SEA was an answer to this situation of 'Eurosclerosis'.

The Act committed the member states to completing the internal market by 1992. It made this possible by a significant extension of majority voting

Figure 1.1 The European Community

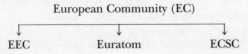

European Community (EC)

EEC   Euratom   ECSC

(see below); it developed the Community's powers in economic and social fields; it enhanced the role of the European Parliament; it formalized cooperation in foreign policy; and it recognized the European Council (a regular meeting of the heads of state and governments) as the supreme body. None of these points had previously featured in the treaties.

More specifically, the Act reformed the decision-making process of the three founding treaties. The three main changes related to the Rome Treaty. First, majority voting in the Council of Ministers was allowed concerning the completion of the single market, economic and social cohesion, and research and technology. The Council of Ministers (not to be confused with the European Council just mentioned) brings together the member states' ministers and is the legislative body. Second, a cooperation mechanism was introduced concerning the relationship between the European Parliament (whose powers are very limited relative to those of national parliaments) and the Council of Ministers. Third, an additional court, the Court of First Instance, was to be grafted onto the Court of Justice (which watches over the proper legal application and interpretation of the treaties). Moreover, the Act inserted into the Rome Treaty new provisions concerning convergence of economic and monetary policy. It also modified provisions concerning social policy and subjected social improvement proposals to majority voting, making them compulsory on member states.

1.1.3 The European Union

A further revision of the treaties was the Treaty on European Union (TEU), or Treaty of Maastricht, which was signed in 1992 and which constituted the European Union. The TEU was prompted by the collapse of the Soviet Union and by the end of the Cold War. Eastern European countries previously within the sphere of influence of the Soviet Union were expected to apply for EC membership. It was recognized that reform of the EC institutions was needed in order to facilitate the process of decision making within a community which is expected to grow to some twenty members by 2005. (In 1995 Austria, Finland and Sweden joined the EU.) While the official reason for a revision of the decision-making process focused on the need to make it less cumbersome, the real reason is that the economically powerful states want to retain their political power over the smaller and poorer states after the latter's accession to the EU. Second, German unification in October 1990 reawakened strong concern about German power. France's traditional response was to try to contain this power through further integration. This meant the introduction of the Economic and Monetary Union (EMU). Third, there was a recognition that further economic integration (the EMU) was needed not only for political but also for economic reasons. The crisis of the Exchange Rate Mechanism (ERM) in 1992–93 (see chapter 4) showed that this was a real concern.

The TEU is based on three pillars. The first is the EC, and thus it comprises the three communities (ECSC, EEC, Euratom). The second is a

Common Foreign and Security Policy (CFSP) and the third covers Justice and Home Affairs (JHA). The policies contained in the last two pillars are given greater prominence than before. Schematically, this is represented in figure 1.2. ˙

Figure 1.2 The European Union

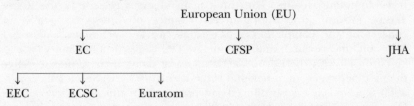

The existence of the three pillars is not a federalist solution. This would have had the CFSP and JHA integrated in the EC framework but it was rejected. Yet there are many elements of a supranational character in the EU. The sphere of competence of the EC has been extended and a greater use is made of qualified majority voting within the Council of Ministers. This is a voting system assigning a proportional weight to the vote of the member states according to their population size. The power of the European Parliament has been enhanced. The Commission (which initiates proposals for legislation and which manages and executes the Union policies) has become more independent from national governments. The CFSP and the JHA, although separate from the EC, have been drawn closer to it. They are managed through the EC institutions, financed partially under its budget, and subject to the same revision clauses. Perhaps the most prominent provision of the Maastricht Treaty concerns the conditions and timetable for achieving the EMU and the single European currency (the Euro) by 2002. The European System of Central Banks (ESCB) will have to be fully independent and will have as absolute priority the fight against inflation. As argued in chapter 4, this independence and this priority represent specific interests.

The TEU left a number of important issues unresolved. These were not simply technical. Rather, they arose from the above-mentioned changes, namely the expected application by the Eastern European countries to join the EU (as a consequence of the collapse of the Soviet Union); the need to further integrate Germany, thus checking as much as possible its predominant weight after German unification; and the need to proceed towards the EMU. Thus a revision of the Treaty was called for. Agreement on the modalities and content of this revision was reached through the 1996 Intergovernmental Conference (IGC). An IGC is a negotiation between governments outside the framework of the Union's procedures and institutions. Through this negotiation, the member states agree to alter both the legal and institutional framework and policy procedures. However, the IGCs do not directly develop the specific content of policies. Their negotiations are usually shaped by reports and recommendations previously prepared by expert officials under the guidance and coordination of the Council of Ministers. There have been six IGCs in the Union's history: one in 1950–1 (which resulted in the Paris Treaty instituting the ECSC), one in 1955–7 (which resulted in the Treaty of Rome instituting the EEC and Euratom), one in 1985 (which resulted in the signing of the Single European Act) and two in 1990–1 (one on political union and one on monetary union) which resulted in the signing of the TEU in Maastricht. The Treaty on European Union, which amends the other treaties but does not replace them, was the first to schedule a subsequent IGC to review its working. This was launched in March 1996 in Turin and was concluded in June 1997. It led to the Treaty of Amsterdam in 1997.

The questions faced by the 1996 IGC revolved around five basic topics. First, there was the issue of 'bringing the EU closer to the citizens'. This is a fuzzy concept. Basically, it should be understood within the context of the increasing resistance in large sectors of the European populations towards the EMU and the sacrifices it entails (see chapter 4). The EU institutions have to become more transparent for the ordinary citizen and the EU process of decision making has to be more democratic if the EMU project is to be sold to the public at large.

Second, there was the question as to the issues for which unanimity in decision making should be required. It was argued that, with the future extension of the EU to other states, greater flexibility should be built into the process of decision making. The principle of majority voting is already being applied in a number of cases (see section 1.3 below), but the question is whether it should be extended and how. The demand that Council's decisions should be taken not unanimously but by qualified majority hid (a) the concern by the greater member states to retain their predominant weight and (b) the wish by Germany and France to proceed on the road to the EMU, the single currency, and ultimately a federalist European state more quickly than the pace at which the UK is willing to advance. Fourteen states were in favour of introducing qualified majority in the second and third pillar of the EU, namely the CFSP and the JHA. The UK was against it. Related to this there is the question of the composition of the Commission. According to the European Parliament, the greater states should renounce one of their two commissioners, rather than asking the smaller states to give up their commissioner.

Third, there was the question of the Western European Union (WEU), the European defence union. The UK was in favour of keeping the WEU under, and as an autonomous arm of, NATO, while Germany and France wanted to bring it under the second pillar of the EU, the CFSP. Here too, this difference reveals the wish of the UK to resist the movement towards a federalist European state which is favoured more by Germany and France. Moreover, the European Parliament was against retaining the three pillars and would have liked to bring the CFSP (as well as the JHA) under the EC. This, it was held, would stimulate the formation of a common foreign policy, which at present is practically non-existent (as the recent failure to intervene in ex-Yugoslavia shows). At the same time, this would increase the democratic content of foreign policy. Aside from these differences of opinion (and interests), the importance of the WEU is bound to grow together with the growing economic weight of the EU. Economic power and military power reinforce each other. A future united Europe will have to have a military arm at its disposal.

Fourth, opinions diverged widely between the UK and other member states concerning criminality, migrants and refugees. For the UK these are areas of police and internal affairs which, therefore, should be the exclusive concern of each member state. Other member states were in favour of a greater integration of these policies (see chapter 8).

Finally, the unemployment issue was bound to play a role in the negotiations. While unemployment in the EU is close to 19 million, the fight against unemployment is subordinated to the fight against inflation. Some would have liked to include unemployment in the convergence criteria for joining the EMU (see chapter 4), but others were against it.

The Treaty of Amsterdam, signed in 1997, is based on these preparatory negotiations. The outcome has been disappointing even for those holding only moderate expectations. While it was decided that accession negotiations with applicant nations could begin shortly after the signing of the Treaty, no agreement was reached as to how the process of decision making within the Union should change following the enlargement. Practically no changes have been made in Foreign and Security Policy.[8] The WEU has not been integrated into the EU, contrary to the wishes of France and Germany, due to Britain's opposition. The possibility for some countries to proceed towards closer integration in specific areas (flexibility) has been greatly restricted.

Further, the power of the European Parliament has been somewhat enlarged and the number of decision-making procedures, previously amounting to more than twenty, has been brought down to the three basic procedures: consultation, cooperation, and co-decision (see section 1.3 below). The Schengen System (see chapter 8), on asylum and migration policies but also on criminal activities, has been integrated into the TEU. This is a positive development, in spite of the anti-labour content of the Schengen System, since both the Parliament and the Court of Justice will have some power to influence policies in this area. The fundamental human rights have been incorporated in the Treaty of Amsterdam. The Court of Justice can be called upon to decide upon cases of violation of these rights and a member state violating these rights can lose some of its rights, including its voting rights in the Council. This is a bland measure, given that no provision is made for its expulsion from the Union. Finally, while all countries agreed on the need for a coordinated strategy for employment, no extra EU funds have been freed for it and job creation remains an exclusive responsibility of national governments.[9] All in all, the results are meager indeed (*Europa van Morgen*, 1997; Louis, 1997).

1.1.4 The Enlargements

As already mentioned, the EU has undergone several enlargements. The recapitulation below includes also the probable next enlargement around the year 2005

- 1973: Denmark, Ireland, UK.
- 1981: Greece.
- 1986: Spain, Portugal.
- 1995: Austria, Finland, Sweden.
- 2005?: Czech Republic, Poland, Hungary, Slovenia, Croatia.

Of these enlargements, the most relevant are the 1973 and the future ones, possibly in 2005. The former because it raised issues which still play a role in the divergence of opinions between the UK and the rest of the EU. The latter because it will shape the future of the Community. Let us begin with the 1973 accession.

1.1.4.1 The Accession of the UK
From the very beginning the UK was in favour of a free trade area while the Six wanted a customs union. Moreover, the UK was contrary to the federalist aim to create, ultimately, a united states of Europe. There are two reasons for the UK's attitude. First, the UK thought it would keep its special relation with the US (which had been galvanized by the Allied victory in the Second World War) and with the Commonwealth. Second, the UK thought that it would keep its role as a world power. This economic predominance was the basis of British financial strength and thus of the role of the pound sterling as an international currency. This, in its turn, entailed substantial economic advantages (similar to those enjoyed nowadays by the US dollar, to be discussed in chapter 4) which would have been limited by an economic and monetary union and would have been lost with the introduction of a single currency. Because of these and other differences, Britain withdrew from the negotiations aimed at setting up the EEC. This came into being on 1 January 1958 without the UK. As a reaction to the establishment of the EEC, the UK, together with Norway, Sweden, Denmark, Austria and Switzerland, set up a free trade area. On 4 January 1960, the Stockholm Convention established EFTA. Since then, EFTA has shed some members (due to accession to the Community) and gained some new members. At present (2000), EFTA comprises Norway, Iceland, Liechtenstein and Switzerland.

Soon after EFTA had been formed, the UK started to reassess its position. To begin with, the Common Market was having considerable success. Second, the sterling area was less and less able to guarantee British exports. In 1953, 47 per cent of British exports went to the sterling area and 27 per cent to Western Europe. By 1962, the percentages had become 34 per cent and 37 per cent (Mandel, 1970, p. 68). Third, British capital realized that 'the appearance of "European" firms, through the interpenetration of capital in Common Market countries, capable of reaching the size of American corporations, would ultimately no longer leave British industry any room for an independent place in the world market' (Mandel, 1970, p. 69). Thus, in 1961 Britain applied for membership of the EEC. The negotiations which followed were difficult and laborious. Eventually no agreement was reached and the negotiations were indefinitely adjourned in January 1963. The reasons for this failure were complex. Only two will be briefly mentioned here. On agricultural policy, the UK admitted it had to join the Common Agricultural Policy (CAP) but wanted a transition period of twelve to fifteen years, while the EEC held that the CAP would have to be applied by 1969. On the tariffs front, the UK accepted the common external tariff around the EEC but called for a 20 per cent cut as well as several exceptions for the products of the Commonwealth countries.

The change of government in the UK in 1964 gave a new impulse to its determination to join the EEC. The new Labour government submitted a second application for membership in 1966. This time both parties showed more flexibility in the negotiations and yet these too resulted in failure, basically because of General de Gaulle's hostility to Britain's accession. This hostility was fundamentally of a political nature, that is, 'De Gaulle did not want competition from the United Kingdom for the leadership of the EEC' (Bulmer, 1994, p. 19). When General de Gaulle resigned in 1969, negotiations were opened for a third time and successfully completed in 1971. On 1 January 1973, the UK joined the EEC together with Ireland, Denmark and Norway. However, Norway did not actually join because of the negative outcome of a national referendum, which failed to produce the necessary votes for membership.[10]

In 1991, the EC and EFTA formed the European Economic Area (EEA). This

> provides for the free movement of goods both ways. There will also be freedom to supply services across the EEA.... Individuals will be free to move and work over the whole of the EEA (with mutual recognition of qualifications) and capital movements will be freed (although this is subject to some exceptions). The EFTA states will adopt many of the Community's existing laws. In the case of competition rules (cartels, dominant positions, state aids) EFTA will take these on board but set up a separate body to deal with cases with specific relevance to EFTA members. Merger control will, however, remain in the hands of the Brussels Commission. EFTA states will not be allowed to vote on EC legislation. (Swann, 1994, pp. 357–8)

This is made up of all the fifteen EU members and all the four EFTA members, except Switzerland, which only belongs to EFTA.

1.1.4.2 The Enlargements to the East

To date, fifteen applications are pending.[11] What follows will focuses only on the Central and Eastern European Countries, or CEECs, that is, Hungary, Poland, Romania, Slovakia, Bulgaria, the Czech Republic, Estonia, Latvia, Lithuania, Slovenia.

The procedure for the accession of these countries calls for the Commission to produce opinions on each country's application. These opinions cover for each applicant a description of the economic and political situation, an evaluation of the ability to implement the EU agreements and laws, an indication of the issues which might arise during the negotiations, and a recommendation concerning the starting of the negotiations (*Europa van Morgen*, 1996, p. 238). The criteria for accession are that the applicants (a) will be committed to the rule of law and respect both human rights and minority rights, (b) have established a market economy capable of coping with competition within the EU and (c) accept the EU agreements and laws, including the EMU (the so-called *acquis communautaire*).

The most important instrument for financial assistance during the transition period is PHARE.[12] PHARE's 1989–9 budget amounts to ECU 11bn, of which ECU 7bn is for the 1995–99 period. For 2000–6, PHARE will be endowed with a yearly budget of Euro 1.5bn. These funds are basically earmarked for 'the restructuring of the economy and the strengthening of democracy' (*Europa van Morgen*, 1996, p. 240). But the reality is different. Particularly revealing is the criticism moved by the European Parliament in 1994 that PHARE money was being spent only for studies and that these were not carried out by local consultants. As a result, these studies told the target countries what they already knew. Far from being an oversight, this procedure promotes the flow of information from the CEECs to the EU, rather than the other way around, and this in its turn provides the sort of information which facilitates both privatization and the flow of foreign direct investments from the EU to the CEECs.[13]

In addition, the following funds have been made available: ECU 3.7bn by the European Investment Bank (for bilateral assistance programs); ECU 3.6bn by the European Bank for Reconstruction and Development; ECU 2.9bn by the EU for balance of payments loans; plus loans by the ECSC and Euratom and bilateral investment guarantees and credit insurance arrangements by the IMF, the World Bank, the Paris Club and the London Club. Moreover, the EU has signed the Europe Agreements in association with the CEECs which abolish all quantitative restrictions and tariffs on all exports of industrial products from the applicants to the EU over an originally intended ten-year period. There are, however, exceptions, that is, the 'sensitive' sectors, such as textiles and coal. Agriculture is also excluded. The Agreements with Poland and Hungary entered fully into force on 1 February 1994, the others on 1 February 1995.[14]

The whole process will be subject to what has been euphemistically called a 'structured dialogue', that is, to talks during the meetings of the European Council and of the Council of Ministers in the following domains: foreign affairs, finance, economic affairs, agriculture, transportation, telecommunication, research and environment, justice and internal affairs, and culture and education (*Europa van Morgen*, 1996, p. 241). On the basis of these talks, the EU leaders will have to decide whether to start negotiations with all countries or to 'select front-runners and compensate those left behind with financial aid' (*Europa van Morgen*, 1996, p. 241). The issue is sensitive. Germany wants a first wave including Poland, the Czech Republic and Hungary (because they fall within its sphere of influence) while the US and the Scandinavian countries favour early entry of the Baltic states (*Europa van Morgen*, 1996) for strategic reasons. The causes and effects of the enlargement to the East will be discussed in chapter 6.

1.2 The Main Bodies of the European Union

Having run quickly through the most important moments of the history of the EU, let us now get acquainted with its main bodies. To understand how the EU works, we must consider its most important institutions. This section will briefly sketch their basic features and tasks. This preliminary information will provide the basis for an analysis of the EU decision-making process that will be carried out in the next two sections.

The *European Council* (or European Summit), established in 1974, comprises the fifteen heads of state or government, the fifteen foreign ministers, the Commission president and a vice-president. Originally conceived as an opportunity for informal discussion and agreement between heads of state and government, it has become an increasingly important element of the EU. Its supreme position has been formally recognized by the SEA.[15] it meets at least twice a year in the form of European Summits. The European Council submits a report to the European Parliament after each Summit as well as an annual written report on the progress achieved by the Union. The European Council takes political decisions which are then transposed into laws by the Council of Ministers. It sets priorities, gives political direction, and negotiates on issues which the Council of Ministers is unable to resolve. Its strategy-setting role concerns not only internal policies but also key issues of foreign policy.

The *Council of Ministers* (usually, simply the Council) consists of the ministers of the fifteen member states. The Council is subdivided into different councils such as the Council of Agricultural Ministers (which deals with the Common Agricultural Policy), the Council of Economic and Finance Ministers (ECOFIN, for short, which deals with matters such as the European Monetary System), and the Council of Foreign Ministers. The Council is empowered to take decisions by unanimity or by qualified majority vote, that is, according to a system assigning voting weight proportional to a country's size. The member countries' votes are weighted as follows: Germany, France, Italy and the UK 10 votes each; Spain 8 votes; Belgium, Greece, the Netherlands, Portugal 5 votes each; Austria and Sweden 4 votes each; Denmark, Ireland and Finland 3 votes each; Luxembourg 2 votes. For a proposal to be accepted, at last 62 votes have to be cast in favour. The presidency rotates between the member states every six months.

The Council of Ministers is the legislative authority. The draft proposals, perhaps inspired by the European Council and proposed by the Commission, become the law of the Community only if the Council agrees. As already mentioned, the Council is not a fixed group of persons, in the way that the Commission is, but meets in the form of the Agriculture Council, the Economic and Finance Council, and so on. The ministers of foreign affairs and of agriculture are the senior body, and the former (usually referred to as the General Council) tend to be called in when colleagues in specialist fields are locked in disagreement. Each member state has its national delegations in Brussels, the Permanent Representations, headed by the Permanent Representatives, who are normally very senior diplomats. The Committee of the Permanent Representatives, called Coreper, prepares the Council's meetings.

While originally all decisions had to be taken unanimously, the SEA (1987) introduced the principle of qualified majority (see above) in fields such as agriculture, fisheries, the internal market, environment and transport. The Council decides by unanimity on taxation, industry, culture, regional and social funds, and research and technology. This concerns the first pillar of the EU, the EC. Unanimity is required also in the other two pillars, Justice and Home Affairs (JHA) and Common Foreign and Security Policy (CFSP). Moreover, the Luxembourg Compromise, agreed upon in 1966, rules that on matters of vital national interest discussion should continue until consensus has been reached. This has slowed down decision making.

The *European Commission* consists of twenty members (commissioners) supported by 15,000 civil servants. The five larger member states (France, the UK, Germany, Spain and Italy) have two commissioners, the other ten states have one. The commissioners are appointed by the national governments for five-year renewable terms but are expected to detach themselves from national loyalty. One of these twenty commissioners is appointed president by the European Council and two are appointed as vice-presidents. The president and vice-presidents hold office for two-year renewable terms. The Commission must be approved by the European Parliament. Each commissioner has specific portfolios (which comprise either just one specific policy area, such as agriculture, or a number of policy areas, such as the internal market, industrial affairs and relations with the Parliament). These are the twenty-six Directorate-Generals. Each commissioner has a number of advisers which constitute his or her cabinet. At the head of each Directorate-General there is a director who is responsible to the commissioner and who is responsible for the political and organizational work of the Directorate-General.

The Commission has four basic tasks. First of all, it has the exclusive right of initiative, that is, it proposes legislation. Community law cannot be made without a Commission proposal. The only exception is in the two areas of intergovernmental cooperation covered by the TEU, the CFSP and the JHA, where the Commission can submit proposals in the same way as national governments. In drafting a proposal, the Commission must respect the principle of subsidiarity, that is, it proposes EU legislation only if it will be more effective than that of the individual member states. A draft

legislation can concern a directive, a decision, a regulations, a recommendation or an opinion. Only the first three have the force of law. More
specifically:

- Regulations have general application. They are binding in their entirety
  and are directly applicable (i.e. without the need for national measures)
  in all member states.
- Directives are binding, as to the objectives to be achieved, upon each
  member state to which they are addressed, but it is left to the member
  states to decide how and with which means to implement them.
- Decisions are binding in their entirety upon those to whom they are
  addressed. A decision might be addressed to any or all member states, to
  undertakings or to individuals.
- Recommendations and opinions are not binding.

Second, the Commission acts as a mediator between the different governments trying, by means of negotiation, to find an acceptable compromise.

Third, the Commission acts as a guardian of the treaties by ensuring that
the EU laws are upheld,[16] that is, that individuals, companies or member
states do not act in ways contrary to the treaties or to specific policies laid
down by the Council of Ministers. For example, if firms enter into an
agreement which restricts competition (see chapter 4), the Commission
can seek a voluntary termination of such an agreement or, if necessary,
may issue a formal decision prohibiting such an agreement and ultimately
impose a fine. If a member state refuses to comply with the Commission's
decisions, directives or regulations, the Commission can take it to the Court
of Justice.

Fourth, the Commission represents the external interests of the EU, that
is, in negotiations with individuals, companies or states outside the EU.

The *European Parliament* consists of 626 members (MEPs) directly
elected since 1979 for five years. It convenes once a year for a twelve-week
period. It is divided into committees that are more or less a copy of the
Commission's Directorate-Generals. All important political currents (num-
bering close to 100 political parties) are represented within the European
Parliament. They are organized in a relatively small number of political
parties (presently eight). The number of representatives elected in each
member state is as follows: Germany 99; France, Italy and the UK 87 each;
Spain 64; the Netherlands 31; Belgium, Greece, and Portugal 25 each;
Sweden 22; Austria 21; Finland and Denmark 16 each; Ireland 15; Luxembourg 6.

The European Parliament has basically three functions. First, it has a
legislative power, which, however, is very limited in scope (see section 1.3).
The Parliament's function is primarily consultative and only very partially
legislative. The second function of the Parliament is the supervision of the
executive. The Parliament can call to account the Commission and to a
much lesser degree the Council of Ministers. It appoints the president and
members of the Commission every five years and regularly interrogates its

members. It can dismiss the Commission but has done so only once, in 1999, following evidence of corruption by some commissioners too blatant to be ignored. However, even if it can dismiss the Commission, it has no effective sanction against the Commission's decisions and has no control over the selection of the new commissioners. The Council's members too must respond to the Parliament's written questions. Third, the Parliament has budgetary powers. It approves the Union's budget each year; it can propose modifications and amendments of the Commission's proposals; it has the last word on agricultural spending and costs arising from international agreements, but it must decide in cooperation with the Council on other expenditure, such as education, social programmes, regional funds, environmental and cultural projects. In exceptional circumstances it has voted to reject the budget.

The *European System of Central Banks* (ESCB), which hinges on the *European Central Bank* (ECB), is a particularly important body because it operates in the only area, monetary policy, in which the member states have completely relinquished their sovereign powers by joining the Economic and Monetary Union (not all members of the EU have joined the EMU, see chapter 4 below). The ESCB is composed of the ECB and of the national central banks of the EMU countries. The latter have been reduced to operating bodies carrying out the decisions taken by the ECB. The ECB has a 'primary objective', that of maintaining price stability. To achieve this objective, the ECB carries out several tasks. The most important are: to define and implement the monetary policy; to conduct foreign exchange operations; to hold and manage the official reserves of the EMU member states; and to promote the smooth operation of payment systems. The ECB must be consulted on any draft legislation drafted in its field of competence by either the Union or any member state (article 105). It has the exclusive right to authorize the issue of banknotes in the EMU area (article 105a of the TEU) and it is formally independent of any EU institution and member state (article 107). Finally, in order to carry out its tasks, the ECB can make regulations (which are binding in their entirety and are directly applicable in all member states) and take decisions (which are binding in their entirety but only upon those to whom they are addressed). It can impose fines upon those who fail to comply with these regulations and decisions (article 108a).

These six major bodies are supported by a number of other institutions which, while less central, perform important functions.

The *European Investment Bank* is the EU's financing institution. It obtains the bulk of its resources on the capital markets that it loans for capital investment. Loans are allocated according to the demand of the economic operators on the basis of policy priorities. These are large-scale and long-term projects (a) for the economic progress of the less developed regions,[17] (b) for improving the trans-European networks in transport, telecommunications and energy transfer; (c) for enhancing industry's international competitiveness; (d) for protecting the environment; and (e) for achieving secure energy supplies. The Bank claims to be the largest financial institution in the world. In 1999 it lent a total of Euro 31.8bn. While the EU is the main focus of its activities, the Bank also supports the financial aspects of the Union's cooperation polices with non-member states. Together with the Commission and the banking sector, the Bank has set up the *European Investment Fund*, whose basic aim is to provide long-term guarantees for the above-mentioned trans-European networks as well as for small and medium-sized enterprises.

Another important financial institution is the *European Bank for Reconstruction and Development*. Set up in 1990, its aim is to aid the transition to market capitalism of the Central and Eastern European countries and of the former Soviet Union Republics. It focuses on infrastructure projects and technology transfer. It operates as part of the PHARE programme (see section 1.1.4.2).

Outside the monetary and financial sphere, the following institutions should be mentioned. The *Court of Justice* is composed of fifteen judges and nine advocates-general. These latter's general task is to deliver independent and impartial opinion on cases brought before it. Its basic tasks are (a) to ensure that the European treaties are interpreted and applied in accordance with the law and (b) to fine member states if they do not comply with its judgements.

Since 1989 the *Court of First Instance* has been attached to the Court of Justice. It has fifteen judges appointed by the member states and deals with actions brought by individuals and businesses. While the Court of First Instance focuses on the judicial protection of individual interests, the Court of Justice's fundamental task is to ensure uniform interpretation of Community law.

The *Court of Auditors* has fifteen members, one per member state. Its function is to check that (a) all revenue has been collected, (b) expenditure is incurred lawfully and (c) financial management is sound. Every recipient of Community aid must satisfy the Court that it has respected the Union's moral, administrative and accounting principles. This holds for European institutions, for national, regional and local administrations, as well as for all other recipients, inside and outside the EU. It publishes its observations on the EU's financial management in its Annual Report.

In addition to these major bodies, there are more than 2,000 committees, subcommittees and working parties assisting the Community institutions in the formulation of policy and the prosecution of business. Moreover, surrounding the EU institutions, there are numerous lobby groups, about 500 of them, which chiefly focus their attention on the Commission. One of these committees is the *Economic and Social Committee* (ECOSOC), which is formed by interest groups and has an advisory role. Its main task is to issue opinions on matters referred to by the Council or the Commission. The ECOSOC represents three interest groups: the employers (group I), the employees (group II) and other interest groups (group III). Its 222 members are appointed by the Council from lists submitted by national governments. It must be consulted by the Council before this latter takes action on a number of issues. However, no great weight is assigned to its advisory role.

Another committee is the *Committee of the Regions*, which must be consulted by the Council or the Commission in a number of areas where regional interests are involved, such as education, youth, culture, public health, economic and social cohesion, and trans-European transport, telecommunications and energy networks. It too has 222 members, who are regional presidents, mayors of cities, or chairs of city and county councils. A constant theme running through its opinions is the safeguard of the principle of subsidiarity.

1.3 Decision Making within the European Union

We can now inquire into decision making within the EU. Basically, there are three types of procedures.

1.3.1 The Proposal or Consultative Procedure

This is still the most widely adopted type of decision-making process. Basically, the Commission proposes legislation and the Council has the power to adopt it or not. A proposal is prepared by a commission department on the responsibility of a commissioner. The draft goes before the Commission as a whole and is adopted by simple majority. The Commission proposal is then sent to the Council (step 1 in figure 1.3) which decides whether other bodies should be consulted or not. The European Parliament has to be consulted on politically important measures (compulsory consultation), but the Council might seek the Parliament's opinion in other cases as well (optional consultation). The Parliament's opinion is then sent both to the Council and to the Commission (step 2) but the Council is not obliged to take account of the Parliament's view. The opinion of the ECOSOC might also be sought, but this too is not binding on the Council.

After the Parliament and the ECOSOC have been consulted, the Commission amends the initial draft, which is then sent to the Council (step 3). The draft is first discussed by specialized working parties and then by the Permanent Representatives Committee.[18] The draft is then either adopted by the Council, thus becoming law, or rejected. In case of rejection, the

Figure 1.3   The consultation procedure

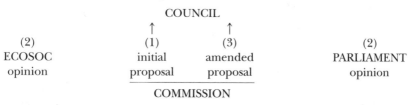

Council can only alter the draft by unanimous vote. This is a rare occurrence. In case of lack of unanimity, the proposal has to go back to the Commission, which has to come up with an acceptable alternative. After approval, the final text is published in all the nine official languages of the EU (Danish, Dutch, English, French, German, Greek, Italian, Portuguese and Spanish) and published in the *Official Journal of the European Communities*. When Community and national law conflict, the requirement of Community law must be regarded as paramount. Figure 1.3 summarizes this process.

1.3.2 The Cooperation Procedure

In the consultative procedure, the only one envisaged by the original Treaty of Rome, the power of the Parliament is practically nil. However, this power has increased over the years. Subsequent treaties have enlarged the power of the Parliament, which now can modify and reject laws. More specifically, there are two other types of procedures. In the cooperation procedure the Parliament can improve or amend a bill. In this case two readings are required. This procedure is applicable to questions concerning the European funds for regional development, research, transport, milieu and development aid.

The procedure starts with the Commission proposal, which is sent both to the Parliament and to the Council (step 1 in figure 1.4). The Parliament notifies the Council of its opinion (step 2), and the Council, on the basis

Figure 1.4 The cooperation procedure

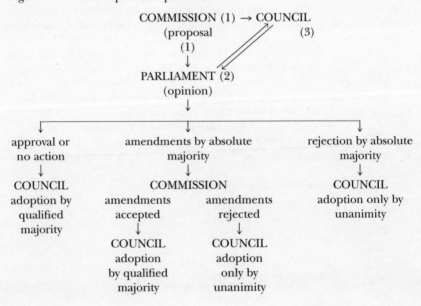

of this opinion as well as of the Commission proposal and of its own deliberation, adopts a common position which is sent to the Parliament for a second reading (step 3). Within three months, the Parliament can:

- refrain from reacting, in which case the draft is deemed to be accepted;
- accept the Council's common position, and in this case the draft is accepted;
- reject the Council's common position, in which case the Council can still adopt the draft on condition of unanimous vote;
- propose amendments to the common position.

In this latter case, the question is whether the Commission accepts the amendments. If it does, the Council may adopt the draft by qualified majority (but unanimity is required if the Council diverges from the Commission's proposal). If it does not, the Council needs unanimity to adopt the draft proposal. The Council can also block legislation by not taking any decision on the Parliament's amendments or on the Commission's amended proposals. This procedure is summarized in figure 1.4.

1.3.3 The Co-decision Procedure

In this procedure, both the Parliament and the Council have a veto right. This procedure is applied to questions concerning the internal market, the free movement of persons, consumers' safety, education, culture, health and trans-European networks.

Again, the Commission's proposal is sent both to the Council and to the Parliament. After a first reading, the Parliament sends its opinion and amendments to the Council. The Council, acting by a qualified majority, may:

- approve the EP's amendments, in which case the text is approved;
- approve the Commission proposal if the Parliament has not proposed any amendments;
- adopt a common position. This is sent to the Parliament. The Parliament can approve or reject the Council's common position. In the former case the text is approved, in the latter case it is rejected. But the Parliament can also propose amendments to the Council's common position. In this case, the Parliament sends these amendments to the Commission and to the Council. The Council, having heard the Commission's opinion, may approve the Parliament's amendments, in which case the text is adopted. Or it can reject the Parliament's amendments. In this case a Conciliation Committee is nominated. It must be composed of members of the Council and of the Parliament in equal numbers. The task of this Committee is to produce a joint text. If it does not manage to do this, the draft is definitely rejected. If it does produce a joint text, the text is approved only if it is approved both by the Parliament and by the Council. This procedure is summarized in figure 1.5, where CM stands

Figure 1.5 The co-decision procedure

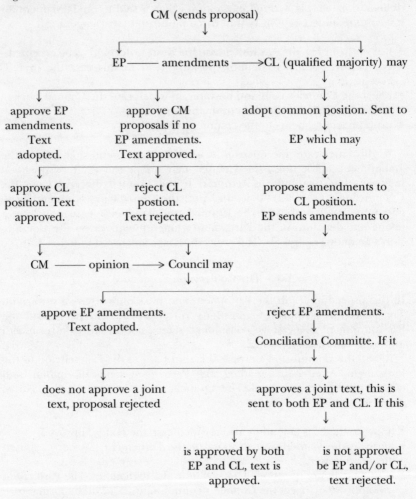

CM (sends proposal)

EP——— amendments ———→CL (qualified majority) may

approve EP
amendments.
Text
adopted.

approve CM
proposals if no
EP amendments.
Text approved.

adopt common position. Sent to

EP which may

approve CL
position. Text
approved.

reject CL
postion.
Text rejected.

propose amendments to
CL position.
EP sends amendments to

CM ——— opinion ———→ Council may

appove EP amendments.
Text adopted.

reject EP amendments.

Conciliation Committe. If it

does not approve a joint
text, proposal rejected

approves a joint text, this is
sent to both EP and CL. If this

is approved by both
EP and CL, text is
approved.

is not approved
be EP and/or CL,
text rejected.

for Commission, CL for Council (of Ministers) and EP for European
Parliament.

As it emerges from a comparison among the three procedures, the
greater the power to the EU, the more complex the process of decision
making. This is not by chance. To see why this is so, we must turn to the
next section, which deals with a question of the greatest significance for
the EU.

1.4 The Question of Democracy

Let us now assess the process of decision making within the EU. Let us begin with the Parliament. Its legislative power is very limited in spite of the introduction of the co-decision procedure. This broadening of the power of the only elected European body has a largely symbolic and cosmetic significance. As more functions are transferred from the national governments to the powerful but unaccountable institutions of the EU, this move is meant to hide the real nature of the power relations within the EU. It is not by chance that, the greater this (limited) transfer of power, the more confusing the procedure in order to complicate the Parliament's exercise of power. At the same time, the Byzantine nature of the co-decision procedure conveys the impression of a relationship of cause and effect between greater democracy and increased inefficiency.

In essence, the difference between national parliaments and the European Parliament is that the former legislate while the latter has primarily a consultative function. This is referred to as the democratic deficit of the EU. The co-decision procedure is far from filling this deficit.[19] But this notion of democratic deficit is insufficient. Even within the confines of parliamentary democracy, insufficient democracy in decision making within the EU goes much further than the relation between the Parliament, on the one hand, and the Council and the Commission, on the other, concerning the acceptance, modification and rejection of European directives and regulations. This is already written, crystallized, legislation. In it, the boundaries of the discussion are already set, that is, some interests are already represented while others have been excluded a priori. The other, equally important, question then is: which social groups influence the content of the legislation submitted by the Commission and discussed by the Council, that is, which social groups manage to have their interests inscribed in the Commission's proposals to the detriment of other groups?

If the question is thus posed, the EU decision-making process emerges as one of negotiation both between and within two sets of actors. On the one hand, there is the triad of European Council, Council of Ministers and European Commission. On the other, there are those lobbies, basically representing national capitals' interests, powerful enough to influence both politicians and Eurocrats within the European institutions. If these interest groups are taken into account, the other side of the democratic deficit emerges as the result of the privileged access some social groups have to the Commission's proposals and to the Council's decisions. This complex process starts with the prioritization of some interests, to the detriment of other interests, in the Commission's proposals. It ends with the negotiation between the Commission, the Council and the Parliament (a negotiation in which the same lobbies weigh heavily) as to the final form taken by that legislation.

Consider the European Council. We have seen that each treaty has been preceded by an IGC. In it, expert officials prepare the reports and recommendations on the basis of which the European Council negotiates the terms of the treaty. These officials are not independent but are guided and coordinated by the Council of Ministers itself. In this indirect, but very effective, way, it is the European Council (in its interrelation with the Council of Ministers), rather than the European Parliament, that has shaped and continues to shape the EU. It is true that a treaty, once signed, has to be ratified by the national parliaments (or possibly directly by the nation through a referendum). But both the parliaments and the referenda can only react to proposals which have already been made and accepted.

Once the general policy lines have been drawn by the European Council, specific decisions are taken by the Council of Ministers on the basis of proposals made by the Commission. This latter's role is not simply that of a broker. Rather, substantial power can derive from the possibility to initiate legislation since, as just said, some interests are represented right away in the proposals and other interests are not. As for the Council, decisions are taken on the basis of preparatory work done by the *Committee of Permanent Representatives*. This latter is made up of national officials who negotiate behind the scenes and usually agree upon deals which are then simply ratified by the Council. As *The Economist* (1997) puts it, 'About 90% of Council decisions are taken before ministers even get entwined. And ministers often prove bad even at agreeing on the 10% that are too controversial for officials to resolve, especially when they need unanimous approval' (p. 59). The Council's decisions are taken in great secrecy: the Council is 'the only law-making body of the democratic world that takes decisions behind closed doors' (p. 59). The Committee of Permanent Representatives adds another element of secrecy to the EU decision-making process (Corporate Europe Observatory, 1977 ch. 1.2, p. 1). Democratic deficit and lack of transparency as to how decisions are taken go hand in hand.

The commonly held notion is that the Council represents national, that is, a nation's, interests (through national ministers) while the Commission represents supranational, that is, Europe's, interests. This is hardly a faithful representation of reality. The Council does express national interests, but it does not express a nation's interests. For each nation, the interests represented by its ministers are those of that nation's classes and groups of all sorts, and in the last instance of that nation's capital as formulated after they have been negotiated with that nation's labour. They are not the interests of an undifferentiated, homogeneous nation. The Commission mediates between these national interests and represents them in such a way that they are acceptable, through concessions and mediations, to the greatest possible sector of the EU even if, in the last analysis, these proposals prioritize the interest of big capital (see below). This is mystified, as if the Commission had detached itself from any national interests and served the interests of 'Europe'. On the contrary, as we shall soon see, both the Council and the Commission have been, and still are, heavily influenced by national classes and groups acting through their lobbies. As just mentioned, by far the most influential of these interest groups are those representing oligopoly capital. A short overview of the basic features of the EU is sufficient to prove this point.

It was mentioned in section 1.1.1 that the first step towards the EU, the ECSC, was born at the initiative, and to foster the interests, of oligopoly capital, that is, French and German coal and steel capital. The ECSC served as a model for the EEC (Accattatis, 1996), and this latter too was born in order to create a market sufficiently large to absorb the potential production of European oligopolies (as well as for the other reasons mentioned in section 1.1). From the very beginning, then, it was the interests of European large corporations which European integration was principally (but not exclusively) meant to serve, as opposed to the interests of other classes, as well as of smaller capitals, both within and outside Europe. These absorption difficulties, in their turn, should be placed within a theory of crises which will be dealt with in chapter 3. The following chapters will provide other examples. For instance, chapter 4 will argue that the European Union's competition policy is regulated to the advantage of European oligopolies and that it is these oligopolies, under the leadership of German oligopolies, which have been instrumental for the realization of the Economic and Monetary Union. Or, to give another example, chapter 7 will argue that the formation of international agricultural prices favours big corporations and that Europe's Common Agricultural Policy has favoured disproportionally the large agricultural units.

The question then is: how can capital, especially big capital, have such an overpowering influence on the nature and working of the Union's institutions? The answer is simple: through a highly efficient web of lobby groups which parallel similar groups in the various national realities and which can exercise their influence because the Council's and Commission's members are very receptive to their messages. A (necessarily short) review of some of the major interest groups will prove this point.[20]

Perhaps the most influential of all these groups is the *European Roundtable of Industrialists* (ERT), which was founded in 1983 by Umberto Agnelli of Fiat, Wisse Dekker of Philips and Pehr Gyllenhammer of Volvo. The ERT has dramatically increased contacts among European corporations. Its members are forty-five 'captains of industry', that is, the Chief Executive Officers of the most important European oligopolies, also called transnational corporations, which in 1997 had a combined turnover of ECU 550bn and three million employees worldwide. The ERT has some ten working groups covering major areas of interest (e.g. competition, education). Decisions are taken on the basis of the work of these working groups by the ERT members in Plenary Sessions. As the Corporate Europe Observatory (1997) puts it, 'more than just another lobby organization trying to benefit from the European integration process, the ERT was formed with the expressed intention of reviving European integration and shaping it to the preferences of European transnational corporations' (2.1, p. 1). The ERT has been a driving force behind all the major reforms since the 1980s and more generally behind the institutionalization of neo-liberalist policies within the EU.[21] Let us consider some major examples.

- *The internal market.* From the very beginning, the ERT has been enthusi-astically supported by the Commission.

> This new alliance between the European Commission and the ERT played a crucial role during preparations for the Internal Market. In 1985, ERT chairman Wisse Dekker launched his proposal and timetable for the removal of all obstacles to trade within the European Economic Com-munity. The European Commission was easily convinced. This pressure from industrial leaders for unification of European markets was precisely the momentum towards further European integration that the Commis-sion was seeking. Shortly afterwards, Commission President Jacques Delors held a speech in the European Parliament which closely paralleled Dek-ker's proposal. Delors set 1992 as the deadline for the Internal Market, just two years later than the ERT's optimistic 1990 target. A few months later, Lord Cockfield, Commissioner for Industry, published his White Paper which became the basis of the 1986 Single European Act. . . . Behind this quick success lay an intensive lobbying offensive, waged by the ERT. (Corporate European Observatory, 1997, 2.1, p. 3)

In the following years the speedy implementation of the Single European Act was ensured by close cooperation between the Commission and the ERT's Internal Market Support Committee.

- *The Trans-European Networks* (TENs). This is a gigantic investments plan in infrastructures, including high-speed train links, expansions of airports and 12,000 kilometres of new motorways, which was first proposed by the ERT in a 1994 report. The ERT made this one of its priorities and worked side by side with the Commission, which 'funded many ERT activities on transport issues'. The ERT

> was heavily involved in the detailed shaping of TENs. It was for instance one of the seven road lobby groups in the official 'Motorway Working Group' which put together the road network program. . . . Since 1993, the ERT has transferred most of its activities in the area of transport to its infrastructure institute ECIS, the European Centre for Infrastructure Stud-ies. (Corporate European Observatory, 1997, 2.1, p. 4)

There is no mention in these plans of the enormous environmental damage inherent in them.

- *Policies on growth, competition and employment.* In the autumn of 1993 the ERT prepared its report 'Beating the Crisis'. In December 1993 Delors's 'White Paper on Growth, Competitiveness and Employment' was released. The two reports were prepared in close cooperation between the ERT and the Commission and 'are strikingly uniform in their calls for deregulation, flexible labor markets and transport infrastructure investments' (Corporate European Observatory, 1997, 2.1, p. 5). The White Paper was endorsed by the European Council in December 1993 in Brussels.
- *The Maastricht Treaty and the Economic and Monetary Union.*

The ERT was very active in negotiations about the Maastricht Treaty [and] met regularly with European commissioners [as well as with] powerful national policy-makers in their respective governments.... As early as 1985, the ERT had argued that the Internal Market must be completed with a single currency. The EMU continued to be a leading ERT demand in its 1991 report *Reshaping Europe.* This report also presented a timetable for EMU implementation which bears remarkable similarity to the one incorporated in the Maastricht Treaty a few months later. However, the main work preparing the ground for the EMU was not done by the ERT, but rather by [one of its offsprings] the *Association for the Monetary Union of Europe (AMUE).* The AMUE was founded in 1987 by five transnational corporations, each of which was also represented in the ERT. (Corporate European Observatory, 1997, 2.1, p. 5)

The AMUE enjoys the same privileged access to high decision-making bodies as the ERT and its cooperation with European oligopolies and the EU is close. The Commission not only provides financial support to the AMUE but also frequently consults it on monetary questions. The AMUE also has close contacts with the European Central Bank. Its first chairman was Wisse Dekker, who was also the chairman of Philips.

The ERT wields power also through official EU groups. The creation of the *Competitiveness Advisory Group* (CAG) should be mentioned. This is an official EU working group which provides an example of the intimate relationship between the Commission and the ERT. The ERT first proposed its creation in 1993. The CAG was set up in 1995 and its members were selected personally by Jacques Santer, then the Commission president. In it, leading ERT members have been given a central role. It will come as no surprise, then, that the policies advocated by the CAG in its bi-annual reports bear striking similarities to those promoted by the ERT.

The *European Centre for Infrastructure Studies* (ECIS) has been mentioned above. This is another spin-off of the ERT. It was founded in 1992 by Umberto Agnelli of Fiat. Even though officially it is a research bureau, its function is to work out, in close cooperation with the Commission, the implementation of TENs. It prepares, among other things, conferences to 'educate Commission officials' (Corporate Europe Observatory, 1997, 2.2, p. 1). The following is an indication of ECIS's success. In December 1995, the European Transport Commissioner presented to the media a report on the advantages of the PBKAL high-speed train network (which includes the Amsterdam–Paris and the Brussels–Cologne tracks). The author of this report was a member of ECIS. The next report on the PBKAL was also written by ECIS on behalf of the Commission. The data upon which the Commission argues for the TENs, including the supposed economic advantages, are thus based on ECIS calculations which have been challenged as unjustified by the European Federation for Transport and Environment. Neither the ECIS nor the Commission mention the ecological damage of the TENs, for example the consequences of the huge quantity of energy used by high-speed trains or the gas emission from the transport sector.

The ERT has been a driving force also behind the *Transatlantic Business Dialogue* (TABD). This is a policy-making body which was set up in 1995 at the initiative of the Commission and of the US Department of Commerce. The TABD has been instrumental for the removal of trade and investment barriers across the Atlantic. Here too the ERT is present with eleven ERT companies as its members. This goes a long way towards explaining why the TABD wants to remove 'environment, safety, health and worker regulations' (Corporate European Observatory, 1997, 2.4, p. 23). These are perceived by corporations as being obstacles to trade and investment flows (see further chapter 6). In 1998, the US and the EU announced their intention to start negotiations to establish a Transatlantic Economic Partnership (TEP). This will be a binding trade and investment agreement which mimics the TABD (and thus the business) agenda.

This short list, while far from being complete, should be sufficient to indicate the symbiotic relation between big business and EU institutions, especially the Commission.[22] Even within the confines of parliamentary democracy, the democratic deficit is much more than Parliament's extremely limited legislative power. It is also oligopoly capital's ability to tailor the Commission's proposals to its interests, thus inscribing those interests into the decisions taken by the Council, with or without Parliament's co-decision, before those decisions are taken. Having said this, it is necessary to stress that EU institutions are not simply oligopoly capital's spokespersons. Similarly to national institutions, EU institutions are the arena in which different interests clash. These institutions, the Commission and the Council to begin with, must often mediate among different classes' and groups' interests, rather than simply imposing oligopoly capital's interests upon those of other social actors. In other words, they must broker different and often contrasting interests and mould them into a common position acceptable to everybody (even though all parties involved might have to make concessions) but ultimately functional for the retention by oligopoly capital of its leading role.

For example, small and medium-sized capital, the trade unions, consumer organizations, environmental groups, and so on, do engage in lobbying at the European level. However, their access to the loci of decision making is either precluded or severely restricted. Their ability to counter oligopolies' weight is minimal. The case of the *European Trade Union Confederation* (ETUC) is exemplary. It groups sixty-two national trade union confederations from twenty-eight Western, Central and Eastern European countries and its membership comprises 59 per cent of the organized labour force in Europe. In spite of this, its influence on the Commission is at best partial and in any case limited to the weakest of the Directorate-Generals, that is, DG 5 (Social Affairs) and DG 10 (Communications). Moreover, even if the ETUC had a first-class, rather than a second-class, access to EU institutions, the question is whether this would make much of a difference given that it too has made the neo-liberal project its own.[23]

The question of democracy will inform the rest of this work and will inspire both its tactical and its strategic dimensions. Tactically, the question is how to give this process the highest possible democratic content by limiting the EU's expansionist goals, by checking the power of the multi-nationals, by reducing unemployment, poverty, and racial, sexual and ethnic discrimination, by decreasing the differences between regional and national levels of development, by overcoming the divisions among the national labouring classes, by strengthening their combined power and by countering the (effects of the) international appropriation of value inherent in international price formation. All these themes will be explored in the following chapters. But more important is the strategic question, that is, how to turn the Europe of the industrial and financial multinationals not into a vague 'Europe of the citizens', but into the Europe of labour, into a Europe based on equality and solidarity.[24] The last chapter of this work will attempt to answer this most difficult of questions.

The Ideology of Economic Integration

2.1 Trade and Specialization

The previous pages have only hinted at the economic forces behind the origin and development of the EU. It is now time to inquire in detail into the nature of these forces. Before doing that, however, we must review conventional economics' theory of economic integration. This will be the task of this chapter. This first section deals with the question as to why and for whom trade and specialization are advantageous. Orthodox economics gives a number of answers. The most often cited are (a) the Ricardian theory of comparative advantages, (b) the theory of opportunity costs and (c) the Heckscher–Ohlin theorem and its extension, the factor–price equalization theorem.

2.1.1 Ricardian Comparative Advantages

All textbooks pay tribute to Ricardo's theory of comparative advantages. Even though this theory has been abandoned in its original form (for reasons to be mentioned shortly), it is essential to discuss it briefly because other, modern, interpretations rest on the same basic principle and thus, as argued below, are subject to the same criticism. Ricardo's famous example is reproduced in table 2.1, where (hours of) labour is the only factor of production.

In terms of *absolute advantages*, that is, in terms of a comparison for each commodity (wine and clothing) between the labour time needed to produce it in each country (Portugal and England), Portugal is more productive in both branches. In fact, it takes Portugal fewer hours to produce both one unit of wine and one unit of clothing than it takes England. If capital were mobile across national boundaries as it is within a country,

Table 2.1 Ricardo's comparative advantages (hours of labour)

	Portugal	*England*
Wine	80	120
Clothing	90	100

Source: Ricardo, 1966, ch. 7.

Portugal would specialize in both wine and clothing. Specialization would be dictated by absolute advantages.[1]

This, however, is not the path followed first by Ricardo and then by the modern theory of international trade. Ricardo's approach is based on the hypothesis of international capital immobility. This means that both Portugal and England must produce either both goods or only one in order to be able to import the other one. If Portugal were to produce both wine and clothing, it would have to spend $80 + 90 = 170$ hours of labour. It is more convenient for it to produce two units of wine (which cost 160 hours of labour) and trade one unit of wine for one unit of English clothing. England would have to spend $120 + 100 = 220$ hours of labour in order to produce one unit of both goods. It is more convenient for England to produce two units of clothing (for a cost of 200 hours) and trade one unit of clothing for one unit of Portuguese wine. In other words, international capital immobility leads to specialization in terms of *comparative advantages*, that is, to the saving of universal labour. This is why this specialization is rational.[2] It is difficult to imagine a more powerful argument in favour of England's specialization in manufacture and of Portugal's 'specialization' in agricultural products (raw materials).

Yet, there are at least four reasons why Ricardo's theory should be discarded. First, since modern economies are characterized by capital mobility, the theory is irrelevant for modern-day capitalism. Second, the theory does not fit historical evidence. History shows clearly that Portugal's specialization in raw materials has been due to quite different factors than Ricardo's comparative advantages. As A. G. Frank (1972) recounts:

> Since the destruction of the Spanish Armada by the English in 1588 and the economic colonization and de-industrialization of Portugal by means of a series of commercial treaties which culminated in the Methuen Treaty of 1703, Great Britain had virtually eliminated the Iberian countries from participation in world capitalist development. The process was exemplified by the exchange of English textiles – an industrial product – for Portuguese wine – an agricultural product: this trade agreement was made famous by Ricardo, who used it to justify the exploitation of Portugal by England on the basis of a supposed natural law of comparative advantages. (p. 46)

Since Ricardo's theory assumes implicitly that international specialization leads to a harmonious and well-balanced development in which all parties concerned gain, development and underdevelopment as two sides of the same coin fall outside its scope. Even if the system could operate unimpeded, international trade and specialization are governed by international unequal power relations, so that some gain at the cost of others (see chapters 3 and 4).

Third, if in Portugal one unit of wine ($1w$) requires less labour than one unit of clothing ($1c$), the labour time needed for $1w$ compared to (divided by) the labour time needed to produce $1c$ ($80/90 = 0.8888$) is less than the time needed to produce $1c$ compared to (divided by) the time needed to produce $1w$ $(90/80 = 1.125)$. Portugal's comparative advantage in wine is measured by $80h/90h$. The opposite holds for England. This is how the theory is submitted. But one does not simply compare two quantities of labour time. One compares one quantity of labour needed to produce one unit of a certain good to another quantity of labour needed to produce another good. That is,

(1) $80h/90h = (80h/1w)/(90h/1c) = (80h/1w) \times (1c/90h) = (80h/90h) \times (1c/1w)$

But $1c/1w$ is an irrational expression. Comparative advantages rest on the impossible quantitative comparison of two heterogeneous goods. Moreover, $80h/90h$ is also an irrational expression. The labours that create the specific aspects of commodities (wine versus clothing) are specific types of labour and as such incommensurable, just are as the commodities they create. This is the *incommensurability problem* that invalidates comparative advantages at their very core. No degree of improvement can rescue them. The reduction to homogeneous quantities of labour can be performed, but this is a problem neither Ricardo nor orthodox economics is aware of. It arises, and can be solved, only within Marxian economics (see section 2.3.2 below).

Fourth, and most importantly, the theory assumes that in a capitalist system countries specialize in those sectors in which labour can be saved. This is pure fantasy. Under capitalism production is for profit and countries specialize in those sectors in which their capitalists can realize the highest profit rates. Since the two principles do not coincide, the theory offers no guidelines as to the patterns of international specialization and trade in a capitalist economy. The same critique applies to absolute advantages. The fact that in Portugal it takes less labour to produce both wine and clothing than in England tells us nothing about profitability differentials. Both absolute and comparative advantages do not help us understand capitalism.

The previous point can also be put differently. The ratios $(80h/1w)$ and $(90h/1c)$ are actually the reciprocal of the productivities in the two sectors. Therefore, the ratio $80h/90h$ implies the comparison between productivities *across* sectors rather than *within* sectors. But, in a capitalist system, productivity differentials can be meaningfully compared only within sectors. In this case, they do indicate profitability differentials. Such a comparison is meaningless across sectors. It is meaningless to say that a computer producer is more productive than a car manufacturer because, given an equal investment, the former can make ten computers and the latter 'only' one car. There is no reason to assume that the computer producer can realize higher profits than the car manufacturer and thus to assume that that country specializes in, and exports, computers.

Orthodox economics has indeed abandoned Ricardian comparative advantages, but not because of the reasons just submitted. Rather, orthodox economics has two orders of criticism, a fundamental and a non-fundamental one. The non-fundamental objection focuses on the theory's restrictive assumptions, such as 'two countries, two commodities, two factors, perfect competition in product and factor markets, international immobility and national mobility of factors, identical production functions and qualitative similarity of production factors between countries' (Kiljunen, 1986, p. 99). It is usually submitted that the theory could be made to fit reality more closely by dropping these limiting assumptions. The more fundamental objections are that (a) labour is not the only factor of production and (b) different types of labour cannot be compared because of the different types of skills (which make different types of labour incommensurable). These objections can be and have been answered (a) by pointing out that, while commodities are the outcome of a great number of inputs, all inputs can be reduced to either present or past labour, and (b) by reducing skilled to unskilled (see Carchedi and de Haan, 1996). Therefore these arguments cannot be used to abandon the Ricardian comparative advantages. The real reason why orthodox economics has dropped this theory in this form is that (a) it leaves the door open for a theorization of exploitation and (b) it is not amenable to a marginalist approach. Orthodox theory abandons Ricardo for the wrong reasons and develops it in the wrong direction, into the theory of opportunity costs.

2.1.2 The Theory of Opportunity Costs

In this new form, the theory of comparative advantages holds that, given two commodities, the *opportunity cost of a commodity* is the quantity of the second commodity which must be given up in order to release just enough factors of production, or resources, to be able to produce one additional unit of the first commodity.

Consider table 2.2, in which with 1 unit of resources, $1R$, it is possible to produce ¼ unit of wheat in the UK, 4 units of wheat in the US, and 1 unit of cloth both in the UK and in the US.

What does the theory tell us? To produce one additional unit of clothing, the UK must withdraw one unit of resources from the wheat sector and thus must give up ¼ units of wheat. In the US, to produce one additional unit of clothing, one unit of resources has to be drawn from the wheat sector and thus 4 units of wheat must be given up. To minimize the total loss deriving from the withdrawal of resources from the wheat sector, it is the UK that should withdraw resources from that sector rather than the US. Therefore, it is the UK that has to specialize in cloth. Or, the UK has a comparative advantage in clothing because it has to give up less wheat than the US in order to free one unit of resources with which to produce one

Table 2.2 Opportunity costs

	UK	US
Wheat	¼	4
Cloth	1	1

additional unit of clothing. The nation with the lower opportunity cost for a commodity has a comparative advantage in that commodity and a comparative disadvantage in the other commodity. This approach differs from the Ricardian one (a) because of its marginalist nature and (b) because labour is subsumed under the more general category of resources.

In spite of the just-mentioned differences, the original Ricardian errors emerge here too. First of all, the above-mentioned pattern of specialization makes sense only if the economy's working principle would be to minimize output losses when allocating international resources. This is not the case in a world ruled by capital: resources are shifted where profits can be maximized. Second, opportunity costs too rest on an economic inconsistency. To see this, let:

$1R$ = one unit of resources.
$1w$ = one unit of wheat.
$1c$ = one unit of clothing.
O = output.
Rc = productivity in the clothing sector.
Rw = productivity in the wheat sector.

Since productivity = $O/1R$, in the UK $Rc = 1$ and $Rw = ¼$. In the US $Rc = 1$ and $Rw = 4$. The UK specializes in clothing because $Rc/Rw = (1/1)/(¼/1) = 4$ is greater than $Rw/Rc = ¼$. The opposite holds for the US, where $Rc/Rw = ¼$ and $Rw/Rc = 4$. The US specializes in wheat. But productivities cannot be compared in different sectors. That is, $Rc/Rw = (1c/1R)/(1w/1R) = (1c/1R) \times (1R/1w) = 1c/1w$, which is a nonsensical relation. On the other hand, if productivities are compared within sectors across countries (as they should be), the US specializes in wheat, and cloth is produced by both the UK and the US. Notice that this is not a feature of this particular numerical example, given that the theory requires *one* (extra, marginal) unit of cloth in both countries.

Introducing prices, either in physical terms or in money terms, does not solve the incommensurability problem. As seen above, given two goods, x and y, the opportunity cost of x is given by the quantity of y which must be given up in order to release sufficient resources to produce an extra unit of x, that is, $(y/1R)/(x/1R) = y/x$. Similarly, the opportunity cost of y is x/y. Consider now the price of x. This is the quantity of y which can be received in exchange for x, that is, the quantity of y relative to that of x, or y/x. Similarly, the price of y is x/y. In symbols, $Px = y/x$ and $Py = x/y$. Relative prices in physical terms are the same as opportunity costs. This is important because it shows that the incommensurability problem has its roots in the notion of relative prices in physical terms.

The question now is: why not express the Ricardian, or the opportunity costs, comparative advantages in money terms? In this case, it could be submitted, the logical inconsistency inherent in the quantitative comparison of heterogeneous, and thus incommensurable, quantities could be avoided. Let Mx and My be the quantity of money needed to produce $1x$

and $1y$. Under the assumption that the resources (money) needed to produce $1x$ and $1y$ are equal, Mx and My cancel each other out. Or,

$$(2) \quad \frac{Px}{Py} = \frac{Mx}{x} : \frac{My}{y} = \frac{Mx}{x} \cdot \frac{y}{My} = \frac{y}{x}$$

But relation (2) is far from providing an answer to the incommensurability problem. While it is possible to divide Mx by My, y/x makes no sense. Moreover, if y/x cannot be carried out, Mx/My too remains indeterminate. Mx exchanges for My in a definite proportion because x and y must exchange in a definite proportion. Now, whether we assume that a commodity has an objective value (as in the labour theory of value) or a subjective value based on preferences (as in neo-classical theory), it is this value which determines the money-price of that commodity and not vice versa. Therefore, as long as x and y are conceived in physical terms, that is, as long as we do not know (because of the incommensurability problem) why x and y exchange in those proportions, we cannot know why Mx exchanges for My. Mx/My, while in itself a valid expression, conceals, rather than resolves, an irrational relation. Only after x and y cease to be seen as physical entities can a common denominator be found and it becomes possible quantitatively to compare them and thus their monetary form. Only then does Mx/My express a rational relation. This requires, as we shall see, that labour is given back its central role.[3]

The basic difference between the Ricardian and the opportunity costs theory is that the latter (a) takes a marginalist view and (b) surrenders the notion of labour as the source of value. The focus on the margin wipes the different economic agents' unequal relations of power from economic theory. The advantage can only be for the powerful. The subjective notion of value, the individual's evaluation of the commodities as the commodities' value, cannot but rest on their physical, specific characteristics. This is the ultimate origin of the inevitability of the incommensurability problem. The defence of the interests of the powerful cannot but rest on a fundamental theoretical inconsistency.

2.1.3 The Heckscher–Ohlin Theorem

The third pillar in orthodox trade theory is the Heckscher–Ohlin theorem. This states that a nation will export the commodity whose production requires the intensive use of the nation's relatively abundant and cheap factor and import the commodity whose production requires the intensive use of the nation's relatively scarce and expensive factor. The element of novelty, relative to the Ricardian theory (which focuses only on labour) and the opportunity costs theory (which focuses on all resources, including labour), is (a) that emphasis is placed on the relative abundance of the factors of production and (b) that the two factors of production upon which attention is focused are capital (K) and labour (L). The country with a relative abundance of labour should specialize in labour-intensive goods and the country with relative abundance of capital should specialize in capital-intensive goods.

This inherent 'rationality' is brought about by international trade and by the emergence of a single (international) price for each good produced by both countries. Owing to this price convergence, each country specializes (partially) in the production of, and thus exports, that good which requires an intensive use of the relatively abundant factor of production. In fact, the international price of the labour-intensive good, being between the low national price in the labour-rich country and the high national price in the labour-scarce country, must be higher than the former and lower than the latter. It follows that the labour-rich country will export that good and the capital-rich country will not. The same holds for the capital-intensive good that will be exported by the capital-rich country.

After what has been said above, it will be clear that as long as capital refers to physical means of production and labour refers to the different types of labour needed to produce different types of capital goods, the relative abundance of capital ($K/L>1$) or of labour ($K/L<1$) is as illogical as x/y. Aggregation in terms of money would not work either, for the reason highlighted above, that is, because money has to express something all types of K and of L have in common rather than their different qualities.[4] The Heckscher–Ohlin theorem cannot explain comparative advantages because it cannot define factor abundance. Nevertheless, the theory is still being seen as a founding stone of international economics. The reason is not difficult to see. This is the implicit conclusion inherent in this 'theory': the country with relative abundance of labour should specialize in those goods which do not require advanced industrialization and, vice versa, the industrialized countries should continue to specialize in those goods which require a higher level of technological development. It is immediately clear that this is both a recipe and a rationalization for the continuation of technological and thus economic dependence.

These are the consequences for the relations between countries. But the theory also has important consequences for the relations between capital and labour. To see this, consider the extension of the Heckscher–Ohlin theorem, the *factor–price equalization theorem*. Disregard, for the sake of argument, the aggregation problem and take two countries. Country 1 has relatively more L than K and country 2 has relatively more K than L. The factor–price equalization theorem says that international trade will bring about the equalization of returns to K and L in both countries. That is, international trade will equalize both the (absolute and relative) wage rate (w) and the (absolute and relative) rate of interest (r) in both countries.[5] Thus, in this respect, international trade is a substitute for the international mobility of the factors of production. The argument goes as follows.

In country 1, w/r is lower than in country 2, due to the relative abundance of labour. In the same country, r/w is higher than in country 2 due to the relative scarcity of capital. Let us introduce now two goods, x (labour-intensive) and y (capital-intensive). If, as comparative advantages hold, country 1 specializes in x (labour-intensive), the demand for labour increases more than the demand for capital. Consequently, w increases more than r. Given that, initially, w/r was lower in country 1 than in country 2, w/r converges to the w/r of country 2 on this account. In country 2, w/r is higher than in country 1 (due to labour's relative scarcity) and r/w is lower than in country 1 due to capital's relative abundance. If country 2 specializes in y (capital-intensive), the demand for capital grows faster than that for labour and r grows faster than w. Given that, initially, r/w was lower in country 2 than in country 1, r/w in country 2 moves towards that of country 1. In short w/r in both countries tends to converge towards a common value.

What, then, are the consequences of factor–price equalization for labour? To express the system's inner rationality, international trade must equalize returns. If r/w is lower in the capital-rich country, and if an increased production in capital-intensive goods increases r, then w must decrease. The inner rationality of this theory is that it is rational for wages to fall in the technologically developed countries (where wages are higher because, it is said, labour is relatively less abundant). It follows that it is irrational for workers (unions) to resist wage cuts. The Heckscher–Ohlin theorem and the factor–price equalization theorem argue for the best of all possible worlds for capital in the technologically leading countries, that is, the imperialist countries: both specialization in technologically advanced sectors and decreasing wages.

Given the shaky foundations upon which the theory rests, it comes as no surprise that, as well known, empirical tests of the Heckscher–Ohlin theorem (the Leontieff paradox) have failed to corroborate it.[6] On balance, then,

> empirical evidence broadly supports the Ricardian model's prediction that countries will export goods in which their labour is especially productive. Most international economists, however, regard the Ricardian model as too limited to serve as their basic model of international trade. By contrast, the Heckscher–Ohlin model has long occupied a central place in trade theory because it allows a simultaneous treatment of issues of income distribution and the pattern of trade. So the model that predicts trade best is too limiting for other purposes, while there is by now strong evidence against the pure Heckscher–Ohlin model.
>
> The best answer at this point seems to be to return to the Ricardian idea that the trade pattern is largely driven by international differences in technology rather than resources. (Krugman and Obstefeld, 1994, pp. 78–9)

To conclude, the above-mentioned theories are irrelevant theoretical constructions which speculate on what the patterns of trade and specialization would be if the world were a society of nations whose common purpose were that of saving international labour. But neither does capitalism work on the basis of saving labour, nor would a society of nations based on saving labour opt for this way to do so. If a country 'specializes' in labour-intensive (low-technology) products, it remains subject to loss of value through the international price system (see chapter 3), insufficient capital accumulation, further technological backwardness, and either de-industrialization or dependent development (see chapter 4). For a country trying to break out of economic dependency (so-called 'underdevelopment') and poverty it might be much better to try to develop its own technology than to import it and keep producing with low-technology methods (Carchedi, 1991, ch. 8).

2.2 Tariffs and Trade

Orthodox economics argues that, if trade is beneficial to all parties concerned, obstacles to trade should be removed so that countries can specialize in those products for which they have a comparative advantage. It is at this point that the theory of economic integration comes in. Let us review briefly its basic elements. Consider the figure 2.1, which depicts the welfare effects of a tariff.

The *dd* line is the demand line, which is downwards-sloping because it reflects the assumed behaviour that if the price of *x* decreases, the quantity demanded increases (and vice versa). The *ss* line is the supply curve, which is upwards-sloping because it is assumed that if the price of *x* increases, the producers are willing to supply more of it (and vice versa). The same good can be imported from outside the country, that is, from the rest of the world. *P1* and *P2* are two world price levels. Suppose that the world price is *P1*. This is the price at which *x* is imported and sold on the internal market,

Figure 2.1 Welfare effects of tariffs

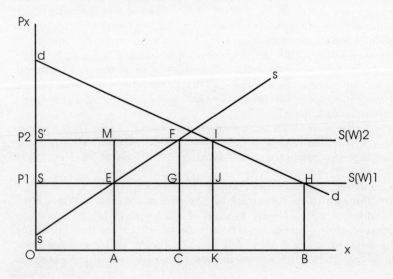

without tariffs. The price line is drawn horizontally because it is assumed that no matter how much of x is internally produced, the world price does not change. The quantity OA is supplied internally because the internal producers' marginal costs (MC), as given by the supply curve, are lower than the import price, $P1$, which is also the marginal revenue (MR) curve for the importing country. Since each national enterprise produces up to the point where $MC = MR$, the aggregate national output is OA. From point A onwards, national production stops and x is imported. Imports grow up to the point where the quantity supplied (through internal production plus imports) is equal to the quantity demanded, that is, up to point B. H is then the equilibrium point. The domestic quantity demanded is OB, domestic production is OA, and imports (to supplement domestic production) are AB. The supply curve is not ss any more (as in the case of lack of a competing source of supply, that is, the world) but sEH and beyond.

Suppose now a tariff, $P1P2$, is imposed. The effect is to raise the price of the domestic market to $OP2$. The supply curve is now sFI and beyond. Now, OC is produced internally (for this quantity the marginal cost of producing x is lower than the marginal revenue) and CK is imported. KB is neither imported nor produced because it is not wanted any more, due to the fall in the quantity demanded (from OB to OK), as a result of the higher market price (from $OP1$ to $OP2$). The *welfare effects* are as follows.

Before the imposition of the tariff, internal production was equal to OA. Each point on the horizontal segment OA represents producers with a certain marginal cost, which is the distance between that point and the ss line. The difference between the marginal costs and the marginal revenue (the $P1$ line) is the *producer surplus* (rent) for each producer on the OA segment. Therefore, the triangle sSE is the (aggregate) producer surplus. After the tariff, internal production increases to OC due to the fact that the less efficient enterprises can now produce because of the upward movement of the marginal revenue line (from $P1$ to $P2$). The producer surplus is now $sS'F$. The difference $SS'FE$ is then the *net producer surplus*, due to increased internal production, itself a consequence of the imposition of the tariff.

Consider now the segment CK. The cost of importing it before tariff was $CGJK$. After the tariff, the cost is the same but there accrues to the country a *tariff revenue* equal to $GFIJ$. This is a benefit for the government. However, this is at the same time a real loss for the consumers.

Let us introduce now the notion of *consumer surplus*. This is the difference between what the consumers are willing to pay and what they actually pay. Take total consumption before tariff, OB. If one assumes that the price the consumers are willing to pay is a measure of the welfare they derive from the consumption of that good, the total welfare deriving from the consumption of OB is equal to the area under the demand curve, that is, $OdHB$. However, consumers pay only $OSHB$. Therefore, the consumer surplus is SdH. Similarly, after the introduction of the tariff, the consumer surplus is $S'dI$. Therefore, the loss of consumer surplus due to the introduction of the tariff is $SS'IH$. However, this loss is compensated by the producer surplus *SS'FE* and by the tariff revenue *GFIJ*. The two triangles *EFG* and *JIH* are the *net welfare loss* due to the imposition of the tariff.

These two triangles can be further analysed. Under the assumption that *P2* is not only the import price but also the price charged by the national producers, the consumers must bear an extra expenditure *EMFG* on the extra quantity produced, *AC*. In fact, before the tariff, *AC* was imported and the consumers had to pay *AEGC*. After the tariff, the same quantity is produced internally and the consumers must pay *AMFC*. The difference is *EMFG*. Of this, *EMF* is compensated by the producer gain but *EFG* is not compensated by anybody's gain. It is the net consumer loss due to the fact that less efficient enterprises have been drawn into production. *EFG* is called the *efficiency loss*. The other triangle, *JIH*, is also a consumer loss, but this is due to the fact that consumption has dropped by *KB*.

A first critical comment is now in place. The problem of illegitimate comparison (the incommensurability problem) looms large here too. To derive the net welfare effects, both the tariff revenue (*GFIJ*) and the net producer surplus (*SS'FE*) are subtracted from the consumer loss (*SS'IH*). But the former two quantities are a real gain, extra money both the state and the employers receive due to the imposition of the tariff. On the other hand, the latter quantity (the loss of consumer surplus) is a psychological notion, an imaginary quantity which, important as it might be for the psychological welfare of the consumers, cannot be added to or subtracted from a real one. Also, it is impossible to add individual satisfactions, given that they are by definition different and have no common denominator that can unify them. The constituent categories of the net welfare effect are heterogeneous so that this notion is logically inconsistent. But let us proceed.

Having introduced the notion of welfare effect, let us turn to the way in which this theoretical apparatus is used to analyse the welfare effects of a customs union. Consider figure 2.2. Now, instead of postulating the initial country I and the rest of the world, we postulate three countries: the initial one, I, plus countries II and III. The supply curve of these latter are *SS*(CII) and *SS*(CIII). The numbers 1 and 2 refer to the time before and after the tariff.

Again, the fact that the supply curves of II and III are horizontal indicates that the quantity demanded by I for the products of II and III does not affect these latter's prices. Also, II is supposed to be more productive than III, that is, any quantity can be supplied by II at a lower marginal cost (and thus price) than that of III. This is indicated by the lower position of *SS*(CII) relative to *SS*(CIII). Let us assume that I has imposed an equal tariff on the imports of both II and III (this is called a non-discriminatory tariff). This has raised the supply curves from *SS*(CII)1 to *SS*(CII)2 and from *SS*(CIII)1 to *SS*(CIII)2. After the tariff, the supply curve of II is still lower than that of III. The supply curve is *sAS*(CII)2, country I produces *OB* and imports *BC* from country II. The equilibrium price is *OP1* and the equilibrium point is *E*.

Suppose now countries I and II form a customs union, thus abolishing

Figure 2.2   Trade creation

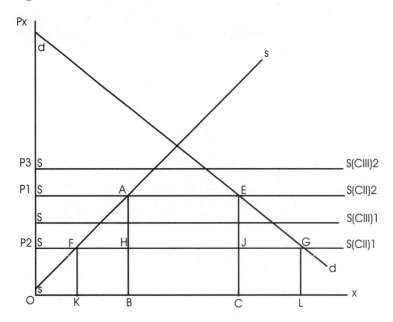

internal tariffs but introducing a common external tariff, in this case against III. Now country II can supply country I's internal market at price *P2*. The supply curve becomes *sFS*(CII)1, the equilibrium point is *G*, total demand and supply is *OL*, internal supply contracts from *OB* to *OK*, and imports (from II) rise from *BC* to *KL*. In this case, there is *trade creation*, that is, trade has increased (between I and II) by *KB* plus *CL*. Moreover, this increased import comes from the most efficient source, that is, from II rather than from III. The higher efficiency of II relative to III is indicated by the fact that the marginal cost line of II, *SS*(CII), is lower than that of III, *SS*(CIII). The higher efficiency of II relative to I is indicated by the lower marginal cost line in II, *SS*(CII)1, than that of I, the *ss* line, for *KL*. The effects of abolishing the tariff between I and II (customs union) are positive. There is a net consumer surplus equal to *FAH* (the efficiency gain) and *JEG* (due to increased consumption). The objections moved to figure 2.1 can be repeated here *tout court*.

Let us now consider a different case. This is depicted in figure 2.3. Now it is country III which is more efficient than country II as indicated by the lower level of *SS*(CIII) relative to *SS*(CII). Here too the imposition of a tariff by I on both II and III shifts their supply curves from SS(CII)1 to SS(CII)2 and from SS(CIII)1 to SS(CIII)2. Now the supply curve is *sAS*(CIII)2 and beyond, equilibrium is reached at *E*, *OB* is produced by country I, and *BL* is imported from III (the most productive outside supplier).

Figure 2.3 Trade diversion

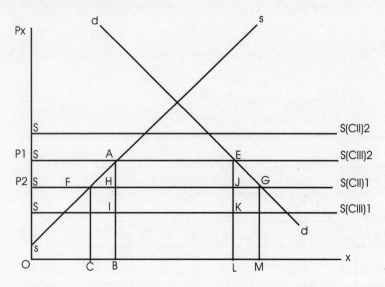

Consider now the formation of a customs union between I and II (II is now the less efficient outside supplier). The price falls from *OP1* to *OP2* and country III (which can only supply at *OP1* because it has to bear the tariff) is excluded from trade. The supply curve is *sFS*(CII)1, equilibrium is reached at *G* and country I produces *OC* and imports *CM* from II. While before the customs union imports equalled *BL*, after it they equal *CM*. The difference, *CB* plus *LM*, is trade creation. The quantity *BL* represents commodities that keep being imported after the customs union as well as before it. Only, the union causes a change in the exporting country, from country III to country II. This is called *trade diversion*. Since there is no clear-cut trade creation or trade diversion, the net welfare effects are mixed. *BL* is now imported from II (the less efficient producer), rather than from III (the more efficient producer), as before the customs union. This loss of welfare is represented by *IHJK*. In fact, before the union, country I imported *BL* from III at a cost of *BIKL*. After the union the same quantity is imported from II at a cost of *BHJL*. The difference is a loss. However, there are also positive welfare effects, namely *FAH* and *JEG*. If these two triangles are greater than the rectangle *IHJK*, the net welfare effect is positive. If they are not, the outcome is negative.

The same criticisms applied to figure 2.1 and 2.2 can be restated concerning 2.3: the notion of total welfare effect is logically inconsistent. Unless someone finds the method to add apples and pears, the theories discussed in this and the previous section are not worth the paper they are written on. Moreover, they rely upon the neo-classical notion of demand and supply in order to theorize prices and equilibrium. This notion will be criticized in the next section.

2.3 The Fallacies of Equilibrium

One of the basic notions inherent in orthodox theory is that the economy, by which it means the capitalist economy, if unhampered, tends to (or reaches) a state of equilibrium. This is clearly theorized in the neo-classical tradition but it is already inherent in Ricardo's model, given its emphasis on the optimal allocation of resources. The theory of customs union introduced in the previous section is a clear example of equilibrium analysis. This section will subject equilibrium analysis to critical review. It will consider both partial equilibrium theory, in which the price of a good is determined only by the demand and supply of that good, and general equilibrium theory, in which other factors are allowed to play a role in price determination.

2.3.1 Partial Equilibrium Theory

Figures 2.1, 2.2 and 2.3 are examples of partial equilibrium theory (PET). As is immediately evident, the tendency towards the equilibrium price is vitally dependent upon the downwards slope of the demand curve and on the upwards slope of the supply curve. Equilibrium thus depends on the tendency prices have to fall if demand is lower (or if the supply is higher) than the equilibrium quantity and to rise if demand is greater (or if the supply is lower) than the equilibrium quantity. This hypothesis can be criticized from different perspectives. Each one of them would be sufficient to cast serious doubts on PET.

2.3.1.1 Empirical Evidence
It is a matter of common knowledge that the shape of the demand curve does not fit a whole array of goods, such as status goods and financial goods. While the practical importance of the former can be considered to be limited, the same cannot be said of the latter: nowadays the size of the financial markets is fifty times greater than that of the markets involving exports of goods and services. Or, by 1995, the daily turnover of foreign exchange transactions (US$1,300bn) had exceeded the world's foreign exchange reserves (estimated at US$1,200bn). These US$1,300bn are in the hands of a relatively small number of banks, companies and above all 'institutional investors'. These latter are (a) pension funds, (b) mutual funds and (c) speculative or hedge funds. These investors might just as well demand less of certain financial instruments if their price falls or more if their price rises. The unbridgeable gulf which separates this reality from the neo-classical economics (NCE) demand curve is shown by the fact that in 1991 the top 100 US, European and Japanese pension funds managed almost US$8,000bn, about one third of the world's income.

But even more importantly, the capitalists' demand for means of production and labour (power) can regularly and significantly diverge from the pattern exhibited by the NCE demand curve. It is true that capital's demand for those inputs might conform to the downwards slope of the demand curve (a logical consequence of the attempt to maximize the rate of profit). But it is equally true that the demand for those inputs depends principally on the (phase of the) economic cycle and on the relative competitiveness of each capitalist within each phase of the cycle. In high economic conjuncture, capitalists must buy more inputs even if their price rises; and in a phase of economic downturn, capitalists might buy less inputs even if their prices fall. Or, independently of the cycle, some capitalists experiencing financial difficulties might buy fewer inputs even if their prices fall, and other financially sound capitalists might buy more inputs even if their prices rise.

Finally, it would appear that the shape of the demand curve reflects the demand for at least one category of goods: consumer goods. But even the demand for these goods might fail to behave as the neo-classical curve predicts. If consumers are worried about their future, they might not react favourably to a price fall, and if consumer confidence increases, they might increase their demand even if prices rise. It follows that all goods, from consumer to investment goods, from status to financial goods, may or may not behave as presupposed by the downwards slope of the demand curve. In short, in terms of empirical observation, that shape is indeterminate and therefore equilibrium prices are indeterminate.

2.3.1.2 Theoretical Indeterminacy

What follows will focus only on the demand curve because, once this is proved to be indeterminate, there is no need to invalidate the supply curve in order to show that no equilibrium point can be theorized.

In order to draw the demand curve, PET first presupposes all possible prices corresponding to all possible quantities demanded, including the equilibrium price and quantity that it wants to find. It then proceeds to 'determine' the equilibrium price (and quantity) where the demand curve intersects the supply curve. But the demand curve is drawn on the basis of certain combinations of prices and quantities and therefore it is only a graphical restatement of those combinations. Since one of those combinations is the equilibrium one, the demand curve simply repeats the assumption that the specific combination of price and quantity demanded is the equilibrium one. It follows that equilibrium cannot be proved on the basis of the intersection of the demand and supply curves. In other words, if the aim is to explain the formation of the equilibrium price and quantity, then the theory is circular since that price and quantity have already been postulated as one of all possible combinations of prices and quantities.

How, then, can PET validly prove, rather than simply assume, equilibrium? How, in other words, can one escape the above-mentioned circularity? To prove the necessarily downwards slope of the demand curve and thus equilibrium, one must hypothesize a pattern of human behaviour which is not that postulated by the demand curve and from which the pattern of that curve can be derived. If the shape of the demand curve can be derived from this initial hypothesis in a theoretically consistent way, then the equilibrium hypothesis inherent in the shape of the demand curve will have been shown to be a theoretically valid and non-circular conclusion flowing from those premises. Orthodox theory disposes of five candidates for this task.

(1) *Marginal utility theory* is based on the so-called 'law of diminishing returns', according to which, as more of a good is consumed, the extra utility derived from the consumption of each successive unit becomes smaller. The demand curve is derived as follows. Call Px and Py the price of x and y, and MUx and MUy the marginal utility of x and y, that is, the extra satisfaction derived from the consumption of one extra unit of x and y. The consumer reaches equilibrium at $MUx/Px = MUy/Py$. In fact, if $MUx/Px > MUy/Py$, the consumer spends more on x and vice versa if $MUy/Py > MUx/Px$. Suppose now that, starting from this condition of equilibrium, Px falls relative to Py. Then $MUx/Px > MUy/Py$, that is, the utility from the last penny spent on x is greater than the utility from the last penny spent on y. The consumer will buy more of x (and less of y) until equilibrium is again achieved. It follows that if the Px falls, the quantity demanded of x increases (and vice versa). The pattern of demand has been derived from some premises, the law of decreasing marginal returns, in a non-circular way.[7]

The problem here is that utility plays a role in consumption, not in exchange. The act of exchange abstracts from the physical qualities of the commodity. At the moment of exchange the trading agents are not interested in the traded commodity's utility. To account for exchange, that is, trade, in terms of subsequent consumption leaves trade as trade (as opposed to trade as a precondition of consumption) unaccounted for. But even if one were to disregard this point, the demand curve thus derived is irrelevant. This is a consequence of the fact that the demand function is based upon the *ceteris paribus* condition (CPC). This, in itself, is not objectionable. Given the complexity of real life, the CPC might be unavoidable. Rather, it is its incorrect use (in terms of the aims to be achieved) which is disputable. Its use is correct if it serves as a first approximation in theory building, that is, if it can be dropped, after it has served this purpose, without prejudice to the theory which has been built upon it. Its use is incorrect if, once it has been introduced, it cannot be dropped without impugning the theory it has helped to create. This latter is the case of NCE demand curve.

In PET, the downwards slope shape of the demand curve can be drawn on the basis of a specific assumption. In specifying the relation between the prices and the quantities demanded of a certain good, x, all other factors influencing those prices and quantities (including the prices and quantities demanded of other goods and the consumers' disposable income) are assumed not to change. That is, the shape of the demand curve depends upon the CPC. If other factors were allowed to influence a good's demand and price, the relation between prices and quantities demanded of that good would become indeterminate. One needs the CPC. However, the CPC is untenable both in terms of how individuals really behave and in terms of how the economy really works.

Consider first individual behaviour. People do not react to a good's price variation by assuming the CPC. Rather, they react by taking into account the greatest possible number of variables influencing their decisions, like (relative) price changes in other goods, forecast income, future (un)employment possibilities, and so on. Behaviourist studies have shown that people 'use selective heuristic and means–end analysis to explore a small number of promising alternatives' (Simon, 1979, p. 73). For example, given a fall in the price of x, consumers might decide what to do with the extra disposable income by assuming the CPC and buy more x. But they might just as well base their decisions on forecast changes in the price of x and of other commodities, or they might increase the purchase of other commodities, rather than of x, or they might save the extra disposable income, and so on.

Consider now the theory. In NCE, the demand for x is affected not only by x's price change but also by changes in the price of other commodities, say y, and by income changes. These are the cross elasticity of demand and the income elasticity of demand. The theory then adds (a) the effects of the changes in x's own price alone upon the quantity demanded of x to (b) the effects of the changes in y's price alone upon the quantity demanded of x and (c) the effects of the changes in income alone also upon the quantity demanded of x. In this way, it arrives at the determination of changes in the demand for x due to all these factors.

But this procedure not only is not exhaustive of all possible factors affecting demand, it is also based on a wrong method. The summation of the effects of all factors in order to find their combined effect upon a good's demand is internally inconsistent if those effects have been individually computed on the basis of the CPC. For example, let us add the own elasticity of demand, which is based on the CPC, to the cross elasticity of demand, which is also based on the CPC. This, far from giving the combined and contemporaneous determination of the demand for x (due to changes in the price of both x and of y at the same time), creates an insoluble inconsistency. At any given moment, the superimposition of two or more CPCs implies that the same factor (x's own price) is kept constant (under the hypothesis of cross elasticity of demand) and at the same time is made to vary (under the assumption of own elasticity of demand). The superimposition of two or more static assumptions does not depict movement.[8] Or, the marginal utility hypothesis cannot explain multiple, and thus real, patterns of demand determination. It follows that the demand and supply curves cannot show the selection of the equilibrium price and quantity in case of multiple determination of demand, the only real case. Notice that it does not help to invoke other possible explanations of economic behaviour. Let us deal with them quickly.

(2) *The maximization hypothesis* assumes that 'the average individual, when

confronted with real choice in exchange, will choose "more" rather than "less"' (J. M. Buchanan, 1962a, p. 18). What does this means within the setting of a market economy? It means that people choose more of something if its price falls and less if its price rises (Buchanan, 1962b, p. 34). We are back at square one. This is nothing more than a restatement of the assumptions behind the demand function and as such is subject to the circularity critique submitted above.

(3) The same holds for *rational expectations*, which are forecasts of the future behaviour of a variable based on all available information and on an effective knowledge of the economy. Here too a certain type of rationality is presupposed (that is, these forecasts are based on the assumption that if prices fall, demand rises, and vice versa).

(4) *The satisficing hypothesis*, on the other hand, holds that 'for most problems that Man encounters in the real world, no procedure that he can carry out with his information processing equipment will enable him to discover the optimal solution' (Simon, 1976, p. 72). If this is so, then the inescapable conclusion is that equilibrium must be excluded. But if equilibrium is a theoretical impossibility, so are equilibrium prices.

(5) Finally, one could rest content with the observation of *revealed preferences* and thus of the downwards slope of the demand curve (and choose to ignore other macroscopic instances which do not conform to this desired behaviour). But this is tantamount to abandoning all claims to theoretical explanation.

2.3.1.3 Verification

The neo-classical demand curve is, by its own admission, untestable. This follows from the implicit assumption of a timeless reality, itself a consequence of a mistaken application of the CPC. Marshall was aware of this feature: 'we do not suppose for time to be allowed for any alteration in the character of tastes of the man itself' (quoted in Robinson, 1962, p. 50). This timeless depiction of reality is the reason why any empirical observation of actual human behaviour meant to corroborate the shape of the demand curve, being based on observations in different points in time, can neither support nor disclaim, that is, is irrelevant to, the theory itself. We might be able to observe that an individual, having to choose among the same good at different prices, might choose the good with the lowest price. This, however, does not imply that, if the price were to drop between time 1 and time 2, that individual would buy more of that good at time 2 than at time 1. His or her taste or his or her income could have changed in the meantime. If time is introduced, the theory becomes untestable and thus, in terms of the Popperian methodology to which neo-classical economists adhere, metaphysical.

To sum up, no matter which hypothesis is chosen to support the neo-classical demand curve, in terms of their own theory, neo-classical (partial) equilibrium analysis is untestable, practically irrelevant, and not corroborated by unambiguous empirical observation. The whole of the modern theory of economic integration, then, being based on this type of demand theory, collapses not only because of the critique submitted in the previous sections but on these grounds as well.

2.3.1.4 Ideology

If the above arguments are valid, how can we explain the appeal the neo-classical demand curve has upon students of economics and the public at large? There are several reasons. To begin with, owing to the educational system in most countries, students of economics are isolated from critique and alternative explanations. As far as the public at large is concerned, mass media and other means of indoctrination play an indirect, but very effective, role.

But there is more to it. To see this, a brief excursus in the theory of ideology is needed. An *ideology* is a form of knowledge mystifying class interests. To be credible, however, it must not only relate to people's life experience but also offer a plausible explanation of that life experience. It is then through the plausibility of this explanation that the mystified class interests are accepted by those whose interests are contrary to the interests represented by that ideology. The strength of an ideology *vis-à-vis* other ideologies (the measure in which it is generally accepted) is then determined by two mutually reinforcing factors: its plausibility and its access to the means of knowledge formation and communication such as schools, mass media, churches, and so on. Let us apply these general concepts to the NCE demand curve.

To begin with, the demand function does depict most people's daily behaviour, only it offers an interpretation that, besides being inherently inconsistent for the reasons submitted above, also excludes alternative views of that behaviour. An alternative account should begin by focusing on purchasing power. The indisputable fact is that most people dispose of a limited purchasing power, relative to the needs they want to (and must) satisfy. Therefore, at any given level of their income, the component share of their income earmarked for the satisfaction of each need is relatively fixed. Under these conditions, the demand curve will probably (but not necessarily) behave as anticipated by NCE. Only, the reason is radically different from those adduced by NCE.

An increase in the quantity demanded (or consumed) of a certain good implies an increase in the purchasing power allocated to that good. Given people's limited purchasing power relative to the needs to be satisfied,[9] the lower demand for a good associated with higher prices is the result of the fact that, with increasing purchases, the purchasing power which can be allocated to that good must decline (Linder, 1977, p. 120). The demand curve does not depict an ahistorical and socially neutral behaviour, the supposed result of, say, the lower marginal utility deriving from increased consumption. Although the curve does reflect psychological propensities, these, far from being inherent in human nature, are the result of social conditions, that is, are socially determined. It is this socially determined condition (lack of purchasing power relative to the needs to be satisfied) which the demand curve reflects in a distorted and theoretically mistaken way.

The next question is then: how does this distortion take place? The answer presupposes that we inquire into the notion of human beings (that is, of 'natural' human behaviour) inherent in, and thus implicitly submitted by, the neo-classical demand curve. Consider the following: if the demand for a certain good rises, the sellers profit from the buyer's greater need by raising their commodities' prices; if demand falls, the buyers profit from the sellers' need to sell their commodities by forcing prices down. It is this egoistic and exploitative behaviour which is inherent in the shape of the supply and demand curves. Is this behaviour rational? Indeed it is. But this is so only within the context of exploitative societies. It has absolutely nothing to do with 'human nature', as, for example, utility theory submits. Under capitalism it is rational to be egoistic because to live and survive in a capitalist system one has to be egoistic (and this holds to begin with for capitalists). But humans can be both altruistic and egoistic. While capitalist societies foster egoism, anthropological studies show that there have been societies whose organizing principle has been altruism. Moreover, both types of behaviour can be observed even in capitalist society.

The next question follows: in whose interest is the view of human beings and of society inherent in the neo-classical demand curve? To begin with, explanations in terms of decreasing marginal utility reflect the experience of the rich, for whom sufficient purchasing power is no problem. This view, then, wipes out the sad fact that differences in purchasing power do exist and do play a role in demand. Explanations in terms of insufficient purchasing power, on the other hand, reflect the experience and thus the view of the relatively poor, for whom insufficient purchasing power *is* a problem. But the question is not simply one of rich versus poor.

The focus on poverty versus wealth circumscribes analysis on the distribution of wealth. The deeper question is one of production of wealth, that is, of the social classes participating in the capitalist production process. At the highest level of abstraction, these are the capitalist and the working class. In neo-classical economics, the supply of labour is determined by each individual's choice between real income and leisure (given a wage rate and the initial endowments in hours). The crucial distinction between the owners of the means of production, who hire the labourers, and the latter, who are compelled to offer their labour power to the former, is obliterated. It thus becomes impossible to inquire into who works for whom and thus into the production and appropriation of value at the level of production, that is, before the redistribution inherent in exchange.

It follows that, whenever the downwards slope of the demand curve is accepted as being naturally rational, it is the social rationality of a certain type of behaviour which is implicitly accepted as being a type of rationality inherent in human beings. (The abundant use of mathematics contributes a great deal to creating an image of objectivity and neutrality.) Whenever it is accepted that the neo-classical demand curve depicts a rationality inherent in human beings rather than a socially determined rationality, it is the superiority of the exploitative and egoistic nature of the capitalist system (which expresses that rationality) which is implicitly accepted. Conversely, it is the 'irrationality' of social systems based on cooperation and altruism that is declared to be irrational, that is, contrary to human nature. If this system is the most rational, it is in the interest of everybody, capitalists and labourers alike, to hold onto it. All this is contained in the shape of the NCE demand curve and is unconsciously internalized by unaware students of economics.

The strength of the ideology behind the NCE demand curve is that it offers an explanation of a real state of affairs (the need to lower demand if prices rise due to a limited purchasing power) which is actually experienced by people. At the same time, the 'explanation' of that state of affairs offered by NCE smuggles in the notion that capitalist rationality (that is, egoistic behaviour) is nothing less than human rationality and that this class society is the most rational (because ahistorically human) type of society. A type of society that expresses the interests of a class can be depicted as also being the expression of those classes whose interests would be best served by an alternative and radically different form of social organization. But, in spite of its 'intuitive' appeal, the demand curve as in PET can be defended neither on theoretical nor on empirical grounds.

If this is the case, there is no longer any guarantee that the demand and supply curves meet. If they do not, they cannot meet at the point of equilibrium. Just as the advantages and disadvantages of trade cannot be explained in terms of comparative advantages, or of opportunity costs, or of the Heckscher–Ohlin theorem, the advantages and disadvantages from customs unions cannot be explained in terms of the demand and supply curves and thus in terms of partial equilibrium analysis. But even more fundamentally, the assumption that the economy tends towards equilibrium becomes unsubstantiated, that is, the whole neo-classical construction is undermined at its very foundations. Equilibrium is an article of faith.[10]

2.3.2 General Equilibrium Theory[11]

But orthodox theory has another rabbit in its hat. This is general equilibrium theory (GET). Suppose two countries, country 1 and country 2, and two goods, x and y. Suppose country 1 produces a certain quantity of x and y in a situation of autarky. After opening up to trade, given a certain international price, country 1 produces at equilibrium more x and less y. That is, it specializes in x and will trade x against y. Suppose that the international price of x is $Px = \frac{1}{2}$. Country 1 exchanges 2 units of x for one unit of y. If it exchanges $40x$ it gets $20y$. This is point H in figure 2.4. Suppose now that $Px = 1$ and that at that price country 1 exchanges $1x$ for $1y$. If it exchanges $60x$, it gets $60y$. This is point E in figure 2.4. More points can be derived in a similar manner. If we now join all these points, we get country 1's offer curve or reciprocal demand curve (which is the curve on which point H is placed). This shows the various quantities of y (the imported good) country 1 demands in order to offer (export) various

Figure 2.4   Equilibrium between country 1 and country 2

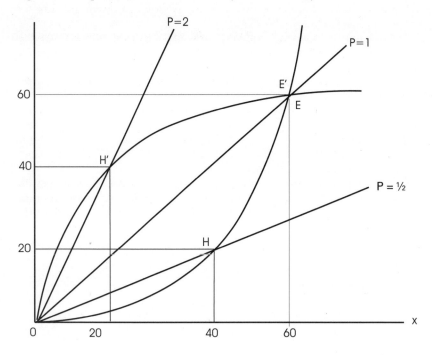

quantities of x (the export commodity) at various prices. Thus, the offer curve shows the country's disposition to import and export different quantities at different relative prices.

Consider now country 2. It specializes in y and exports it against x. At $Px = 2$, country 2 exchanges $2y$ for $1x$. If it exchanges $40y$ it gets $20x$ (point H' in figure 2.4). If the price of x falls to $Px = 1$, country 2 exchanges $1y$ for $1x$. If it exchanges $60y$, it gets $60x$ (point E' in figure 2.4). By deriving more points in a similar manner, we get country 2's offer, or reciprocal demand, curve. This shows the various quantities country 2 requires of x (the import good) to export the various quantities of y (the export good) at different prices. If we now draw the two offer curves together, we get figure 2.4.

This figure depicts graphically the equilibrium price equal to 1, at which both countries are willing to exchange $60x$ for $60y$. At $Px = \frac{1}{2}$, country 1 offers $40x$ for $20y$. However, country 2 demands a greater quantity of x. This is given by a point on the x axis perpendicularly below the point of intersection of the extended $Px = \frac{1}{2}$ line and the offer curve of country 2. This, to repeat, shows the offer of y by country 2 and its demand for x. This *excess demand* of x by country 2 would force up the price of x, until it reaches $Px = 1$. Similarly, at $Px = 2$, country 2 is willing to buy $20x$ and offers $40y$. But country 1 offers a greater quantity of x, which is given by the point on the x axis perpendicularly below the intersection of the extended $Px =$ 2 line and country 1's offer curve. This *excess supply* of x by country 1 would force down the price of x, to $Px = 1$.

What has been gained by abandoning PET in favor of GET? GET is not a radical departure but only an extension of PET. As such it is open to the same criticisms. The most important for the present purposes is that the curves of reciprocal demand have the same price behaviour as the demand curves in PET. The excess demand of x forces Px up and the excess supply of x forces Px down. This notion has been amply criticized above.

It is conceptually easy to extend this procedure to an n sector model in which, as in figure 2.4, the reciprocal offer curves of each of the n categories of commodities depends also upon the price of the other $n-1$ commodities. That is, given n goods, Pi $(i = 1, 2 \dots n)$ are the prices of the n goods, xi $(i = 1, 2 \dots n)$ are the total quantities demanded of each of the n good, and yi $(i = 1, 2 \dots n)$ are the total quantities offered of each of the n goods. Then, the demand functions are

$$xi = xi \ (P1, P2 \dots Pn) \ (i = 1, 2 \dots n)$$

the offer functions are

$$yi = yi \ (P1, P2 \dots Pn) \ (i = 1, 2 \dots n)$$

and the system is in equilibrium if

$$ei \ (P1, P2 \dots Pn) = xi \ (P1, P2 \dots Pn) - yi \ (P1, P2 \dots Pn) = 0 \ (i = 1, 2 \dots n)$$

These are mathematically complex formulations[12] of concepts that have been shown to be void of any analytical content. No matter the degree of mathematical sophistication, the basic fault remains. In spite of this criticism, neo-classical partial and general equilibrium analyses continue to be taught simply because they are the most powerful ideology, that is, the ideology of the powerful. One conclusion becomes inescapable: orthodox economics is a credo, the institutes teaching it (to begin with, the university system) its church, and orthodox economists its priests. Managers, on the other hand, having to deal with the real world, know that enterprises aim at the maximum *dis*equilibrium between receipts and costs, whether they manage to sell all their commodities or not.

If trade and economic integration cannot be explained by orthodox economics, why do nations trade and pursue economic integration? The answer presupposes that we step out of orthodox economics and into the labour theory of value. This will be done in the next and following chapters. The last task of this chapter will be that of arguing that a solid answer presupposes inevitably the notion of value as human labour. Without this notion, exchange and thus trade cannot be explained. To show this, an argument by exclusion will be followed, that is, it will be shown that any other theory falls short of the task. There are actually only three serious candidates.

The first is the thesis that exchange is explained by utility, that is, by the economic agent's subjective evaluation of the commodity's physical qualities. The above has disposed of this hypothesis. Utility can explain neither the demand and supply of goods nor their exchange and thus their trade. If subjective evaluations should be discarded, exchange must rest upon some objective (i.e. inherent) element common to the commodities exchanged. In this case, the different quantities of this common element inherent in the two commodities would make possible their exchange in definite quantities. For example, all commodities contain, directly or indirectly, iron either as iron or as other components which are reducible to iron. In this case, it could be held, the different quantities of iron in the different commodities could explain the proportions in which commodities exchange against each other.[13] However, the different quantities of iron in the different commodities is also what accounts for the physical differences between commodities. The same concept, then, is made to perform two opposite functions: to explain what makes commodities different and what cancels those differences. This concept is internally contradictory. The same holds for any other commodity.

There remains then only one possibility: that all commodities share the feature of being products of human labour. But labour, just as iron, both creates the aspects peculiar to each commodity (their differences) and is what is common to all of them. The concept of labour as substance of value is internally contradictory too. There is, however, a feature specific to human labour which allows us to resolve the problem at hand. Chapter 3 will introduce the notions of concrete and abstract labour. To anticipate, concrete labour is the expenditure of human energy in a specific way. It creates the specific aspects of goods, those aspects that make it possible for them to be used in some specific ways, that is, their use value. Abstract labour, on the other hand, is the expenditure of the same human energy irrespective of the specific aspects of this expenditure, for example as so many calories. The higher the abstract labour contained in a commodity, the higher its value. This solves the problem that has played such a prominent role in this chapter. Abstract labour provides at one and the same stroke both the qualitative equalization of different commodities (the feature that makes exchange possible) and the quantitative proportions in which commodities exchange (according to the social evaluation of the different quantities of labour contained in them). Labour, in its double form as concrete and abstract, can explain the specificity of the various commodities, their common substance (their value), and the quantities in which they exchange against each other. The rest of this work will be based on this notion of value.

A Value Theory of European Economic Integration

3.1 Profits, Trade and Integration

Chapter 2 has argued that neo-classical economics can explain neither trade nor economic integration. Thus the benefits deriving from international trade, that is, comparative advantages and optimal allocation of resources, turn out to be fairy tales based on a highly inconsistent body of theory. Daily observation supports this point. Chapter 2 has also argued that the only valid notion upon which to build an economic theory is that of value as human labour. From this perspective, the answer to the above questions is quite simple. First of all, it is not nations that carry out, and gain or lose from, international trade. Rather, it is capitals that produce and exchange, also internationally, their products. Capitals need to trade, that is, exchange, simply because they need to realize the value contained in their products at the highest possible (rate of) profit. Thus they aim at the highest feasible rate of profit on their investments. Failure to do so spells lower profitability and possibly bankruptcy. Nations, that is, the nation states, only provide the institutional framework and facilities for capital.

This is the empirically observable slice of reality. Managers know this; only the economists seem unable to grasp it. Neo-classical economics' thesis that the capitalist system tends towards equilibrium not only is undermined (see chapter 2), it is actually replaced, through value theory, by the thesis that the capitalist system, far from tending towards equilibrium, tends towards recessions and crises. Value theory shows how it is capitals themselves (actually, the technologically most advanced capitals) that, in their need to produce and realize higher and higher rates of profit, actually are the cause of economic crises. This will be one of the major themes of this chapter.

Put in slightly different terms, profitability is the reason why capitals move across national frontiers. In their constant quest for the highest rates of profit, the most dynamic capitals seek access to (a) foreign inputs, labour power and financial capital, (b) foreign commodity markets and (c) foreign direct and indirect investment opportunities. They seek to realize abroad those higher profits that cannot be realized at home due to insufficient purchasing power. This insufficiency, in its turn, is caused by the crisis-prone nature of the capitalist economies. They thus engage in a relentless fight for the world's purchasing power, that is, for the world's (surplus) value. International trade and capital movements are thus the manifestation of this fight. The outcome of this conflict is far from being mutually advantageous for all parties involved. Given that the commodities' value cannot be created in the act of exchange (it is created only in production), if one trade partner gains, the other loses. This skewed redistribution of value reinforces the tendency towards capital concentration and centralization inherent in technological competition and thus towards the emergence of oligopolies and multinational enterprises.

Those capital units, and by extension those nations, which gain the most from all this are basically those which are already ahead of the others, usually the oligopolies in the so-called 'developed' countries. It is they that are the motor of world's trade, both when it expands and when it recedes, and which amass an increasing share of the world's wealth. Economic integration makes this greater freedom permanent. But it is neither an automatic nor a necessarily favourable outcome for everybody. Resistance to integration, far from being an irrational economic policy, simply expresses the interests of those who stand to lose from it. And the push towards integration mounts only under favourable conditions, basically when the interests of the powerful coincide, even if some will gain more from integration than others. The rest of this work will use this conceptual framework in order to research the process that has led to European economic integration.

Following the conclusions reached in chapter 2, section 3.2 above, the first task is that of providing a firm theoretical ground to the labour-based notion of value. In the course of doing this, it will also be necessary to respond to the most commonly heard criticism of this position. This will be done in this first section. On this basis, section 3.2 will argue that the capitalist economy does not tend towards equilibrium but towards crises and unemployment through recurrent booms and busts. Finally, section 3.3 will draw on this analysis and submit that the tendency towards crises causes a tendency towards capital concentration and centralization so that oligopolies become the basic unit of economic life. It is against this background that EU competition policy can be understood.

Consider first the production process. What can be empirically observed is the following. The entrepreneur, that is, the owner of money capital, both purchases the means of production and hires labourers, that is, it purchases the labourer's possibility to expend labour, also called labour power. These two categories of inputs are set to work and the end result is the product, or output. The output is also called *commodities*, that is, goods, both material goods and knowledge, produced for sale. This product is sold on the market for a price that must be higher than the price of the initial inputs. The difference is called profit.

Consider the outcome of the production process, the commodity. A commodity must have two qualities. First, the purchasers must have some use for it, or it will not be sold. This is unquestioned. We can say that the product has (is) a *use value*. Second, the same product must have a value, or it will not be sold for a certain price (i.e. in a certain proportion for other products). This too is an undisputed issue. The disagreements, however, arise when the nature of value is considered.[1] Chapter 2, section 3.2 above has argued that the only feature which makes commodities exchangeable (in definite quantities) is the labour which has been necessary to produce them, also called the *labour contained* in them. This notion must now be clarified.

Each commodity requires, in order to be made, its own particular type of labour. There are thus as many different types of labour as there are categories of commodities. At the same time, within each type of labour, there are different levels of skills at which labour is expended. And, finally, labour is expended at different levels of intensity, according to circumstances. It would seem to follow that (a) if labour is not the same for different commodities, it cannot be that feature which those commodities have in common, and (b) if it is expended at different levels of intensity, it cannot function as an invariable unit of measure. On both accounts, labour could be neither value nor the measure of value. There would seem to be here a crucial contradiction similar to that pointed out in discussing the iron-based 'theory' of value. But this is not the case.

If commodities are both different from each other and share something in common (or they would not be exchangeable), then the labour that has gone into their production must also have a double quality. On the one hand, the production of each good requires a specific type of labour, and it is because of its specificity that that type of labour creates the distinctive qualities of that good, its use value. This is called *concrete labour* because it creates the concreteness of commodities. On the other hand, all types of labour have a common quality, that of being expenditures of human labour power in general (as measured, for example, in terms of calories expended, no matter what one does). This is called *abstract labour* because it abstracts from the concreteness, from the specificity, of the labour performed. It is clear, then, that *the quality common to all commodities is abstract*, rather than concrete, *labour*. Or, while concrete labour creates use values (the *differentia specifica*), abstract labour creates value (the common quality). We can now see why labour is the element that creates both diversity (as concrete labour) and similarity (as abstract labour): its double quality creates at the same time both the specific features and the common feature. International trade theory falls into the insoluble difficulties mentioned in chapter 2 above because it disregards abstract labour and focuses only on concrete labour (and thus only on the use value of commodities).

The distinction between concrete and abstract labour allows us to perform a double reduction. First, (abstract) labour of higher intensity counts as a multiple of labour of lower intensity, that is, it produces more value than that produced by lower-intensity labour.[2] Second, different values are produced in the same length of time by labourers with different levels of skills (qualifications) because the value of the labourers' labour power (the labour which has gone in the production of the commodities

which have been necessary to produce that labour power, including training and education) is different according to the level of skills required to
produce commodities. In short, in the determination of commodities'
value, more intense labour counts as a multiple of less intense labour.
Similarly, skilled labour counts as a multiple of unskilled labour because
more labour has been necessary to form the skilled labourer's labour
power. This is why, *ceteris paribus*, commodities requiring skilled labour can
be sold at a price higher than that of commodities requiring unskilled
labour.

Thus, the labour contained in different commodities can be compared
because (a) it is abstract labour and (b) skilled labour can be reduced to
unskilled labour and more intensive labour to less intensive labour. But
this is not sufficient. The labour contained in a commodity is given not
only by the labour that has been freshly expended by the labourers. It is
also given by the labour contained in its means of production. Here, one
meets a different critique. It has been argued that, since the means of
production as inputs of this commodity are also a product of the previous
period, to find the labour contained in them, one would have to determine
the labour contained in *their* means of production, and so on in an infinite
regression in time. The same would apply to labour power, that is, to the
labour contained in the commodities which have been necessary to form
labour power. The answer to this critique is simple.

Consider a production period, $t0-t1$ and let us focus on the labour newly
expended during that period. If a proper system of survey could be set up,
these hours could be counted, their intensity (e.g. calories consumed)
measured, and their level of skills ascertained. The reduction of more to less
intensive labour and of skilled to unskilled labour could be performed. The
total number of hours would increase accordingly. The fact that such a
system is not available represents a practical, not a theoretical, difficulty.
Suppose, then, that we do dispose of such data. In this case, these hours of
labour find their monetary expression in total wages and profits. It follows
that the remaining quantity of money is the monetary expression of the
social valuation of the hours of labour contained in the means of production.
To find these hours, it is sufficient to apply the same ratio 'total wages and
salaries/hours of new labour' to the total price of the means of production.
For example, if total wages and salaries paid at $t1$ are US$15bn and if, after
conversion, the total of new hours of labour expended during $t0-t1$ is 1bn,
the ratio is 15, that is, 15 dollars represent one hour of new labour. If at $t1$
the monetary base is US$30bn, US$30−US$15 = US$15 is the monetary
expression of the social valuation of the hours of labour contained in the
means of production, which is 1bn hours of past labour. This is the *value
realized* at $t1$ by the means of production as outputs of the $t0-t1$ period.

Consider now the next production period, $t1-t2$.[3] The labour realized
by those means of production as outputs of $t0-t1$ is by definition also the
labour contained in them as inputs of $t1-t2$.[4] Or, at $t1$, the value realized by
those means of production as outputs of $t0-t1$ and the value contained in
them as inputs of $t1-t2$ cannot but coincide. There is thus no need to

regress infinitely back in time in order to find the labour contained in the
means of production used for a certain output: one period back is sufficient
(and the social valuation of those means of production one period back is
empirically observable). This having been done, it is possible to compute
the social valuation of those means of production at $t2$, as inputs of the
output of $t1-t2$. This is done by following the procedure set up in the
previous paragraph, that is, by computing the social valuation of those
means of production at $t2$. Thus, given $t1-t2$, we can compute the
difference between the value contained in the means of production at $t1$
(which, to repeat, is the value they realize as outputs of the previous
production process, the $t0-t1$ period) and the value they realize at $t2$, that
is, the proportion of the value realized by the commodities produced
during $t1-t2$ imputable to these means of production.

The infinite regression critique is worthless once it is understood that
the value contained in the means of production is not given by the number
of hours which have been necessary to make them in the past. Rather, that
value is given by the social valuation of those hours one period back, that
is, by the number of hours they have realized as outputs of the previous
production period.

The same procedure applies to the value of labour power. This is the
number of hours of societal labour which are necessary to reproduce it,
that is, to produce the collective labourer's means of consumption. This is
given by the proportion of total money wages and profits going to wages.
For example, if money wages are two-thirds of total wages and profits, then
two-thirds of the total hours of new labour expended during $t0-t1$ is
needed for the reproduction (is the value) of labour power at $t1$ as the
end-point of $t0-t1$. This quantity enters $t1-t2$ as the number of hours
contained in the commodity labour power.[5] We thus have the value
contained both in both the means of production and in labour power at t
1 as the starting-point of $t1-t2$.

Keeping this in mind, we can determine the labour contained in any
individual commodity, say A. Given $t1-t2$, we compute first the value
contained in its means of production at $t1$, the initial moment of $t1-t2$.
This is the value realized by them at $t1$ as outputs of $t0-t1$. This value is
equal to their share of the total value realized by the means of production
at $t1$, the end-point of $t0-t1$. This share, in its turn, is given by dividing
the price of A's means of production by the total price of the means of
production. Next we compute the value of the labour power that has been
used to produce A. We know both the value of labour power in terms of
hours of labour and the proportion of total wages going to A's labourers.
Then, the number of hours contained in the means of consumption going
to A's labourers, that is, the value of the labour power needed to produce
A, is given by applying to the total hours of labour going to the collective
labourer the share of the wages paid to A's labourers relative to total wages.
Unlike the value of the means of production (which is computed at $t1$),
the value of labour power is computed at $t2$.

Finally, we compute the surplus labour contained in A. The procedure is similar to that used for the value of labour power. By adding the hours of labour contained in the means of production (computed at $t1$) to those contained in the means of consumption (computed at $t2$) and to those representing surplus value (also computed at $t2$), we obtain the value contained in A at $t2$.

The above allows us to dispose of the 'circularity critique' as well (for more details, see Carchedi, 1991). In computing the value of a commodity, it is said, the means of production are expressed at their value contained as inputs but at their price (value realized) as outputs. Since the same commodity is bought and sold at the same price (value), there is an inconsistency here. This critique is worthless. Take two periods, say $t0–t1$ and $t1–t2$. $t1$ is both the end-point of $t0–t1$ and the starting-point of $t1–t2$. At $t1$, the means of production are sold as outputs of $t0–t1$ at their realized value (price) and are bought as inputs of $t1–t2$ at the same price. This latter, however, becomes the value contained in those means of production as inputs of the production period $t0–t1$. The same quantitity of value is both value realized, from the point of view of the producers in $t0–t1$, and value contained from the point of view of the producers in $t1–t2$. This as far as $t1$ is concerned. If we now consider $t2$, there is no reason to assume that the social valuation of the means of production (their value realized as outputs of $t0–t1$ and thus their value contained as inputs of $t1–t2$) should be equal to their social valuation at $t2$.

The circularity critique is based on a double mistake. First, the correct comparison is between the value contained in the means of production as inputs of $t1–t2$, and thus at $t1$, and the value they realize at $t2$ as inputs of the output produced during the same period. This is confused with the incorrect comparison between their value contained as inputs at $t1$ and the value realized by the outputs of which they are the inputs at $t2$. It is this latter comparision which is referred to by the circularity critique. Since these two values are not the same, the critics apply a number of 'solutions' to this problem in order to find this equality. But the two values cannot be the same because the value of the means of production produced during $t1–t2$ is equal to the value of the means of production used as inputs of the same process plus the new value produced and added to their value. The two values could be equal only if no new values were added, that is, only in case of a completely mechanized production process (in which no labourers are employed and thus no new value is created). This is not the case considered by the critics.

But, second, and more importantly, the circularity critique assumes not only that the value contained in the means of production as inputs of $t1–t2$ should be equal to the value realized by the means of production produced with those means of production (the output of $t1–t2$). It actually does not differentiate, and thus assumes the identity between, the means of production as inputs of $t1–t2$ and as outputs of the same production process. This could be the case only if time did not exist. And this is indeed the hidden assumption behind the circularity critique, a timeless reality. If there is a logic to madness, this is it.

An important conclusion can now be reached. The notion of abstract labour (value) contained has a double dimension. On the one hand it is the *physical expenditure* of human energy, past and present, gone into the production of that commodity. On the other hand, each amount of that expenditure, say an hour, either freshly expended or frozen in the means of production, counts as labour of a certain quantity because of the *social valuation* both of the labour embodied in the means of production and of the labour newly added to those means of production (because of the double reduction mentioned above). The two dimensions (the physical and the social) are inseparable. To hold that labour embodied is only a physical quantity of human energy (simply so many hours) is a naturalistic notion which crashes against the impossibility of measuring the labour contained in past outputs; to hold that labour embodied is only a social valuation would cancel the objective basis of value and fall into some of the sorts of subjectivist notions of value criticized above. The labour *embodied* in commodities is the *social valuation* of the (past and present) expenditure of the human energy that has been *actually necessary* to produce those commodities.[6]

There are several reasons why the notion of labour embodied has been given such a detailed treatment. Here, only two will be mentioned. First, this notion allows the quantification of the value contained in the commodity labour power (and thus the surplus value accruing to the owners of the means of production) not purely as a monetary phenomenon (i.e. at the level of exchange) but first of all as a production phenomenon. This means that value is quantified before this period's exchange (but obviously after the previous period's exchange, or realization). The importance of this is that it becomes possible to quantify surplus value at the level of production, as the difference between the 'hours' paid to the labourers at the end of this period and the hours they have been working during it.[7] *Exploitation* manifests itself at the level of exchange but arises in the production sphere. This by the way is the ultimate limit of all redistribution schemes aimed at superseding the capitalist system.

Second, this notion of value makes it possible to quantify the value contained in the output of a production process before it is sold, and thus to theorize and quantify the loss/gain, in terms of labour hours, inherent in the exchange of commodities (unequal exchange). Both of these aspects will play a prominent role in this and the following chapter. It should not be forgotten, however, that the value contained in a commodity is value destined to be exchanged (i.e. the commodity must be sold) and to realize itself as money. This is why it is also called *exchange value*.

Up to here, the analysis has focused on grounding the notion of value on labour. But this is not sufficient. There are several conditions for labour to become value in a capitalist society. First, given that concrete and abstract labour are two indivisible aspects of labour, labour, to be exchange value, must both create (and thus modify or preserve) use values and be expenditure of human energy abstracting from the specific aspects of the labour performed. This means that activities which (a) do not create (or modify, or preserve) use values and (b) are carried out to force other people to act upon use values (the work of control and surveillance) cannot create value even if they too are expenditures of human energy. This point will be dealt in some details further down in dealing with unproductive labour and non-labour. Second, what has just been said applies to both material commodities and mental commodities (knowledge). But the production of knowledge is a topic which cannot be examined here.[8]

Third, given that in capitalist society production is carried out by some (the labourers) for others (the entrepreneurs, or owners of the means of production), labour can be exchange value only if carried out under these specific production relations. Labour expended outside capitalist production relations can produce use values (and thus wealth) but does not produce value. Capitalist production relations are the *social form* of value and labour is the *substance of value.*

Fourth, the product belongs to the owners of the means of production, who do not consume it but must sell it, that is, convert it into money. If the sale does not take place, labour has been expended, exchange value has been produced, but it has not been realized. It as if it had never been expended. *Exchange value*, then, is labour as abstract labour that is performed under capitalist production relations and that, therefore, must manifest itself as money.[9] Moreover, the same labour, as concrete labour, must transform use values. Only if all these condition are satisfied does labour become value.

This notion of value has been derived from the incontrovertible empirical observation that in a capitalist economy (a) some people own the means of production and others do not; (b) that the latter must work for the former; (c) that all participate in a process of production the outcome of which must be sold for money; (d) that this sale implies that the product has some use for the purchasers (or it will not be sold); and (e) that, for the system to reproduce itself, the proceeds of this sale must be sufficient for the owners of the means of production to make a profit. What is not empirically observable is (a) that machines do not create value and (b) that the owners of the means of production appropriate value from their employees (rather than produce it). This is *surplus value*, which, when the output is sold, takes the form of money profits. These two points are usually hotly disputed.

Let us consider the first point, that is, that only people (and thus not machines) create value. To see this, consider a limit case, a fully automated economy. In this instance there would be no labourers. The system would no longer be a capitalist one and no value, as defined above, could be created. It could be argued that the owners of the means of production could sell their products to each other. But then they would exchange their use values for their own consumption and would no longer be capitalists but independent producers. A fully automated capitalist economy is unthinkable. This shows that machines, that is, the means of production, do not create value. However, they do create use values.[10] Actually, as we shall see shortly, machines increase the productivity of labour (and thus the appropriation of value), and this is why they are constantly applied to the production process. The opinion that machines can create value can be held on the basis of the observation that more advanced machines do produce more use values and because no distinction is made between concrete and abstract labour.

If machines do not create any new value, their value must be transferred to that of the product (or the entrepreneur would not recover the value of the machine through the sale of the product). This implies that each moment of work is a moment of wear and tear and thus of transfer of a part of that machine's value to the value of the product. Since the wear and tear affects the machine as a specific object, as a use value, it must be a specific type of labour which, by diminishing the use value of that machine, transfers its value to that of the product. That is, the exchange value of the machine is transferred to that of the product through concrete labour. But the same moment of labour is also abstract labour and thus the creation of new value. Up to a certain point, the new value created is equal to the *value of the labourers' labour power*, that is, the value of the commodities which are deemed necessary, under specific historical and social circumstances, to reproduce the labourers. From that point on, extra value, or surplus value, is created which, as it will be argued in a moment, is appropriated by the owners of the means of production.

Each moment of labour, then, both transfers the value of the means of production to the output (through concrete labour) and creates the new value contained in the output (through abstract labour). A part of this new value is the labourers' wages (necessary labour) and the other is profits (surplus value or surplus labour). It is in this way that the value of the commodity is formed. During the process of production, the value of the means of production does not change (it is simply transferred to that of the product). This is why the money, capital, invested in the means of production is called *constant capital*. The value invested in labour power, on the contrary, does change (it increases, since it creates surplus value). This is why the capital invested in labour power is called *variable capital*. If V is a commodity's value, c is constant capital, v is variable capital, and s is surplus value, then

$$(1) \quad V = c + v + s$$

on the basis of which we can define the *rate of surplus value* as $s' = s/v$ and the *rate of profit* as $p' = s/(c+v)$.

Relation (1) accounts for the value contained in each commodity. This, as anticipated above and as shown in more detail below, is not the same as the value realized by it. This discrepancy is due to the transfer of value due to technological competition and to discrepancies between demand and supply. However, at the aggregate level, given that the value lost by a commodity is gained by some other commodity, the value contained must coincide with the value realized. Thus, relation (1) accounts also for the value realized at the aggregate level and for the economic agents' purchasing power. The value realized by the capitalists for their commodities is the *capitalists' purchasing power*. They receive sufficient capital to purchase again the means of production (c), to purchase again their own means of consumption (s), and to pay the labourers their wages (v). The last is also the *labourers' purchasing power*. With variable capital (v), the labourers purchase their means of consumption from the capitalists while the capitalists purchase both the means of production and their own means of consumption (s) from each other.

Wages are then both the share of total value going to the labourers (tendentially, the value of their labour power) and these latter's purchasing power. Contra orthodox economics, *real wages* refer neither to money wages corrected for inflation nor to wages' purchasing power in terms of means of consumption (use values). Rather, unless differently specified, real wages are understood as that share of the total value produced going to the labourers, irrespective of whether this share is represented by a greater or smaller quantity of money and irrespective of whether it can buy a greater or smaller quantity of use values, that is, of means of consumption. Real wages can change because of changes in the size of the labour force employed and/or because (given a certain monetary expression of value) the value of labour power changes and/or because total money wages fall or rise relative to the monetary expression of the value of labour power. The latter two cases correspond to a change in the rate of surplus value.

The second hotly debated point concerns the notion that profit is value appropriated from the labourers by the entrepreneurs. Orthodox economics is squarely opposed to this idea. Rather, it submits that profit is the entrepreneurs' reward for their participation in the production of value (broadly understood as production proper, distribution, exchange, and including the financial and speculative spheres). The arguments most commonly put forward are the following.

First, it is held that entrepreneurs are rewarded for abstaining from consumption. Whatever the merits of abstinence and whatever the reasons for rewarding it, it is impossible to argue that one creates something (value) by not participating in its consumption.

Second, it is submitted that entrepreneurs are rewarded for selling the products in the most advantageous way possible. Commercial activities are certainly essential for capitalist production but they can only realize, rather than produce, value. Take a two-people, one-commodity economy. If they engage in constant sales/purchases of that commodity, one might get richer at the expense of the other (and vice versa), but the value at their disposal, that commodity, does not in any way increase in spite of possible inflationary phenomena. The same applies to nations and to trade relations between nations.

Third, the entrepreneurs are supposedly rewarded for taking risks. Whatever the merits of, and the reasons for rewarding, this behaviour, neither the quantity nor the value of commodities is affected by it.

Fourth, it is submitted that entrepreneurs are rewarded for performing the managerial function. This is a more serious argument. Before dealing with it, an important distinction must be made. We have seen that the production process produces both use values and value, the two aspects of commodities. Since the labourers produce not for themselves but for the capitalists, a series of means of control is required. This ranges from the most brutal coercion to the most subtle forms of persuasion, and passes through a wage policy deliberately designed to spur and/or to divide the labour force. It is conceived and implemented both by the entrepreneurs themselves and by those to whom this function is delegated. Thus, the typical function performed by the capitalists, as representatives of capital, is to control and discipline labour. This is called the *function of capital*, and this aspect of the production process is called the *surplus value producing process*. The labourers, on the other hand, perform the *function of labour*. This means that they deal with use values either by transforming them (and these are the productive labourers, that is, productive of value and surplus value) or not (and these are the unproductive labourers, as in the commercial activities). They perform the other aspect of the production process, the *labour process* (the process which deals with use values either by transforming them, as in production, or not, as in exchange). In short, the *production process* is the combination of the labour process and of the surplus value producing process.

This allows us to conceptualize the *managerial function*. This encompasses both the function of capital and (aspects of) the function of labour, such as the work of coordination and unity of the labour process (which includes the combination of the factors of production). The managerial function is performed not only by the capitalists but also by all those to whom the function of capital is delegated, from the CEO, through various layers of managers, down to first line supervisors. Those who control other people (and those who are controlled can be labourers and/or other agents performing the function of capital), inasmuch as they perform this function, neither participate in the transformation of use values (and thus cannot create value) nor deal with use values without changing them (as in commercial activities). Rather, they *force/persuade* other people to perform the function of labour or the function of capital. Put in the simplest way, if one must force/convince other people to transform use values, one cannot participate in that transformation. Therefore, the capitalists and all those who perform the function of capital create value only inasmuch as they perform the function of labour. But in this case, and only inasmuch as they perform this function, they are not capitalists. Inasmuch as they perform the function of capital, they cannot create value. If they do not create value, they must expropriate and appropriate, in the form of profit, a share of the value produced by the labourers. The way they do that is by forcing the labourers, directly or indirectly, through coercion or persuasion, to work for a time longer than the time needed to produce the labourers' wage goods, that is, to provide surplus labour. The notion that capitalists, managers and all the bureaucratic apparatus at their service create value rests on the failure to draw these basic distinctions.[11]

Fifth, it is proposed that entrepreneurs are rewarded for the introduction of innovations. Here too, a distinction should be made. If new technologies are applied to the labour process, the entrepreneur has performed one of the aspects of the function of labour and thus has contributed to the creation of (surplus) value. If they are aspects of the function of capital, then the entrepreneur is part of the process of expropriation and appropriation of value (surplus value).

To sum up, it can be held that capitalists and managers create value only because of the failure to distinguish between production and realization of value, or between objective factors of production and subjective motivations, or between the function of capital and the function of labour.

We can now examine some important differences between the approach submitted here and the orthodox view. In terms of the neo-classical synthesis, the relationship between income, or output (Y), consumption (C), investments (I) and savings (S) is given by

$$(2) \quad Y = C + I = C + S$$

First, the categories in relation (1) are in terms of value (as defined above). In relation (2) the production and realization of surplus value (s), and thus the conflicting nature of capitalist production and realization, is absent. Or, while relation (2) conceals the fundamental social contradiction of a capitalist society, that is, the production of value by some through the function of labour and the appropriation of value by some other through the function of capital, relation (1) reveals them. This can be clearly seen if the two definitions of rate of profit emerging from (1) and (2) are compared. According to relation (1), the rate of profit is the ratio of surplus value to the sum of constant and variable capital. According to relation (2), the profit rate is the ratio of profits to capital stock (plants and equipment). Exploitation as expropriation of surplus labour is absent from a notion of rate of profit in which it is capital stock rather than labour which generates profits, that is, surplus value.

Second, relation (2) implies equilibrium (even though possibly at less than full employment) while relation (1) does not. Relation (1) indicates the value contained in commodities, whether this is realized or not. More specifically, as a rule the value contained in any commodity will deviate from the value it realizes (see below) while the value contained in total production can or cannot be fully realized. Moreover, in relation (1) only labour can be the substance of value. This implies, as we shall see shortly, that even if all the total value produced were to be realized, that is, even if there were equality between demand and supply, the inexorable march of the capitalist system towards depression and crises could not be halted. Relation (2), on the other hand, implies equilibrium since investments are defined as equal to savings. Given that in real life this is usually not the case, orthodox economics considers inventories as investments. But, while investments produce new value, inventories are past, already produced but yet unrealized, value. Contra orthodox economics, capitalists know very well the difference between a certain quantity of money as unsold inventories and the same quantity invested in means of production and labour power.[12]

Third, this has repercussions for the multiplier. In Keynesian economics an initial increase in investment produces a rise in income several times greater. The ratio between the change in income and the change in investments is the multiplier. The mechanism is as follows. An initial investment translates into an equal increase in income. A part of this greater income is saved and the other is consumed. This greater consumption in its turn is an income increase that leads to yet further consumption and saving, and so on. At each round, consumption and income increase less than in the previous round due to the fact that some income is not consumed but saved. In this theory, then, income and thus wealth (value) increase due to successive rounds of consumption and *in the absence of further investments*. However, in the absence of investments, and thus of extra production, people can only purchase and consume goods which have already been produced but not yet sold. The multiplier, then, indicates not by how much value (wealth) has increased (aside from the first injection of investments) but rather by how many goods lying idle (value previously produced) have been sold (have been realized). Moreover, for this initial investment to produce extra value (extra income), capital has to be invested in the productive sphere, that is, labour has to be productive labour, as defined above (see also Carchedi, 1991a, ch. 5).

Fourth, relation (2) implies that psychological motivations are the prime mover of the economy. In relation (2), S and I are equal *in accounting terms* (as just mentioned, on the basis of nonsensical accounting principles). But *in real terms*, they are not. To explain this, the notion is introduced that I and S, while always equal in accounting terms, can and do differ in terms of the plans of the economic agents. It is then the difference between planned S and planned I (subjective factors) which determines the course of economic life. Relation (1), on the other hand, implies that the course of the economy is determined by objective factors, the production and realization of (surplus) value. The economic agents' motivations are but the way in which this objective movement manifests itself through the individuals' consciousness. Therefore, in relation (1), the real inequalities between D and S (supply), that is, disequilibrium, become one of the theory's building blocks.

Fifth, while both (1) and (2) assume that $D = S$, the meaning attached to this equality is radically different. Relation (2) assumes that in reality all products are, or tend to be, sold and that at this point the economy has reached equilibrium, whether this is the level of full employment or not. In terms of relation (1), equilibrium on the market is no equilibrium at the level of the production and realization of value (i.e. the production price is no equilibrium price). As already mentioned, even if all commodities were sold, the system would still tend towards crises due to the crisis-prone nature of capitalism, itself a consequence of technological competition. Let us see why.

One of the basic contradictions inherent in capitalist production is that between the production of use values and of (exchange) value. That is, the introduction of technological innovations (TIs) usually implies the shedding of labour so that an increasing quantity of output is produced with a downsized labour force. Given that only labourers can produce value, an increasing quantity of use values contains a decreasing quantity of value and thus of surplus value. If abstraction is made of the many countertendencies, some of which will be dealt with shortly, the average rate of profit (ARP), defined as total surplus value divided by the total capital invested, cannot but fall.[13] To see this, let us distinguish the sector producing means of production (sector I) from that producing means of consumption (sector II).

Consider first the case of a productivity increase in sector II with concomitant unemployment in that sector. This increase has not been carried out homogeneously in the whole sector. Some producers of means of consumption have introduced technological innovations (thus shedding labour) while some other capitals have failed to do so. More use values (means of consumption) are produced per unit of capital in sector II due to the technological leaders. However, less value is produced by them (in that sector). Let us provide a simple example.

Consider the $t0-t1$ period. Let us assume that initially, at $t0$, to each unit of value (V) there corresponds one unit of money (M). Then, the *monetary expression of value* (M/V) is 1. Suppose $200V = 200M$ are invested in constant capital and that $100V = 100M$ are invested in variable capital, as in table 3.1. In this table c = constant capital, v = variable capital, s = surplus value, V = value, MP = means of production, MC = means of consumption and M = money. The rate of surplus value (s/v) is assumed to be 100 per cent and each sector is represented by one capital unit.

During $t0-t1$ a value of 400 is produced. At $t1$, as the *end-point* of $t0-t1$, under the assumption that all products are sold, sector I realizes a rate of profit equal to $20/100 = 20$ per cent. Capitals IIa and IIb realize a rate of profit equal to $40/100 = 40$ per cent each.[14] Unit prices are different: $120M/100MP = 1.2V = 1.2M$ in I and $280V/200MC = 1.4V = 1.4M$ in II. We focus on sector II. Since the rate of surplus value is 100 per cent, labour buys $100MC$ at $100 \times 1.4 = 140M$ and capital does the same. Therefore wages must be $140M$ and profits too.[15] This means that at $t1$ as *the starting-point* of $t1-t2$ the value of labour power has increased from $100V = 100M$ to $140V = 140M$.[16]

Table 3.1 Productivity increase in the wage goods sector: initial situation

		Output
I	$80c + 20v + 20s = 120V = 120M$	$100MP$
IIa	$60c + 40v + 40s = 140V = 140M$	$100MC$
IIb	$60c + 40v + 40s = 140V = 140M$	$100MC$
	$200c + 100v + 100s = 400V = 400M$	

Consider now a different situation in which IIa is more productive than IIb. It now produces 150MC instead of 100MC while having shed labour. This is indicated by a greater c (70 instead of 60) and a lower v (30 instead of 40). Since, for sake of comparison, the rate of exploitation ($s/v = 100$) is assumed not to change, s too decreases to 30.

The rate of profit of sector I remains unchanged. Sector II produces a value of 270V = 270M which is embodied in 250MC.[17] The output unit price in II is 270M/250MC = 1.08M. Capital IIa realizes 1.08M $\times$ 150MC = 162M and its rate of profit is $(162 - 100)/100$ = 62 per cent. Capital IIb realizes 100MC $\times$ 1.08M = 108M and its rate of profit is 8 per cent. Capital IIa gains at the expense of capital IIb even though it produced less value. Labour gets 135M to buy 125MC, and so does capital. All the means of consumption can be sold. As long as the output prices of the MC fall with wages and profits, there are no realization problems. At the level of realization, that is, in terms of demand and supply, the market is in equilibrium. However, the technological leader in II has increased its rate of profit from 40 per cent to 62 per cent while the technological laggard has seen its rate of profit fall from 40 per cent to 8 per cent. A further step in the same direction might erode completely IIb's profits and cause its bankruptcy. If IIb goes out of business, it cannot buy any more MP from I. Overproduction arises also in I.

At first, owing to falling output unit prices being more than compensated by rising productivity, lower real wages might command a higher quantity of MC than the quantity commanded before the increase in productivity. In table 3.1 a total wage of 140M can buy 100MC while in table 3.2 a total wage of 135M can buy 125MC. This explains why the negative effects that technological innovations have on labour's purchasing power might at first not be visible. However, once the technological laggards start experiencing profitability difficulties, there is augmenting pressure on real wages, that is, on total money wages, to fall relative to the monetary expression of labour power. If this happens, labour's purchasing power becomes insufficient to purchase its previous share of MC.

A temporary relief can come from shifting this purchasing power to capital. But there are limits to the capitalists' capacity to absorb means of consumption in spite of conspicuous consumption and the production of luxuries. Realization problems start appearing in sector II. The more real wages are reduced, the greater the realization problems in sector II. The

Table 3.2 Productivity increase in the wage goods sector: results

		Output
I	$80c + 20v + 20s = 120V = 120M$	100MP
IIa	$70c + 30v + 30s = 130V = 130M$	150MC
IIb	$60c + 40v + 40s = 140V = 140M$	100MC
	$210c + 90v + 90s = 390V = 390M$	

higher real wages are pushed (through demand stimulation) in order to increase labour's purchasing power, the smaller the realization problem but the greater the profitability problem. Both Keynesian and neo-liberalist policies are impotent *vis-à-vis* depression and crises. As we shall see later, inflationary policies are no solution either.[18] The more capitals in II reduce wages in order to increase profits, the more realization problems appear in II. The more capitals in II close down, the more realization problems appear also in I.

But wage policies are only one option. The other is for the technological laggards to increase their own rate of profit (and to avoid realization difficulties) by investing in more productive techniques. But this, while improving their own situation, causes more unemployment and worsens, rather than relieves, the economy's profitability and realization problems.[19] The economy has fallen into a downwards spiral. The greater the business failures, the more severe the realization difficulties of the survivors. Orthodox economics perceives this process in a typically topsy-turvy fashion. Less value has been produced (by the technological leaders in sector II) and thus less value can be realized in that sector. However, a greater share of this reduced quantity of value is appropriated by the technological leaders. The technological laggards start experiencing profitability problems. Real wages are reduced. This creates realization problems. This discrepancy between demand for and supply of means of consumption is the final result of this chain of causation but is perceived by orthodox economics as its initial cause.

Consider next a productivity increase in the capital goods sector, again accompanied by decreased employment in that sector. Table 3.3 gives the initial situation.

The rate of profit is 20 per cent in I and 40 per cent in II. Again, we disregard the effects of capital mobility on the production of value and thus the tendential formation of an average rate of profit. Suppose now a situation in which Ia is more productive than Ib, which means that Ia produces more MP per unit of capital invested while disposing of 'redundant' labour force (see table 3.4).

Now the output unit price in I falls from $240M/200MP = 1.2$ in table 3.3 to $230M/230MP = 1$ in table 3.4. Capital Ia realizes $1M \times 130MP = 130M$ and thus a rate of profit equal to 30 per cent, up from 20 per cent. Capital Ib realizes $1M \times 100MP = 100M$ and thus a rate of profit equal to zero,

Table 3.3 Productivity increase in the capital goods sector: initital situation

		Output
Ia	$80c + 20v + 20s = 120V = 120M$	$100MP$
Ib	$80c + 20v + 20s = 120V = 120M$	$100MP$
II	$60c + 40v + 40s = 140V = 140M$	$100MC$
	$220c + 80v + 80s = 380V = 380M$	

Table 3.4   Productivity increase in the capital goods sector: results

		Output
Ia	$90c + 10v + 10s = 110V = 110M$	$130MP$
Ib	$80c + 20v + 20s = 120V = 120M$	$100MP$
II	$60c + 40v + 40s = 140V = 140M$	$100MC$
	$230c + 70v + 70s = 370V = 370M$	

down from 20 per cent. Ia gains at the expense of Ib even though it produces less value. Ib can continue to operate but will succumb as soon as some other capital in sector I introduces the new technologies. As long as Ib survives, there is market equilibrium. But as Ib goes bust, Ia cannot sell its *MP* to Ib and II cannot sell its *MC* to Ib's labourers. Insufficient purchasing power arises both in I and in II as companies in I go bankrupt, and in II as companies in I reduce wages in order to stem falling profitability. This is all the ultimate result of the decreased production of value.[20]

To sum up, owing to TIs in sector II, the more the technological laggards in that sector reduce their wages in order to counter falling profitability, the stronger is the tendency towards overproduction, that is, the labourers' insufficient purchasing power, in II. The more companies in II go bankrupt, the greater the overproduction in I, that is, the insufficient purchasing power by capitalists in II to buy sector I's MP. If TIs take place in sector I, again the more the technological laggards in that sector reduce their wages in order to counter falling profitability, the stronger is the tendency towards overproduction, that is, the labourers' insufficient purchasing power, in II. The more companies in I go bankrupt, the greater the overproduction in II, that is, the greater labour's insufficient purchasing power.

Up to here we have disregarded capital movements and their effect on the production and distribution of value. That is, the effects of the diminished production of value by the technological leaders have been felt only by the laggards in the same sector. If we now introduce capital mobility, for each level of technological development there arises a tendency towards the equalization of the different sectors' rates of profit into an average rate of profit. It should be emphasized that this is only a tendency and that in reality profit rates differentials do not disappear. However, the hypothesis of an average rate of profit is useful to determine the tendential price levels in all sectors if TIs are introduced in one sector and thus to determine the appropriation of value associated with the changed level of value produced and with its changed redistribution. This redistribution, that is, appropriation of value, affects all sectors of the economy even if TIs are introduced in just one sector. For example, in table 3.2, that is, before the equalization of the rates of profit due to capital movement, sector I realizes a profit rate of 20 per cent, IIa of 62 per cent and IIb of 8 per cent. There is no equalization of profit rates either among the two sectors or within sector II. If we now assume an equalized profit rate across sectors, the average rate of profit is

$90/300 = 30$ per cent. Then, I realizes $130V = 130M$ and II realizes $260V = 260M$. The unit price of the MC is $260M/250MC = 1.04M$ and IIa realizes $1.04 \times 150 = 156M$ while IIb realizes $1.04 \times 100 = 104M$.

The price level at which all capitals[21] realize the average rate of profit is called the *production price*. This is a moving target, for two reasons. First, each time a TI is introduced, this tendential price changes. Second, even in the absence of further TIs, production prices would differ from the real prices, or *market prices*, because of shifts in demand among sectors which alter those sectors' profitability. However, shifts in demand are not unrelated to profitability. In fact, a higher rate of profit (for some capitals) in one sector relative to other sectors determines a capital influx in that sector and thus an increased volume of production. Market prices (and thus profitability) tend to fall and demand for those commodities tend to increase. The opposite holds for capitals in sectors with lower rates of profit than those of other sectors. However, this should not all be taken as implying an equilibrium between demand and supply. Here too the difference with orthodox economics is sharp. Productivity levels, and thus profit differentials and capital movements, determine demand and supply. In orthodox economics demand and supply are disjoined from production.

It should be emphasized that TIs do not automatically *engender unemployment*, they do so *only tendentially*. TIs generate unemployment because the variable capital (labourers) employed per unit of capital usually falls (the saving on labour costs is just a powerful incentive to innovate as the increase in efficiency). However, the introduction of new technologies can be accompanied by increased employment if (a) new branches of production are opened up and (b) if the number of labourers shed by each unit of capital is more than offset by an increase in the number of units of capital invested, that is, by an increase in the total capital invested. In other words, the tendency is for TIs to generate unemployment (if the same or a smaller quantity of capital is invested on the basis of 'labour-saving' technologies) but the counter-tendency is the opposite, that is, is given by the creation of more employment for capital as a whole even if each unit of capital uses less variable capital and more constant capital.

While the tendency (technological unemployment per unit of capital invested) is always present, it manifests itself as higher societal unemployment only in periods of crises, that is, of decreased capital accumulation. In periods of economic boom it manifests itself as its own counter-tendency (higher societal employment). The rest of this work will return to, and elaborate upon, this theme.

It could be argued that the analysis above could be carried out without having to resort to the notion of value. It would be sufficient to assume that the quantity of money (M) falls in spite of the increased productivity and of the increased production of use values. The fall in profitability following TI could be explained in terms of falling prices of use values. Bankruptcies would explain lower purchasing power without having to resort to a fall in value rate of profit. Yet, there are at least three reasons why this option is foreclosed:

- First and foremost, the dismissal of value has a devastating effect on economic theory since (as Marx shows in masterly fashion in *Capital* Volume I) only value can explain exchange.[22] If exchange cannot be accounted for, production (in an exchange economy) remains unaccounted for as well.
- Even if one were to disregard this point, exclusive focus on the use value aspect of commodities makes it impossible to theorize a lower M with increased productivity.[23]
- Suppose finally that one were to accept that M decreases if productivity increases. Then, one would have to accept that TI (embedded in the capitalist production relations) is the ultimate cause of crises and that crises are unavoidable. This would be a radical break with orthodoxy, whose fundamental notion is that TI is the root and motor of economic growth.

To end this section, a last point. Up to here the focus has been on the production and appropriation of (surplus) value and thus on only two classes, capitalists and labourers. This is the hub of capitalist economies and these are its two fundamental classes. However, it is clear that the class structure of any capitalist society is articulated in more than these two classes. Even at the level of capitalist production relations, one can theorize both the old and the new middle classes. Moreover, while the capitalist production relations are the fundamental ones, a capitalist system encompasses also other production relations, such as those defining independent producers and peasants. Finally, if political and ideological factors are considered, both fractions of classes and social groups cutting across classes emerge (Carchedi, 1977, 1991). This more detailed class analysis, irreplaceable in a different context, is omitted here since focus on the two fundamental classes is sufficient for the purpose of this work, which is that of revealing the inner dynamics of capitalism and thus of the European Union.

3.2 The Illusions of the EC Treaty

Article 2 of the EC Treaty lists the objectives of the European Union. They are

> to promote throughout the Community a harmonious and balanced development of economic activities, sustainable and non-inflationary growth respecting the environment, a high degree of convergence of economic performance, a high level of employment and of social protection, the raising of the standard of living and quality of life, and economic and social cohesion and solidarity among member states.

Such an idyllic situation can be painted only by using the neo-classical economics brush, that is, only by assuming (contrary to all empirical observations) the optimal allocation of resources in a crisis-free economy tending towards equilibrium. The logical faults marring this theory have been exposed in the previous chapter. The first section of this chapter has argued that, from a different perspective, capitalism appears as a crisis-prone economic system. The ultimate cause of crises has been identified in technological development within capitalist production relations. It is now time to analyse the form of manifestation of crises: the economic cycle. In the course of this analysis, it will become clear that the aims of article 2 of the EC Treaty are mutually inconsistent.

While the introduction of labour-saving technologies within capitalist production relations, and thus the contradiction between a decreasing quantity of value contained in an increasing quantity of use values, is the ultimate cause of economic crises, these latter manifest themselves in cyclical form.[24] Consider first economic recovery. Existing capitals expand their investments and thus, given a certain technology, their employment. On the one hand, more means of consumption, means of production and luxury goods are produced. On the other, more labour power is productively employed. This means that more (surplus) value, and thus more purchasing power for both capitalists and labourers, is created. The former have the purchasing power to absorb capital and luxury goods, the latter to absorb consumption goods. Also, new enterprises arise and new sectors of production emerge, thus further increasing investments and employment. Capital grows and accumulates. But this situation cannot last forever.

During the recovery, the demand, and thus the price, of raw materials and labour power increases. Profits are compressed. But even if this were not the case, individual capitals would still aim at growing (i.e. at increasing their profitability) at the expense of each other. This is their inner drive, apologetically perceived by orthodox economics as the law of the survival of the fittest. The major way for capitalists to compete within sectors is by introducing technological innovations. This move is spurred not only by the need to save on rising input costs, but also by the need to improve efficiency, that is, the units of output per unit of capital invested, and thus competitiveness and profitability. As seen in the previous section, these new investments produce less value per unit of capital invested. However, given their higher productivity, they realize a higher rate of profit. The ARP decreases and the rates of profit of the technological laggards decrease even more. The latter's reduced profitability spurs them to adopt the more efficient technologies.[25]

Initially, the extra employment caused by expanded reproduction and by the creation of new sectors of production is greater than the unemployment caused by technological innovations and capital concentration and centralization. The extra production is matched by the extra purchasing power needed to absorb it. The new technologies, by casting off labour per unit of capital invested, cause a fall in the ARP. However, given that more units of capital have been invested, the total surplus value, and thus the total mass of profits, increases. This conceals the fall in the ARP. However, the non-innovative capitals start experiencing realization difficulties. But, at a certain point, owing to increasing technological competition as well as to capital concentration and centralization, the number of people laid off surpasses the number of people absorbed by the labour market. Unemployment starts appearing.[26] Realization difficulties are temporarily delayed by drawing upon reserves and through the payment of unemployment benefits and other anti-cyclical measures (see below) but eventually must become manifest. The rate of utilization of productive capacity falls, that is, a part of the means of production remains unutilized. At this point the virtuous cycle becomes a vicious cycle.

The more enterprises seek to avoid the effects of the upcoming slack, the more they 'rationalize', that is, shed people. This has positive effects for the innovative companies but negative effects on the weaker enterprises, some of which go bankrupt. Each time an enterprise goes bust, capital, that is, capitalist production relations, is destroyed. Each time capital is destroyed, less value can be produced and consequently less value can be realized. But also, given the interconnection between the production and distribution units in the economy, each time an enterprise goes bankrupt, other enterprises experience difficulties (e.g. because of default on debts). The crisis expands from those enterprises and sectors where it began to the rest of the economy. This destruction of individual capitals has a beneficial function for capital as a whole. It destroys those capitals which, in terms of capitalist competition, are weaker because less able to compete. The ARP falls.[27]

But the same forces that cause crises cause also the end of crises and the beginning of a new period of recovery and boom. The destruction of capital, as production relations, is at the same time the condition for the overcoming of crises. As sufficient capital has been destroyed, those capital units which have survived the clean-up, and which realize high profit rates due to their advanced techniques, can cater to a larger share of the market. This share of the market was previously catered to by less efficient capitals which operated under increasingly difficult conditions (that is, lower profit rates) and which eventually had to resort to closures and unemployment. With the disappearance of these capitals, the same share of the market can be supplied by the more efficient capitals. They have survived the crisis and, owing to their higher profitability and thus possibility to accumulate, can expand their activities, thus increasing employment and the production of (surplus) value (purchasing power). Higher profitability without realization difficulties is made possible by growing employment at relatively low levels of real wages.

Growth becomes self-sustaining due to the increasing production of both value (higher purchasing power) and surplus value (higher profits). This renewed economic dynamism extends itself to the less dynamic businesses and sectors. These capitals' conditions of survival might not be threatened any more because of the general increase in society's purchasing power. For them, simple, instead of expanded, reproduction might be all the system has in store.[28] Recovery begins anew. This movement is summed up as a falling ARP during stagnation and crises and as a rising ARP in periods of economic growth and boom (Carchedi, 1991a, ch. 5).

Crises are thus due not to underconsumption (overproduction) of use values[29] but to underproduction of (surplus) value due to TI embedded in capitalist production relations. They become visible as (a) destruction of capital as social relations, that is, bankruptcies, closures, and unemployment; (b) devalorization of capital if some capitalists must undersell their products[30] or if bankrupt capitals are taken over by the stronger ones and their means of production are acquired at sell-out prices[31] (c) destruction of capital as finished commodities (if the products of the bankrupt capitals are not sold and are destroyed as use values due to either the action of natural elements or to technological competition which makes them obsolete) and as unfinished commodities (if the interruption of the production process leaves the product unfinished);[32] (d) difficulties of realization, if the decreased purchasing power is not matched by lower prices; and (e) financial, monetary and budgetary crisis as well as inflationary processes (see below). All these manifestations of crises find their expression in the cyclical movement of the average rate of profit. Let us provide some empirical substantiation for the theory submitted above. (The following three figures are taken from Freeman, 1999).[33]

Figure 3.1 shows clearly the inverse relation between the movement in capital stock and the rate of profit, both measured in value terms. 'Statistical analysis confirms that 80 per cent of the variation in the value rate of profit is explained by changes in the capital–labour ratio' (Freeman, 1999, p. 8). This figure

> picks out critical turning points. The peak of 1914 signals the exhaustion of the third industrial revolution and the wave of classical imperialist expansion of the 1890s. The long irregular decline to 1939 accompanies the prolonged interwar general crisis and the 1933 peak marks the great depression. The long boom of 1945–1962, the onset of a phase of profitability crisis in 1962, and the sharp turning point of 1980 all stand out. (Freeman, 1999, p. 8)

Figure 3.2 shows that, even though capitalists react to their own money rates of profit, the average money rate of profit fluctuates around the average value rate of profit due to the fact that it is changes in value production and distribution which determine the movement of the economy (the economic cycle). At the aggregate level, money quantities express value quantities and, while diverging from the latter, are cyclically attracted to them. The reason for this is that if less value is produced, less value can be realized (and vice versa). As we shall see below, an increase in the quantity of money can only postpone the fall in the average rate of profit, while an increase in the surplus value produced and realized translates into an increased quantity of use values and thus in the monetary authorities increasing the quantity of money in circulation.

The same inverse relation between capital stock (constant capital) and rate of profit is empirically evident also in money terms, as in figure 3.3.

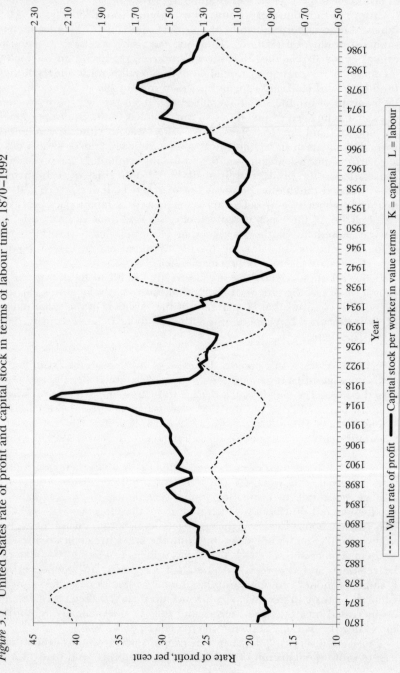

Figure 3.1 United States rate of profit and capital stock in terms of labour time, 1870–1992

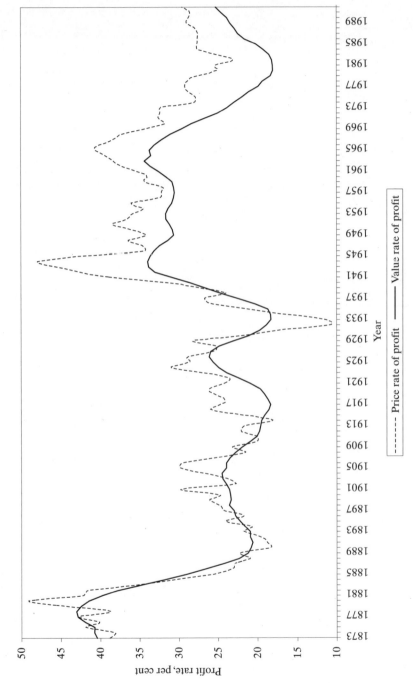

Figure 3.2 Money and labour-time profit rates compared

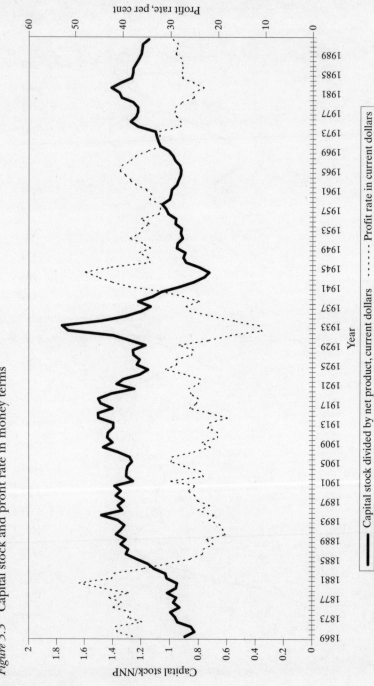

Figure 3.3 Capital stock and profit rate in money terms

——— Capital stock divided by net product, current dollars - - - - - - Profit rate in current dollars

NNP = Net National Product.

The two terms should be inverted here, namely NNP/Capital stock (in order to measure profit). (Freeman's oversight.) – G.C.

Having sketched the causes and course of the economic cycle, let us consider some lines of criticism that might be made to this approach. The approach just sketched runs counter to the commonly held but mistaken idea that an increased productivity raises the ARP, rather than decreasing it. There are many reasons for this misconception. The following are the most common ones.

First, most economic theories consider only one aspect of productivity increases: the greater physical output per unit of capital invested. These theories see only physical quantities and disregard the value (labour) dimension. Thus, they cannot understand how a greater physical productivity can lead to a falling ARP.

Second, higher output per unit of capital can be achieved either through TI or through greater intensity of labour and longer working days (absolute surplus value). While in the former case less value and thus less surplus value is produced (given that labour is shed) so that the ARP falls, in the latter case more (surplus) value is produced, so that the ARP rises. Usually no distinction is made between these two cases, so that confusion arises as to the effects of the introduction of TI on the creation of value and on the ARP.

Third, the innovators do realize a greater rate of profit, at the expense of the value appropriated by other producers, thus causing a fall in the ARP. An acritical extension to all capitals of the effects of TI on the innovators' profit rate leads to the erroneous conclusion that TI must increase the ARP.

Fourth, exploitation is not synonymous with poverty. High rates of surplus value do not necessarily imply greater poverty in terms of use values (the level at which people perceive wealth). In the technologically advanced countries high exploitation rates can be achieved through greater efficiency and thus through higher productivity in the wage goods sectors. This creates the possibility that those countries' labourers receive more wage goods with lower labour contained. The situation is different in technologically backward countries. Here, high rates of surplus value are achieved through (a) the implementation of relatively inefficient techniques, (b) high labour intensity and longer working days and (c) towering inflation rates (combined with devaluations, as we shall see below). The second and third factors are much more important in the underdeveloped countries than in the developed ones. Their effect is that people's lives are burned up in a much shorter time than in the developed counties, that is, that their labour power does not get the chance to reconstitute itself fully. In particular, inflation has a devastating effect on the labourers's purchasing power. In this case, greater poverty in terms of use values does indicate a greater extraction of surplus value.[34]

There are thus sound reasons for accepting the thesis that TIs reduce the ARP because they generate unemployment (and equally sound reasons for rejecting the critique of this thesis). However, this is not an absolute law. Capital tries to check this fall either due to its inner working or through conscious policies. Since the effects are contradictory, the analysis will be carried out in terms of the tendency (the introduction of TIs and concomitant unemployment) and counter-tendencies. In other words, even if the inner dynamics of the cycle can be explained purely in terms of the tendency, a more complete analysis must take the counter-tendencies into account.

Let us begin with some definitions. The previous section has submitted that the fall in the ARP, defined on the basis of relation (1) above as $p' = s/(c + v)$, is caused by technological innovations accompanied by unemployment, that is, by an increase in constant capital relative to variable capital per unit of capital invested. The relation between constant and variable capital, or $q = c/v$, is called *organic composition of capital*. Since the replacement of people by machines within each capital unit is a constant tendency, the organic composition of capital tends always to rise and the ARP tends always to fall. However, this tendency becomes manifest only if the counter-tendencies are not strong enough to overpower it. When the counter-tendencies get the upper end, the ARP rises. However, after a while they exhaust themselves and the tendency (the fall in the ARP) emerges again. There are two major counter-tendencies.

The first counter-tendency is an increase in the *rate of surplus value*, defined above as $s' = s/v$. The relation between the rate of profit (p'), the organic composition of capital (q) and the rate of surplus value (s') is as follows:[35]

$$(3) \quad p' = s'/(q + 1)$$

This relation shows how a rise in q causes a fall in p' and how a rise in s' causes a rise in p'. The point is that these two factors have a different status. An increase in q (and thus a fall in the ARP) is the tendency while a greater s' (and thus a rise in the ARP) is the counter-tendency. In other words, the ARP has a tendency to fall, and this is why the capitalist economy tends towards crises. This thesis must now be shown and further articulated.

It is usually adduced that a rise in q could in theory increase indefinitely while there are limits to an increase in s'. These limits are first of all socio-cultural, given that labourers grow accustomed to a certain level of living, and then biological, given that the longer the working day and/or the more intense the labour, the more difficult it becomes to raise that length or intensity further. What is referred to here is an increase in absolute surplus value, that is, greater intensity of labour and longer working days. Put in these terms, this argument is not convincing, given that q cannot increase indefinitely. At a certain point there would be no labour employed any more and then we would have a different socio-economic system. A less categorical version stresses that the limits posed to an increase in s' would be reached before those encountered by a rise in q. This version is more acceptable. Yet there is a more compelling reason why the rise in q overpowers that in s'. This is that while a rise in q has only negative consequences for the ARP, a rise in s' has both a positive and a negative consequence. The positive effect is an increase in the extraction of surplus value (the level of production), while the negative effect is the increasing difficulty encountered in realizing it (the level of realization). Beyond a certain point the two effects balance each other out (i.e. the extra value and surplus value and thus the increase in the rate of profit cannot be realized) so that on balance only the effects of a greater q remain. Let us see why.

Consider first an increase in absolute surplus value, that is, longer working days and higher intensity of labour, in sector II (which produces means of consumption). More surplus value and more use values (means of consumption) are produced. If the capitalists can absorb this extra production (value), profitability increases without realization problems. But, as already repeatedly mentioned, this option exhausts itself rapidly. If the entire extra product can be absorbed by labour, then there has not been an increase in surplus value but a wage rise. But this is not the way capitalism works. Any point in-between implies realization problems. Consider now greater intensity and longer days in sector I (which produces means of production). The quantity of means of consumption does not change, while more means of production are produced. In principle there are no realization problems.[36] However, given labour mobility (as well as institutional factors such as the action of the trade unions), there is a tendency towards the equalization of s'. This equalization will cause a rise in s' in sector II and thus will cause realization difficulties in sector II. The positive effect on the ARP deriving from an increase in the rate of absolute surplus value at the level of production is neutralized by a negative effect the same rate has at the level of realization.

The second counter-tendency emerges because a greater productivity in sector I engenders a fall in the means of production's unit value (price). Once the means of production become inputs of subsequent production processes, the organic composition of capital decreases. More value and surplus value is then produced per unit of capital invested in these sectors and the rate of profit rises. But, again, this is only a counter-tendency. In fact, the new means of production are not only cheaper but also more efficient, that is, labour saving. Once introduced, the capitalists profit not only from their lower cost (value) but also (and principally) from the possibility they offer to shed labour force. The tendency (a rise in q) will re-emerge within the counter-tendency (a fall in q). Thus, the cheapening of the means of production can only postpone unemployment and crises, not avoid them. The same applies to the case of product innovations, that is, to the emergence of new sectors of production, whose organic composition is lower than the average (e.g. software). Here too, after a while, capital's necessity to replace people by machine will re-emerge. In short, counter-tendencies postpone the upcoming crisis but cannot avoid it. The history of capitalism is there to confirm this.

The same conclusion applies to those conscious policies aimed at eliminating the cycle or at least at reducing its amplitude.[37] First, governments engage in *monetary policies*. Consider, initially, interest rates reductions aimed at stimulating consumption and production. To begin with, if the producers' and the consumers' mood is gloomy, they might not respond to lower interest rates by increasing production or consumption. Their pessimism might be aggravated by the realization that consumers are already saddled by high levels of indebtedness.[38] Also, of those who do react to lower interest rates, only some will engage in production of value (the only way to weaken or reverse the tendency to crises). Some will engage in unproductive activities (i.e. in the sphere of circulation), some will refinance debts or engage in speculative activities, and some might increase purchases. As long as the production of value has not increased, it will be inventories that are sold rather then new output being stimulated by those monetary measures.[39] Prices cannot but rise.

The point, however, is that the positive effects on the production of value brought about by lower interest rates cannot turn depression and crises into their opposite. In a situation of economic malaise, few will find outlets for profitable productive investments. The majority will borrow in order to beef up their meagre purchasing power and/or for unproductive investments (e.g. attempts to sell existing investments under the pressure of realization difficulties) and/or for speculative activities. This puts extra pressure on prices. This is why these policies in times of economic malaise must cause inflation even though they might have a limited impact on production, employment and profitability (the counter-tendency). This is also why higher interest rates can decrease inflation but cannot but worsen the economic situation. Fine tuning is a myth.

It could be argued that inflation has positive effects on profit rates either by decreasing wages or by increasing output prices. Consider, first, a decrease in the value of labour power and thus in labour's purchasing power. This can be achieved through a rise in the price of wage goods greater than the rise in wages. Lower wages equal higher profit rates, *ceteris paribus*. This holds certainly for individual capitalists. But on the macroeconomic level this can increase profit rates only initially. Subsequently, it cannot but create realization problems in sector II (see above). Consider next an increase in the price of the means of production. This would not work for the same reasons that an increase in output prices does not work. Given that the outputs of this period are also the inputs of the next period, if the price of the outputs of this period rise, the prices of the inputs of the next period are also by definition greater. This reduces the rate of profit in the next period, *ceteris paribus* (and aside from the redistribution inherent in the different rates at which different prices increase). From that point on, a constant inflationary process is needed to avoid lower money profits at the end of each period, that is, to prevent money profit rates from falling in accordance with the fall in value profit rates. This self-reproducing inflationary process is aggravated every time an attempt is made to neutralize a new fall in the public's purchasing power through a new injection of money. Inflation can delay but not avoid the fall in the ARP. This is why it is a counter-tendency aimed at checking the tendency towards economic crises. It delays crises while at the same time depreciating money (i.e. through a fall in money's purchasing power).[40]

There are two misconceptions surrounding inflation. The first is that it is the result of mistaken calculations, that is, of excessive increases in the quantity of money (including credit) relative to the stability of the unit prices of both resources and outputs. This thesis can be taken seriously only if somebody can explain why the same mistakes are made time and again. In reality, the monetary authorities must allow inflation. But this must not exceed a certain limit. If it does, international competitiveness is weakened, devaluation becomes inevitable, and the renewal of foreign debt in the form of fixed income assets is discouraged (see next section). The rate of inflation is then the result of the degree to which the monetary authorities are willing to weigh its positive and negative effects under the pressure of the different social classes and groups acting in their own interest. The fixing of a required rate of inflation, as in the Maastricht criteria (see next chapter), is always in the interests of some and against the interests of others.

The second misconception identifies the source of inflation in wage increases higher than the increase in sector II's productivity. But 'high' wages are an excuse used by the employers' organizations and the monetary authorities in order to get back a part of the value lost through higher wages. The key variable linking wages to inflation is the power relations among classes, that is, capital's ability to reduce real wages through inflation, which is the reverse of labour's militancy. Low wages (i.e. high profits) and low prices (i.e. a favourable competitive position) are the ideal situation for capital. It is this situation which is canonized by orthodox economics as the most rational one because it is supposedly the most favourable for all. The argument is that low inflation leads to high employment through greater markets shares, higher profits and higher investments. The bottom line is 'if the cost of labour is reduced, firms will be encouraged to take on more workers' (European Commission, 1994b, p. 4). But if lower wages increase profits, they also discourage their realization. Moreover, higher profits need not result in higher productive investments (they can lead to unproductive consumption or financial investments), and these latter do not lead necessarily to higher employment (if invested in labour-saving techniques). The relation between low wages and high employment passing through low inflation is nothing more than the rationalization of capital's wishes, that is, low labour militancy, as if it were the most rational state of affairs for all. To show this, the cause of high inflation (and thus high unemployment) must be found in high wages. This is the alpha and omega of orthodox inflation theory.

Let us now consider the second type of anti-crisis measures, *fiscal policies*. Lower taxes are assumed to stimulate demand for capital and wage goods by increasing both profits and wages. Here too the relief is only at most temporary and in any case not automatic. First, lower taxes might but do not necessarily increase demand. People might save the extra purchasing power or use it for speculative purposes. Second, if taxes are lowered, state revenues decline, and with them the possibility for the state to stimulate demand (e.g. through state procurements, state subsidies and various benefits). Third, and most importantly, if the extra income is spent on consumption, it is existing inventories which are sold. If it is invested, the same reasoning applied to monetary polices suggests that only a limited share of these investments will generate (surplus) value and that the rest will be invested in unproductive or speculative spheres. Here too fiscal policies can only be a counter-tendency.

Third, there are *budgetary policies*. We have seen that in times of economic depression both investments and purchases of consumer goods slow down. Money is hoarded rather than spent. It would seem that these ailing sales could be countered through state borrowings that are then used to stimulate demand (e.g. through state procurements). But this is not the case. On the one hand, what has been said regarding the insufficiency of monetary and fiscal policies to start a stable recovery holds here too and need not be repeated.[41]

On the other hand, the money borrowed must be paid back. If debts are rolled over by means of further debts, a financial crisis of the state is in the making due to the mounting debts on interests. At this point, governments can resort to two main strategies. The first one is to default. This can happen indirectly through inflation and taxation. Inasmuch as the state repays its debt with devalued money, a part of that debt is not paid back. Through repayment with devalued money, the state appropriates a part of the value whose monetary expression it has borrowed. This has a negative effect both on profits and on demand. Or, the value (money) needed to repay state debts can be appropriated by the state through taxation. Again, this might have a negative effect on profits and demand. But the state can also resort to open default, through insolvency. This is of course a measure of last resort. When the state defaults on its debts, either openly or indirectly, either partially or totally, either the capitalist class or the labourers are forced to accept *post festum* a reduction either of profits or of wages. A part of profits and/or wages reveals itself to have been illusory. That value has been simply consumed by the state. Alternatively, governments can resort to privatization. This is a way in which capital attempts to ward off the fall in the average profit rate. But state ownership, large as it may be, is limited, hence this strategy is limited too.

It has been mentioned above that the state can borrow or appropriate value in order to finance state procurements. An important case is the state-induced production of weapons. The state's purchasing power is value appropriated from both capitalists and labourers and thus is a diminution of these two categories' purchasing power. What is gained on the one hand is lost on the other.[42] Moreover, the more a nation's resources are spent on the production of weapons, the less are they available for the production of the means of production and of the means of consumption. In a competitive setting, this is a recipe for troubles. However, the production of weapons has the advantage of being much less sensitive to the different phases of the cycle than other types of expenditure given the non-reproductive nature of these goods. It has the further advantage that it is neither extra production of consumption goods nor extra production of capital goods (which would aggravate realization problems in both sectors).

Inasmuch as weapons are not used, it is production of useless things and thus wasted labour in order to keep the system going. Inasmuch as they are used, they destroy other goods as well as people. The judgement about the rationality (in terms of the satisfaction of human needs) and morality of such a system is left to the reader. The EU is certainly not innocent in this respect. 'In 1995, nine EU countries ranked in the world first 30 positions for exports of major conventional weapons, of which Germany, United Kingdom, France, Netherlands, and Italy in the third, fourth, fifth, seventh and eighth positions, respectively' (Finardi et al., 1998, p. 1).

To conclude, in spite of the many counter-tendencies, crises are unavoidable. The capitalist system reproduces itself through a cyclical succession of depressions, crises, recoveries and booms. The effects of crises, however, are felt less in that bloc of nations that are technologically advanced (the imperialist bloc) and more in those countries that are the technological laggards. To anticipate chapters 4 and 6, the technologically advanced nations export a part of the increased quantity of products following a productivity increase. What is realized is value produced in other countries, thus achieving a greater ARP in the exporting country at the expense of the value appropriated by other countries. The nations that have been left behind can resort to devaluation in order to increase their exports. In this case, they surrender a part of the value produced.

To end this section, a few remarks are in order. First, the analysis above implies a two-class model of the economy and thus of society. Of course, in a real society (economy) there are more than two classes (see Carchedi, 1975, 1977, 1983, 1987, 1989, 1990, 1991a). This (otherwise very important) fact does not invalidate the above because whatever value (and thus purchasing power) is appropriated by other classes cannot be appropriated by the two fundamental classes. If part of the (smaller) mass of total value is given to other than the two fundamental classes, there is a simple redistribution of value. If that quota comes from wages, a part of the diminished purchasing power of the working class goes to other classes, but the realization difficulties remain unsolved. If that quota comes from profits, the ARP falls.

Second, data on GNP and profit rates cannot be used to support or falsify a crises theory based on value categories, since they are computed by using categories which do not coincide with value categories. To judge the state of the economy, unemployment, bankruptcies and the masses' insufficient purchasing power are more reliable indicators than official figures on both GNP and profit rates.[43] For example, we can observe in the capitalist developed nations wide fluctuations in the enterprises' mortality rate in periods of crisis and also, since the early 1970s, a long-term high rate of unemployment which, even though fluctuating, shows an increasing trend.

Third, disregard of the value dimension leads to the erroneous conclusion that a social category's income, or share of GNP, corresponds to the value produced by it (where value, differently from what has been submitted above, is the monetary expression of use values). In reality, the income perceived by a class or social group measures the value realized by it through the sale of its commodities (including labour power). This is different, as shown above, from the value produced (labour worked) by it. For the labourers, the difference is given by surplus value; for the capitalists, it is the difference between the value contained in their products and the value realized through the price mechanism.

Fourth, owing to the international redistribution (appropriation) of value, GDP figures are not the money measure of the value produced in a certain nation: they express the value realized by that nation. This appropriation goes from the weaker (dominated) to the stronger (imperialist) countries. It follows that, in the economically stronger nations, the three above-mentioned indicators of the state of an economy (unemployment, bankruptcies and insufficient purchasing power) understate the scale of recession and crises. These topics will be dealt with in the next chapter. The task of this chapter is that of showing how hopelessly misconceived and mystifying are the aims stated in article 2 of the EC Treaty. Given the importance of article 2, the EC Treaty (and the following ones) turns out to be a system of practical rules chasing illusory ends.

3.3 From International Prices to Monetary Crises

We have seen in chapter 2 that orthodox theory cannot be relied upon to explain international trade. The current chapter has expounded the basic laws of development of capitalism and highlighted the difficulties capital encounters in realizing the value it produces. The thesis which follows logically from the above is that the ultimate cause of international trade, and its inner rationality, is the need for capitals to realize the highest possible profit rate, if need be abroad. It is within this perspective that the formation of economic and trade blocs, including the European Union, should be placed.

We have also seen that capitals are moved by a constant quest for profits. This quest causes both technological innovations, that is, competition within sectors, and capital movements across sectors, that is, competition across sectors. It is through this double and interrelated process that prices emerge. These prices favour the technological leaders and punish the technological laggards, that is, the former appropriate surplus value from the latter. The thesis to be argued for in this section is that this holds also for different countries.

The first task then is to explain the prices at which commodities exchange. This requires a value theory of national prices first and then one of international prices. Since different countries have different currencies, a theory of exchange rates will have to be provided. This will allow us to see the unequal exchange inherent in international trade and thus the appropriation of value by the technologically advanced capitalist countries. It is through these exchange rates that the technological leaders maximize their profit rates. The other countries, being dependent upon the former, must cede part of their surplus value if they engage in international trade. They too aim at maximizing their profit rate, but they do so under unfavourable circumstances.

3.3.1 International Prices

To illustrate the basic elements of the labour theory of price formation, let us assume a three-sector economy as in table 3.5.

This and the following tables can be read either in value terms (as defined in section 3.1 above) or in money terms, since the former can be derived from the latter.[44] Each sector is represented by only one capital that invests one unit of capital, subdivided in constant capital (c) and variable capital (v). Thus, the total capital invested by each capital is always equal to 100 (i.e. c and v can be read as percentages). The assumption of only one capital for each sector does not prevent a theorization of a multiplicity of capitals within sectors. It only means that, given price competition, each capital within a sector buys its means of production and labour power at the same price (for the same value), that is, at the average value, and sells its products for the same price. That sector, then, can be represented either by one unit of capital or by a multiple of it. This is the tendential situation that we can assume to coincide with the real situation because it rests on a real movement (price competition). Different input and output prices would not invalidate the analysis, they would only enrich it.

Table 3.5   The tendential equalization of profit rates

	$c + v + s = V$		$PrPr\,(C)$	$PrPr\,(C) - V$	OCC	O	$PrPr\,(O)$
Sector A	$80c + 20v + 20s = 120V$	120	0	4	100	1.2
Sector B	$90c + 10v + 10s = 110V$	120	10	9	120	1.0
Sector C	$70c + 30v + 30s = 130V$	120	-10	2.3	130	0.9
Total	$240c + 60v + 60s = 360V$	360				

As mentioned above, the ratio c/v is called organic composition of capital (OCC, fifth column in table 3.5), the ratio $s/(c + v)$ is called the rate of profit (not shown in the table), and the ratio s/v is called the rate of surplus value (also not shown in the table). This latter is a measure of how much of the new value produced is appropriated by capital. We assume a certain rate of surplus value, for example 100 per cent, that is, we assume that labour produces as much surplus value as the value of its labour power. The rate of surplus value is assumed equal in all three sectors because of the assumption that labour is free to move from one sector (where that rate is higher) to the other (where it is lower). Again, it is warranted to assume equal rates of surplus value because this hypothesis is based on a real movement (labour mobility). Here too different rates would not change the analysis.

The total surplus value is 60, the total value produced is 360, and the average rate of profit (ARP), that is, $s/(c + v)$ for all three sectors, is 60/300 = 20 per cent. If capitals are mobile across sectors, they leave the low-profitability sectors to enter the high-profitability ones. Tendentially, therefore, each sector realizes the ARP. This assumption too is methodologically sound because it strikes its roots in a real movement (capital mobility across sectors). Thus, the value tendentially realized by each sector is equal to the average value of the inputs $(c + v)$ plus the average rate of profit. This is the *price of production* per unit of capital, $PrPr(C)$ in table 3.5, which is equal for all capitals.[45]

Three equalities have been assumed: of prices within sectors, of rates of surplus value both within and across sectors, and of rates of profits also within and across sectors. This has been done in order to focus on only one feature: the difference between the value contained in the commodities and the value which would be realized through their sale if they were to be sold at their price of production. This is the $PrPr(C)-V$ column. For example, sector B produces an output (O) of 120 commodities whose value is $V = 110$ but sells them at $PrPr(C) = 120$ if the three rates of profit are equalized. It appropriates a value of 10. This is also called *unequal exchange*. Since the total value appropriated must be equal to the value produced, the sum of the $PrPr(C)$ column must be equal to zero. Finally, the last column gives the price of production per unit of output, $PrPr(O)$.

The relation between the OCC and profitability in table 3.5 should be clarified. Technological innovations reduce variable capital and increase constant capital (i.e. increase the OCC) per unit of capital invested. Within sectors this it taken to be a sign that productivity (units of output per unit of capital invested) has increased. Higher productivity translates into higher profitability due to price equalization (see examples in tables 3.1 and 3.2 above). Given that only the value produced can be realized, the higher profits of the technological innovators must be offset by lower profits for the technological laggards. The former appropriate surplus value from the latter.

But table 3.5 does not refer to three different capitals within a sector. Rather, it refers to three capitals, each representing a sector. As argued in chapter 2, productivity differentials cannot be computed in any meaningful way across sectors. Thus, in table 3.5, there is no reason to assume that sector B (high OCC) is more productive and thus more profitable than sector C (low OCC). There is thus no reason to assume capital movement from C to B either unless we assume that sector B has increased its productivity relative to the previous level. It can thus sell its higher output at, say, the same price. Given society's total purchasing power, prices will have to fall in (and thus value will be lost by) other sectors up to the point where (tendentially) all rates of profit are equal. This is the first assumption behind table 3.5. The second one is that demand equals supply, in the sense that demand is such that all capitals sell all their output and realize the average rate of profit, 20 per cent.[46] If demand does not equal supply, the actual prices, also called *market prices*, fluctuate around these tendential prices, the prices at which all capitals realize the ARP, that is, the production prices.

Let us now introduce technological innovations. Consider table 3.6, where V is the value produced (contained), O is the output, VTR is the value tendentially realized and $VTR–V$ is unequal exchange.

Table 3.6 is an extension of table 3.5 in that each sector is now represented by three capitals: the above mode, the modal and the below mode capitals.[47] The difference with table 3.5 is that now the average rate of profit is tendentially realized only by the *modal productivity capitals* within each sector: those which use the modal technique and which therefore produce the bulk of the products in that sector. This follows logically from the following three points. First, the hypothesis that tendentially all capitals within sectors use the same technique is methodologically warranted because it rests on a real process, technological competition. Given that all capitals aim at the highest profit rates, they aim at the most efficient technique. This allows us to theorize a tendency towards a common technique. Second, at any given point in time, there will be a scale of techniques so that the average will not be the highest technique. Or, the ARP is realized tendentially by the average-productivity, and not by the high-productivity, capitals.[48] Third, the notion of mode, rather than of mean, has been chosen because it represents better the present situation (oligopolistic competition) in which a restricted number of producers produce the bulk of commodities. It follows from these three points that modal capitals realize tendentially the average rate of profit, while above-

Table 3.6 Prices of production before technological change

	Below mode	Modal	Above mode
Sector A I		II	III
V	$75c + 25v + 25s = 125V$	$80c + 20v + 20s = 120V$	$85c + 15v + 15s = 115V$
O	90	100	110
VTR	108	120	132
$VTR–V$	-17	0	17
Sector B I		II	III
V	$85c + 15v + 15s = 115V$	$90c + 10v + 10s = 110V$	$95c + 5v + 5s = 105V$
O	50	60	70
VTR	100	120	140
$VTR–V$	-15	10	35
Sector C I		II	III
V	$65c + 35v + 35s = 135V$	$70c + 30v + 30s = 130V$	$75c + 25v + 25s = 125V$
O	120	130	140
VTR	110.8	120	129.2
$VTR–V$	-24.2	-10	4.2

and below-mode capitals tendentially realize higher and lower than average rates of profit.

In table 3.6, the total surplus value produced is $s = 180$ and the total capital invested is $(c + v) = 900$. Thus the average rate of profit is ARP = $180/900 = 20$ per cent. This is profit rate all modal capitals realize (i.e. capitals AII, BII and CII). The total value each modal capital realizes is arrived at by adding this rate of profit to the capital invested (which is always equal to 100 because we consider the percentage composition of the capitals invested). This is the price of production per unit of capital invested. Unit prices are derived by dividing this price by the modal output. They are the prices of the commodities produced under average conditions of profitability. Thus, the unit price of sector A is $120/100 = 1.2$, that of B is $120/60 = 2$, and that of sector C is $120/130 = 0.923$. Non-modal capitals realize tendentially this unit price times their own output so that their tendential rate of profit differs from that of the modal ones according to their level of productivity. For example, capital AIII realizes VTR = $1.2 \times 110 = 132$ and thus a rate of profit of $132/100 = 32$ per cent, a value higher than the average (20 per cent).

Here too the implicit assumption is that $D = S$. Within this new context, this means that social demand is such that all commodities are sold (minus unwanted inventories) at the price realized by modal capitals, that is, that demand is such that all modal capitals realize the ARP.[49] If we now drop the $D = S$ assumption, in a certain sector modal capitals might realize a profit rate greater than the ARP while the modal capitals in another sector might realize a rate of profit smaller than the ARP. These are the market prices, fluctuations around the production prices. Consider now the introduction of TI and its effects on profitability (table 3.7).

Table 3.7 is a modification of table 3.6. In that table, capital BI (an arbitrary choice) invests $(c + v) = (85 + 15) = 100$ and realizes VTR = 100 (i.e. it loses a potential profit of 15). Since it does not make any profit, if it wants to improve its competitive position, it can either move to another sector or shift to more efficient technologies. Table 3.7 has been constructed on the hypothesis that BI introduces BII's technology, the modal one. Now BI's rate of profit rises while the ARP falls. *Ceteris paribus*, this means that the rate of profit of all other capitals has fallen (i.e. that their profits have decreased or that their losses have increased). Let us see how.

Given that BI's constant capital has risen and its variable capital and surplus value have fallen, the total surplus value falls from 180 to 175 while the total capital invested remains 900. The total value available for redistribution through the price mechanism is then 1,075. Let us shift for a moment to table 3.8. The ARP is $175/900 = 19.44$ per cent, less than 20 per cent. The value tendentially realized by all three modal capitals is 119.44 (see VTR(M) in table 3.8). The value of the commodities produced under average conditions of productivity/profitability is then $119.44/100 = 1.1944$ for A (lower than 1.2 in table 3.6), $119.44/60 = 1.9907$ for B (lower than 2), and $119.44/130 = 0.9188$ for C (lower than 0.923) (see VTR/0 in

Table 3.7   Prices of production after technological change

	Below mode	Modal	Above mode
Sector A I		II	III
V	$75c + 25v + 25s = 125V$	$80c + 20v + 20s = 120V$	$85c + 15v + 15s = 115V$
O	90	100	110
VTR	105.5	117.3	129
VTR− *V*	− 19.5	− 2.7	14
Sector B I		II	III
V	$90c + 10v + 10s = 110V$	$90c + 10v + 10s = 110V$	$95c + 5v + 5s = 105V$
O	60	60	70
VTR	117.3	117.3	136.8
VTR− *V*	7.3	7.3	31.8
Sector C I		II	III
V	$65c + 35v + 35s = 135V$	$70c + 30v + 30s = 130V$	$75c + 25v + 25s = 125V$
O	120	130	140
VTR	108.2	117.3	126.3
VTR− *V*	− 26.8	− 12.7	1.3

table 3.8). Multiplication of these *VTR/ O* by the total output in each sector gives the unadjusted total value tendentially realized in each sector, as in the third column of table 3.8. These totals are called unadjusted because if we add the sector totals we get 1,095, whereas the value available for distribution is only 1,075 (the sum of the nine *V*s in table 3.7). Since only the value produced can be distributed, prices have to fall. Under the assumption that all commodities realize equally less (this assumption is needed to maintain an equal ARP in all three sectors), a distributional ratio equal to $R = 1,075/1,095 = 0.9817$ must be applied. This is done in the last column of table 3.8, whose total is 1,075.

The unit prices (*VTR/ O*) are now 1.1944 × 0.9817 = 1.1725 for A, 1.9907 × 0.9817 = 1.9543 for B and 0.9188 × 0.9817 = 0.9019 for C. Multiplication of these prices by each capital's outputs gives the figures in table 3.7. The sum of each capital's *VTR− V* is equal to zero, that is, all the value has been realized through this new redistribution.[50] Comparison of tables 3.6

Table 3.8   Value tendentially realized (VTR) after the application of the distributional ratio

	VTR(M)	*VTR/O*	*Unadjusted total VTR*	Adjusted total *VTR*
A	119.44	1.1944	1.1944 × 300 = 358.33	R × 358.33 = 351.665
B	119.44	1.9907	1.9907 × 190 = 378.23	R × 378.23 = 371.309
C	119.44	0.9188	0.9188 × 390 = 358.33	R × 358.33 = 351.665

and 3.7 reveals that capital BI (the technological innovators) has realized a greater rate of profit while contributing less to the production of surplus value. All other capitals realize less. Capitals BII and BIII realize less because of capital BI's increased productivity. Capitals in sectors A and C realize less because of the assumption that unit prices fall in all three sectors while the purchasing power in sector B is sufficiently great to absorb all the extra production. In other words, there has been a redistribution of surplus value from sectors A and C to sector B.

Let us now extend this analysis to the international scene, as in table 3.9, whose purpose is to exemplify the redistribution of value, or unequal exchange, inherent in international price formation. Here we have two countries, Italy and France. The assumptions are the same as in the previous tables, with some differences. First, sectors A and B are common to both countries while C belongs only to Italy and D only to France. Consequently, different OCC in C and D cannot indicate different levels of productivity. Second, we assume that A's modal productivity in Italy (capital AII) is equal to the highest productivity France can reach (capital BIII). Italy is then the international leader in A and the ARP will be realized by AII in Italy and by AIII in France. France's modal productivity in B (capital BII) is equal to Italy's highest productivity in the same sector (AIII). France is the international leader in B and the ARP will be realized by BII and by BIII. Consequently, capitals BII in Italy and AII in France realize a rate of profit smaller than the international average in spite of their being the modal capitals on the national scale. What counts now is international levels of modal techniques.

The way the figures in table 3.9 are arrived at is similar to that in the previous tables. In this table, total $s = 405$, total capital invested = 1,800, and the ARP = 405/1,800 = 22.5 per cent. The VTR by modal capital per unit of capital would then be 122.5. The *VTR* per unit of output is arrived at by dividing this figure by the modal output. For example, in A it is 122.5/100 = 1.225, both for AII in Italy and for AIII in France. Since the value which would be realized on the basis of these prices would amount to 2,154, and since the value actually produced is 2,205, a distributional ratio must be applied equal to 2,205/2,154 = 1.0237. Multiplication of this ratio by the modal prices gives us the adjusted prices. For example, 122.5 × 1.0237 = 125.4. These are then the prices upon which the *VTR* by all capitals can be computed. Finally, if we subtract *V* from *VTR* we obtain the unequal exchange inherent in price formation.

The discussion above has been carried out in terms of value. But value must be expressed as money. Therefore, under the assumption that to each unit of value there corresponds a unit of money (or a multiple of it), the tables above can also be read in monetary terms. However, in table 3.9 there are two countries and thus two currencies. International production and distribution, thus, implies the conversion of one currency into the other, and the analysis of this real movement implies a theory of exchange rates. This will be the task of the next section.

Table 3.9 International prices of production

	ITALY		
	I	II	III
Sector A	Below mode	Modal	Above mode
V	$75c + 25v + 25s = 125V$	$80c + 20v + 20s = 120V$	$85c + 15v + 15s = 115V$
O	90	100	110
VTR	112.85	125.4	137.92
$VTR - V$	-12.15	5.4	22.92
Sector B	Below mode	Modal	Above mode
V	$80c + 20v + 20s = 120V$	$85c + 15v + 15s = 115V$	$90c + 10v + 10s = 110V$
O	50	55	60
VTR	104.48	114.93	125.4
$VTR - V$	-15.52	-0.07	15.4
Sector C	Below mode	Modal	Above mode
V	$65c + 35v + 35s = 135V$	$70c + 30v + 30s = 130V$	$75c + 25v + 25s = 125V$
O	50	60	70
VTR	104.48	125.4	146.27
$VTR - V$	-30.52	-4.6	21.27

	FRANCE		
	I	II	III
Sector A	Below mode	Modal	Above mode
V	$70c + 30v + 30s = 130V$	$75c + 25v + 25s = 125V$	$80c + 20v + 20s = 120V$
O	85	90	100
VTR	106.57	112.84	125.4
$VTR - V$	-23.43	-12.16	5.4
Sector B	Below mode	Modal	Above mode
V	$85c + 15v + 15s = 115V$	$90c + 10v + 10s = 110V$	$95c + 5v + 5s = 105V$
O	55	60	70
VTR	114.93	125.4	146.27
$VTR - V$	-0.07	15.4	41.27
Sector D	Below mode	Modal	Above mode
V	$60c + 40v + 40s = 140V$	$65c + 35v + 35s = 135V$	$70c + 30v + 30s = 130V$
O	120	130	140
VTR	115.73	125.4	135
$VTR - V$	-24.27	-9.6	5

3.3.2 A Value Theory of Exchange Rates

We have seen that if a capital in a country improves its productivity, it boosts the quantity of use values per unit of capital invested while decreasing the value produced. If that capital sells its greater output on the foreign market, it appropriates a greater quantity of foreign currency which, upon exchange in the national currency, results in a higher profit rate.[51] The innovative capital has increased its profit rate while causing the production of less international value, thus contributing to the formation of realization difficulties. Through commodity exports, that capital also exports those difficulties. Other capitals in the same country might follow its lead. As long as this process is restricted, the rate of exchange is not affected. However, if one or more sectors in that country experience a continuous and generalized productivity increase, the demand by other countries for that country's currency increases, thus generating an upwards pressure on, and eventually an appreciation[52] of, that currency. There is a fall in the *rate of exchange*, defined as the rate at which the national currency is converted into one unit of the foreign currency.[53] While greater appropriation of international value due to increased efficiency benefits only the innovative exporters, appreciation benefits all holders of that currency, whether in the productive or in the financial and speculative sphere.

As argued in chapter 2, comparisons between productivity differentials are meaningful within sectors but meaningless across sectors. It is then impossible to construct a multi-sector indicator of productivity and relate it to exchange rates. Nevertheless, it is possible to relate exchange rates to changes over time in productivity differentials within sectors. Starting from a given situation (different countries with different economic structures and their exchange rates), any increases in any country's productivity in any sector will tend to revalue or appreciate its currency. The ultimate impact on its exchange rate is then the summation of the effects of all productivity changes in all sectors. The pressure to appreciate is therefore directly proportional to the technological lead gained in any sector and to the number of sectors in which this leadership has been attained. The obverse is the case for the technological laggards.

But this notion of technological leadership is not yet sufficient. In an economy there is a hierarchy of sectors according to their strategic importance for capital accumulation and thus for international trade. Then, a *country* can be defined as a *technological leader*

- where only one sector is considered if its average productivity in that sector is higher than in other countries; and
- where more than one sector is considered if that country leads technologically in the major high-technology and innovative sectors (e.g. the high-technology products to be considered in chapter 4, section 2 below).

Consider now two specific categories: the importers and the exporters. Following appreciation, all exporters (and not only the innovative ones) appropriate more international value in its money form for each unit exported (disregarding for the time being whether exports are discouraged or not).[54] All importers need less national currency to purchase foreign currencies and thus foreign goods. Appropriation of value increases in this case as well.[55] But appreciation affects also the quantities both imported and exported. The dearer national currency encourages imports (assuming that imports' prices in foreign currencies remain unchanged). The share of international value appropriated on this account (in the form of foreign money and thus as importers' profits) increases. On the other hand, exports are discouraged (the foreign importers need more foreign currencies to buy the same quantity of national currency and thus of goods priced in that currency). The share of international value appropriated falls, realization difficulties increase and profitability levels fall. The above can be put in terms of tendencies and counter-tendencies.

Owing to technological advance in the export sectors and concomitant higher productivity with shedding of labour by a country's innovative exporters, the mass of (surplus) value produced decreases so that both profitability and realization difficulties increase in that country while that country's currency appreciates. The *tendency* is the countering of the profitability crisis through the appropriation of a greater relative share of that decreased mass of international value both by the exporters (more foreign money is received for each commodity exported) and by the importers (less national money is spent for each commodity imported). The *counter-tendency* is the restraint imposed upon the greater appropriation of international value due to smaller exports and thus the decreased possibility of shifting the realization difficulties abroad. While technological innovations diminish the quantity of value produced, appreciation does not. It only redistributes that decreased quantity.

What strategies are there for the technological laggards? They too can try to increase their productivity. In this case, they improve their own economic situation (appropriation of value) while further contributing to the aggravation of the general situation (lower international value produced). If higher efficiency is not viable and if the technological leaders' appreciation is not sufficient for the laggards to increase their exports, the option is open for depreciation. Here too the effects can be analysed in tendential terms. The *tendency* is the worsening of the profitability crisis through a loss of value, that is, the realization of a smaller relative share of a smaller mass of international value. This holds for the exporters (they receive less foreign money/value for each unit of export priced in national money), for the importers (they must give up more national money/value for each unit of imports priced in foreign money) and generally speaking for all holders of the national currency. The *counter-tendency* is the reduction of the loss of value inherent in greater exports following depreciation because such a loss is smaller than that which would occur if there were no exports (sales) at all. The greater the exports, the greater the loss of value but the smaller the difference between this loss and the potential loss inherent in no exports at all. In terms of the functioning of the system, it is important to distinguish the tendency from the counter-tendency. It is the tendency that explains the dynamism of the system. The innovative country (innovative exporters and through them all exporters and importers) is rewarded for its increased productivity through the appropriation of more international value, that is, by shifting abroad its profitability difficulties. The country lagging behind is punished through a loss of value and thus by importing profitability crises. This movement is checked by the counter-tendency: for the leaders, the slowing down of exports and thus of the international value appropriated and of the possibility of exporting the difficulties of realization; for the laggards, the increased exports and thus the slowing down of the profitability (and realization) crises. The working of the exchange rates is, in spite of its specific characteristics, just another way to reward *tendentially* the technological leaders within the international capitalist context at the expense of those who have been left behind in the technological race.[56]

Orthodox economics ignores the value dimension. It only sees the importers' greater profits and the exporters' lower profits in case of appreciation and the importers' lower profits and the exporters' greater profits in case of depreciation.[57] It sees neither the appropriation of value following appreciation nor the expropriation of value following depreciation. Also, orthodox economics does not place this redistribution of value within the context of that decreasing production of international value that is at the root of depreciations and appreciations. It believes that stable exchange rates contribute to an equilibrium situation whereas stable rates hide the redistribution of a decreasing quantity of value. Similarly, depreciations and appreciations might work towards redressing the balance of payments. But this implies neither equal exchange nor a tendency towards equilibrium. Stable prices, whether in a national or an international context, and equilibrium in the balance of payments cannot hold back the incoming crisis. But perhaps even more important, orthodox economics does not see how crises, and thus this redistribution of a smaller quantity of international value, are made to pay by the international collective labourer. Let us see how.

The above has stressed technological laggards' resort to depreciation in order to appropriate that international value which cannot be appropriated through superior technologies. This concerns the relation between competing capitals. But there is another way for the technological laggards to achieve the same aim, one that concerns the relation between capital and labour. The technological laggards can resort to forcing their labourers to work longer and/or more intensively, thus achieving a higher production both of (surplus) value and of use values. The result is an increased rate of absolute surplus value. But the working day, as well as people's physical endurance, is limited and the labourers might resists these higher rates of surplus value. Then, real wages must be lowered through inflation, that is, through an increase in the price of wage goods greater than a possible increase in nominal wages. But higher prices in national currency impede exports unless they are offset by lower international prices. Hence depreciation. On this account too, the laggard countries, inasmuch as they try to avoid a loss of foreign markets and thus of profitability through inflation, tend to depreciate their currency. The loss of foreign markets and of international value might be checked but that country's labourers are definitely worse off.

This outcome is reinforced because depreciation in its turn can further strengthen inflation. Through depreciation, import prices in the national currency increase, thus decreasing importers' profits. If at all possible, importers pass these price increases over to national purchasers. If imports are means of production, higher input prices decrease the next production period's profits. Capitals will try to restore profitability levels by decreasing real wages. If imports are wage goods, these goods' higher prices increase profits but decrease labour's purchasing power (wages). The result is the masses' increasing impoverishment, with all the social tensions and problems associated with it. If this process goes on far enough, a country might be left with a worthless currency. This is what happened in many Latin American countries in the 1970s and 1980s. The combination of technological lag, inflation and depreciation leads to the well-known incredible conditions of misery in those countries as well to the military dictatorships and authoritarian regimes which are often needed to impose these conditions on the labourers (in case the neo-liberalist ideology fails to convince them that it is in their own interest to tighten their own belt even more). There are many ways in which crises become manifest as a deterioration of the masses' levels of living. The example of monetary crises in the next section will illustrate this perverse mechanism.

To close this section, two further specific aspects must be stressed. First, the analysis above presupposes that all countries are more or less equally able to compete technologically. This is only a first approximation. We will see that the capitalist world is subdivided into two blocs of countries, the dominant and the dominated, or dependent, ones (also called the developed and the underdeveloped countries[58]). The characteristic feature of the dominated bloc is that they might be able to introduce more efficient technologies but that they remain one step behind the dominant bloc's high technologies. The appropriation of value inherent in the dependent countries' consistently lower degree of productivity relative to the dominant ones is a constant feature of the capitalist world. Chapter 4 below will discuss these features in detail.

Second, the countries whose currency is the international one enjoy a very peculiar privilege, 'seigniorage'. This is the possibility to pay for real value with paper with no intrinsic value. It is thus another form of appropriation of value. Since the post-war period, this is the case for the US dollar. The US enjoys a privilege similar to that of a central bank when it prints paper money: by using that money to purchase foreign commodities, it too appropriates a share of international value. Of course there are limits to this privilege. The greater quantity of dollars diminishes their purchasing power[59] as well as the willingness of foreigners to hold them both as a means of payment and as a reserve currency. This erodes the status of the dollar as the international currency and thus the possibility of profiting from seigniorage. Moreover, money creation can be inflationary. This can lead to depreciation and to further erosion of the dollar's status as the international currency.[60] How has this come about?

After the Second World War, in the period of absolute US economic domination, both the First and the Third World not only did not object to receiving, but actually wanted, US dollars both because the dollar was covered by great gold reserves and because dollars allowed the purchase of cheaper and better quality US goods. This was possible because of the unscathed and more productive US economy. This is why the dollar was 'as good as gold'. The international monetary system agreed upon at Bretton Woods in 1944, in which the dollar was given a fixed gold value and the other currencies were anchored to the dollar in a system of fixed exchange rates, reflected this state of affairs. But this system could function smoothly only inasmuch as it reflected the technological superiority of the US. Once the US began to lose its absolute competitive advantage, the system of fixed exchange rates began to crack. On the one hand, the dollar was not allowed to devalue by the Bretton Woods system because its depreciation would have dented its role as international currency and its seigniorage. On the other hand, devaluation was needed as a measure to prop up US international competitiveness (in 1950, the percentage share of world industrial production was 47.8 for the US and 1.6 for Japan; in 1985 it was 39.3 and 11.5 respectively).

The US was caught in a dilemma. The solution was found in the 'soft landing' of the dollar, that is, in a gradual devaluation of the dollar in order to avoid undermining international confidence in it. But this implied a change from fixed to flexible exchange rates and the suspension of the dollar's gold convertibility. This took place in 1971. This dented the dollar's status as the international currency. Gradually, two rivals have begun to emerge as potential international currencies: the Euro and the yen. The dollar has not lost its seigniorage but its position of privilege is being increasingly threatened.[61] Chapter 5 will develop further this theme.

3.3.3 Monetary Crises, the Euro and the Dominated Bloc

The above provides the framework within which to analyse international monetary crises. Only two causes will be mentioned, those of immediate interest for this work. The first pertains to the relation between the dominant countries of the centre. The three basic points are as follows. First, there are huge quantities of dollars owned outside the US. The seigniorage attached to the US dollar has made it possible for the US to finance its current account deficits by printing money in payment for real commodities (the US has become, since 1985, the world's largest debtor country). Huge current account deficits, that is, huge appropriation of value from other countries, imply huge quantities of US dollars kept by foreign investors. Second, the more the US dollar loses its dominant position, the less it is demanded as a means of international payments and reserve currency, the less it can serve as an anchor for the value of other currencies, the more it must allow depreciation, and the more it is subject to speculation.[62] But, and this is the third point, the dollar is still the major currency in international transactions and is still used as a major reserve currency. Therefore, any speculative attacks against it cannot but reverberate greatly amplified through the rest of the world economy.

The recent advent of the Euro might further destabilize the international monetary system. This on condition that the Euro will become a true rival of the dollar (see chapters 4 and 5 below) thus claiming seigniorage. The Euro's new role will further weaken the dollar and increase international speculators' room for manoeuvre against it. At the same time, what has been said about the dollar holds also for the Euro, as long as it has not reached absolute predominance (a very hypothetical proposition): speculations against it will send reverberations through the whole international monetary system. However, there is one way in which the Euro does stabilize international monetary markets. The Euro replaces the national currencies of the Economic and Monetary Union (EMU). Therefore, it cancels automatically monetary crises within the EMU. Before the EMU, for example, usually a massive sale of dollars caused an appreciation of the German mark (a safe currency). This could not but create tensions within the European Monetary System (see next chapter). Or, to give another example, speculative attacks against the Italian lira and the English pound led to the 1992 monetary crisis within the EMS. This sort of crisis is no longer possible. But this advantage does not cancel the possibility of wider international monetary crises, between the US and the EU.

The second cause of international monetary crises pertains to the relation between the countries of the centre and the dominated bloc.[63] As depression and crises in the centre set in, the money capital that cannot find profitable investments in the productive sphere (see section 3.2 above) finds its way into the stock market. As more capital flows into it, stock prices rise and fictitious capital is created. This explains why rising and even euphoric stock prices might hide an economic malaise and usher in a sudden stock exchange crisis. With the increasing internationalization of capital and the adoption of new telecommunications technologies, huge sums of capital roam the stock markets of the world in an instant search for the highest feasible rate of profit.

Great profits (and great losses) can be made overnight in the stock exchange and currency markets all over the world, even if exchange rate differentials are small, due to the sheer size of the currencies exchanged. These capital movements can bring about wide fluctuations in the rates of exchange. This aspect has been amply underlined by financial publications as a new element in the monetary crises: 'Global investors become increasingly able to switch from economy to economy at the tap of a computer key ... with more than $1 trillion looking for a home in the foreign exchange market every day, even a slight deviation from the straight and narrow can invite a savaging' (*Business Week*, 16 January 1995, p. 20). In 1998, this sum had been estimated to have reached 2 trillion dollars. What has not been evidenced in these writings is the just-mentioned origin of these massive quantities of currencies looking for instant profits. There is thus a clear link between the present still unresolved profitability crisis and this new form of monetary turbulence.[64]

Under these circumstances, rising stock prices do not reflect a real increase in capitalization (value). Rather, this rise is fed by money that has been created in order to check and delay the emergence of crises, that is, it reflects a previous inflationary process. But, since money creation (inflation) can only postpone crises, sooner or later the crisis erupts. Bankruptcies surface at the weakest junctures of the economy. Stock prices fall, credit shrinks, more closures follow, and the crisis spills over from the stock market to the financial institutions and to the real, productive, sphere. While it looks as if crises originate in the stock market and in the monetary and currency spheres, in reality they originate in the productive realm (due to less production of value) but can manifest themselves first in the other spheres.

A wrong diagnosis cannot but lead to wrong recommendations. If one believes that crises do indeed originate in the financial domain and/or in the stock exchange, one is led to seek relief in the manipulation of the money quantity. For example, for the 'crowding-out' thesis, the international financial markets absorb an increasing quantity of money and this crowds out investments in the real economy. It is this shortage of financial means for real investments which, it is submitted, causes depression and crises. Thus the remedy is sought in the provision of sufficient money liquidity (for productive purposes)[65] and in stemming massive speculative movements (e.g. the Tobin tax). In reality, it is the lack of profitable opportunities in the productive spheres which breeds an increasing quantity of money and thus the need for swelling financial and speculative investments.

A first conclusion follows. The huge sums of capital originating in the centre and looking for profitable channels in the stock markets of the dominated bloc, including the emerging markets, delay the crisis in the centre and cushion its effects. In fact, that capital, if invested in the stock markets and financial institutions of the centre, would claim a share of total profits as dividends and interests without generating any new profits in the centre; if invested in the dominated bloc, it rakes the savings (value) generated in those countries, thus gaining higher profit rates and augmenting the availability of credit. At the same time, however, the effects of the crisis are unloaded on the dominated countries. Let us see how.

Stock market crises can cause monetary crises and both can spill over from one country to another. Suppose the stock exchange in country A collapses due to precipitous sale of stocks (shares and bonds). The reasons for this behaviour will become clear shortly. Foreign investors sell those stocks and receive a quantity of country A's currency that they offer on the stock exchange for foreign currencies. This might lead to a first wave of depreciation of country A's currency. The holders of country A's stocks see the risk of being stuck with assets whose value is falling both because of those assets' falling prices (in terms of the national currency) and because of the depreciation of the national currency. Further waves of sales and depreciations might follow. This process intensifies further if investors perceive a danger for enterprises to run into re-financing difficulties (given the decreasing interest investors show in purchasing stocks and bonds) with consequent danger of bankruptcies and defaults. Falling assets prices and depreciation feed upon each other. At this point country A's stock exchange crisis and the monetary crisis can spill over to other countries, for example B.

There are basically two channels through which this spill-over mechanism works. First, a depreciation of A's currency increases its international competitiveness.[66] If B competes on the international markets with A, B might be compelled to depreciate its own currency.[67] But B's competitive depreciation implies lower purchasing power for the foreign investors holding B's stocks denominated in B's currency. Sales of B's stocks and currency, and thus a further depreciation, might follow, possibly reinforced by fears of financial difficulties for B's enterprises, risks of bankruptcies, and defaults in B.

Second, if A's stock exchange crashes, and thus if foreign capital out-flows, investors might anticipate an interest rate hike to attract foreign financial capital. Investors in B can anticipate either a flow of capital from B to A or an interest rise in B too. In both cases, this is supposed to have negative effects on investments, output, income and employment, thus creating financial difficulties for both enterprises and consumers in B. These anticipated financial difficulties spur a sale of B's stocks and the expected higher interest rate stimulates the sale of B's bonds (whose interest rate is lower than the expected one). The process of depreciation and falling stock prices is further strengthened, especially if the rate of interest is actually increased.[68]

This flow of capital, if it goes from the centre to the dominated bloc, can find an outlet either in the productive sphere or in the financial/speculative one. In the former case, given appropriate conditions that vary from case to case, a period of economic growth in the dominated countries might follow. This is the case of the so-called 'Asian tigers'. But the Asian model, based on advanced technologies and low real wages, runs into difficulties after an initial period of industrialization. Dependency on exports for the realization of surplus value in an increasingly saturated world market becomes problematic and the lower export prices needed to penetrate the world markets lead to lower profits and profit rates.[69] 'In dollar terms, the average [of the Asian tigers' export growth] in 1995 was almost 23 per cent; in 1996 it was only 5.6 per cent. . . . European and Japanese markets were sluggish and competition from low-costs exports from China was beginning to bite' (Strange, 1998, p. 103).

Real wages in those dominated countries experiencing industrialization might also rise, thus contributing to the profitability crisis. As the credit system is called upon to save tottering businesses, bad loans start becoming the way this potential crisis becomes manifest. They are, however, not the cause of crisis, contrary to conventional wisdom. This tendency towards crises is reinforced if, as is usually the case, capital is invested in the financial/speculative sphere or if it is appropriated by corrupt civilian or military elites. After a while the cost of servicing that debt will weigh more and more heavily on the country. Public debt is added to private debt.

As the situation in these countries deteriorates, the condition is set for foreign financial capital (usually from the centre) to leave them, thus not only taking with it interests and dividends (value produced in the dominated countries) but also catalysing (rather than provoking) bankruptcies and unemployment in those countries. Except that this capital withdrawal is not gradual but abrupt. For example, bad loans start becoming threatening only after a certain critical mass has been reached. At that point, one or a few major defaults might cause a chain reaction of bankruptcies first in the financial and then in the real sectors. As some major investors, fearing this outcome, leave, others follow in a 'herd-like' behaviour. A stock exchange and currency crisis follows. This sudden withdrawal of capital is similar to the withdrawing of credit by national financial institutions when the crisis sets in, but it is much quicker and uncontrolled and therefore much more disruptive. While the working class in the centre suffers less due to capital export, the working class of the dominated countries receives the full impact of the crisis when that capital is suddenly withdrawn.

The process through which a stock exchange and monetary crisis spreads from one country to the other (see above) can further both widen to other countries and reinforce the vicious circle in the country in which it first emerged. The social consequences are usually very grave for those who already have very little, especially if the monetary crisis affects the dominated countries where the largest areas of absolute poverty and destitution can be found. As mentioned above, they suffer from unemployment. But this is not the only evil. If capital is withdrawn and if credit shrinks, inflation will eventually be resorted to. The enterprises' increasing financial difficulties, and thus the lower profitability deriving both from these difficulties and from the increased price of imports following depreciation, are met with an inflationary process in order to further decrease real wages and increase profits. This affects not only the imported goods but also those locally produced goods which are consumed by the (very) poor. Higher prices of consumer goods plus higher unemployment cannot but have a devastating impact on the poor and the weakest, as the 1997–8 Asian monetary crisis clearly illustrates. From the point of view of value theory, this simply means that those who pay for a country's monetary crisis in terms of great human suffering are those who are least able to pay, and who, in any case, are not responsible, for it.

Contrary to the analysis above, a number of alternative explanations have been offered by orthodox economics. How is it possible, exclaim the orthodox economists, that a country with strong 'fundamentals' (such as high trade surpluses) can suffer monetary and stock exchange crises? The alternatives on offer are as follows. They have been submitted in recent discussions over the East Asian crisis:

- the crisis is caused by the IMF and its restrictive monetary policies, that is, a country hit by the crisis has a liquidity rather than a solvency problem;
- the crisis is caused by foreign speculators, an understandable move for some Asian ruling elites;[70]
- the crisis has been caused by changes in investors 'sentiments', that is, perceptions, which might be triggered off by external circumstances; these crises of confidence can become self-fulfilling prophecies;
- the crisis is caused by deregulation and liberalization in some Asian countries which have led to misallocation of resources and overinvestment (e.g. in the property sector);
- the crisis is caused by 'crony capitalism', that is, the appropriation of capital inflows not by productive capitalists but by corrupt political elites;
- the crisis is caused by the Asian 'model' itself, that is, by government intervention including industrial policies, directed credits and protectionist policies. This thesis is the most amusing of all, given that before the eruption of the crisis the same features were used to explain the success of the Asian 'model'.

In the last analysis, all these views blame human errors as the cause of crises, thus leaving open the obvious question as to why the same mistakes are repeated time and time again. The fact is that all these factors are consequences of a deeper cause. This is the crisis of profitability in the centre, one aspect of which being huge quantities of money looking for profitable investments in the dominated countries. These capital inflows cannot but reproduce in the receiving countries the contradictions which caused the profitability crisis in the centre to begin with. At the same time they are a precipitant of crises. This becomes visible on the basis of value theory.

First, if capital inflows are productively invested and if new, labour-saving, technologies are introduced, after an initial period of growth the decreasing volume of value and surplus value incorporated in a increasing quantity of use values forces those producers to seek an outlet in the centre, that is, in those countries where the profitability and thus the realization crisis has originated. Realization difficulties emerge followed by a profitability crisis. Second, the same holds if, independently from technological innovations, the country in question, following foreign direct investments, pursues an export-led model of economic development in a period of world economic recession. Contracting markets in the centre cannot but impact negatively on the exporting dominated countries. This second case, however, can only be understood as a sub-case, a temporary suspension as it were, of the first case: the lack of purchasing power following the introduction of more efficient technologies within capitalist production relations.[71] Third, if capital is used for financial and speculative purposes, the foreign investors' profits cannot but be realized at the expense of the local capitalists and/or workers.

It is this third type of capital inflows which catches the eye. Short-term loans to the dominated countries piled up in huge amounts in Asia, Russia and Brazil. As investors became worried and withdrew their money, a financial and monetary (exchange rate) crisis erupted. But even if capital controls were to be introduced, even if other suggestions were followed (like flexible exchange rates to avoid sudden depreciations, bankruptcy laws which allow companies to resume borrowing before the old debts are extinguished, or provisions for international lenders in their loans agreements to prevent them from withdrawing their money if a crisis is developing), it would be the form of manifestation of crisis which would change and nothing more; there would be a shift of the burden among the different economic players.

To extract this extra surplus value, local policy makers shift back and forth (see below) from neo-liberalist policies (high interest rates and austerity measures) to Keynesian policies (expansionary policies and exchange rate flexibility), each time rediscovering the negative aspects of the previous policy and the positive aspects of the alternative policy. But both are essentially redistributive policies[72] that, inasmuch as they relieve the profitability crisis in the centre, cannot but exacerbate it in the dominated bloc.[73] But this mechanism unfolds itself only inasmuch as the centre has not exited its own economic crisis. After the crisis has passed, that is, after a massive capital destruction in the centre (possibly initiated in the dominated countries), a new cycle begins in which some of the dominated countries can undergo a further stage of dependent development.

The IMF and the World Bank play centre-stage in all this. Their role is basically that of facilitating the centre's financial investments in the dominated countries. Gradual and foreseeable depreciations do not hamper new investments and make it possible to withdraw existing investments if their value is eroded beyond what the (international) investors consider to be an acceptable level. On the other hand, sudden depreciations (or only their possibility) discourage investments by endangering them in local currencies. This is why the IMF 'recommends' a policy of high interest rates if a country is forced to devalue. High interest rates are supposed to attract foreign capital, thus slowing down depreciation, and to check economic growth, thus slowing down inflation. Since depreciations are basically caused by inflation, the IMF's recipe for the 'developing' countries is monotonous: low inflation. But if the dominated countries must earn the foreign currencies needed to import from the centre, if this requires low prices, and if low prices cannot (should not) be achieved through competitive depreciations, only one avenue is left open: low real wages. Hence the IMF's obsession with austerity measures.

Of course, the IMF mystifies reality. First of all, low levels of inflation are prescribed as a method to force 'underdeveloped' countries to renounce competitive depreciations and compete by increasing their productive capacity, thus becoming competitors of the countries of the centre. This is pie in the sky. This system regenerates both the centre and the dominated countries. Some of these latter might achieve a state of dependent industrialization (see chapter 4 below) thus both generating the purchasing power needed to absorb the centre's excess output and losing (surplus) value to the more efficient capitals in the centre (through the price mechanism). Second, high interest rates are supposed to support this anti-inflation, anti-depreciation policy while their real function is to ensure high profit rates for international finance capital. Third, free capital movement across borders is supposed to allocate international resources optimally while in actual fact it corresponds to the interests of capital from the centre: that of keeping borrowing from the rest of the world in order to retain a level of living higher than would otherwise be possible. And finally restrictive policies are supposed to make nations more efficient after an initial period of belt-tightening, while in reality it is not the 'nation' which must tighten its belt, but the poor, the world proletariat, who are forced to do so and for whom the chances of escaping poverty and deprivation sink further and further.

In these matters, as in all social phenomena, the objective laws of movement manifest themselves through the consciousness of concrete individuals. Investors keep an eye on three orders of indicators:

- First, they watch the level of indebtedness and foreign reserves. More specifically, they watch (a) the level of enterprises' indebtedness relative to their production capacity and profitability, that is, relative to their capacity to repay their debts and, (b) a country's foreign debt relative to its capacity to repay it, that is, relative to its exports, to the inflow of foreign investments (including financial packages from international institutions like the IMF and the World Bank), and to its foreign reserves. It is on this basis that (foreign) investors assess the risk of bankruptcies and defaults. If such a risk looms large, a massive capital outflow follows, with consequent negative effects for the stock exchange and exchange rates.

- Alternatively, investors keep an eye on the exchange rate, that is, on the possibility of a depreciation of the currency. If it is assessed that a depreciation will spur a massive sale of stocks and bonds, large capital outflows follow, again with the above-mentioned negative consequences for the stock exchange and the currency both of that country and of the other countries liable to be 'infected' by this economic malaise.[74]

- Finally, investors keep an eye on the social and political conditions of a country, such as political movements and strikes, and more generally on a country's 'social peace' (even if based on ferocious repression). Social peace is supposed to affect the capacity to repay private and state debt (which are supposedly caused by 'too high' wages and thus by too low profitability) and, through it, the level of the exchange rate. Investors are thus satisfied if 'austerity' policies (e.g. budget cuts) are applied, that is, if real wages are further reduced.

On the basis of these remarks, it is now possible to highlight some differences and similarities between the stock exchange and monetary crises in the 1980s, on the one hand, and in the 1990s, on the other. In the 1980s, speculative capital movements originated in the great masses of money capital (to begin with, dollars) which, not finding an outlet in the productive sphere of the centre, wandered the financial markets of the world in search of the highest possible rate of profit. The chief players were transnational banks. This was still the case in the 1990s, the difference being quantitative, that is, speculative capital movements had greatly increased. The chief players were insurance, pension and hedge funds.

Second, and more importantly, in the 1980s the dominated countries pursued an export-oriented policy based on low real wages. The mechanism was simple: if nominal wages could not be reduced, high (sometimes huge) rates of inflation were pursued as a way to reduce real wages. This called for equally vast depreciations that made the currency worthless. But this discouraged foreign investments, the strategic variable in those countries' plans for rapid industrialization and economic development. Three inter-related factors contributed to change this. First, as said above, the flow of financial capital looking for profitable outlets greatly increased in the 1990s. Second, the 1990s witnessed the fall of the Soviet Union and the concomitant rise of neo-liberalism to the world's ruling ideology. As one government after another embarked on a policy of privatization (usually at give-away prices), the demand for foreign capital inflows expanded to match the greater supply. 'Globalization' plus privatization created the conditions for massive capital investments in the dominated countries. But this required a 'safe environment' for such investments, that is, low levels of depreciation and thus of inflation. And third, the greater integration of the dominated countries into the economies of the centre was facilitated by the breakdown of the non-aligned countries' movement.

This new policy met and still meets the needs both of foreign investors, who want these capitals to be made safe from depreciations, and of the receiving countries, who want these capitals not to be erratic but firmly established, something which again rules out sudden and violent deprecia-tions. Moreover, competitive depreciations are seen by the centre as 'unfair' competition because they make the centre's exports to the dominated bloc more expensive. All this is served with an ideological neo-liberalist sauce stressing the need to renounce depreciation and inflation in order for the dominated countries to achieve a level of technological and economic development comparable to that of the centre. This ideology has gained the status of an unchallenged truth since the demise of the Soviet Union in 1989.

It is because of these reasons that the dominated countries, sometimes under the stimulus of, and sometimes being compelled by, the IMF, started to pursue in the 1990s a policy based on low depreciation, low inflation and stable exchange rates (rather than on high rates of depreciation and inflation and on utterly unstable exchange rates as in the 1980s). Sometimes, the value of a currency is tied to that of the US dollar as a way to rule out inflation.[75] But, after an initial period of economic growth, the same mechanism which causes economic crises in the centre is reproduced in the industrializing dominated countries. Moreover, high capital inflows (coupled with the high interest rates needed to attract and keep foreign capitals) cannot but cause high levels of indebtedness and eventually bankruptcies. Economic crises are ushered in by monetary and stock exchange crises. Exchange rates are left free to fluctuate, the currency is depreciated, and inflation emerges again. It is in this light that the Mexican crisis of 1994–95, the Asian crisis of 1997–98, the Russian crisis of 1998 and the Brazilian crisis of 1999 can be properly seen.[76]

However, in the first years of the second millennium, as the effects of this policy become more and more manifest, the pendulum seems to be ready to switch again towards an approach in the dominated countries based on fiscal expansion, low interest rates, capital controls (e.g. through a system of rationing dollars by the Central Bank) and possibly inflation.[77] This change will be made inevitable if the present financial and monetary crisis provokes a worldwide recession. This is another manifestation of the way policy makers react to the objective laws of capitalist development by switching from restrictive to expansionary (Keynesian) policies and back again in a vain attempt to hold back the emergence of crises. This is the reason behind the critique that is being mounted against the IMF.

In the last analysis, then, the investors' decisions, right or wrong, are based on real, objective factors, that is, on a country's capacity to achieve sufficient levels of profitability and international competitiveness. Those investors who can forecast correctly these objective factors gain, the others lose. But, as mentioned above, this is a redistribution within the class of (financial) capitalists. The real losers become visible only in terms of class analysis. Only class analysis can reveal the reasons for this drama, the culprits, and the victims.

The Economic and Monetary Union

4.1 Old and New Imperialism

Chapter 1 has argued for the inherent imperialist nature of the European project from its very beginning. We must now dwell on this issue in detail. Imperialism's major character traits are as follows:

- The imperialist centre grows at the expense of the dominated bloc through the appropriation of value inherent in the system of international prices arising from inter-oligopolistic competition in the centre (something that is perceived by the dominated country as a deterioration of the terms of trade).
- This appropriation of value is constant over a relatively long period of time because based on permanent technological and thus efficiency differentials between the two blocs, itself the outcome of a cumulative process between appropriation of value (i.e. capital formation), investment in research and development and technological innovations.
- The reproduction of this self-reinforcing process is ensured by international institutions and appropriate institutional arrangements (e.g. patents ownership) as well as by military power if need be.
- This constant advantage makes it possible for the technological leaders (thus the centre) to undersell their competitors (this is a deviation of international market prices from international production prices).
- At this point, three tendencies arise within this inter-blocs dynamics, according to the ability of the dominated countries to resist imperialist relations:
  - First, the centre's market share grows at the expense of that of some of the dominated bloc to such an extent that local industry in the latter is destroyed. This is classic colonialism.
  - Alternatively, some of the dominated countries can resist this destructive process and engage in a process of dependent development (see below).
  - Or, finally, by way of exception, a dominated country can break out of this relation of domination and join the imperialist centre. This change affects the internal composition of the two blocs but erases neither their existence nor their differences.

Traditionally, research on imperialism has centred on the first of these latter three cases, that is, on the relation between the 'mother' countries and their colonies. In this *colonial* type of imperialism:

- the colonies must deliver raw materials to, and import manufactured products from, the colonial centre; and
- because of this, the colonies undergo little if any capitalist economic growth and diversification.

But there is also a newer type of imperialist relation (holding for some South American and Asian countries, for example). Within it, the dependent countries can achieve a degree of capitalist economic growth and diversification. However, this is *dependent development and capitalist accumulation* in the sense that:

- capital in the dependent countries adjusts production and more generally its economic activity to the markets in the centre (export orientation) and diversifies its internal structure accordingly, rather than the other way around;
- the centre exports to the dependent countries what these latter need (including capital as aid and infrastructures) for this process of dependence to continue;
- the dependent countries produce what the centre needs through the use of advanced but not cutting-edge techniques (i.e. more labour-intensive techniques) so as to ensure both a transfer of value to the centre and continued technological dependence;
- given that they cannot compete with the centre on the basis of more advanced technologies, the dependent countries must 'save' on labour costs. This means that wages in terms of use values can be relatively high in the centre and (sometimes absolutely) low in the dependent countries.[1]

Colonialism means that the imperialist country robs the colonies of their raw materials and uses their markets as an outlet for its own (industrial) products. The colonies' resources are squeezed out and local industries (if they existed) attacked up to the point where they disappear. At this point the colonies' capacity to absorb the centre's output is destroyed and they are abandoned to their fate. Even if local industries do survive, no substantial process of industrialization and capitalist development takes place in any case.[2] This is a process of reversed development and/or underdevelopment. Dependent development means that it is the market of the centre that is important for the dependent countries as an outlet for these countries' production, 'commissioned', as it were, by the centre itself. Some dependent countries can undergo even a substantial process of capitalist development, but of this dependent type. Of course, the distinction between these two types of imperialism is analytical. In real life, they can coexist in hybrid forms in which one of the two types of imperialist relations is more pronounced.

The thesis submitted here is that, besides the imperialist relations some of the EU countries have with some of the dominated countries (both within and outside the EU), the EU *as a whole* has also a set of imperialist relations with (some of) the countries of the dominated bloc. To see this, consider the following. From a class analysis perspective, to say that a country has imperialist relations with another country is only a short-cut to indicate that:

- capitalist enterprises in the former country have such relations with (i.e. they appropriate value systematically from) enterprises (or 'independent' producers) in the latter country; and
- these relations need a set of national institutions handing down a set of legally binding instruments and military means making (the continuation of) those relations possible.

Nowadays, imperialist relations exist not only between some imperial powers and some dominated countries. They also exist between the impe- rialist bloc as a whole (the centre of capitalism, the developed countries) and the dominated bloc (the periphery, the underdeveloped countries) either for some countries individually or as a whole. The element which makes this systematic and collective appropriation of value possible is a set of international institutions, like the IMF, the World Bank, the WTO and the NATO, which act as the agents of capital in the centre. But it would be improper to refer to these institutions as pursuing their own imperialist policies. They only represent the interests of the centre *vis-à-vis* the dominated bloc and mediate those interests within the dominant bloc, given that common interests *vis-à-vis* the dominated bloc do not exclude contradictory interests within the dominant bloc.

The case is different for the EU. While the EU is not (yet) a state entity, it has the legal instruments to legislate and thus to regulate sections of the economy and of other spheres of the member states' society. Through the formulation of these common interests, these institutions make it possible for all member states to participate in the systematic appropriation of value from non-EU countries. Here, differently from the case of the IMF and other similar institutions, EU institutions not only represent and mediate common (but contradictory) national interests *vis-à-vis* non-EU countries. They also formulate in a relatively independent way those common interests because the member states have relinquished part of their sovereignty to these institutions. The imperialism of EU member states thus acquires new frontiers. One implication is that those member countries which, taken separately, would not enjoy the privileges of belonging to the centre participate (even if in a subordinate position) in these privileges when they join the EU. Thus, strictly speaking, *EU imperialism* refers to:

- the imperialist relations between the capitalist enterprises of the EU countries and those of the non-EU countries;

- the unequal shares in which this value is split up among the EU countries;
- the EU institutions, and thus to the legally binding sets of rules and laws handed down by those institutions (e.g. the Lomé Conventions and the recent ACP–EU Agreement with the African, Caribbean and Pacific [ACP] countries and the Association Agreements with the Central and Eastern European Countries [CEECs]), which make those relations possible; and
- the military might needed to enforce compliance with these rules and laws upon reluctant countries (as we shall see, the Western European Union).

Of course, the imperialism of the EU as a whole (EU imperialism proper) is strictly interconnected with the imperialism of the EU member countries (national imperialisms). As of now, EU imperialism proper might still be less relevant than national imperialisms, but this situation is bound to change as the process of European unification proceeds. For the purposes of this work, it is not necessary to distinguish between the separate effects of these two aspects of EU imperialism.

Once imperialist relations have been established in the industrial sphere (as being either a colonialist or a dependent development relation), all other relations can be seen in the same light. Thus, the true nature of the Economic and Monetary Union comes into view both as an attempt to rival the dollar's seigniorage and as a major step towards that political unification without which further economic domination is hampered (see further below in this chapter). The Western European Union can be seen as an attempt by the EU to develop its own military arm in order to fulfil fully its own imperialist urge (see chapter 6). The Common Agricultural Policy emerges as a policy aimed at imposing on the weaker countries outside the EU a dependent type of agricultural development (see chapter 7). And the Schengen System can be seen as regulating the reproduction of EU labour power according to the need of the EU itself (see chapter 8). These are major examples of the institutionalized appropriation of international value upon which the European project revolves.

4.2 The Competitiveness of the European Union

The above has argued for the primary importance of technological competitiveness and for the advantages deriving from it to the European Union as one of the major economic blocs. In this section we will inquire empirically into the level of competitiveness of the European Union, into the Union's competition policy, and into the advantages deriving to the EU from this higher competitiveness and policy.

According to the EC Treaty, the activities of the member states and of the Community will be 'conducted in accordance with the principle of an open market economy and of free competition' (article 3a.1). Translated in terms of the approach submitted in this work, this article calls for a discussion of the following two points:

- the competitive position of the EU (both as a whole and of its member countries) in relation to the economic units' size and competitiveness; and
- the forms taken by competition, the actual meaning of 'free' competition, and the actual interest served by a policy of free competition.

4.2.1 The EU and International Competitiveness

In this work productivity has been conceived of as being:

- the effect of the application of new, labour-saving, technologies (rather than of an increased rate of surplus value); and
- measured as the ratio of units of output per unit of capital invested.

An analysis of productivity differentials both within the EU and between the EU and the rest of the world, then, would have to rely on data collected according to these principles. The notions of technological leadership submitted in chapter 3, section 3 would then allow us to determine whether this role could be adjudicated to the EU (or to any of its member states). Unfortunately, such data are not available. We must then resort to indirect and at best only approximate indications of productivity levels.

One such index, for which data are available, is international trade in high-technology products (HTPs).[3] This is a vague indication of a country's technological leadership, given that trade figures in HTPs are influenced by a host of other factors besides productivity, such as exchange rates. Nevertheless, trade figures in HTPs do provide some basis for an international comparison in terms of technologies and productivities. Table 4.1 shows the major world traders in HTPs.

In 1997, the EU, the US and Japan accounted for 51.2 per cent of the world's imports and for 61.2 per cent of world exports of HTPs. The major exporter was the US (27.4 per cent of world trade). The EU's share was

Table 4.1   Major world traders in HTPs, 1997

| | Imports | | Exports | | Balance |
	ECU bn	World %	ECU bn	World %	ECU bn
EU	60.1	20.4	52.6	17.2	−7.5
US	68.3	23.1	83.7	27.4	+15.4
Singapore	25.8	8.8	23.6	7.7	−2.2
Japan	22.7	7.7	50.5	16.6	+27.8

Source: Eurostat, Statistics in Focus, External Trade, No. 11, Luxembourg, 1998, p. 3.

Table 4.2 Absolute values (ECU) and percentage shares of HTP imports by EU, US and Japan, 1997

EU (60.2bn)	US (68.3bn)	Japan (22.7bn)
38.7 from US	25 from ASE6	51.4 from the US
12.4 from Japan	22.2 from Japan	20.6 from ASE6
11.7 from ASE6[a]	16.4 from the EU	9.7 from the EU
4.5 from EFTA[b]	7.1 from Singapore	5.1 from Singapore

[a] Hong Kong, Indonesia, Malaysia, Philippines, South Korea, Thailand
[b] European Free Trade Area: Iceland, Norway, Switzerland

Source: Eurostat, *Statistics in Focus, External Trade,* No. 11, Luxembourg, 1998, p. 4.

slightly higher than Japan's. However, while Japan had a surplus in HTPs of 27.8bn (ECU), the EU had a deficit of 7.5bn. In terms of the trade balance, Japan was the foremost technological leader (+27.8bn), followed by the US (+15.5bn), Singapore (-2.3bn) and the EU (-7.5bn). But it should be added that the EU's trade balance has improved over the years. In 1990 it was -19bn (Eurostat, op. cit.). These figures can be further broken down as shown in Table 4.2.

Thus, the EU imported most HTPs from the US and Japan, the US from ASE6 and Japan, and Japan from the US and ASE6.[4] As for exports, table 4.3 shows that in 1997 the EU exported most of its HTPs to the US and to ASE6, the US to the EU and to ASE6, and Japan to the US and to ASE6.[5]

Let us now look at the main HTPs traded by the EU (table 4.4).

In 1997, the largest surpluses were in aerospace (+6.3bn) and telecommunications (+2.3bn). The largest deficits were in computers and office machines (-10.3) and electronics (-7.8bn).

A large amount of HTPs are traded within the EU, as shown by table 4.5. Intra-EU exports are greater than extra-EU exports but intra-EU imports are smaller than extra-EU imports. The five countries mentioned in table 4.5 accounted for 85 per cent of intra-EU exports and 67 per cent of intra-EU imports as well as for 85 per cent of extra-EU exports and 84 per cent of extra-EU imports.

We can now draw some conclusions. It is obvious from the list of the

Table 4.3 Absolute values (ECU) and percentage shares of HTP exports by EU, US, and Japan, 1997

EU (52.6bn)	US(83.7bn)	Japan(50.5bn)
27.5 to the US	25.4 to the EU	31.3 to the US
12.3 to ASE6	17.4 to ASE6	27.8 to ASE6
7.6 to EFTA	11.5 to Japan	15.9 to the EU
7.4 to the Mediterranean basin	6.4 to Singapore	9.4 to Singapore

Source: Eurostat, *Statistics in Focus, External Trade,* No. 11, Luxembourg, 1998, p. 5.

Table 4.4 EU imports and exports by main HTP, 1997

	Imports		Exports		Balance
	ECU bn	%	ECU bn	%	ECU bn
Electronics	22.5	31.5	14.7	23.9	−7.8
Aerospace	20.7	29.0	27.0	43.8	+6.3
Computers, office machines	17.5	24.5	7.2	11.7	−10.3
Machinery	3.5	4.9	3.8	6.1	+0.3
Scientific and medical	3.1	4.4	4.0	6.4	+0.9
Chemicals	1.3	1.8	1.0	1.6	−0.3
Telecommunications	0.6	0.8	2.9	4.8	+2.3

Source: Eurostat, *Statistics in Focus, External Trade*, No. 11, Luxembourg, 1998, pp. 7 and 9.

sectors defining HTPs that only large and technologically advanced firms can engage in the production, and the successful competition for the markets, of those goods. These are oligopolistic firms. The notion of oligopoly employed here rests not only on its being a technological leader and on its large share of the market but also on its dominant position on the basis of this technological and market leadership. This dominant position refers not only to a large and technologically advanced firm's relation to other smaller, or less powerful, firms within the same sector, that is, to the power any large firm has to impose its will consciously upon smaller firms within a certain sector. This does occur through a whole array of legal, semi-legal and outright illegal practices but is only one aspect of the matter. In fact, oligopolies compete both with each other and with non-oligopolistic firms also across sectoral boundaries.

A firm becomes an *oligopoly* if its technological and market leadership are such that, through its participation in the competitive process (both across and within sectors, both with other technological and market leaders and with smaller and less technologically advanced firms), it shapes those

Table 4.5 Trade in HTPs by major member states, 1997 (ECU bn)

	Extra-EU			Intra-EU		
	Imports	Exports	Balance	Imports	Exports	Balance
D	14.7	12.5	−2.2	12.6	14.2	1.6
F	16.6	21.8	5.2	15.4	17.2	1.8
UK	16.2	11.5	−4.7	7.1	11.3	4.2
NL	9.5	3.3	−6.2	4.1	11.1	7.0
I	3.3	3.2	−0.1	5.7	3.7	−2.0
Total	71.5	61.6	−9.9		68.0	

Source: Eurostat, *Statistics in Focus, External Trade*, No. 11, Luxembourg, 1998, p. 2.

terms of competition, which must then be accepted by those who do not have that power. For example, the prices which emerge from oligopolistic competition become also the prices the non-oligopolistic firms must accept; or, market sharing between oligopolies excludes the non-oligopolistic firms but the opposite is not the case. These terms of competition become the boundaries within which the non-oligopolistic firms compete both against each other and (if they can) against the oligopolies. Non-oligopolistic firms can and do compete with oligopolistic ones as well as, of course, with each other, but they cannot affect or influence the terms (e.g. prices) upon which this competition takes place. There are thus, within each modern capitalist economy, two sectors of *firms*, the *oligopolistic sector* and the *dominated sector*. The line discriminating these two sectors rests on the necessary acceptance by the dominated sector of the terms of competition emerging objectively from the competition both within and outside the oligopolistic sector and which objectively favour this sector.

The above is no argument for the *necessarily* greater efficiency of oligopolies. There is no univocal relationship between size and productivity. Large-scale units are neither more efficient nor necessarily proportionally more efficient as their size increases. But the opposite is equally false. There is no necessary relationship between large-scale enterprises and inefficiency. What is true is that, given the present scope of capital concentration and centralization, oligopolies are *often* the only enterprises able to develop (or purchase) and apply new and more efficient technologies on such a scale as to keep their share or conquer greater shares of the market. Smaller units can (and indeed occasionally do) develop and apply new and more efficient technologies, but they lack the critical mass which allows them to get into the dominant oligopolistic sector, Even if their rate of profit might be greater than that of the oligopolistic sector, the terms of competition objectively or consciously imposed by the oligopolies are such that these smaller units as a rule will not grow to seriously challenge the oligopolies' dominant position. Occasionally, a smaller and technologically advanced capital unit can grow to become an oligopoly and an oligopoly can lose its technological leadership and dwindle in size, thus losing its dominant position. But these changes internal to the oligopolistic and the dominated sector do not affect the existence of the division between these sectors. Of course, each of these two broad sectors is subdivided into a number of commodity-specific sectors.

Then, even if oligopolies are not always and not necessarily the most efficient enterprises, the most efficient enterprises are usually oligopolies. This holds even more for the most strategic and dynamic sectors of modern capitalist economies, the high-technology sectors. Owing to their economic power, oligopolies have their ways and means to get their interests defined and represented both by their own national institutions and, through them, by international institutions as well. This process of representation is almost never immediate and transparent. It involves multi-party negotiations often conducted in arcane terms. Yet it is the oligopolistic sector that, directly or indirectly, dictates the rules of the game.

Capital concentration and centralization do not stop at national frontiers but lead to the formation of international oligopolies, also called multinational enterprises, which account for the greatest bulk of global output and trade. Given that the greatest number of these firms is concentrated in a small minority of countries, the world is subdivided into two blocs of *countries*: the *imperialist centre* and the *dominated bloc*. The notion of imperialism, and thus of the imperialist relations between these two blocs, will be elucidated in following chapters. Here suffice it to anticipate that the centre is formed by the technologically leading countries (as defined above). This bloc appropriates value from the dominated bloc (the technological laggards) through the international prices system in a systematic and permanent (rather than accidental) way, thus being able to accumulate capital and invest it in technological innovations and further reinforcing its technological lead. Some countries are practically wiped out as international competitors whereas other countries can reach a measure of development while at the same time being dependent upon the technological leaders. Moreover, each of these two blocs is internally articulated in a variety of relations of power and domination. This is the case also for the EU, which belongs to the imperialist centre.

Table 4.5 above would seem to indicate a dominant position by French oligopoly capital within the EU. However, French surpluses in HTPs are entirely due to the aerospace branch (Eurostat, *Statistics in Focus, External Trade*, No. 3, Luxembourg, 1997, p. 11). This is too narrow a basis for technological leadership. We must then turn to other indicators, such as the number of persons employed in high-technology sectors (table 4.6).[6]

Table 4.6 Employment in high-technology sectors, major countries

Germany	France	Italy	UK	EU-15
3.8m 10.5%	1.4m 6.5%	1.4m 7.0%	1.7m 6.8%	10.7m 7.2%

Source: Eurostat, *Statistics in Focus, Research and Development*, No. 1, Luxembourg, 1988, Table 1, p. 3.

The situation presented by table 4.6 differs radically from that suggested by table 4.5. In table 4.6 it is Germany (i.e. German oligopolies) which holds by far the dominant position. Of the major producers of HTPs, Germany is the only one whose employment in these sectors (10.5 per cent of its total employment) is higher than the European average (7.2 per cent). More importantly, Germany's employment in HTPs accounts for more than a third of that of each of the three other major producers. These results are even more telling if it is considered that over three-quarters of persons employed in the high-technology sectors are found in these four countries. Perhaps even more significant are data on regional concentration. Of the top ten regions in terms of the percentage of their total employment in high-technology sectors, six are in Germany (with percentages varying from 17.3 to 9.5), two in Italy, one in France and one in the UK.

Besides the two above-mentioned indicators, a third one is available, patent activities. This is the most suitable for our present purposes. In fact, data on patent activities record not only the outcome of scientific discoveries and the possibility of their economic application but also the exclusion from these applications of those who do not have access to patents. In terms of technological competition and of the appropriation of value due to a technological lead (through the price mechanism), these data are by far the most significant because they freeze, as it were, the technological lead of those who possess these patents. And here the true picture emerges in all its vividness. Writing in 1995, Mihevc pointed out that 'At present only one per cent of patents are owned by persons or companies in the Third World and, of those, 84 per cent are owned by foreigners and less than 5 per cent are actually used for production in the Third World' (p. 172). This incredibly skewed pattern is reproduced within the centre, including the EU. Table 4.7 presents the share of patent applications in 1996 for the fifteen EU member states.[7]

Table 4.7 Patent applications as a percentage of total EU applications, 1996

HPCs	FRG	F	UK	I	NL	SW		
	41.4	16.3	11.9	8.02	5.89	5.33		
LPCs	B	FIN	A	DK	SP	IRL	GR	LUX	P
	2.53	2.46	2.24	1.91	1.36	0.39	0.11	0.10	0.04

HPC stands for high patenting countries and LPC for low patenting countries.

Source: Eurostat, *Statistics in Focus, Research and Development,* No. 2, Luxembourg, 1988, Table 1, p. 2.

Germany's share is no less than 41.4 per cent of all EU patent applications in 1996, which is more than the combined shares of France, Italy and the UK. However, it should be remarked that in the 1989–96 period the low patenting countries achieved a much higher rate of growth in patent applications than did the high patenting countries. Germany's leading position in HTPs is confirmed also if the most active patenting regions in the EU are considered. Of the five most active regions, four are German and one is French.

To conclude this first section, in spite of their well-known deficiencies, empirical data support the thesis that, given the sheer size of capital investments needed to engage in competition in the high-technology sectors,

• the most efficient companies are usually oligopolies, and,
• within the EU, it is the German oligopolies which lead in the technologically advanced sectors, and thus in the rest of the economy.

There seems to be little doubt that Germany is Europe's technological leader. More precisely, it is German oligopolies which are Europe's oligopolies leaders and it is this advanced, oligopolistic sector which leads the rest of Europe's capital in the technological race.

4.2.2 The European Union's Competition Policy

The above shows that the European economies neither are in nor tend towards free, or perfect, competition. Yet orthodox economics holds on stubbornly to this worthless economic concept. There are many variations on the theme. Young and Metcalfe (1994, pp. 120–2) distinguish between several notions of competition. The *neo-classical* view stresses perfect, or free, competition as the ideal state and considers any deviation from it as a distortion that should be corrected by a proper policy. *Perfect competition* is usually defined as a state in which a number of conditions apply. The two most directly relevant ones for the present discussion are: (a) no enterprise can affect market prices through its own actions; and (b) both buyers and sellers are free to enter and exit the market. While it is recognized that this is an 'ideal' state which does not exist in reality, its theorization is the basis of all strands of orthodox economics because, it is argued, this is the state towards which the economy should (or does) tend.[8]

A more realistic notion is that of *workable competition*. It eschews perfect competition as a realistic objective and aims for a market with an 'acceptable' degree of competition. This is more a policy-oriented than a theoretical concept. The difficulty with this approach is that, in the absence of a theoretical concept of what is acceptable, the acceptable degree of competition becomes a matter of subjective assessment or of relations of power between the economic agents.

A third approach is the *Austrian view*. It criticizes the neo-classical approach as being essentially static and stresses that competition is a continuous process of entrepreneurial rivalry in which the pursuit of profits (rather than the maximization principle) is the basic driving factor of the capitalist economy. The difference between the Austrian and the neo-classical view is that for the former profits include also what the latter regards as super-normal profits. These latter arise not necessarily from monopoly power but from superior efficiency and technologies. Therefore, super-normal profits are necessary and should not be penalized by state policies. The efficiency gains from innovations may outweigh any short-term inefficiencies resulting from market imperfections.

It is usually held that the Community's competition policy is inspired by all these three notions in that it combines the static nature of the neo-classical view (emphasizing the virtues of free competition) with the more dynamic view of the Austrian school (stressing efficiency gains from innovations rather than the negative aspects of market imperfections) and with a more policy-oriented view of competition (highlighted by the notion of workable competition). This is not the view adopted in this work. It argues that the three above-mentioned notions are ideological standpoints which, at best, can only partially represent capitalist reality and thus the competitive process characterizing it. After what has been said in chapter 1 about the influence transnational corporations have on the process of decision making within the EU, it will come as no surprise that the function of competition policy is that of promoting the interests of big capital rather than those of labour or those of small or medium-sized capital (even though a balancing of different interests is a basic function of this policy as well as of other EU policies). As the CEO reports, the UEAPME (the European Union of Craftsmen and Small and Medium-Sized Enterprises) is denied access to both the Social Dialogue and the Competitiveness Advisory Group, that is, to those high-powered groups which are influential in shaping the policies of the EU.

Basically, there are two ways for capitals to compete: within sectors and among sectors. Within sectors, capitals engage in technological competition, thus trying to achieve ever greater levels of efficiency, or productivity. Among sectors, capitals engage in competition by moving to those sectors where the highest feasible profit rates can be realized. Since, usually, a rise in profit rates in a sector results from the introduction of new and more efficient technologies, capital moves as a rule to those sectors which undergo a process of technological innovation.[9] There are of course many other forms of competition (e.g. the search for cheaper inputs), but these two are paramount because they account for the dynamic nature of capitalism (and thus for the production and appropriation of value and surplus value), thus ensuring the reproduction of the capitalist system. A first task of competition policy, then, if it has to be functional for the reproduction of the capitalist system, must be that of prohibiting barriers to capital mobility (barriers to entry) and of fostering the free development and application of technological innovations. The stronger capitals gain from this policy, the others do not. EU competition policy ensures this freedom, thus favouring Europe's oligopolies. Let us see how.

Given the size of investments needed both to start a new enterprise and to develop and introduce new technologies, a policy emphasizing freedom of capital movement (both within and between sectors) and of technological competition objectively favours oligopoly capital to the disadvantage of the dominated sector. For example, the prices emerging from the technologies adopted by the oligopolies cause both the oligopolies' higher profits and the smaller enterprises' lower profits, inasmuch as these latter cannot afford to introduce those technologies. A policy aiming at safeguarding the 'free' introduction of these technologies cannot but favour those who can afford them. The same applies to capital mobility. The higher the degree of monopolization in a certain sector, the more difficult will it be for an enterprise in the dominated bloc to enter it. The prohibition of bid rigging seems to be in the interest of the dominated firms, given that only the oligopolies usually engage in this practice. However, given that only the oligopolies can bid for the large and more profitable contracts, such rules are only a way to regulate competition between oligopolies (for reasons to be explained in a second) rather than a way to ensure equal terms of competition to the non-oligopolistic firms. A policy of free competition, then, fosters objectively the powerful economic units, that is, the oligopolies.[10]

The legal equality of non-oligopolistic and oligopolistic capitals ignores the unequal power relations between these two blocs. It ignores the fact that the non-oligopolistic enterprises are formally free to compete with the oligopolies but on the terms (prices, technologies, etc.) emerging from the competition among oligopolies. This shows the ideological nature of the neo-classical view of competition policy: by arguing that all capitals should be equally free to compete, this view preaches equality while effectively fostering unequal and preferential treatment.

This is a first aspect of the EU's competition policy. There are at least three more aspects. The second one concerns the role of the European institutions in safeguarding the interests of national capitals by forbidding certain competitive practices such as price collusion, cartels, bid rigging, and so on. The reason why these practices are given illegal status is purely economic. Contrary to the accepted competitive practices, these practices do not increase but actually weaken European oligopolies' (and thus the European nations') competitive power *vis-à-vis* non-European capitals. For example, if a firm secures a procurement through bid rigging rather than higher efficiency (and thus lower prices), it damages (the growth of) more efficient firms and thus (of) the economy as a whole. These practices must thus be checked by a policy whose aim is not so much the fostering of the competitive position of the oligopolistic sector against the dominated one. Rather, the aim is that of preventing the weakening of the competitive position of the European dominant sector, and thus of the (European) economy, as a whole. Oligopolies must be protected, as it were, against themselves. The EU's various bodies intervene regularly not only to promote the foreign expansion of European capital but also to secure procurements without which specific European oligopolies would be irremediably damaged.

Illegal practices are called, in official terminology, abuse of market power or abuse of the dominant position. Anti-trust legislation does not fight the oligopolies' dominant position (actually, it favours it, notwithstanding its claims to the contrary), but it does fight the abuse of it if it leads to practices weakening the competitive strength of the European oligopolistic sector as a whole. This function is given an ideological twist by official ideology. Since illegal practices can cause prices higher than those which would emerge if these practices did not exist, anti-trust legislation is said to be in the interest of consumers. In reality, as argued above, the aim of anti-trust legislation has very little to do with consumers. The protection of the interests of consumers (if this is the case) is a by-product (in spite of claims to the contrary) rather than being the primary purpose of this legislation. The protection of the interests of the tiny majority of the powerful is smuggled into the collective consciousness as being the protection of the overwhelming majority of society.

The third aim of European competition policy, one which is more tied to the present economic, political and ideological conjuncture, is that of favouring the privatization of state enterprises, often accused (rightly or wrongly) of being incompetent, bureaucratic, inefficient, and so on. The usual argument is that these enterprises are protected from the salutary effects of 'market forces' and thus should be exposed to them, that is, privatized. Of course, it is the best and more profitable slices of the state enterprises that are put up for sale, often after the state has invested great sums to modernize and streamline them. If they are sold before having been made more efficient, they are usually given away for a fraction of their value.

This belief in the 'rationality' of private capital is what explains a feature that at first sight could be puzzling. Given the great importance of technological competition, one would expect the EU to allocate consider-able resources to science and technology policy. Yet the opposite is the case. In the EU, research and development is basically a matter of private investments as well as of the national states' support. The private sector, especially large corporations, and the public sector can and do engage in European collaborative projects, some of which have been very successful, like the Airbus airliner and the European Space Agency (ESA). Concorde had for many years been considered to be a technically successful aero-plane. However, owing to the recent (July 2000) crash in Paris, which has revealed major design flaws, the plane has been withdrawn and may be scrapped. Yet these instances of European collaboration have been spurred and directed not by the EU but by agreements between member states. The EU plays a practically insignificant role in this area, as can be seen by the fact that national expenditures dwarf EU expenditures.

The reason for the embryonic form of the EU programmes in the field of scientific and technological research, especially if this is compared to the role played by the MITI in Japan, is not difficult to find. EU funds for research in science and technology do not promote science and technology in an amorphous 'Europe'. Rather, they favour the scientific and technolog-ical lead of those undertakings and nations involved in those projects. Given the importance of such a lead for competitive advantages also within the EU, it is not surprising that research and development in the EU is still a matter of national governments and especially of the private sector, that is, of the oligopolistic sector.

Finally, a fourth element of EU competition policy is that the very general formulation in which this policy is cast leaves ample room for interpretation when it comes to concrete decisions. Given that decisions have to be taken on a case-by-case basis and without clear-cut operational principles, chances are that the more powerful are the capital units involved, the greater the likelihood that the final decision will be favourable to them rather than to 'free competition'.

Young and Metcalfe (1994) mention two relevant examples.

In 1988 an arrangement between AEI and Reyroll Parsons to set up a joint manufacturing company (Vacuum Interrupters Limited) was granted exemption in spite of being the sole European supplier, entirely on the grounds that the associated product innovations would benefit consumers. (p. 133)

In another example, in 1990 the Commission allowed a joint venture between Alcatel Esaci and ANT Nachrichten Technik to produce electronic components for satellites 'on grounds that it strengthened European industry relative to foreign competition . . . notwithstanding the fact that this agreement was judged adversely to affect competition within the EC' (p. 133). Moreover, article 90 of the EC Treaty states that undertakings providing 'services of general economic interest or having the character of a revenue-producing monopoly' can be exempted from the rules of the Treaty if the application of these rules would obstruct the performance of their particular tasks.

To sum up, *EU competition policy* should be seen as a complex body of legislation deriving from the contradictory needs of European capital. This policy:

• fosters the interests of the oligopolistic sector (while claiming the opposite) *vis-à-vis* the dominated one;
• protects this sector from injuring itself by forbidding forms of competition (price collusion, price discrimination, bid rigging, barriers to entry, cartel forming, etc.) which would weaken it rather than strengthen it;
• defends it against foreign oligopolies at critical conjunctures;
• under favourable circumstances, breaks up and privatizes state monopolies, thus favouring private oligopolies; and
• is formulated in such a way as to leave ample room for the most powerful oligopolies to push through decisions favourable to them.

This is not a straightforward process but a complex one informed by contradictory interests at various levels, that is, within and between sectors, within and between blocs, within and between European states, and within and between the (different institutions of the) EU and the rest of the world.

All these five elements are recognizable in articles 85 and 86 of the EC Treaty, which are the pillars of EU competition policy. Article 85 prohibits all agreements, decisions and practices among undertakings that affect trade by preventing, restricting or distorting competition. In particular, it mentions price fixing, limits to 'production, market, technical development, or investment', market sharing, the application of different conditions to equivalent transactions, and making the stipulation of a contract subject to conditions having no connection with that contract. However, such agreements, decisions and practices are allowed in case they improve production and distribution or foster technical and economic progress 'while allowing consumers a fair share of the resulting benefit'. While article 85 prohibits agreements between two or more undertakings which affect trade between member countries, article 86 prohibits the abuse of a dominant position by one or more undertakings not resting upon an agreement with other undertakings. Such abuse may consist of the imposition of unfair purchases or prices or other trading conditions, of conditions resulting in competitive disadvantages, of obligations unrelated to the transaction engaged in, and of restrictions on supply, market or technical development. Article 86 does not specify what constitutes a dominant position.

Cases of suspected infringement of articles 85 and 86 are investigated by the Commission on 'application by a member state or by its own initiative' (article 89 EC). Anti-competitive practices are fined by the Commission up to 10 per cent of the transgressing parties' turnover. Firms can appeal initially to the European Court of First Instance and then to the European Court of Justice. According to Kemp (1992), the 'Commission's record on attacking cartels and concerted practices is impressive, for it has vigorously pursued and successfully secured the termination of a substantial number and varieties of concerted practices' (p. 72). However, the analysis above allows us to see whose interests are represented behind the smoke-screen of the official formulations and concrete decisions.

This chapter has highlighted the basic elements that allow us to place the process of European (economic) integration in its proper perspective. This process is spurred by the need the European nations have to aggregate in order to compete with the two other major blocs, the United States and Japan.[11] It is capital's need for, and interest in, a new imperialist bloc that spurred the EEC and its common market as a first step towards this ultimate end. This movement took place under the leadership of 'Germany', that is, of Europe's oligopolistic capital, within which German oligopolies play a leading role. The 'German' leadership was accepted because it allows for a common advantage, the extraction of greater surplus value by European capital at the point of production. This is the thesis which will be argued for in the next section.

4.3 The Economic and Monetary Union and the Euro

The above can now be used to inquire into the European Monetary Union (EMU).[12] To begin with, it is useful to consider how orthodox literature approaches the theme of a monetary union. The key concept here is that of an optimum currency area (OCA). Emphasis in what follows will be on the US and the EMU. The discussion was started in 1961 by Mundell. His argument runs as follows:

> Suppose that the world consists of two countries, Canada and the United States, each of which has separate currencies. Also assume that the continent is divided into two regions which do not correspond to national boundaries – the East, which produces goods like cars, and the West which produces goods like lumber products. (p. 659)

Initially, the two regions are blessed by full employment. Suppose now a shift in demand, from cars to lumber products. The immediate impact will be unemployment in the East and excess demand for labour in the West. If the US wants to relieve unemployment in the East it can increase the quantity of money, but then it creates inflationary pressures in the West. Or, if the US wants to increase car production, it can devalue the US dollar, but this will increase exports of lumber products as well as fuel inflation in the West. The same holds for Canada. Flexible exchange rates do not correct the balance of payments between the two regions (even though they may correct the balance of payments between the two countries). They are thus not necessarily better than fixed exchange rates.

Suppose, however, there is labour mobility between regions. In this case, labour migration to the West restores equilibrium not only in the labour market but also in the balance of payments because the purchase of cars by the Eastern workers who have moved to the West now constitutes not home demand but extra Eastern exports and because the purchase of lumber products now constitutes not Western exports but home demand. In this case, owing to interregional labour mobility, there is no need for changes in the rate of exchange, and fixed exchange rates, and by extension a common currency, is the best policy. Notice that labour must not be free to migrate to other regions, or equilibrium might not be restored. Thus, 'the optimum currency area is the region – defined in terms of internal factor mobility and external factor immobility' (Mundell, 1961, p. 661) as well as in terms of the activity in which it is specialized (cars or lumber products).

It is not difficult to see this theory's shortcomings. First of all, it relies on equilibrium. Or, the assumption is that countries try to stabilize output. This bears no resemblance to reality. Countries, that is, their capitals, try to maximize, not stabilize, output, and they do this only if this serves to maximize profit rates. The theory is silent on how it would cope with a realistic, non-equilibrium, situation. Second, to stabilize the initial, equilibrium situation, labour must be not only homogeneous or multi-skilled (a lumberjack must be able to replace a car engineer and vice versa) but also perfectly mobile. Since this is not the case, an OCA becomes a very small area specializing in one line of production. It fits thus neither the US nor the EMU. As such the theory is practically useless and historically irrelevant.

Two years later, McKinnon (1963) advanced a modified version of an OCA. This is an

> area within which monetary-fiscal policy and flexible external exchange rates can be used to give the best resolution of three (sometimes conflicting) objectives: (1) the maintenance of full employment; (2) the maintenance of balanced international payments; (3) the maintenance of a stable internal average price level. (p. 717)

Here too emphasis is on small areas. In such areas, the ratio of tradable to non-tradable goods is large and 'the prices of the former are fairly well fixed in the outside currency' (p. 722). Importable goods may be more important than domestically produced goods so that the currency should be pegged 'to maintain its value in terms of importables' (p. 722). But this is virtually the same as pegging the domestic currency to the outside currency. Thus, a number of small areas whose economy is open to each other and which peg their currency to a representative bundle of imports should peg their currencies to each other. By extension, they should form a single currency area. These arguments, McKinnon argues, 'give us some insight into why each of the fifty states in the United States could not efficiently issue its own currency, aside from the inconvenience of money changing' (p. 722).

Here too, it is not difficult to see that emphasis on small areas cannot explain the rise of the EMU. As for the US, as Boisson (1999) rightly remarks (p. 4), that currency area has emerged as the result of a civil war and not because of a 'rational' economic process. Practical uselessness and historical irrelevance are the features of this theory as well.

Finally, Kenen (1969) advances yet another notion of the OCA. For Kenen, well-diversified national economies will be less subject to negative external shocks. In fact, 'a country that engages in a number of activities is also apt to export a wide range of products' (p. 49). If disturbances in exports are 'fairly well randomized' (p. 53), external shocks tend to average out. Flexible exchange rates are not needed and it is in their interest to form a single currency area. This theory would seem to explain the rise of the EMU but certainly does not fit the US experience. But actually it explains neither the EMU nor any other OCA. In fact, the whole construction rests on an absurd hypothesis: that the export sector is such that an increase in the export of some goods is countered by a decrease in the export of some other goods. In actual fact, a decrease in the external demand for some goods tends to reverberate to the rest of the economy rather than to be averaged out by an increase in the export of some other goods.

Notice finally the implications of this theory. The well-diversified countries, the countries of the imperialist centre, should form a single currency area while the so-called 'less developed countries' should choose a system of national currencies and flexible exchange rates. The analysis above allows us to see what lies behind such proposals: on the one hand the formation of a world currency with the seigniorage reverting to the countries of the centre (the notion of seigniorage will be explained further down in this and the following chapters); and, on the other, devaluations for the dominated countries with concomitant loss of value and reproduction of their state of dependency. To sum up, OCAs, as theorized by conventional economics, are a figment of the imagination. The thesis to be developed in what follows is that single currency areas emerge as the result of a complex and contradictory process of mediation of class interests under the leadership of a class which is the major beneficiary of the creation of that single currency. To this end, it is useful to begin with a short history of the EMU and then with an analysis of the precursor of the EMU, the European Monetary System (EMS).

The original 1958 Rome Treaty did not call for the creation of an Economic and Monetary Union (EMU). A first decision to proceed from a common market to an EMU was taken later, at the 1969 Hague Summit. This first attempt failed, for reasons to be discussed shortly, and was shelved at the 1974 Paris Summit. A second attempt has been made with the 1992 TEU and is currently near completion. The TEU amends the 1958 Rome Treaty, which is now called Treaty Establishing the European Community, or EC Treaty for short.

The notion of an EMU can be best understood by examining article 3a of the EC Treaty. Article 3a(1) refers to the economic aspect of the EMU, which is basically a common market plus a close coordination between the national economic policies. The monetary aspect refers either only to the full convertibility of the national currencies at irrevocably fixed exchange rates or also to the adoption of a single currency. While the 1969–74 experiment could not proceed further than an attempt to fix the rates of exchange, the TEU, article 3a(2), aims explicitly at the introduction of a single currency.

Before focusing on the present attempt, a few words on the 1969–74 attempt are in order. In 1969, the motivation for the creation of an EMU was three-fold. To begin with, the great season of social movements started by the May 1968 events led to an inflationary policy in France. In 1969 France devalued and Germany revalued. This had negative consequences for the Common Agricultural Policy (CAP). As chapter 7 will explain, the prices of agricultural products were fixed in terms of a unit of account. It was deemed of great importance that exchange rates should be relatively fixed and stable. In fact, if a national currency devalued, farmers' incomes and agricultural prices in terms of that currency rose automatically. This was not particularly objectionable. But if a member country revalued, the effects on farmers' incomes and prices were the opposite, and this was politically unacceptable. The 1969 exchange rate changes modified the fragile equilibrium that had been reached within the European Economic Community. Anticipations of possible future monetary crises and of their disruptive effects on the CAP spurred policy makers to work to create an EMU.

Second, as has been explained in chapter 3, fixed exchange rates (and this holds even more for a single currency) among countries with different degrees of economic power favour the most powerful of them. Within the EU, this is Germany (see section 4.2 above). The latter decides, even if in an indirect and often conflicting way, the Community's economic, fiscal and monetary policy. Therefore, Germany and the stronger countries favoured an EMU on condition that the EMU's policy would be an extension of their own national policies (basically, low rates of inflation and no depreciations). The weaker countries, on the other hand, had to accept the idea of an EMU, for fear of jeopardizing their membership in the common market. At the same time they welcomed the possibility to influence the Community's policy through their membership in the Community's policy-making institutions. Third, an EMU would have spurred

further political integration and cooperation among the different manifestations of European capital, a not insignificant factor in those tumultuous
times of social confrontation.

The sequence of events which led to this attempt are of secondary
importance (for an analysis, see Swann, 1995, ch. 7). Within the present
context, it is more relevant to analyse this scheme's basic features and
reasons for failure. The major step towards the institution of an EMU was
the reintroduction in March 1972 of a system of relatively fixed exchange
rates. This system has been called the snake in the tunnel (the precursor
of the European Monetary System to be analysed below). The tunnel was
the wider band of fluctuation of European currencies relative to the US
dollar, while the snake was the narrower band of fluctuations of these
currencies relative to each other.[13] Currencies were to be kept within these
bands through foreign exchange market interventions and, on a more
structural level, through the coordination of national economic policies.
This scheme was unsuccessful. On the one hand, exchange rates proved to
be far from fixed. Within a relatively short time period, some countries
(the UK, Ireland and Italy) left this system definitely, other countries exited
it but rejoined it later on (Denmark and France), and many countries had
to change their central rates (i.e. either to depreciate or to appreciate).
On the other hand, the coordination of national economic policies failed
to materialize.

Again, the reasons for this failure should be sought in the political
sphere. First, the high level of combativeness of the European working
classes forced the member states to cope with the different national
situations with different economic policies, thus effectively precluding
concerted economic action. Second, the outright US supremacy was challenged by the equally high level of combativeness of the Third World's
working classes and by the emergence of Europe and Japan as major
economic competitors. This meant the loss by the dollar of its role as the
undisputed international currency and thus the possibility for it to be
subject to speculative attacks. But speculative attacks on the dollar could
not but have repercussions on all other currencies and thus on exchange
rates. Sales of dollars were usually matched by increased demand for marks,
and this could not but have disruptive effects on the ERM. The weaker the
dollar, the less it could function as an anchor for the value of other
currencies. This could not but shake the stability of European exchange
rates.

More generally, given that capitalist development is by definition unequal
development, convergence of economic policies can be achieved only if it
can be imposed upon the weaker countries, which, as a rule, will suffer
from such a convergence (something which does not exclude that these
countries might derive not only disadvantages but also some advantages
form such an arrangement). This, in its turn, is much more difficult to
achieve in a period of social strife (as in 1969–74) than in a period of
unchallenged capitalist domination, as at present.

At the beginning of the 1990s, with the fall of the USSR and with German reunification, a new situation emerged which was again favourable to the launching of an EMU, but now for partly different reasons and in a partly modified form. On the one hand, the greater German economic and political power, as a result of reunification, increased Germany's objective possibilities of introducing a monetary union as a means to consolidate its leadership on Europe. The Community reacted to this shift in power relations in its traditional manner, namely by trying to contain Germany's greater power in a 'constructive' way, that is, by furthering its integration in a common European project. On the other hand, contrary to the early 1970s, the early 1990s were a period of consolidated capitalist power. This made it possible to unload the costs of the EMU upon the European working class (see below). It is this new situation which drives the European Union towards the EMU. Article 2 of the EC Treaty explicitly refers to an EMU as one of the means to achieve the EU's objectives.

The EC Treaty envisages three stages. In the first stage, which was assumed to have been completed by the time the Treaty had been written, all member states' exchange rates would be moved within the narrow bands of the ERM. Capital controls would be phased out but realignments would still be permitted (see further down for a detailed description of the ERM). In stage 2, which started as anticipated by the Treaty on 1 January 1994, the margins of fluctuations would be reduced, realignments would be allowed only in exceptional circumstances, the convergence of the national economies would be substantially realized, and the European Monetary Institute, the forerunner of the European Central Bank, would be set up. Stage 3 would commence at the earliest on 1 January 1997, if the majority of the member countries satisfied the convergence criteria (see below). However, if such a majority were to fail to materialize (as it did), the EMU would be formed on the basis of those countries which did achieve the convergence criteria, not later than 1 January 1999, and on the basis of a selection to be made not later than 1 July 1998. Stage 3 was indeed launched on 1 January 1999. The single currency, the Euro, was introduced, the European Central Bank (ECB) was formed, and this was put at the head of the European System of Central Banks (ESCB). Finally, in 2002 the Euro coins and notes will be introduced.

Having dwelt briefly on the history of the EMU, lets us now turn to an analysis of the European Monetary System (EMS), the precursor of the EMU. An understanding of the latter is conditional upon an analysis of the former.

The two basic features of the EMS were the *Exchange Rate Mechanism*, or ERM, and the *European Currency Unit*, or ECU. The ECU was not a real currency, such as the US dollar or the German mark. Rather, it was a unit of account whose basic function was that of serving as a means of settlement between central banks. Initially, it also had three other functions, namely that of being (a) the denominator for the determination of central rates in the EMS, (b) the reference unit for the construction and the operation of the divergence indicators, and (c) the denominator for the operations performed both in the intervention and in the credit mechanisms. These three functions will be examined shortly. In the course of the years, the ECU had become a major currency of denomination of Eurobond issues and increasingly a vehicle of private transactions. Nevertheless, this was a much more restricted role than that which would be attributed to the Euro, the successor of the ECU.

Let us consider the ECU more closely. At its inception, the ECU was created by accrediting to each central bank a quantity of ECUs equal to 20 per cent of its gold reserves and 20 per cent of its US dollar reserves.[14] Once the ECU price of US$1 (and thus of 1 ounce of gold) was found (we shall see shortly that it was set at ECU 1.3001831 for the US dollar), it became possible to compute the quantity of ECUs each central bank swapped in exchange for its dollar and gold reserves. These swaps were renewed four times a year, at the beginning of each quarter.[15] This was done by the European Monetary Cooperation Fund.[16] It follows that the ECUs swapped by central banks for their gold and dollar reserves were variable according to the market price of the US dollar and gold as well as to the reserves they held.

The tying of the value of the ECU to that of the dollar and to that of the member states' dollar reserves was a recognition of the relative supcriority of the US economy relative to the European ones. The recent transformation of the ECU into the Euro has sanctioned the Euro's willingness not only to put an end to this dependence but also to challenge the dominant position of the dollar in the international financial sphere. This, of course, reflects the willingness of the EU to challenge the US on the international economic scene. But this movement, external to the EU, goes hand in hand with an equally important movement inside it. To see this let us consider the composition of the ECU.

In the ECU, all the currencies of the member states were represented in different quantities. The quantities in which the member states' currencies were represented in the ECU were called bilateral central rates against the ECU, or *central rates* for short. For example, when it was introduced in 1978, the ECU had the composition shown in column (a) of table 4.8.

Column (b) gives the exchange rates against the US dollar on 1 December 1978. Column (c) is derived by dividing (a) by (b) and thus gives the equivalent in dollars of column (a), that is, of the quantities of the national currencies going into ECU 1 expressed in dollars. The total of column (c), that is, 1.3001831, is the value in dollars of ECU 1. Column (d) gives the value of ECU 1 in the different national currencies. It is obtained by multiplying the value of ECU 1 in dollars (1.3001831) by each rate in column (b). Thus, ECU 1 was equal to DM 2.51689, FF 5.78516, and so on. Finally, column (e) is the expression in dollars of the weight of each currency in ECU 1. It is obtained by dividing each item in column (c) by the total (1.3001831).

We have seen in section 3.3, that a country's exchange rate is both an expression of, and is functional for, that country's economic power (or lack of it) and interests. If the ECU had been made up only of marks, the weight of the marks in the ECU (expressed in US$) would have been 100

Table 4.8   Equivalents in national currencies of ECU 1 and weightings

(a)	(b)	(c)	(d)	(e) (%)
0.828 DM	1.9358	0.4277301	2.51689	32.9
1.15 FF	4.4495	0.2584560	5.78516	19.9
0.0885 UKL	1.9364	0.1713514	0.671443	13.2
109.0 ITL	853.00	0.1277842	1109.06	9.8
0.286 HFL	2.1035	0.1359638	2.73494	10.5
3.66 BFR	30.6675	0.1193445	39.8734	9.2
0.140 LFR	30.6675	0.0045650	39.8734	0.4
0.217 DKR	5.3885	0.0402709	7.00604	3.1
0.00759 IRL	1.9364	0.0146972	0.671443	1.2
		1.3001831		100.0

Source: Columns (a), (b), (c) and (d) from Communication of the calculation of the equivalents of the ECU and of the European Unit of Account published by the Commission, 28 December 1978. This Communication is reproduced as Document 7 in Ypersele, 1985, p. 128.

per cent and the demand and supply of the ECU would have been moved only by the factors affecting the demand and supply of the mark and ultimately by Germany's economic power. A change in the exchange rate of the mark would have been reflected in an equal change in that of the ECU. The fluctuation of the ECU on the exchange rate markets would have been tied only to the German economy and thus would have been functional only for Germany's economic policy. Since the mark weighted more in the composition of the ECU than any other currency (about 33 per cent, see column (e) in table 4.8), the value of the ECU reflected the interests and economic position of German capital more than those of other national capitals. This is a clear, quantitative, expression of Germany's ability to impose a value of the ECU closer to its own interests due to its economic superiority. In short, it is a quantitative expression of Germany's domination within the European project. This situation has remained basically unchanged up to the transformation of the ECU into the Euro.

The German leadership hypothesis should not be seen as the dominance of one country upon the others (even less by one central bank upon the others) but (a) as the internally contradictory dominance by German advanced capital upon Europe's advanced capital and (b) by this advanced sector upon the rest of Europe's capital. Also, contrary to some commentators' opinion (e.g. Bladen-Hovell and Symons, 1994, p. 337), the German leadership hypothesis does not imply Germany's absolute power (more precisely, German oligopoly capital's absolute power) to impose its policies. Rather, various fractions of national capitals express their interests through state and supra-state institutions (including both the national central banks and the European Central Bank) which must not only negotiate and mediate these contradictory interests but must also articulate them with those of other classes and fractions of classes and defend this complex of interests against the interests of non-EU countries. Finally, the discussion as to whether the imperialist countries act collectively against the dominated bloc or engage in inter-imperialist clashes seems to be outdated in the context of the EU. The countries (capitals) of the EU do both. The peculiarity is that within the EU there is a dominant, advanced, capital sector led by German advanced capital. This bloc engages in rivalries within itself and with the rest of European capital while at the same time representing the interests of the EU as a whole *vis-à-vis* non-EU countries.[17] But let us return to the ECU.

Once the value of the ECU (relative to the US$) had been fixed, a system for restricting the ECU's fluctuations around this level had to be devised in order for this privileged situation for German capital not to be dented. This was done as follows. Through their fixed value relative to the ECU (column (d) of table 4.8), national currencies had a fixed value relative to each other. These were called cross bilateral central rates or *cross central rates* for short. For example, DM 2.51689 were equal to FF 5.78516. Since the market cross rates diverged from these values due to the effects of demand and supply of currencies, the member states undertook to keep their currencies' fluctuations within relatively narrow limits. These limits of fluctuations were called *bands* or *bilateral limits*. Up to 1992, these limits were set at 2.25 per cent above and 2.25 per cent below the cross rates (Italy was allowed a ±6 per cent band but adopted the ±2.25 per cent band in 1990). After the 1993 crisis, these bands were widened to ±15 per cent (except for Germany and the Netherlands, which retained the ±2.25 per cent band).[18] To keep currencies within their bilateral limits, central banks and governments had to intervene. In the case of a weak currency, they resorted to restrictive monetary policies (a rise in interest rates or a credit crunch), to support operations using a diversity of currencies, to a tightening of fiscal and income policy, or to a realignment of the central rate (devaluation). The opposite applied in the case of a strong currency.

We can now see how the bilateral bands restricted the technological laggards' possibility of using anti-cyclical measures. Take a certain sector (e.g. cars) and consider the example of Germany (higher productivity) and Italy (lower productivity). Germany, given its higher productivity, was more competitive on foreign markets. Also, greater productivity allowed greater material welfare for German labour.[19] German capital's pursuance of higher profits, then, was less dependent upon high inflation. Moreover, inflation would have dented price competitiveness thus requiring devaluation, something Germany was reluctant to do because, as we shall see shortly, this would have checked its aim to make of the mark an international currency. Inflation, then, was enemy number one in Germany. Italy's situation was the opposite. Lower productivity levels created the conditions for inflationary policies as a means to reduce the level of real wages (i.e. to increase the rate of surplus value and thus the rate of profit). To safeguard its international competitiveness, Italy had to resort to devaluation.[20] But the relatively high value of the ECU relative to the US dollar and the relative fixity of the exchange rates within the ERM greatly limited the less efficient country's possibility to resort to competitive devaluation.

Suppose, for example, that the Italian government considered resorting to money creation to stimulate the economy, that is, profitability. This might have generated inflationary pressures and consequent devaluation of the lira. However, the bilateral bands ruled out large exchange rate fluctuations. Consequently, Italy, if it did not want to devalue by modifying its central rates (as in column (a) in table 4.8), had either to accept a deterioration of its balance of trade or reduce the rate of inflation. In this indirect way, that is, through the ERM, Germany could set a limit to the Italian rate of inflation thus restricting the (limited) effectiveness of this anti-cyclical measure in Italy. Or, suppose that Germany lowered its interest rate in order to check pressures on the mark. Inasmuch as interest rate differentials played a role in financial capital movements, financial operators sold marks and bought lire. This put pressure on the lira to revalue and on the mark to devalue. If this process threatened to send the lira through the upper band, Italy had to lower its interest rate in order to relieve the pressure on the lira. But this might have had unwanted inflationary effects.[21]

In this way, this seemingly neutral mechanism fostered specific economic policies and interests, those of the leading sectors of Europe's capital under the leadership of German oligopolies, that is, under 'German leadership'. This had specific consequences for Europe's labour. Since technological laggards had to renounce inflation and devaluation, their capitals had to compete through longer working days (or weeks) and higher intensity of labour, that is, by imposing higher rates of absolute surplus value at the point of production. This was fostered by the dismantling of social security systems and the increased legal possibility of arbitrarily dismissing labourers, nowadays called labour flexibility. The ERM forced technological laggards to extract more (absolute) surplus value at the point of production rather than through redistribution mechanisms (inflation). This made it possible for Germany too to raise its rate of absolute surplus value, as German entrepreneurs too demand more 'freedom' to deal with labour. This, then, was the economic significance of the ERM for labour. At the same time, this system seemed to be imposed by a distant bureaucracy whereas it was the result of conscious anti-labour economic policies.

The law according to which technological leaders tend to revalue their currencies and technological laggards tend to devalue theirs is stronger than the conscious attempts to check it. In fact, during the EMS, the mark was only revalued and the Italian lira was only devalued. As for inflation, if 1980 = 100, consumer prices in Germany had risen to 121 by 1987 but to 214 in Italy. However, if the weight of the ERM became intolerable for the weaker countries in terms of unemployment, loss of foreign markets and foreign currency, popular discontent or simply speculative movements, only one solution was left: leaving the ERM. This is indeed what happened to Italy and the UK in September 1992.[22]

What held for the ERM and the ECU holds *mutatis mutandi* for the EMU/Euro. The advantages of the EMU/Euro for capital are numerous. According to official economic doctrine, the EMU is supposed to create a zone of monetary stability and this in its turn is supposed to contribute to the achievement of a stable, equilibrium and crisis-free economy. This, of course, bears no relation to reality, which obstinately continues to be in an unstable, disequilibrium and crisis-prone state. Also, official economics submit that the discipline imposed by the EMU will induce greater competitiveness through the introduction of technological innovations. But what has been said above shows that both the ERM and the EMU force laggard countries to extract more absolute surplus value at the point of production, something which, if anything, slows down the introduction of technological innovations. If these latter countries introduce TI, they do that in spite of, and not thanks to, the EMS/EMU. On a less ideological plane, official ideology stresses the Euro's common advantages, like better trade conditions deriving from savings on exchange rate costs and hedging, or the simplification which could be achieved in managing the Common Agricultural Policy. However, this is not the heart of the matter. Neither is it of decisive importance to know that the computer industry will gain from a greatly increased demand while the car industry will suffer from reduced demand.

What then are the advantages deriving to capital from monetary integration? Let us begin with the advantages deriving from the introduction of the EMS *and* which are still valid under the EMU. We have seen that advanced capital and thus capital as a whole gains from the possibility of renouncing inflation and devaluation and from increased rates of surplus value at the point of production. This has some important ramifications.

First, in post-Second World War Europe, high rates of inflation have been a means to increase the rate of surplus value, and thus the rate of profit, in periods of heightened labour militancy. But inflation corrodes not only labour's income but also that of all other classes, including those which are traditional allies of capital, thus being a possible cause of generalized discontent with the national governments' economic policies. High rates of absolute surplus value at the point of production avoid this drawback. Second, while inflationary measures increase the average rate of profit by redistributing the value produced, higher rates of absolute surplus value at the point of production increase both the average rate of profit and the economic base (the production of value and of commodities). Third, contrary to inflationary measures, high rates of absolute surplus value at the point of production foster an increased direct control on labour within the labour process itself and the (ideological, political and organizational) weakening of labour's organizations.

Finally, this economic policy is carried out under a double deception. On the one hand, an anti-labour policy wanted by national governments (on behalf of their capitals) is disguised as if it were an economic policy imposed by some distant bureaucracy, for which the member states are not responsible, and reflecting some socially neutral rationality. On the other hand, an economic policy ultimately in the interest of (the technologically advanced) industrial capital appears as if it were imposed by (German) financial capital. In reality, financial capital forces industrial capital to renounce the competitive instruments of the poor countries (inflation and devaluation), it calls industrial capital to task, and thus is functional for the greater creation of (surplus) value rather than simply for a more favourable redistribution of the (surplus) value created. Supra-national financial capital (the European Central Bank) enjoys a measure of relative autonomy in the interest of the expanded reproduction of the most advanced European industrial capitals. Without this 'independence' the ECB cannot perform this basic task, and it is for this reason that so much fuss is made of the issue concerning the ECB's 'independence'. But it should be clear that the ECB is *at best* independent of political parties and national governments but totally subservient to the interests of (the most advanced sectors) of European capital.

The Euro, and thus German leadership, is accepted by the other European countries because the bill is paid by labour.[23] The economic significance of the EMU and of the Euro for labour cannot but be negative. The more the EU countries are tied to Germany (i.e. to the project of Europe's advanced capital under the leadership of the German one), the greater the expropriation of value from labour. This is the class content both of the EMS and of the EMU. The latter is a continuation and an expansion of the economic strategy instituted by the former. It is for this reason that an analysis of the EMS is a necessary precondition for a proper understanding of the EMU. But there is also another reason. Within the EMU, the ERM has not disappeared but ties the non-EMU members to the Euro. This is the ERMII, which was established on 1 January 1999.

The difference between the ERM and the ERMII is that the Euro has replaced the ECU as the pivot of the central rates of non-Euro currencies (European Commission, 1996). More specifically, participation in the ERMII is voluntary for all non-Euro area member states: Greece, Denmark, the UK and Sweden. The two former countries joined the ERMII, the latter two declined to join. The intervention rates are determined by adding or subtracting the agreed bandwidth, expressed as a percentage, to or from the bilateral central rates. As a general rule, for the currency of each member state participating in the mechanism a central rate against the Euro and a standard fluctuation band of ±15 per cent are defined. On 1 January 1999, the Euro central rates and the compulsory intervention rates were established for the two non-Euro countries. The ±15 per cent band was applied to the Greek drachma (upper rate 406.075, central rate 353.109, lower rate 300.143). However, a narrower band of ±2.25 per cent was agreed upon for the Danish krone (upper rate 7.62824, central rate 7.46038, lower rate 7.2925). With Greece scheduled to join the EMU in 2002 and Denmark having opted for non-membership (on 28 September 2000), the ERMII will shortly apply only to this latter country. However, it will increase in significance once new member states join the EU but not the EMU.

These bands are in principle supported by automatic unlimited intervention at the margins, with very short-term financing available unless the interventions are at odds with the objective of price stability. This last point is important in that it frees the ECB from mandatory interventions. Supposedly, monetary stability and convergence towards the single currency were a much more significant aim for the EU than the enlargement to the EU countries that have not (yet) joined the EMU. In practice this means that the ECB will decide from case to case whether it will support a currency by means of interventions. The ECB and the 'out' countries have the right to propose (discreetly) the realignment of a rate in relation to the Euro. A country that refuses to devalue will no longer be supported by the ECB. After what has been said above it will be clear that the ERMII ties the economic policy of the non-Euro members to that of the Euro area and thus to the interests of its dominant capitalist fraction under German leadership. In this way, the introduction of the EMU and of the Euro, a further step towards not only European integration but also a strengthening of German advanced capital's dominant position, will be paid by labour both in the Euro area and outside it.

Let us now consider the advantages for Europe's capital *specific to* the introduction of *the EMU*. What follows analyses only the interests of Germany, on the one hand, and of the rest of the EMU countries, on the other. *For Germany*, the EMU and the Euro are important because:

- the conversion of ECU 1 into Euro 1 has fixed irrevocably the value of the Euro at a level consonant with the needs of Europe's (and in particular, German) advanced capital; and
- the EMU, by managing the Euro according to a policy similar to that followed by the ERM in managing the ECU, is the platform from which Germany's, and more generally oligopolistic capital's, economic interests will be best and further served.

The ECU was important for Germany because it was supposed to be the first step towards the transformation of the mark into the Euro and of the Euro into a world currency serving principally the interests of Europe's advanced capital under the leadership of German oligopolies. The economic base of the mark was too restricted. To become a truly international currency, it had to become the currency used in the whole Community (even though under different clothing), in a market comparable to that of the US and served by an efficient and technologically advanced production system. In the dreams of big capital this would have propelled a volume of Euro-denominated international transactions such that the demand for the Euro would be equal to or surpass that for the dollar. This, in its turn, would facilitate the placing of Euro-denominated financial instruments on non-EMU markets, thus increasing the demand for this currency. Inasmuch as this process would be successful, the world's central banks and other institutional investors would adjust their portfolios from dollar-denominated to Euro-denominated instruments, thus reinforcing this virtuous circle.

But there are two prerequisites for the Euro to become a real challenger of the dollar. The first one, studiously ignored by most texts on the Euro, is that a world currency must be supported both by a sovereign political entity and by an overpowering military force. As of now, the eleven countries making up the EMU lack the political and diplomatic support of a European state. There has been only a very limited transfer of power to the European institutions which has not dented the political sovereignty and independence of the member states. The less powerful states retain a political and diplomatic capability (even though weakened by their subordinate position) to undermine the economic and social policy that is needed to make of the Euro a world currency. Things are made worse by the military dependence of the EU, and of its military arm, the West European Union, upon the USA and NATO. This latter point will be dealt with in detail in chapter 6, section 3 below.

The second prerequisite is that the Euro will need the confidence of international investors. To this end, it will have to be a means of international exchange and a depository of international value at least comparable to the dollar. This means that the Euro will have to be managed according to an economic policy functional for it to become a widely used and traded currency with a constant value (international purchasing power). This coincides with the interests of advanced European capital under the leadership of German advanced capital (even though in a mediated and negotiated way). These interests are worded by the Maastricht convergence criteria and are represented by their relatively strict interpretation and application.[24] It is through these criteria that the other member countries' interests are subordinated to those of Germany.[25] But this will be the case only as long as Germany retains its dominant position within the EU. An economic weakening of Germany both within the EU and *vis-à-vis* other major countries could lead to the pursuance of economic policies incompatible with the above-mentioned conditions for the Euro to become a true world currency. For these reasons, it can be forecast that, in the short and middle term, the Euro will not replace the dollar. At most, it will become a competitor of the dollar. And this is a real worry for the US (see the next chapter).

As for the *less competitive countries* (i.e. those countries with a higher concentration of internationally less competitive capitals), the single currency erases even the restricted possibility offered by the ERM to resort to devaluation (realignments) while the stability criteria will tie even more the weaker countries' economic policies to that of Germany. But there are advantages compensating for these drawbacks. These are first of all those which these countries' capitals derived also from participation in the EMS. As mentioned above, they are the creation of more surplus value contained in more commodities (rather than the redistribution of an unchanged quantity of value and of commodities in favour of capital) based on a greatly increased control and surveillance of labour (and thus on the weakening of its political, ideological and organizational institutions) and tied neither to the generalized worsening of the conditions of life of capital's allies nor to the weakening of the national currencies. At the same time, this system seems to be imposed by a distant bureaucracy whereas it is the result of conscious anti-labour economic policies.[26]

But there are also advantages for these countries specific to their membership in the EMU. First, the conversion of the currencies of the technological laggards into the Euro will allow those countries too to participate in the gains deriving from seigniorage, inasmuch as the Euro does become a rival of and replaces the dollar as the world currency. Second, in a common market, given the free movement of goods, the effects of demand stimulation through inflation might be lost to other member states. The disadvantage of renouncing inflation might be smaller than otherwise. Third, the disadvantages too of renouncing competitive devaluations might be smaller than otherwise. Competitive devaluations create commercial and political tensions and ultimately weaken the EU currencies relative to non-EU currencies. Fourth, a common currency eliminates by definition the monetary crises of, and the speculative movements against, the weaker currencies. These crises can have a disruptive effect on the real economy of all countries but even more on that of the laggard ones.

Common advantages do not imply harmony of interests. Different sectors of capital have different interests and thus foster different economic policies. These are then carried out, in an often mediated way, by different governments with different political connotations. The much-touted necessity for the ECB to be independent is not, contrary to what everybody (from academicians to media commentators) asserts, its need to be able to retain a 'sound' (i.e. non-inflationary) monetary policy in the face of the politicians' pressure for more expansionary (i.e. inflationary) policies. Restrictive policies are not neutral. In the present phase of development of European capital, they serve the purposes of leading capitals which not only do not need inflation as an export-supporting measure but also fear it because of its potentials to provoke industrial strife and a prices–wages spiral possibly resulting in higher real wages. It is they who are the spiritual fathers of the Euro, which for them is equivalent to a strong Euro. Their spokespersons have been German finance capital (supported by European central bankers) as well as those governments that represent the interests of European oligopolies (including the so-called 'social-democratic' governments and parties). They have been able to push through the EMU because of the favourable political conjuncture (the fall of the Soviet Union and the political and ideological defeat of the European working class), because they have represented the interests of smaller capitals as well, because they have managed to portray capital's interests as if they were also the interests of the European working class, and because the decision to join the EMU has been taken in twelve countries (the eleven present members plus the future member, Greece) without asking those countries' citizens. The first time the citizens of a EU state have had the chance to express their opinion through a referendum, in Denmark on 28 September 2000, membership was turned flatly down, in spite of the backing of most of the political establishment and business community.

5

The Geo-politics of the Euro

I have to say that during my time in the U.S. administration and
when subjects related to this came up, I never heard anybody
say, yeah, let's go for U.S. imperialism: That this would have
foreign policy benefits. But I'm sure there are political science
types out there that would talk about that. (J. A. Frankel, former
member of the President's Council of Economic Advisors)

5.1 Introduction

In the previous chapter the analysis of the rise and significance of the Euro
has been related to its fight for supremecy with the US dollar. This has left
unexplored another important dimension: the impact of this fight upon
the dominated bloc. A major aspect of this impact is the process of
dollarization, which has gained a renewed impetus since the 1990s.[1]

On 24 January 2000, the *Los Angeles Times* reported that the US dollar
had become official tender in East Timor, as it prepared for self-rule after
the recently failed attempt by Indonesia savagely to repress the pro-
independence movement (Paterson, 2000). Neither the population nor
official commentators seem to have given much critical thought to the
dollarization of that country. But the announcement by Ecuador earlier in
the same month of its intention to replace the national currency, the sucre,
by the US dollar provoked a flurry of popular protests that hit the news.

To stop the plan, the indigenous people marched on Quito and,

supported by some junior officers in the armed forces, stormed the Congress
building. They announced a new government led by a three-man junta
initially made up of an army colonel, the head of the movement of indigenous people that organized the protests and a former president of the
Supreme Court. (Buckley and Dudley, 2000)

They overthrew the president, Jamil Mahuad, and set up a 'people's
parliament', thus claiming *de facto* political power. This, of course, was not
welcomed by big brother, the US.

The colonel was . . . replaced by General Carlos Mendoza, the armed forces
chief, [who] subsequently dissolved the junta and handed over power to Mr.

Noboa, a former university professor. General Mendoza said he did so after discussions with U.S. officials, who threatened to cut foreign aid and discourage foreign investment in Ecuador if power were not restored to the elected government, The Associated Press reported.' (Buckley and Dudley, 2000)

The new president pledged to push ahead with the dollarization of the sucre. 'Dollarization is a fundamental tool to create stability, growth and democracy, as long as it is complemented by the correct laws,' said Ecuador's new finance minister (Moss, 2000). The bill introducing dollarization was indeed passed on 11 March 2000. A day later Ecuador received a $2bn loan from the IMF and other agencies to help it to switch to the US dollar and to overhaul its economy (MA.GA., 2000). By 10 September 2000, the US dollar had officially replaced the sucre.

The old lesson to be (re)learnt is that the US will do whatever is in its power to suffocate, if need be in blood, any popular movement clashing with its own interests, especially if that movement generates radically alternative democratic institutions. But there is an element of novelty as well. Both some sectors of the Ecuadorian bourgeoisie and the United States have shown that they favour dollarization. The picture is indeed not clear-cut. On the one hand, a fraction of the local bourgeoisie is against dollarization, such as those exporters who can compete only through devaluation. On the other, dollarization seems to enjoy the support of the middle class and of those sectors of the labouring classes whose savings are eroded by the loss of value of the sucre relative to the US dollar. But, on the whole, it seems safe to say that in Ecuador the idea of dollarization has won:

- because it favours principally the interests of the most influential sectors of the bourgeoisie and, in a more contradictory way, of the rest of the capitalist class and of the middle class;
- because it seems to protect the economic interests of the middle class and of a chunk of the Ecuadorian working class by protecting their savings from rampant devaluations;
- because, in the present conjuncture, it emerges as a valuable tool in the arsenal of US economic and foreign policy;
- finally, because of contingent, that is, political, reasons in that it seems to have been a desperate act by the Mahuad administration to retain power (Acosta, 2000).

The first three points have a more general validity. The rest of this chapter will elucidate and elaborate on them.

5.2 Dollarization and Seigniorage

In and of itself, the Ecuadorian economy is of limited practical interest to the US. The repression of the Ecuadorian Indians' movement was due more to political and ideological reasons (the fear of 'contagion' to other countries) than to economic ones.[2] However, the dollarization of major Latin American countries is of much greater interest to the US. The reasons will be examined below. At this juncture, the US does not openly promote dollarization (see below). Rather, it is the dependent countries that are candidly exploring this possibility. In 1999 the presidents of Argentina and of El Salvador called for official dollarization and in 1998 Mexican officials began exploring a monetary union with the United States (Stein, 1999, p. 2), a position urged by Mexican business leaders as well (*Latino Beat*, 1999). Official dollarization 'seems the best choice' for Brazil too (Schuler, 1999b, sect. 6). Peru and even Canada are exploring that idea as well.[3] Besides the above-mentioned countries, government officials or the local press have shown interest in dollarization also in Argentina, Brazil, Ecuador, Indonesia, Mexico, Russia and Venezuela (Schuler, 1999a, table 4). What seemed unthinkable up to very recently is now emerging as a concrete possibility. In this sense, Ecuador's dollarization is important because its example could be instrumental in overcoming other candidates' political and ideological objections. Whether dollarization will spread throughout Latin America and further is still a matter of debate. If it does, it will have a momentous impact on the majority of the population of the countries involved as well as on inter-imperialist relations. It is therefore important to clarify both issues and stakes.[4]

Schuler (1999b) differentiates among three types of dollarization. *Unofficial dollarization* occurs when people hold their financial assets in dollars even if the dollar is not legal tender (or is legal tender but not for daily transactions). A measure of unofficial dollarization is given by Federal Reserve estimates that between 50 per cent and 75 per cent of US dollar notes are held by foreigners and that the monetary base increases 'partly from higher demand for dollars in the United States and partly from higher demand abroad' (Schuler, 1999a, sect. 2). Given that the currency in circulation is about $480bn, $300bn is held abroad. A preferred destination is Latin America: 'Much of Latin America is already *unofficially* dollarized. By 1995, foreign currency deposits as a share of a broad measure of money supply were 44% in Argentina, 82% in Bolivia, 31% in Costa Rica, 55% in Nicaragua, 64% in Peru and 76% in Uruguay' (Stein, 1999, p. 2). It should be noted that a similar movement is discernible for another strong currency: the Bundesbank has estimated that about 40 per cent of DM notes are held by foreigners (Schuler, 1999b, sect. 2). If a different measure of unofficial dollarization is taken, the proportion of foreign-currency deposits in the domestic banking system, then the IMF estimated in 1995 that fifty-two countries were highly or moderately dollarized. If by dollarization one understands the widespread use not of only the US dollar but also of the German mark, then the unofficially dollarized countries comprise most of Latin America, most of the former Soviet Union and various other countries. Clearly, these are only estimates, but they do indicate the magnitude of the problem. The Japanese yen, on the other hand, seems to be of little use abroad.

Semi-official dollarization, or *officially bimonetary systems,* occur in those countries which allow a foreign currency as a second legal tender in everyday payments, even though the foreign currency plays a secondary role relative to the national currency. A half-a-dozen countries use the US dollar (not only the Bahamas but also Cambodia and Laos) and a number of other countries use other currencies as the secondary one, including the French franc (some former French colonies), the German mark (the Balkans), the Hong Kong dollar (Macau and Southern China) and the Russian rouble (Belarus) (Schuler, 1999b).

Official (or full) dollarization is the focus of this chapter. The countries adopting it replace their national currencies with the US dollar. The national currency at most continues to exist in the form of coins having small value. After a country dollarizes it becomes part of the US monetary system and in fact a region of that system. Its supply of money is determined initially by its monetary base (notes and coins both in circulation and as reserves) after the conversion of the local currency into dollars, and from that point on by its balance of payments. The monetary base grows if exports are greater than imports and if capital inflows are greater than capital outflows, and shrinks in the opposite cases. In 1999, twenty-eight countries were using the dollar or some other foreign currency as their predominant currency.[5] Of these, fifteen are not independent and thirteen are independent territories. By far the biggest is Panama, which in 1997 had a population of 2.7 million and a GDP of $8.7bn. This compares with Argentina, the most likely candidate, which in the same year had a population of 33 million and a GDP of $300bn (Schuler, 1999b, sect. 2). Panama has been dollarized since 1904 and is the showcase of the supporters of dollarization. Let us then summarily assess its economic performance.

To begin with, macro-economic data seem to be solid. 'Growth averaged 8.1 percent from 1961–71 and again from 1978–81, and has averaged 2.5 percent in other years' (Bogetic, 1999). However, with 75 per cent of GDP dominated by the service sector related to its geographical position, Panama is hardly a representative Latin American country. As for monetary indicators, 'Inflation has averaged 3 percent per year in the 1961–97 period, almost 2 percent lower than in the United States. Real interest rates have remained in low to mid single digits' (Bogetic, 1999). In 1997 and 1998 the inflation rate was 1.2 per cent and 0.6 per cent respectively (Council for Investment and Development, 1999). Thus, all is well on the monetary front. But let us look at the real economy.

In 1997 and 1998, the unemployment rate was 13.4 per cent. From 1980 to 1989, the population in poverty grew from 27.9 per cent to 31.8 per cent and Panama was one of the four Latin American countries (of the seven for which the data span the entire decade) that experienced an increase in income inequality (World Bank, 1993). 'The elastic supply of labour . . . keeps real wages at subsistence-equivalent levels' (Moreno-Villalaz, 1999, p. 425). Or, to take another angle, the Human Development Index (computed by the United Nations Development Programme) provides a broad measure of human development. A negative figure indicates deterioration.

In 1990, Panama was the fifth worst performing country (-12.91 per cent), surpassed in this unenviable race only by Nepal, Brazil, Ivory Coast and Jamaica. That is, of all the countries in the world, only four had a deterioration of the Human Development Index worse than that of Panama. And yet, official documents are not ashamed to complain about Panama's 'laws that make wages unnecessarily rigid' (Schuler, 1999a, Conclusions). As for the US monetary authorities, the only striking fact the then US Deputy Treasury Secretary Lawrence Summers mentioned in a speech delivered in 1999 on dollarization was that 'dollarized Panama is the only country in Latin America with an active 30-year fixed rate mortgage market' (US Treasury, 1999). Even Summers has precious little to brag about.

Having sketched briefly the geography of the three forms of dollarization, let us now analyse the phenomenon. The first point to be made is that a proper understanding of dollarization presupposes a clear grasp of the notion of international seigniorage. This in its turn presupposes a discussion of national seigniorage, that is, the appropriation of value within a nation from the public by the state due to its power to issue legal tender. In the official literature there are two ways to conceive of seigniorage: as a stock (a one-time gain) and as a flow (a flow of revenue over time). Let us first look at *national seigniorage*, that is, the appropriation of value by the state from its own subjects.

The classic case of *seigniorage as a stock* is that of the sovereign who holds the power to mint coins which cost him less than what he can purchase with them. As applied to modern conditions,

> A \$1 bill costs about 3 cents to print, but the U.S. government can use it to buy \$1 worth of goods. If the bill circulated forever, the net seigniorage would be 97 cents. In reality it is less because after about 18 months the average \$1 bill wears out and needs to be replaced; like other governments, the U.S. government replaces worn-out notes and coins free of charge.[6] More generally, the concept of seigniorage applies not just to the \$1 bill, but to the entire monetary base–notes and coins in circulation, plus bank reserves. Under this approach, gross seigniorage is the *change* in the monetary base over a given period, divided by the average level of prices during the period if one wants to correct for inflation. (Schuler, 1999b, sect. 4, emphasis added)

The above is incorrect. First, if a \$1 bill is replaced, there is no increase in seigniorage because there is no increase in the monetary base. Thus, at any given moment, a change in the monetary base measures a *change* in seigniorage, not its gross quantity. Second, if a period is taken, the seigniorage over that period is computed by dividing the increase in the monetary base by the increase in the price level. This is done in order to compute net seigniorage but also, and more importantly, in order to be able to compare the appropriation of value at different points in time. Third, total seigniorage is not measured by the total monetary base. For each previous period the total monetary base of that period should be divided by a price deflator. This having been said, the following data give an idea of the magnitudes involved. According to Fed data, the monetary base was $50bn in 1960, $81bn in 1970, $162bn in 1980, $314bn in 1990 and $608bn in 1999 (US Federal Reserve, 2000; all data refer to December).[7]

Consider now *seigniorage as a flow of revenues.*

> The income of the Federal Reserve System is derived primarily from the interest on U.S. Government securities that it has acquired through open market operations [from the depository institutions].... After it pays its expenses, the Federal Reserve turns the rest of its earnings over to the U.S. Treasury. About 95 per cent of the Reserve Banks' net earnings have been paid into the Treasury since the Federal Reserve System began its operations in 1914. (US Federal Reserve, 1994, p. 17)

This flow of interests paid by the Treasury to the Fed, roughly $25 billion a year, is considered to be seigniorage. However, this is wrong. Simply, one branch of the state (the Treasury) pays another branch of the state (the Fed). There is simply an internal transfer, a meaningless operation in terms of appropriation of value by the state from the capitalists and labourers. The fact that these interests are rebated to the Treasury makes this point even clearer. Yet official literature considers this flow of interests as seigniorage.

We can now properly understand *international seigniorage,* in relation to dollarization, that is, the appropriation of value by the US from nations adopting either unofficial or official dollarization. Let us start with *unofficial dollarization,* using the notion of seigniorage as a stock. International seigniorage derives to the US from the fact that a big chunk of its monetary base (dollar notes) is kept abroad instead of returning to the US. If a country exports to the US, it gains dollars, paper with no intrinsic value.[8] If that country imports from the US, it gets value and gives back that paper (notes) with no intrinsic value. However, if that country does not use those dollars to purchase back US goods (as happens for other currencies), those dollars represent cost-free imports into the US. This is appropriation of value by the US due to the fact that it issues the world currency (seigniorage). There are basically three reasons why those dollars are not used to purchase US goods: first, they are kept as international reserves; second, they circulate only within the dollarized economies; and, third, they are used in the international markets as a means of international payment. But this use, in its turn, is made possible because the dollar is the money of the hegemonic power, both economically and militarily.[9] 'About 55% to 70% of US dollars already circulate abroad, including about 75% of each year's new dollar issuance' (Stein, 1999, p. 7). As far as Latin America is concerned, it has already been mentioned that much of it is already unofficially dollarized (Stein, 1999, p. 2). This is unofficial dollarization which is at the same time a measure of US international seigniorage.

But it is *official dollarization* that is the focus of this chapter. Let us take the example of Argentina, the country most likely to dollarize officially. In an effort to check the hyperinflation of the 1980s, Argentina passed the 1991 'Convertibility Law', thus instituting a currency board.[10] On the basis of this, the public can convert dollars into pesos and vice versa on demand at a fixed rate of one dollar for one peso. Consequently, for every peso in circulation there must be one US dollar in Argentina's federal bank reserves.[11] In reality, Argentina has more US dollars in its reserves than the peso monetary base, that is, about $30bn in foreign exchange reserves, mostly dollar assets like US Treasuries, against a 15bn peso monetary base. There should be no problem in retiring those pesos and replacing them with dollars. Suppose now that Argentina switched from a currency board system to official dollarization, and let us begin by discussing how the orthodox view sees its effects on seigniorage.

It should be noted that nowadays the focus is on seigniorage as flow and not as stock for reasons which will become clear shortly. Consider the following.

> Under its currency board system, Argentina earns seigniorage of about $750 million per year. Its method of collecting seigniorage is based on the fact that it doesn't actually have many dollar notes on reserve. Its reserves are in the form of short-term dollar-denominated securities (mostly U.S. Treasuries) on which the Argentines earn interest. If Argentina were to dollarize, it would sell these reserve securities for actual U.S. dollars. Argentina would no longer have reserve securities on which to earn interest. Meanwhile, the increased demand for U.S. dollars would allow the Federal Reserve to issue more currency and purchase more securities. In this way, the seigniorage that was previously earned by Argentina would now be earned by the United States. (Stein, 1999, p. 8)

The confusion is remarkable. First of all, there is no mention of the Argentine state's loss of national seigniorage, the stock of value it appropriates from its own subjects and corresponding, in money terms, to the difference between the notes' nominal value and their cost of production. Second, US national seigniorage is misconceived as the flow of interests from the Treasury to the Fed on the securities held by the latter. If the Fed purchases the treasuries held by Argentina, its flow on interests from the Treasury grows. But this is simply a transfer of money in the form of interest from one branch of the state to the other. There is no seigniorage. Third, international seigniorage is here seen as the flow of interests into Argentina due to the US treasuries it holds as international reserves. This confuses interest payments with seigniorage. And fourth, there is no mention of international seigniorage as a stock. In reality, the following would take place.

- The Argentine state loses its national seigniorage since it cannot print its own money any longer.

- There is no increase in the national seigniorage in the US. The greater interests received by the Fed from the Treasury on the US securities the Fed purchases from Argentina are no seigniorage but a transfer of money within the US State. Moreover, the interests go back to the Treasury for about 95 per cent.
- Before dollarization, Argentina receives $750m as interests on US securities. This is no Argentinian seigniorage. *Argentina would gain international seigniorage from the US if it appropriated value from the US in virtue of the fact that the US holds Argentine pesos as international reserves.* Through this confusion, the power relations between the dominant and the dominated country are implicitly reversed.
- Even less is the yearly flow of $750m a seigniorage for the US if it stops paying these interests to Argentina. By selling US treasuries to Argentina, the US contracted a debt with Argentina on which it has to pay interests. If the debt is redeemed, the payment of interests stops. Official literature confuses the termination of the payment of interests by the US with US seigniorage. In this way, as we will see in a moment, the size of the loss of value by Argentina is greatly reduced.[12]
- Argentina swaps $15bn in US treasuries for $15bn of US notes and redeems 15bn pesos. In principle, these $15bn, which were frozen as reserves, can now be used to buy back US goods, that is, the US could lose that much seigniorage. But in practice this is not the case. To begin with, there is no reason to expect that people holding pesos and receiving dollars will use those dollars for imports. If they had wanted to import that much before official dollarization, they could have done so simply by changing their pesos into dollars. Second, a drastic decrease (by a maximum of half) in the monetary base would have serious deflationary effects which would have to be addressed by the authorities long before all the $15bn would be spent on imports. As an IMF official said in a different context, a reduction of the money supply by half would be 'too tough a monetary policy' even for the IMF (Borensztein, 1999). Thus, at least a share of those $15bn would be kept within the Argentine economy, thus representing US seigniorage. There would be only a change in the form of US seigniorage: from international reserves to notes circulating only within Argentina.[13]
- Finally, and most importantly, in the above, quantitative measures of seigniorage have been expressed in money terms. Thus they *grossly underestimate international seigniorage in value terms*, due to the appropriation of value through the formation of international prices.[14]

We have seen that official literature submits two notions of international seigniorage: as stock and as flow. For Argentina, under unofficial dollarization (currency board), the stock measure is $15bn and the flow measure (which is not seigniorage but interests) is $750m, or some other similar figure.[15] However, the stock and the flow notions are seen as alternatives. Thus, this approach reduces Argentina's loss in terms of dollars *either* to $15bn *or* to a yearly $750m outflow. In reality, the loss for Argentina is *both* the seigniorage proper ($15bn or less) *and* the loss of interests on securities ($750m a year).[16] The transition to official dollarization might reduce seigniorage proper but on the other hand it reduces the interest payment inflow.

Having to decide which notion of seigniorage to adopt, both orthodox economists and policy makers almost unanimously choose the flow notion. This has a triple advantage. First, from an economic point of view, as an inducement to dollarization, the US is called to share in Argentina's loss. Aside from the fact that up to now the US has shown no inclination towards loss sharing, the US is called to pay not $15bn (or possibly a part of it) but a part of $750m per year (for a number of years to be negotiated). Almost certainly the total transfer from the US to Argentina (if it does indeed take place) will be less than $15bn. Second, from a political point of view, a yearly flow of money can be suspended and therefore binds the dollarizing country to the whims of the US.[17] And third, from an ideological point of view, through the collapsing of seigniorage into a flow of interests, one loses sight of the appropriation of value by the dominant imperialist power due to its issuing the international currency. Thus, any creditor country can receive seigniorage and the notion of imperialism loses significance.[18] Disregard of seigniorage proper is made even easier by the fact that those not trained to think in terms of value perceive the loss of seigniorage by the US as greater US exports to the dollarizing country, as an inflow of money into the US, and thus as a positive element.[19]

5.3. Dollarization and Social Classes

We can now draw some more general conclusions as to who gains and who loses from dollarization. Let us begin with the dollarizing country. In essence, orthodox economics' argument is simple. The dollarized country cannot print dollars to stimulate the economy. Growth could be stimulated through credit and inflation but this would have adverse effects on prices and international competitivity which could not be countered through devaluations (impossible by definition). If the inflation risk is diminished and the devaluation risk is removed, local savings are stimulated, interest rates fall, expatriated capital returns, and foreign investments increase. This all leads to economic growth. Moreover, if prices cannot be lowered through devaluation (depreciation), wages will have to be contained. Lower wages increase profits and savings and thus investments. Employment grows. So much for Alice in Wonderland.[20]

Labour's point of view is different. First, given the technological (and thus productivity) gap between the US (and other imperialist countries) and Latin America, and given that the prices charged by national producers on the international markets cannot be lowered through devaluation, international competition can be achieved only through lower costs, that is, lower wages. This perverse effect is reinforced by the fact that dollarization is presented as part of a programme of privatization and more generally of neo-liberalist policies. Privatizations (e.g. of basic utilities) lead to higher prices that reverberate on the prices of wage goods. Budget cuts have similar effects. Poverty and social inequality cannot but increase. Second, if competitive devaluation cannot be resorted to, bankruptcies will follow and this will exacerbate unemployment. Third, bankruptcies increase the risk of default on international debt.[21] Foreign pressure on national wage policies will grow. Fourth, in the absence of a monetary policy, the burden of state financing will fall even more upon fiscal and budgetary policies. The fiscal pressure on those who cannot avoid paying taxes (i.e. the poor, especially through indirect taxation) and budget cuts will increase. This reinforces the process just described.

Fifth, there is no certainty (a) that the extra profits are saved, (b) that the extra savings are invested in the country, (c) that they are invested productively, and (d) that they will generate substantial employment (to be competitive, they will have to be as capital-intensive as the foreign competitors). There is thus no essential difference between the 1980s and the 1990s as far as labour's dire conditions are concerned (if anything, they have worsened). While in the 1980s real wages were kept low through (sometimes extremely) high rates of inflation, under complete dollarization the same result is achieved through a reduction of nominal wages (or through a modest increase lower than price hikes).[22] Only, now lower (nominal) wages seem to be 'imposed by dollarization', not by local capital. There is a striking parallelism here with the EU's economic policy following the introduction of the Euro (see Carchedi, 1999b). In Europe too budget cuts and lower real wages seem to be 'imposed by the Euro' instead of by monopoly capital. To sum up, similarly to the EMU, if dollarization will achieve lower inflation rates, it will do so by cutting real wages and by increasing both social inequality and unemployment.[23]

But let us return to capital's view. While lower wages and greater exploitation rates are certainly a great advantage for the local bourgeoisie as a whole, they come with strings attached. Orthodox commentators are quick to list them: loss of seigniorage; loss of an autonomous monetary policy, including the loss of a central bank as a lender of last resort; and loss of exchange rate policy. But orthodox counter-arguments are equally quick to come. The loss of seigniorage has been discussed above. The counter-argument is that this is relatively unimportant compared to other advantages, and that in any case a sharing of this loss (by which is meant the loss of interests on US securities held as reserves at the local central bank) could be negotiated with the US. Then there is the loss of an independent exchange rate policy, basically devaluation to counter inflation and to foster exports. However, some orthodox commentators argue that giving up devaluation can be no sacrifice at all. Devaluation increases the difficulties of those local businesses which have borrowed dollars and which have to re-purchase the same quantity with local currency. Moreover, 'empirical evidence overwhelmingly shows that devaluations in Latin America have proved to be contractionary, not expansionary as in advanced countries' (Testimony of Prof. Guillermo A. Calvo, 1999).

The last objection is that the dollarized country surrenders monetary policy to the US Federal Reserve. There is no opportunity left to adjust the monetary policy to local economic conditions. For example, money injections are no longer available to boost the economy in case of recession or to try to save the banking system in case of financial crises. Moreover, the US has indicated that it does not wish to bear any responsibility for the dollarized country. This means that the banks of the dollarized country would not be allowed to borrow from the Federal Reserve discount window and that the Fed would not adjust its interest rate to suit the needs of the dollarized country (e.g. lower the interest rate if that country experiences economic difficulties or vice versa in case of inflation). Here too there is an orthodox counter-argument. For example, that country's monetary authorities could arrange to have instant credit with large foreign banks in case of crisis (as in Argentina). The same could be done by banks with international connections (Calvo, 1999). Or, 'the central bank can provide liquidity support to local banks if it keeps on hand excess dollar reserves to use for this purpose' (Testimony of Dr Michael Gavin, 1999, point 6). Finally, some commentators hold that already now interest rates in Latin America follow those in the US independently of the phase of their own economic cycle (Frankel, 1999), while others argue that lack of a central bank avoids a policy of easy credit and inflation.

The supporters of dollarization have their own strong argument: dollarization would make monetary crises impossible (unless, of course, there were to be a run on the dollar). This, it is held, is an advantage not only for capital but also for labour. In fact, most of the economic losses due to these crises fall on the poor (Testimony of Dr David Malpass, 1999). Notice, incidentally, that the negative effects of neo-liberalism for the international collective labourer are conveniently rediscovered in an effort to push dollarization through. But, that aside, the orthodox counter-argument here is that what is important for investors and thus for capital movements is not only the 'currency risk' but also the 'country risk', that is, a country's capacity to service its debts.[24] Dollarization would greatly diminish the former but not necessarily the latter risk[25] (Testimony of Dr Liliana Rojas-Suarez, 1999).

The above differences are far from being just a debate between two schools of thought. They are so many arguments expressing *contrasting class interests* within the countries contemplating dollarization (whether the debaters know it or not). In very general terms, larger, export-oriented, capitals will be for dollarization. They are relatively independent both upon the internal market (which will shrink due to lower wages) and upon devaluation (given their high level of international competitivity) and stand to gain from the loss of exchange rate risks. Equally, a powerful support for dollarization is given by financial and speculative capital, which will gain huge profits from the privatizations which will follow dollarization. It is this lobby which makes more inroads into the monetary, political and military decision makers. Less efficient capitals, more dependent upon devaluation and on the internal market (especially of wage goods), are against dollarization but with mixed feelings, given that the high interest rates choking them could be reduced by dollarization. The lower strata of the middle classes may also be in favour of eliminating the local currency due to the risk of devaluation affecting their savings, but will be against low rates of conversion between the dollar and the local currency (which would erode their savings). Those more opposed to dollarization will be those whose interests are served by an 'independent' central bank (i.e. by the possibility to create local money and credit),[26] those sectors of the state bureaucracy whose economic and political power will be wiped out by the privations following dollarization, the working class and the poor (inasmuch as they realize what is at stake), and more generally those who are tied to national independence either for pragmatic or for emotional and ideological reasons.

What about labour? The point has been mentioned above that dollarization, by making monetary crises impossible, would be beneficial to labour, that is, to those who suffer the most from these crises. This argument is instrumental, that is, meant to gather popular support for dollarization, for two reasons. First, the masses do not suffer from monetary crises *per se* but from the financial crises which follow monetary crises and from the fall and disruption in the real economy which follow financial crises. Even if monetary crises were avoided due to dollarization, crises in the financial sphere would still be there, and these would disrupt the economy. Second, in the above argument, the order of causation is inverted. Whereas crises appear first in the monetary sphere, then in the financial sphere, and then in the sphere of the production of value, the order of causation is exactly the opposite. Global investors withdraw their capital if they think that the debtors (institutional or not) cannot honour their commitments. This, in its turn, is an indication of the increasing economic difficulties of that country. Not for nothing are global investors concerned about a country's 'fundamentals'. The real advantage for the masses would be the elimination of crises in the real economy, to begin with.

Labour has little, if anything, to gain. Two points have already been mentioned. First, not only will wages be further reduced, the justification for this will be found in an impersonal development, dollarization, itself an aspect of a so-called 'inevitable movement', globalization. Second, inasmuch as dollarization hurts exports and the disappearance of the lender of last resort makes more difficult the rescue of ailing businesses, labour will be hit by higher unemployment rates. These are general points. Moreover, much depends on how dollarization would be carried out. For example, the dollarizing country needs sufficient dollar reserves to convert the local currency into dollars. If that country gets the necessary dollars through a dollar-denominated loan from, say, the IMF, the repayment of this loan would imply, as is well known, budget cuts with concomitant lower real wages. If that loan is given by the US itself, the advantage could be the yearly (partial) refund of the interests lost on US treasuries. But this 'advantage' would be more than offset by the following:

> If a country has domestic currency in circulation equal to $10 billion at the going exchange rate with the dollar, but only has $5 billion of dollar assets, the United States could extend a loan for the remaining $5 billion. Then the country would be able to convert all domestic currency in circulation into dollars. Instead of paying to the country the seigniorage from the $10 billion, the Federal Reserve would keep part or all of it until the $5 billion loan had been repaid with interest. (Schuler, 1999a, sect. 6)

And, if this were not enough, 'To reflect that some element of risk is involved, the loan should carry an interest rate higher than the rate used to calculate the payment of seigniorage' (Schuler, 1999a, sect. 6).

It is held that dollarization protects savings from currency devaluations. However, savings will be affected in a different way. To begin with, much depends on how dollarization is done. Consider Argentina. It is commonly assumed that dollarization will take place without devaluation, that is, at a rate of conversion of $1 = 1 peso. However, if the peso were to be devalued and less than $15bn were used to replace 15bn pesos, the surplus dollars would be purchasing power available to the government, that is, seigniorage. Thus, less purchasing power would be left to those who saved and indeed to the rest of society. Or, take Ecuador. The rate of conversion was set at $1 = 25,000 sucres. If it had been set at a higher rate, more dollars would have been needed, that is, this rate implies a greater appropriation of value by the government than a higher rate. This is seigniorage, that is, a loss of value by the public at large. Moreover, the 'Ecuadorian model' has its own features affecting specifically savings. In that country deposits have been frozen before dollarization. The plan is to de-congeal them at the rate of $1 = 25,000 sucres after dollarization. Depositors who saved sucres when the rate was $1 = 12,500 sucres will lose half of their savings in terms of purchasing power (not to speak of those who changed their sucres when $1 cost 5,000 sucres). The official argument, that a lower rate of conversion reduces the quantity of dollars needed, hides these facts behind a supposedly technical façade.

Furthermore, wages and thus savings will be reduced after dollarization if prices grow more than wages. It could be objected that dollarization does not imply the loss of wages' purchasing power since prices and wages are converted according to the same rate. But, after dollarization, prices can and will rise more quickly than wages simply because the level of wages is imposed by government institutions and employers' associations while there are no such agencies for the imposition of the level of prices. Only, now prices will not be allowed to rise to very high levels given that devaluations are no longer possible. This holds especially for non-tradables which are not (or are only indirectly) subjected to international competition. These are precisely those goods which are consumed by the working class, like food, transportation, and so on.[27]

5.4 The Euro and Dollarization

Unofficial dollarization has been around for some time. The interesting question is why major countries have expressed an interest in official dollarization in recent years. A first reason is that the high inflation/high devaluation Latin American model of the 1970s and 1980s had become unfeasible. Those policies had resulted, on the one hand, in the destruction of the national currencies' purchasing power and, on the other, in the 'social instability' associated with increasing levels of exploitation and poverty. Resistance to increasing misery had brought a wave of anti-capitalist movements and of military regimes which, to maintain capital's rule and keep the masses at bay, did not hesitate to rival Nazi Germany in their cruelties and crimes. One of the main justifications for these regimes was that only they could prevent those countries from sliding into communism. With the fall of the Soviet Union, these regimes saw a basic aspect of their legitimization vanish. Moreover, almost everywhere popular resistance was crushed, both militarily and ideologically. The situation was ripe for a return to 'normality'. However, the return of 'democracy' had to be conjugated with the maintenance of those traditionally high rates of exploitation. Within the changed political-ideological climate, dollarization represents one, but only one, such opportunity. It is favoured by ample sectors of the local bourgeoisies for a number of reasons, not least because it seems to require and thus legitimizes further neo-liberalist policies.[28]

But it takes two to tango. Dollarization had to become an option for the US as well. The advantages of official vis-à-vis unofficial dollarization for the US should not be sought in the realm of US business (the focus of the commentators). Usually the emphasis is on the elimination of the costs of currency conversion for trade with dollarized countries and on the greater trade and investment opportunities for US companies if (yes, if) dollarization brings about greater economic growth in the dollarized countries. This is not the real thing. The attractiveness of dollarization is that it is not only an extension of seigniorage and a further step towards surrendering the dollarizing country to US imperialism. It is also, and this explains why it has become a real option since the 1990s, a novel strategy to counter the challenge of the Euro. This much is admitted by official sources:

> By increasing the number of countries that use the dollar, official dollarization would help the dollar remain the premier international currency, a state that the Euro is now challenging. Dollarization by one or more large Latin American countries would significantly expand the number of people officially using the dollar, moving the population of the dollar zone ahead of the population of the Euro zone for the time being. (Schuler, 1999b, section 4)

Or, 'If dollarization proved to be successful, the U.S. dollar could become the Western Hemisphere's version of the Euro' (Testimony of Senator Chuck Hagel, 1999).

Dollarization's borders are by no means restricted to Latin America. As a report written for the Joint Economic Committee puts it, 'in principle, dollarization could extend to every country in the Americas, Asia, and the Pacific, plus almost all the former Soviet Union and half or more of Africa' (Schuler, 1999a, sect. 5; Testimony of Senator Jim Bunning, 1999). While dollarization could be extended beyond Latin American countries, it has an added advantage for the US concerning these latter countries. As Falcoff (1999) points out, dollarization could deal a blow to Mercosur,[29] which in theory 'is merely one of the building blocks toward a hemispheric trade area, but in reality it represents Brazil's ambitions to provide a rival pole of attraction to the United States in South America'. For the other member countries (especially Argentina and Uruguay), Mercosur represents 'something for which they have been searching since the collapse of the Soviet Union – a device to allow them to resume their former 'nonalignment' vis-à-vis the United States'. For the US, then, dollarization would kill two birds with one stone: it would check the Euro's challenge and put an end to a rival trading block,[30] thus removing a barrier to the dollar's expansion.

The economic and political advantages for the US are interrelated. Official literature emphasizes the following:

- the saving on transaction costs and the reduction of risks that hamper trade and investment;
- the 'accruing of seigniorage to the US', by which it is erroneously meant that the US will not have to pay interests on the treasuries held by the dollarizing country;[31]
- the increase in trade with those countries; and
- 'maybe some foreign policy benefits to spreading U.S. influence' (Frankel, 1999).

Occasionally, the possibility of a monetary union with the US is discussed (the US Senate Banking Committee has held several hearings on the subject). Inevitably, comparisons are made with the EMU. While commentators are right in believing that at this time this option is not a real possibility, the reasons adduced are acritically borrowed from EU propaganda. For example, it is held that the spur to European integration has been the fear of another war on its territories and that this is not the case for the US. But this and other similar motives played only a secondary role in the construction of the EU. The real fundamental reason for European integration has been the imperialist nature of the European project and especially of European oligopolies under the leadership of German oligopolies. This project required even stricter forms of integration leading to a monetary union (see Carchedi, 1999b). The case is different for the US. It is already the leading imperialist power, especially in Latin America. For it, a monetary union with the dollarizing or already dollarized countries is not only of little use but would also entail the management of those countries' monetary policy (which could be contrary to US interests).

Up to now the US has shown coolness concerning dollarization. This in spite of the advantages to be mentioned shortly. There are several reasons for this coolness. First, dollarization could be seen as the antechamber of a monetary union. Second, a major wave of dollarization would probably put pressure on the Fed to take into consideration the monetary interests of those countries, especially if they are important US trade partners (Bergsten, 1999). This in its turn might weaken confidence in the soundness of the dollar (Acosta, 2000). Third, the issue of seigniorage sharing would be 'pretty hard to explain to Congress' (Frankel, 1999).[32] Finally, and perhaps most importantly, an active and open US support for dollarization might be politically counter-productive and spur nationalist, anti-dollarization, movements.[33] Official statements warning countries to consider carefully giving up their currency[34] should be seen in this light. This 'prudent' attitude is made easier by the desire of (fractions of) the local bourgeoisies to dollarize.[35]

In reality, the advantages accruing to the US are much greater and more substantial than those suggested above. They can be summarized as follows. (The focus is only on what is specific to full dollarization and on Latin America.)

- By making devaluation impossible, dollarization deprives the dollarizing countries of one basic instrument of international competition *vis-à-vis* the US.
- Dollarization, if expanded to Latin America, will strengthen its trade with the US. The appropriation of value inherent in international price formation, also called unequal exchange, will grow (see Carchedi, 1991a, ch. 7).
- US productive and financial investments in that area might also rise (due, for example, to the disappearance of the currency risk or to the further fall in real wages). The repatriation of profits and of interests on financial investments will increase.
- If a country lacks the necessary funds to dollarize, it will have to get them through international debt. As long as the debt is not redeemed, the outflow of interests will contribute to keep the country in a state of either colonialism or dependent development. If the debt is redeemed, its redemption will have to be financed through the export of commodities. As pointed out above, this redemption is US seigniorage.
- Most importantly, a vastly increased dollar area will further strengthen the dollar's premier position, thus strengthening US seigniorage. It will both check the advance of a real rival, the Euro, and effectively kill a rival trade bloc (Mercosur) which could generate its own currency, thus limiting the expansion of US seigniorage (Julia, 2000, pp. 54–5).[36] Right now the dollar accounts for 'only' nearly half of Latin American trade. The other half could become a contested terrain between the dollar and the Euro.[37] As then Deputy Treasury Secretary Lawrence Summers put it: 'The currently modest extent of trade between the United States and individual Latin American countries other than Mexico would limit the

short-term implications for the United States unless dollarization were to become a regional trend' (US Treasury, 1999).[38]

• The above are five facets of US economic imperialism. Given that they are quantified in money terms, they grossly underestimate the appropriation of value from the dollarizing countries. They will reinforce, to the point of institutionalizing it, US political domination upon those dominated countries which 'choose' to dollarize. At the same time, they will weaken the collective labourer's capacity to resist national and international exploitation and political domination.[39]

To conclude, official dollarization, if extended to major countries, would be a new way for the US to increase its imperialist power, a new aspect of inter-imperialist struggle. It would be one of the answers by the US to the real or potential challenges to its economic and monetary supremacy. But it would be at the same time a new weapon in the US arsenal against the dependent countries and in particular against the labouring classes of those countries. Dollarization is already contributing, as unofficial dollarization, to an appropriation of international surplus value on a scale unprecedented in the history of capitalism.[40] It does this through its interrelation with international seigniorage, unequal exchange, profit repatriation and inflow of interests on international investments and debt. Official dollarization would both worsen the already appalling plight of those countries' labouring classes and reinforce US global domination. Of course, all this is denied by official instances and orthodox economics. But the Ecuadorian Indians have not been fooled by propaganda, academic or not. As they put it during their march on Quito, dollarization will 'dollarize poverty, privatize wealth and repress the resistance' (Rother, 2000). They were right. Only, no team of medical luminaries will ever declare them unfit to stand any longer the trial of misery and degradation and no Minister of 'Justice' will ever free them from that prison which is their inhuman condition.[41]

Trade, Development and Wars

6.1 The European Union and World Trade

The two previous chapters have inquired into the relationship between different levels of technological development, the crystallization of the world economy into two major economic blocs, the formation of international prices, international trade, and the appropriation of international value. This analysis can now be made more concrete. This first section reviews those international trade organizations and agreements which masquerade the search for maximum profits by commercial capital in the most powerful countries as if they were aimed at facilitating the attainment of universal comparative advantages through generalized free trade. Section 6.2 builds upon chapter 4, section 1 and considers how the power relations between the EU, on the one side, and two specific groups of countries, on the other, promote either a lack of (capitalist) development or dependent development in those countries. Finally, section 6.3 evaluates the military arm of the EU as a means to impose its trade and (under)development policies on other countries. Let us then begin with a review of world trade, of the world's trade organizations and agreements, and of the place and role of the EU in the world's trade as well as in those organizations and agreements.

6.1.1 GATT

Nowadays, international trade is not left to the unbridled behaviour of the trading 'partners' but is subjected to some 'commonly agreed' rules. The most important structure within which these rules are negotiated is the World Trade Organization, or WTO, the successor of the General Agreement on Tariffs and Trade, or GATT. Through these agreements and organizations, the most powerful countries impose upon other nations a pattern of trade that is to their own advantage. If this pattern of trade requires free trade, this will be the thrust of those agreements. If the most powerful nations require obstacles to trade (protectionism, embargoes, etc.), then this will be the case. This is the alpha and omega of international trade, a point well known to trade negotiators but, not surprisingly, outside the visual range of orthodox international economics. Elucidation of this basic principle requires that we dwell on the contrasting interests not only of the technological leaders *vis-à-vis* the technological laggards but also of the different nations within the two blocs. These contradictory interests are negotiated within the context of the World Trade Organization.[1] To gain a better view of the WTO, let us first deal with its predecessor, GATT.

Conventional accounts of the origins of GATT go back to the Great Crisis of the 1930s. To try to reduce the impact of the crisis on unemployment, the United States passed in 1930 the Smooth–Hawley Tariff Act, which raised import duties by 59 per cent. By 1932 sixty countries had retaliated by raising their tariffs. International trade collapsed to one third of its previous volume. Rounds of competitive devaluations were also resorted to as a means to foster exports. They too had a negative effect on trade. Then, as now, economists thought that trade restrictions were a 'mistake' which aggravated the crisis and that the task of institutions such as GATT would have to be that of preventing the repetition of such mistakes. Ignorance of value analysis precluded then, and still precludes nowadays, the realization:

- that those restrictions were only the natural reaction of national capitals engulfed in a deep profitability crisis;
- that from the point of view of the individual national capitals such a reaction was far from being a mistake; and
- that it is the feature of capitalism that the search for individual advantage leads to generalized ruin rather than to universal advantages.

The Great Crisis was followed by the Second World War, which put the issue of international trade on the back burner. The war created the conditions for a new and powerful cycle of economic growth also in Europe, where it destroyed capital both in its physical shell, that is, as means of production, infrastructures, and so on, and in its social form, through the disappearance of enterprises.

After the war the trade issue emerged again with renewed vigour. The restructuring of the war economy into a peace economy presupposed the smooth working of international trade. Proposals to create an International Trade Organization (ITO) with disciplinary powers were rejected. Instead, an organization was created in 1948, GATT (General Agreements on Tariffs and Trade), whose task was restricted to the provision of a framework within which negotiations could be taken aimed at checking the drift back towards protectionism. To facilitate negotiations, a Secretariat was set up in Geneva. In December 1993, GATT was transformed into the World Trade Organization, or WTO. As we shall see, the WTO enjoys a stronger mandate than that enjoyed by GATT.

Conventional accounts stress two reasons conducing to GATT. The first is the desire to create an institution that, by promoting free trade, would at the same time promote a rational world economic system. Chapter 2 has shown that this is a myth based on an internally contradictory theory. The second reason is that GATT was set up because of fears of a recurrence of the protectionism which disrupted the world economy before, and which led to, the Second World War. But treaties are signed on the basis of present and future situations and not on the basis of what happened in the past. Protectionism might be unwanted by some nations but desired by some other nations. More specifically, protectionism is avoided whenever:

- it hampers the realization abroad of the (surplus) value produced domestically; and
- it is in the interests of the dominant bloc relative to the dominated countries, or of the dominant countries relative to the other countries within the dominant bloc, to do so.

As for the latter point, the end of the Second World War marked the beginning of an era dominated by the US as the dominant superpower. An international organization was needed which could represent the economic and political interests of the US. These were the liberalization of trade (a) in those sectors in which the US was stronger and (b) with those countries with which it was economically and politically advantageous for the US to do so. As we shall see soon, in the trade talks after the formation of the ECC, it was the US that consistently demanded these negotiations. As for the former point, we have seen that the tendency towards crises, which is inherent in the capitalist system, manifests itself as insufficient purchasing power and falling profit rates. Foreign markets provide a solution to the lack of domestic purchasing power by providing an outlet for exports. The profits realizable on foreign markets through this outlet are the form of manifestation of the surplus value appropriated from foreign capitalists through the international price mechanism, that is, through a certain structure of prices and, given that structure, through the working of the system of exchange rates. But this is only a temporary remedy. The capitalists losing surplus value through international trade have in their turn appropriated it from their own labourers.[2] This cannot but have a negative effect on the country losing that value. Chapter 4 has dwelt in some detail on this point.

It follows that international trade must be as free as possible in order for surplus value to be realized abroad. But it is the stronger capitals (and thus countries) which appropriate that surplus value. Thus, free trade must be in the interest of the economically powerful nations. If this is in the interest of other countries as well, so much the better. But, whenever it is in the interest of the dominant countries to impose limits to trade (protectionism), this will be the most probable outcome. This, and not the optimal utilization of resources, is the 'efficiency' which counts in a capitalist system. It is through this kind of 'efficiency' that economic crises can be temporarily shifted from the dominant bloc to the dominated countries.

But within each nation there operate capitals with different economic power and thus with different interests, so that a certain trade regime might be favourable to some but not to others. Since the end of the Second World War, a double movement has emerged. On the one hand, the power of multinational corporations has greatly increased relative to smaller capitals. On the other, the multinationals of some countries have gained at the expense of those of other countries, the major actors being the North

American, the European and the Japanese multinationals.[3] Thus, the national governments, when engaging in trade negotiations, have to balance various contradictory interests. Those of the multinationals are paramount but not the only ones. The effects on employment, the balance of payments, income distribution and the protection of economically or militarily strategic industries are also taken into consideration. The multinationals, that is, the strongest capitals, need a set of national institutions to mediate, and impose in such a mediated way, their own interests *vis-à-vis* those of other social actors.

International institutions perform a similar task within an international setting. This is the general frame within which the various GATT negotiations have taken place. Additionally, each GATT should be understood in terms of the specific circumstances which have given rise to it and which have influenced its outcome. Since GATT's inception there have been eight negotiating rounds. For the purposes of this chapter only the last three, those following the Treaty of Rome in 1958, are dealt with. They are the Kennedy Round (1963–7), the Tokyo Round (1974–9) and the Uruguay Round (1986–93).

6.1.2 The Kennedy Round (1963–67)

The years preceding the Kennedy Round were characterized by vigorous economic growth spurred by greater US production capacity (which had not been dented by the war) and by the rapid reconstruction of the Western European economies. The US needed to export and Western Europe needed to import. European imports required a robust European economic growth. Such growth, therefore, was welcomed in the US. Moreover, economic growth in Europe was aimed at forming a bastion against communism, especially in countries like Italy, Spain and France. These were the two basic reasons behind the Marshall Plan. It is interesting that one of the conditions imposed by the US for its aid was that the European countries should progress towards European unification. This 'is a particularly important point since it indicates that from the very beginning the "European movement" has enjoyed the encouragement and support of the US' (Swann, 1995, p. 5). Because of this and of the other reasons mentioned in chapter 1, the European Economic Community was launched in 1958.

European reconstruction, however, turned out to be a mixed blessing for the US. The growing economic power of the EEC and the possibility that Europe might move towards protectionism were a worrying thought for US policy makers. On the other hand, the US was the mightiest military power, providing the military umbrella for Europe, and the dollar was the unchallenged world currency. These two factors weighed heavily in the relations between Europe and the US. This explains why: (a) it was the US which, in order to reduce the EEC tariffs, took the initiative for the Kennedy Round; (b) this was basically a round of negotiations between the EEC and the US; (c) the US managed to impose tariff reductions on the

EEC; and (d) these reductions were lower than the US had expected and hoped for.

The onset of the Kennedy Round was the passing of the Trade Expansion Act by the US Congress in 1962. This law gave the power to the President to lower tariffs for whole categories of goods (instead of for only one type of good at a time) and to subsidize enterprises and workers hit by the tariff reductions. Neither Japan nor the dominated ('less developed') countries played any significant role in the negotiations. The latter got an institutional channel through which to gain access to the markets of the industrialized countries when UNCTAD (United Nations Conference on Trade and Development) was founded in 1964, thus outside the Kennedy Round. In the end, the European tariffs were reduced by one third and some of the US tariffs were also drastically reduced.

However, the US did not manage to force a reduction of EC tariffs on agricultural products, something the US wanted due to the fact that its agriculture was much more efficient than Europe's. As chapter 7 will detail, reduction of agricultural tariffs would have meant the ruin of many European farmers. This would have had highly undesirable strategic and political consequences. Strategically, at that time Europe was not self-sufficient in this sector. A reduced domestic supply would have implied an even greater dependency on US food products. Given the expansionist nature of the EC project (see chapter 1), this was considered to be strategically undesirable. Politically, farmers formed a powerful lobby that no politician (especially those belonging to Christian Democratic and right-wing parties) could ignore. The EEC put up a strong and concerted resistance to agricultural tariff reductions. Also, the US put its highest priority on the reduction of industrial tariffs and did not want to jeopardize a positive outcome in this field by forcing lower agricultural tariffs on the EEC.

6.1.3 The Tokyo Round (1974–79)

Soon after the Kennedy Round was closed, international economic power relations changed in such a way that a new round of negotiations became necessary. Among the many reasons causing this change, the following three can be mentioned. The first was the deteriorated international economic situation. We have seen in chapter 4 that the dollar's convertibility was suspended in 1971 as a result of the loss by the US of their absolute economic dominance. The devaluation that ensued was followed by sky-rocketing oil prices and by the 1973 oil crisis. A new economic crisis in the Western world unfolded. Contrary to a commonly held opinion, the oil crisis did not cause that crisis. Rather, it acted as a catalyst that ushered in the tendency towards depression and crisis that were already surfacing at the beginning of the 1970s. The crisis not only acted as a brake for international trade, it also caused the emergence of protectionist practices. Given that the Kennedy Round excluded an increase of tariff barriers, countries resorted to the introduction of non-tariff barriers (NTBs), like quota restrictions, export subsidies, industrial standards, health and hygiene regulations, and discrimination against foreign bidders for government procurements.

Owing to the surging economic malaise, protectionism mounted within the EEC, chiefly to protect the weaker industries. This element, together with the loss of EEC competitiveness relative to other countries, led to a reversal in trade flows. While before the oil crisis trade with third countries had increased more than trade within the EEC, starting from 1973 and up to 1981, the opposite became the case. The EEC directed its exports to the OPEC countries. But calls for protectionism became stronger also in the US due to huge trade deficits and to the car industry's difficulties in competing on the US market with smaller Japanese cars which consumed less gasoline (an important point, due to the higher oil prices) than their American rivals.

The second factor at the basis of the need to update the Kennedy Round was the shift in the relation between the US and the EEC. While the US was still the world's hegemonic nation, the accession to the EEC by the UK, Ireland and Denmark in 1973 further increased the EEC's internal market and economic power. The US still provided the military umbrella for Europe and the dollar was still the international currency, but this could not hold back the relative US economic decline. Moreover, the US could retain a greater share of economic might than would have otherwise been the case because the political division among, and the different economic interests of, the EEC member states prevented the EEC from forming a military arm consonant with its economic capability (see section 6.3 below).

The third factor making for the changed international economic scene at the basis of the Tokyo Round was the consolidation of Japan as the third superpower side by side with the US and Europe. This altered its relation both to the US and to the EEC. After the Second World War, it had become imperative for the US first to disarm Japanese imperialism and then, in the face of a resurgence of a Japanese mass labour movement based on 'workers' control of production based on spontaneous shop committees' (Ichiyo, 1987, p. 14), to rebuild Japanese capitalism as an anti-communist bastion. This task was achieved by the Japanese bourgeoisie through mass layoffs and 'red purges'. This ushered in a quasi-absolute control by management over labour. It is within this political climate that the 'superior' Japanese management techniques were introduced. In spite of their differences, all these techniques are based on a mix of, on the one hand, management's paternalistic attitude and the acceptance by labour of management's perspective and, on the other, extremely high rates of surplus value through labour intensity and a length of the working day reminiscent of the first industrial revolution in Europe. The defeat of the working class plus labour shortages following economic growth led to the introduction of modern production techniques which considerably raised technological efficiency. The resulting high profits could be reinvested, thus leading to capital concentration and centralization and to the emergence of giant corporations with enormous productive capacity. The state-bureaucratic apparatus identified (and still does identify) its interest with those of big business (Ichiyo, 1987, p. 24).

At the same time, on the one hand, the US began to spend lavishly in Japan for the production of the weapons necessary for the Korean War. On the other hand, Japan neither had to pay any significant compensation for war damages, nor had to spend as much as the US and the EEC on defence (it spent between 4 per cent and 5 per cent less than the US and between 2 per cent and 3 per cent less than the EEC). These resources could be directed towards productive investments precisely in a period (the post-war period) in which the world capitalist economies were experiencing vigorous growth. Moreover, Japan could profit from the 'most favoured nation' clause through which tariff reductions agreed upon by the US and the EEC had to be extended to all other nations, including Japan. Japan, on the other hand, reduced only very partially its tariffs, quotas and NTBs. This increased considerably Japanese penetration of both the North American and European markets while the latter's exports to Japan were hindered by a distribution system that favoured internally produced commodities. All these factors determined Japan's well-known impressive economic growth after the Second World War. Consequently, between 1968 and 1971, the US trade deficit relative to Japan quadrupled.

It is against this backdrop that the Tokyo Round began in 1974. The US, being more interested in both tariffs and NTB reductions than were its counterparts, took the initiative. However, some important sectors of the US economy were more interested in retaining tariffs against foreign goods, as shown by the many US import restrictions that had to be agreed upon in order for Congress to pass the new legislation. The EEC too was internally divided, with some countries more in favour of trade liberalization than were others. The internal divisions within the two blocs (the US and the EEC), as well as the changing power relations among the three blocs (the US, the EC and Japan), made the Tokyo Round difficult and very laborious.

The EEC, on French insistence, wanted to keep agriculture separate from the rest of the talks, while the US was opposed to it. The US demanded free trade in those farm products in which it was more efficient and expected the EEC to give up its dumping of farm products on world markets at subsidized prices (see chapter 7). The EEC held that its variable levies on farm imports were not a tariff but a form of farm support. The US wanted compensation for these tariffs and the EEC was worried about the retaliatory measures the US could take should compensation not be given. Also, there was no agreement on the tariff cuts that the EEC would have to give to the US on industrial products.

NTBs were also high on the agenda. The US objected to European quota restrictions and on the use of industrial standards and health and hygiene regulations as barriers to trade. The US also opposed discriminating against US firms bidding for European government procurements. The US was against export subsidies but the EEC objected to the imposition of US countervailing duties. Moreover, both the US and the EEC had a common interest relative to Japan and wanted to introduce a safeguard clause aiming at checking sudden and disruptive surges of imports from one source, that is, Japan. The Japanese, of course, objected to this clause. Also, the proliferation of Voluntary Exports Restraints (VERs) between Japanese and European industries came under US attack. As for the dominated (the so-called 'less developed') countries, they were basically spectators of a game which was being played among the three big contenders. For example, the safeguard clause was indeed directed against Japan but it was also aimed at some newly industrialized countries like Brazil, Mexico, Singapore and Korea. Or, tariff preferences were extended to these countries' manufacturing goods only if the countries of the dominant bloc so wished.

The final outcome was that tariffs on industrial products were reduced by 35 per cent, just as in the Kennedy Round. However, the significance of this result was drastically reduced by the fact that many goods were excluded from the negotiations and that Japan offered to reduce only marginally its tariffs on a number of industrial goods, thus provoking retaliation from the EEC, which cut or eliminated its concessions on principal Japanese exports. As a result, there was practically no change in EEC tariffs on Japanese lorries, cars, motorcycles, consumer electronics, semiconductors and microcircuits. Consequently, in the 1980s the US relied on Japanese VERs to try to stop Japanese imports, while many Japanese and European firms invested in the US to circumvent American barriers. All in all, the Tokyo Round was scarcely successful. But it has been pointed out that the very fact that the contenders sat at the negotiating table and achieved some results at a time of mounting protectionism might have been an important factor preventing a full-scale trade war.

6.1.4 The Uruguay Round (1986–93)

Both the Kennedy Round and the Tokyo Round were initiated by the US: the former because of the emergence of the EEC and of the American fear of European protectionism, the latter because of the economic crisis which had hit the US and because of its trade deficit. All countries involved in the negotiations were worried about mounting protectionist tendencies. The same fears were also one of the basic driving forces behind the Uruguay Round. However, there were qualitatively new developments. While the economic power of the US had been almost undisputed during the Kennedy Round, it had been seriously challenged by the EEC during the Tokyo Round. Japan, which was still completely subordinated to the US in the Kennedy Round, had become more prominent in the Tokyo Round. But, and this is the first new development, by the 1980s, Japan had surged to the role of a world power. By the time the Uruguay Round began, the American trade deficit had reached worrying proportions and the Japanese trade surplus accounted for about half of the US trade deficit.

This time too it was America that demanded new trade talks, to begin with in order to stem the flow of Japanese imports. Japan and the EC went along with the American demand for fear of US protectionism, even though mounting unemployment in Europe made the EC reluctant to engage in trade liberalization. Moreover, in 1985 the EC had signed the Single European Act (SEA), whose aim was both to bring to completion the EEC's internal market and to strengthen a common foreign policy. This could have meant that the EC could have become more independent of the US both economically (possibly bending towards more protectionist practices) and militarily. Again, closer economic ties were seen as an antidote for this new development.

A second important development behind the Uruguay Round was the greatly increased role of capital export and its investment in the real economy. This has been a constant feature of capitalist development but in this specific period it had greatly increased due to the need to circumvent trade barriers and produce directly in the foreign market (possible also for third foreign markets). For example, in 1988 the US exported to the EC for a total of US$75bn while the US corporations produced in the EC for a total of US$620bn (Tsoukalis, 1993, pp. 297–8). The direction of capital flows changed too. While traditionally it had been the US corporations that had invested in Europe and Japan, in the 1980s the latter two started to catch up with the former. By 1988 the total of EC investments in the US had become greater then that of the US in the EC. Also, each of the three blocs had developed its own 'back garden': the US had the lion's share of investments in Latin America; the EC in Africa, India and Brazil; and Japan in South Korea and Indonesia.

The third new feature was the growing importance of trade in services, basically transport, tourism, telecommunications and especially financial services. The latter's importance has increased with the explosive growth of financial markets. This growth is usually attributed to the new technologies that greatly facilitate the functioning of financial markets. In reality, the roots of this enormous increase should be sought in the huge quantity of international capital that roams the world's financial markets in search of those investment opportunities that it cannot find in the real economy.

Given the great profits which can be made on the financial markets, and given that these markets were restrained by rules curbing capital movements, it became necessary to deregulate them, that is, to facilitate financial capital investments, something which, obviously, was of interest for capital-rich countries. In the 1980s most Western countries abolished capital controls so that the most efficient and richest financial institutions could invest in, and draw capital from, foreign sources as well. Given that the most efficient providers of financial services were the Western countries, with America in the top position, it was these countries which, after having deregulated, pushed for a liberalization of this sector. A group of developing countries, led by India and Brazil, were opposed to this proposal, due to their weaker competitive position. Additionally, the US complained that the Japanese capital market remained closed due to a series of legal and institutional arrangements.

In 1982 the US, worried by its balance of trade deficit, tried to start a new round of GATT negotiations, but both the EC and Japan turned a deaf ear. Europe was scarcely in the mood to agree to a further round of trade liberalization in the midst of a recession, especially because the US wanted to put agriculture and high technology on the agenda. Japan too did not want to put agriculture on the negotiating table. Moreover, in Japan agricultural protectionism and thus high agricultural prices had led to very high land and thus real estate prices. These prices had been driven high also by Japanese banks which had invested in real estate and whose capital valuation was strongly dependent upon those prices. Agricultural liberalization, and the concomitant lower agricultural prices, would have had serious consequences for the Japanese financial structure. In the face of the European and Japanese reluctance, the US negotiated a series of bilateral agreements with other countries. This, plus fear of US protectionism (and Japan's fear of European protectionism), finally moved these two blocs to accept a new round of negotiations, the Uruguay Round. The difficulties encountered in trying to match the different interests is revealed by the fact that the talks should have lasted four years (as the previous rounds) but were extended to three more years. The results can be grouped as follows.

First, the industrialized countries agreed to cut industrial tariffs from an average of 5 per cent to 3.5 per cent. As a result, more than 40 per cent of all EU imports are now duty-free. This reduction is consonant with the interests of the dominant countries and, within them, of the major economic players, usually their oligopolies, with higher productivity levels.

Second, it was agreed that all trade barriers in agriculture would be converted into tariffs that would be cut in the rich countries by 36 per cent. EU aid to its farmers would be cut by 20 per cent over a six-year period. These reductions also reflect the interests of both the US and the EC. On the one hand, the US was more productive than the EC in agriculture and aimed at liberalizing agricultural trade in order to reduce its trade deficit. On the other hand, the EC pursued a subsidized agricultural policy that by now had resulted in huge surpluses. Both trading blocs favoured a liberalization of this sector. The figures agreed upon were in line with the Common Agricultural Policy (CAP), which disproportionately favours large producers (see chapter 7).

Third, concerning services, investments and intellectual properties, the main result was the signing of the General Agreement on Trade in Services (GATS). The signatories agreed on a non-discrimination clause which ensured that a concession made to one country would apply to all other countries. New rules on trade in intellectual property provided for payments of royalties and strengthened the security of patents, trademarks and copyright. At the same time rules restricting cross-border investment were relaxed. This point was of great importance for the EU, which accounts for 36 per cent of the world's foreign direct investments (FDI) and which receives 19 per cent of global FDI.

As far as intellectual properties (patents, trademarks and copyrights) are concerned, international oligopolies have to protect their inventions and technological advances which often are the result of huge investments in research and development. It was mainly American, European and Japanese multinationals which wanted protection against intellectual 'piracy' from some East Asian countries like Thailand and South Korea. But, more importantly, by limiting access to technological innovations, the dominant bloc institutionalizes the inability of the dominated bloc to compete technologically and thus the latter's transfer of value through the international price system (see chapter 3).[4] Similarly, the removal of obstacles to cross-border investments reflected multinational corporations' need to invest anywhere in the world where opportunities for higher profits are greater. As mentioned above, this need was magnified by the long-term economic crisis that had hit the Western world.

Finally, the dominated countries were interested in protecting their own industries. Moreover, the debt crisis raised the threat of the impossibility for them of paying their debts and thus of halting their imports from the dominant countries. But these latter needed to export to the dominated countries just as badly as the latter needed to import from the former. The debt crisis added thus a new element of urgency to the negotiations. The non-discrimination principle applied to the dependent countries is just a way to avoid their economic breakdown and thus to keep their dependent accumulation going.

A new element was that, for the first time, the dominated countries failed to form a common bloc. On the one hand the newly industrialized countries (NICs) had reached high levels of productivity (through a combination of high tech and high rates of surplus value). Their development was export-oriented, given that high rates of surplus value implied low levels of domestic purchasing power. For them a new GATT basically meant freer entry to the American market. On the other hand, for the other less developed countries, like India and Brazil, the new GATT meant better raw material prices, a price stabilization fund, and a reform of the international financial and monetary system. It was mainly the latter group of the dominated countries which strongly objected to the inclusion in the GATT talks of new rules on services, intellectual property rights and trade-related investment measures. They saw these proposals as unfair – because before new rules could be added, protectionism against them had to be stopped and rolled back – and basically as a means for Western multinationals to conquer world markets.

6.1.5 The World Trade Organization (1995)

As a result of the disappearance of the Soviet Union and the disintegration of the Soviet bloc, the US, the EU and Japan emerged as the undisputed world economic powers. Within this triad, the US partially regained its hegemony, which had been dented by the growing strength of the other two world economic leaders. This reshuffling of the cards is the basic reason behind the transformation of the GATT into the World Trade

Organization (WTO). The WTO is embodied in the Marrakesh Agreement, which was signed at the Marrakesh Ministerial Meeting, on 15 April 1994. It was established on 1 January 1995. It provides:

- the institutional framework for trade agreements negotiations in goods (GATT), services (GATS) and trade-related aspects of intellectual property rights (TRIPs); and
- a set of legal obligations regulating the trade policies of the member states.

The WTO is usually presented as a simple continuation of GATT. But besides continuation, there are also important differences. To begin with, since in 1947 GATT had been conceived as a temporary trade agreement, it neither was a legal entity in its own right nor had an institutional structure. However, soon after its inception, it become clear that it needed a standing body. In the course of the years, an organizational structure gradually emerged. 'As of the early 1990s, a well-oiled GATT machine' had taken shape (Hoekman and Kostecki, 1995, p. 13). The WTO, on the other hand, not only was born with an organizational structure, it is also an international organization with its own legal entity. This juridical change (in itself relatively unimportant) was necessary in view of a second, and this time major, difference between GATT and the WTO, namely the greatly increased powers bestowed upon the WTO. The WTO is not only a forum for achieving agreements (as GATT was), it is also an organization which can and does enforce them. GATT facilitated international trade negotiations but had no mandate beyond this point. The WTO not only provides a framework for multilateral talks, it also administers multinational agreements and enforces them through sanctions. To this end, the decision-making and enforcement processes had to be changed substantially.

Consider the rules which guide the decision-making process within the WTO. These are (a) non-discrimination, (b) reciprocity, (c) market access and (d) fair competition. The first rule, non-discrimination, is embodied in the Most Favoured Nation (MFN) principle. According to this principle, the best treatment (e.g. a tariff reduction) accorded by a WTO member to another WTO member must be extended automatically to all other WTO member countries. Supposedly, MFN 'provide[s] smaller countries with a guarantee that larger countries will not exploit their market power by raising tariffs against them' because the larger countries would then have to apply the same rule to all WTO members (Hoekman and Kostecki, 1995, pp. 26-7). In reality, matters are different.

Take, for example, a tariff reduction. If a country of the centre reduces a tariff for another country of the centre, it must extend this treatment to all other countries and thus to the dominated bloc as well. This has no negative consequences for the countries (capitals) of the centre, given that the dominated bloc is a weak competitor. But if a dominated country opens its market to another dominated country, MFN requires that it extends this treatment to the countries of the centre, which are much more powerful competitors. The consequences for the weak competitors can be damaging. Behind the legal equality, MFN is functional for the interests of the countries (capitals) of the centre.

The second principle, reciprocity, implies that a country's commitments must be met by another country's similar commitments. Here too, the formal, or legal, aspects hide a different economic reality, the effects of the asymmetry in the different countries' economic power. Concretely, 'small nations have little to offer large ones in terms of export potential . . . it is a fact of life that small economies (i.e. most developing countries) have little to bring to the negotiating table' (Hoekman and Kostecki, 1995, p. 29).

The third principle, market access, stresses the commitment to an open trade system. Stated in these terms, this would seem to be a superfluous repetition of WTO aims. In reality, what this rule stresses is that 'multilateral agreements must be translated into domestic law through implementing legislation' (Hoekman and Kostecki, 1995, p. 31). In this way, through the WTO, the major players in international trade, the countries of the centre, ensure that the governments of the dominated bloc introduce legislation functional for the interests of the centre's capitals.

The fourth principle, fair competition, has a specific meaning within the WTO context. Basically it allows for countervailing measures by a country if the effects of international competition become too harmful for that country. This would seem to be a safety valve for the weak competitors, the countries of the dominated block. In reality, here too the legal provisions hide the dominated countries' extremely limited possibilities of applying countervailing measures against the large and powerful nations.

As if all this were not enough, the weakness of the dominated countries is further reinforced in the provisions regarding the settlement of disputes, which are dealt with by the Dispute Settlement Body (DSB). The DSB has the authority to establish a panel. This is made up of three panelists whose names are suggested by the Secretariat and who are retired international civil servants or experts in trade matters.

> There are no conflict of interest rules and the panelists often have little appreciation of domestic law or of government responsibility to protect workers, the environment or human rights. Thus, it is not surprising that every single environmental or public health law challenged at WTO has been ruled illegal. (Working Group on the WTO/MAI, 1999)[5]

The panel writes a report that is submitted both to the DSB and to the parties to the dispute. 'WTO tribunals operate in secret. Documents, hearings and briefs are confidential. . . . There are no outside appeals' (Working Group on the WTO/MAI, 1999). The report must be adopted by the DSB within sixty days, in which case the offending party must comply with the report's recommendations. If the offending party fails to act accordingly, the complainant may ask permission to retaliate. This will be granted because consensus is required to refuse it.

This is a negative consensus. A positive consensus requires that all countries represented in the DSB agree to concede retaliation. Any country, then, has a veto power. Under GATT any country, including the offending party, could block the formation of a panel or the adoption of the panel's report. If the offending party was a dominated country, it had a veto power. Under the WTO, not only has the DSB the right to set up a panel and to adopt its recommendations; also, negative consensus is required to reject these recommendations, that is, all countries (including the complainant) must agree to refuse to retaliate. The dependent countries have thus lost their right to veto.

Formally speaking, the same applies in the opposite case: if the offending party is a country of the centre and the complainant a country of the dominated bloc. However, once more, this legal equality hides a different economic reality. As Hoekman and Kostecki (1995) candidly report, 'if large players are unhappy' with the panel recommendations, they might simply not implement them (p. 50). In this case, the dominated country's retaliation might in all probability be either ineffectual or downright self-damaging. The petitioning country will thus abstain from retaliation. As for the offending country, if it is a country of the centre and if it persists in not implementing the recommendations, in theory it is possible for the WTO to ask it to leave the organization but in reality this is a practical impossibility. The outcome of all this is that the dependent countries have lost their veto rights and that 'large traders cannot . . . be forced to adopt changes they do not like' (Hoekman and Kostecki, 1995, p. 50).

The dominated countries' weakness is exacerbated by three further factors. Due to the disintegration of the Soviet bloc, many of the dominated countries have lost even that limited possibility of finding alternative outlets or supplies in the Council for Mutual Economic Assistance (CMEA). Also, the role for foreign policy considerations in 'cooperation' and trade, and with it the possibility to get favourable trade arrangements for political (i.e. anti-USSR) reasons, shrank. Finally, following the collapse of the anti-colonialist movement, the 'Third World countries' have ceased to act collectively, thus weakening considerably the representation of their common interests. This explains why, 'with the establishment of the WTO . . . most developing countries signaled a greater willingness to abide by the rules of the game' (Hoekman and Kostecki, 1995, p. 10). Of course, the use of the term 'willingness' in this context is highly euphemistic.

The above should have made it clear that the changed rules of the game within the WTO reflect the changed power relations between the dominant and the dominated countries following the disappearance of the Soviet Union and the collapse of the anti-colonialist movement. Given that it is the international oligopolies (usually referred to as transnational corporations) which reap the greatest benefits from trade, and given that these corporations are concentrated in the centre, the WTO rules are advantageous basically for these corporations. Evidence can be provided by considering the different trade categories covered by the WTO. These are the General Agreement on Tariffs and Trade (GATT), the General Agreement on Trade in Services (GATS) and the Agreement on Trade-Related Intellectual Property Rights (TRIPs). While GATT continues to exist under the WTO and its organizational structure has become a part of the WTO's structure, the GATS and the TRIPs were created by the Uruguay Round and are specific to the WTO.

Basically GATT regulates trade policies in material commodities. It covers tariffs, quantitative import restrictions, customs procedures (e.g. pre-shipment inspections in the exporting country on behalf of the importing country), subsidies to import-competing or export industries, state trading, technical regulations and standards, trade-related investment measures and government procurements. In all of these areas, major reductions to trade barriers have been achieved by the various GATT rounds and the WTO will further continue along this road, unless of course strong protectionist measures re-emerge in the countries of the centre.

The same can be said of GATS. Services are broadly defined as intangibles. This category covers areas such as banking, insurance, telecommunications, freight and passengers transport, tourism, consulting, and so on. The countries of the centre lead technologically both in the production of goods and in the provision of services. It is for this reason and thus in the interest of these countries that the aim both of GATT and of GATS is to reduce obstacles to trade as much as possible. The core principle of GATS is, as for GATT, non-discrimination, as reflected in the MFN rule. After what has been said above, it will be clear that these and other similar rules stressing formal equality and reciprocity can only favour the largest traders, the international oligopolies. Greater freedom to trade is thus functional for the interests of the countries of the centre, that is, of the multinationals based in those countries. Whenever this is not the case, anti-protectionist measures are successfully resisted by those very countries that champion free trade. Perhaps the most macroscopic example is agriculture, which has been put back on the agenda only with the Uruguay Round and only because there have been changes in the conditions within both the US and the EU calling for protectionism in this sector (see chapter 7).

Matters are different with regard to trade-related intellectual property rights (TRIPs). Intellectual property can be best understood as privately owned knowledge. Knowledge can be privatized through patents, copyrights, trademarks, and so on, so that competitors are prevented from using it (or from reproducing the goods made with it) without permission, that is, payment. This makes perfect sense from a capitalist perspective. The question, then, is: (a) why has knowledge, as intellectual property (IP), become a trade issue; and (b) how and in whose interest does the WTO regulate trade in IP? The first question is straightforward. Each process of production needs means of production. Each means of production incorporates a certain type of knowledge. Accession to those means of production (usually, through purchase) ensures at the same time accession to that particular type of knowledge. However, if one were able to accede to that knowledge without paying for it, that is, without paying for those means of production, one could build those means of production and thus produce (and sell) those products. Copying of advanced knowledge (usually, techniques) thus goes against the interest of those who have a monopoly of it, mostly the oligopolies in the centre.

It is thus understandable that in the Uruguay Round the countries of the centre, led by the US, argued that the copying of knowledge constitutes piracy and theft while the dominated countries replied that the adoption of OECD levels of protection of IP would have been detrimental for the welfare of their own population. For example, patents on seeds and fertilizers increase the cost of inputs in food production and patents on pharmaceutical products raise the costs of medicines. While this might be true, it would be misconceived to side with the dominated countries on the basis of the just-mentioned welfare arguments.

If countries are essentially one sort of class formation, governments' negotiators represent class interests. Government negotiators care about the welfare of their own populations only inasmuch as this is necessary for the representation of the interests of their own capitalist classes.[6] They object to the protection of patents, trademarks, copyrights, etc. on the basis of welfare arguments. But this is only a thin veil hiding the fear that the introduction of intellectual property rights (IPRs) will make it even more difficult for the technological laggards (capitals) to catch up with the more advanced countries (capitals) and thus to break out of the vicious circle of technological backwardness and loss of value through the price mechanism (see chapters 3 and 4). IPRs have thus become a trade issue because of the profound effects the regulation of the acquisition of knowledge has on trade (and, as we shall see in the next section, on development as well). The WTO, by 'protecting' IP, protects at the same time the interests of the centre, that is, of the multinational, which are essentially a manifestation of capital in the centre. Within this context it is sufficient to repeat some data already mentioned in chapter 4: 'only one per cent of patents are owned by persons or companies in the Third World and, of those, 84 per cent are owned by foreigners' (Mihevc, 1995, p. 172). Or, as the 1999 *Human Development Report* puts it, 'the TRIPS agreement is unbalanced: it provides an enabling environment for multinationals, tightening their dominant ownership of technology, impeding and increasing the cost of transfer to developing countries' (United Nations Development Programme, 1999, p. 35).

If all this is added to the Generalized System of Preferences (GSP), whereby the dominated countries are ensured non-discriminatory trade for their goods in exchange for which they make concession to the dominant countries on manufactured goods, it becomes clear how the countries of the dominated bloc are now at the mercy of the most powerful nations and their multinationals through the WTO. The dominant bloc, and especially the US, has created an organization for the implementation and enforcement of trade regulations embodying basically the interests of its own multinationals. But this is not all. Many dominated countries rely on the export of agricultural goods in order to pay for the imports of manufactured goods. But 'The majority of Third World production of agricultural goods are small rural farmers. In some cases, producing commodities for export means forgoing food production.' (Abugre, quoted in Mihevc, 1995, pp. 146–7.) There is thus a direct relationship of cause and effect between this pattern of trade and hunger in the dominated bloc. Responsibility for it is carried by the WTO, as well as by the World Bank and the IMF. Inasmuch as the farming sector benefits from all these policies, it is the large farmers who benefit while the small ones see their economic conditions deteriorate even further (see chapter 7).

In this connection a few remarks on biotechnology are in order. This is heralded as *the* technology that will allow poor countries to overcome hunger. What has just been said (and what will be added in chapter 7) highlights the basic cause of hunger, which is socio-economic, rather than technical. The technique itself is an expression of those socio-economic conditions, that is, it carries within it the imprint of capital, and cannot provide a lasting and effective solution to the problems arising from those conditions. Let us briefly dwell on this point. By far the greatest quantity of resources invested in research and development in biotechnology is privately funded and increasingly concentrated in pharmaceutical, chemical and seed-producing multinationals. Public research institutions, including universities, are increasingly under *de facto* control by private capital as subsidiaries and joint ventures or through contracts meted out by multinationals. What kind of biotechnology, then, arises from these research institutions?

Biotechnology manipulates existing genetic material. It is estimated that 95 per cent of plant genetic resources are located in the world's poorest countries (Mihevc, 1995, p. 211). Not surprisingly, then, the richest countries, that is, their multinationals, argue against the privatization (by the poorest countries of course) and for the 'common heritage' of these resources. These plant genetic resources are appropriated for free by the multinationals, which proceed to manipulate them through genetic engineering. The outcome (e.g. seeds) is then sold back to the dominated countries at exorbitant prices so that only the largest production units can pay them. These are exactly those units that are export-oriented and that therefore cannot alleviate hunger, let alone overcome it.

It could be argued that these technologies should be made available for free to the dominated bloc. But this goes against the grain of capitalist rationality. For the apologists of capitalism (e.g. Hoekman and Kostecki, 1995, p. 146), patent protection (and concomitant high prices for patented goods) is necessary to induce large-scale units to engage in R&D. Moreover, on a longer-run perspective, the large-scale investments needed by these technologies are usually not available to capitals in the dominated countries. These latter could compete only by appropriating those techniques for free (a reasonable proposition, given that the centre appropriates for free the dominated countries' genetic reservoir). But, again, patents protect one camp and not the other. This stifles whatever possibilities are there for the dominated countries to develop their own food sector, after the traditional, small-scale units have been ruined.

Finally, it could be argued that this is all a consequence of the wrong application of an otherwise neutral technique and that everything would be fine if the dominated bloc had free access to these techniques and if it were to be the receiver of large quantities of capital invested in R&D. But it is at this point that the inherently capitalist nature of these techniques emerges vividly. Biotechnology in agriculture is not geared to developing pest- or disease-resistant types of plants but, given the interest multinationals also have in the production of pesticides, it develops crops which are resistant to increasing applications of herbicides and pesticides. In this way the dominated countries become increasingly dependent upon the use of these chemicals. The socio-economic, not to mention the environmental, effects are disastrous. Only a radically different type of science could redirect this bias.

To conclude, as Mihevc (1995) aptly puts it, WTO rules on IPR 'in effect constitute a form of protectionism granted to' the multinationals, and thus to the centre, which 'favour a protectionist regime in the area of intellectual property rights, while arguing for the principles of free trade in the area of goods and services' (p. 211) as well as in the world's genetic resources. The WTO's basic function is to shape this policy by mediating the different interests of national capitals' different sectors. As Freeman has succinctly put it, the WTO has become, with the IMF and the World Bank, the third leg on which the centre sucks the dominated countries' resources (Freeman, 1998a, 1998b).

6.1.6 The Place of the EU in World Trade

Trade negotiations are carried out by the European Commission on the basis of a mandate by the member states. The importance of extra-EU trade for the EU is summarized by the figures in table 6.1.

As table 6.1 documents, the EU can be considered to be the world's largest trading bloc. Its intra-EU trade is greater still, as shown by table 6.2.

In 1996, the most significant intra-EU surplus countries were the Netherlands (+37.3 per cent of total intra-EU trade), Germany (+19 per cent), Belgium and Luxembourg (+12.4 per cent) and Italy (+10 per cent). The most important deficit countries were Austria (-11.4 per cent), Greece (-8.7 per cent), the UK (-8.2 per cent) and Spain (-6.9 per cent). With

Table 6.1 Percentage share of world trade, 1996

	Exports	Imports
EU	20.2	17.9
US	15.9	19.9
Japan	10.5	8.5

Figures relative to the EU refer to the extra-EU trade.

Source: Eurostat, 1997, pp. 26–8.

Table 6.2   Intra-EU and extra-EU trade, 1996 (ECU bn)

	Export	Import
Extra-EU	623.4	580.0
Intra-EU	1058.4	1011.8

Source: Eurostat, 1997, pp. 11, 12 and 21.

regard to the extra-EU balance, Germany had the highest surplus (32.6 per cent of total extra-EU trade), followed by Italy (+24.7 per cent), France (+16.4 per cent) and Sweden (+12.1 per cent). The largest deficit countries were the Netherlands (-27.2 per cent) and the UK (-17.2 per cent) (Eurostat, 1997, p. 99).

As for the goods traded, table 6.3 shows that the EU imports more raw materials, energy and miscellaneous manufactured goods. Especially significant is the EU's dependence upon the world market for energy, an element of strategic importance, as the next section will argue. On the export side, the EU exports chemicals, manufactured goods, machinery and transport equipment, and to a lesser degree beverages and tobacco. On the whole, the EU imports low-technology products and exports high-technology products. This is in line with the data submitted in chapter 4, section 2.

Table 6.4 gives the external merchandise trade by region. Only the three major trading partners are recorded.

Each member state has closer links with some geographical areas rather than with others. Thus, for Ireland and the UK external trade is greater (in percentage terms) with the US and Japan, for Denmark and Sweden with EFTA, for Germany with the Central and Eastern European Countries, for Italy, Greece and France with the Mediterranean basin, for Portugal

Table 6.3   Extra-EU trade in goods by sector, 1996 (ECU bn)

	Imports	Exports	Balance
Food and live animals	42.0	30.8	-11.2
Beverages and tobacco	3.6	10.3	+6.7
Crude materials, except fuel	35.0	11.4	-23.6
Energy	79.5	15.3	-64.2
Oils, fats and waxes	2.2	1.9	-0.3
Chemical products	44.9	80.7	+35.8
Manufactured goods	75.6	103.5	+27.9
Machinery and transport equipment	187.2	281.7	+94.5
Miscellaneous manufactured goods	94.3	79.5	-14.8
Other	15.5	8.1	-7.4
Total	579.8	623.2	+43.4

Source: Eurostat, 1997, pp. 69–71.

Table 6.4   Extra-EU trade by trading partners, 1996 (ECU bn)

	Imports	Exports	Balance
US	112.5	114.3	+1.8
Japan	52.5	35.6	−16.9
Switzerland	42.6	51.3	+8.7
Total	580.0	623.2	+43.2

Source: Eurostat, 1997, pp. 44–5.

with the African, Caribbean and Pacific countries, and for Spain with Latin America. But, aside from these specific ties, the EU *as a whole* has specific relations with third countries or groups of countries. To this end, it has developed a multi-layered network of free trade, association and other preferential agreements with its trading partners. The substance of these agreements is that they should ensure the domination of the EU as a whole upon third countries or groups of countries. This point will be illustrated by examining two of these agreements: the Lomé Convention with the African, Caribbean and Pacific Countries and the Europe (or Association) Agreements with the Central and Eastern European Countries (CEECs).[7] The next section will substantiate this thesis.

6.2 The European Union and Dependent Development

While the former section has placed EU imperialism within the context of international trade, the present section focuses on specific aspects of EU imperialism *vis-à-vis* two blocs of dominated nations: the African, Caribbean and Pacific countries (ACP) and the Central and Eastern European Countries (CEECs). The thesis submitted here is that the EU as a whole has a colonial type of imperialist relations with the ACP countries but could establish a different type of imperialist relations with some of CEECs. Let us begin with the ACP countries.

EU trade and aid relations with the ACP countries are particularly interesting not only because these countries encompass Europe's former colonies but also because they are the EU's most preferred countries. After three decades of aid and preferential treatment, one would expect these countries to have achieved at least some measure of economic growth. But this is far from being the case. Originally, the Rome Treaty provided for a unilateral association between the EEC (and its member states) and the overseas countries and territories which were still colonies. The 1960s were a period of decolonization. This called for a change in the relation between the Community and the former colonies. The need for a change was strengthened by the UK accession, which raised the issue of the relationship between the enlarged Community and the Commonwealth countries. Eventually, the relationship between the Community and its former colonies was institutionalized by the Lomé Conventions. There have been four of them, in 1975, 1980, 1985 and 1989. This latter took in sixty-nine countries, or one third of the UN. It covered the 1990–2000 period. The fifth came into force in March 2000.

A first feature of the Lomé Conventions is 'development' aid, basically grants, to the ACP countries. For the 1995–2000 period, ECU 12bn of the total ECU 13bn funds is in the form of grants and ECU 1bn in the form of risk capital (loans, equity participation or quasi-capital assistance). The most salient features supposedly favouring the ACP countries' development are Stabex, Sysmin and structural adjustment grants. Stabex, or 'System for the Stabilization of Export Earnings', aims at compensating the ACP countries for the harmful effects of the instability of export earnings for specified products. While disbursement of Stabex moneys under Lomé I and II was not subject to any qualifications, Lomé III introduced some measure of conditionality and Lomé IV tightens further this conditionality. It rules that priority must be given to the sector that has been subject to the loss of earnings. The use of the financial flow is allowed to promote diversification only if the difficulties in that sector have been overcome.[8] Given the structural nature of those difficulties, this condition is actually a prohibition to use Stabex funds for diversification purposes and thus for independent development.

Sysmin stands for 'System for Stabilizing Minerals'. It applies to those ACP countries which are heavily dependent upon the mining sector and which are experiencing difficulties in that sector. In this case, Sysmin makes financial assistance available to re-establish production at the old level, to rationalize, or to diversify. Sysmin is thus an instrument to continue the production of colonies' minerals, an extremely important economic input for the EU. Here too, diversification is an empty word for the reasons just mentioned.

Finally, structural adjustment is defined as a set of policies aiming at reducing imbalances in the economy. It emphasizes long-term development, accelerated growth of output and employment, economic viability and social tolerability. Any casual observer of aid and development policies knows that some of the money 'donated' by the centre must be used to reduce the intolerable consequences of the economic policies imposed by the centre upon the dominated bloc. Lomé grants, then, are crumbs that the EU gives back to the ACP in order to keep the old colonial relations going. The fact that grants are being reduced indicates that the EU is losing interest in these relations.

A second specific feature of the Lomé Conventions is the preferential treatment granted by the EU to exports from the ACP countries. Practically all ACP exports, most of which are primary commodities, enter the EU free of tariffs. The importance of this treatment is revealed by the fact that ACP exports to the EU constitute 40 per cent of their total exports. There have been exceptions, namely agricultural products (see further below).

The evaluation of the Lomé programmes is quite sobering.

Despite free access for industrial exports, and concessions on the protectionist Common Agricultural Policy for most of their agricultural exports, for
more than two decades, ACP exports to Europe have been disappointing.
Their share of the EU market has declined from 6.7% in 1976 to 3.4% in
1993, while developing countries which have received less preferential treatment have performed more successfully. (Davenport et al., 1996, p. 63)

In 1994 this share had further declined to 2.8 (European Centre for
Development Policy Management, 1996, p. 21). 'At the same time, ACP
countries remain heavily dependent on the EU market and have failed to
diversify their exports away from raw materials successfully' (Hewitt and
Koning, 1996, p. 63). There have been a few cases of countries managing
to increase their share of exports but it is doubtful whether this has been
due to preferential treatment. A first conclusion follows: the preferential
system is at best insufficient and at worst an obstacle to even a limited
degree of dependent development.[9]

It is partly because of these critiques (other reasons will be mentioned
shortly) that a new ACP–EU Agreement, replacing the Lomé Convention,
was reached in February 2000. During the next five-year period, Euro
13.5bn are to be channelled to the ACP countries through the European
Development Fund (EDF). Of these, Euro 1.3bn are for regional cooperation and 2.2bn (to be managed by the European Investment Bank) for the
'investment facility', that is, for the development of the private sector (Elf-
Thorffin, 2000, p. 25). These few figures are sufficient to indicate the
different 'philosophy' behind the new Agreement. Given the rampant neo-
liberalist ideology, a greater emphasis is placed on regional cooperation,
on the private sector and trade rather than on aid, which is said to have
failed as a tool of development. In reality, it is not aid which has failed but
this particular sort of 'aid'. What is conveniently forgotten is that 70 per
cent of development assistance has been tied to, that is, recycled by, the
EU (speech by President Obasanjo of Nigeria, quoted in *The ACP-EU
Courier*, p. 27). It therefore takes some imagination to consider this as aid
policy. Moreover, greater financial resources are earmarked for the growth
of the private sector, again conveniently forgetting that this is indeed aid.
By calling 'aid' to governments and public institutions (a bad thing for
orthodox economics) what is in fact export subsidies to EU private companies, and by calling 'Investment Facility' what is in fact aid to the private
sector, the ruling ideology (made their own by the ACP and EU countries)
manages to discredit international co-operation and help, even in its
extremely diluted form as the Lomé Conventions.

But there is one more element to the new Agreement. After the fall of
the Berlin Wall, the geo-political interests of the EU have shifted from the
ACP to the Central and Eastern European Countries (CEEC)[10] Let us then
consider the effects this increased interest by the EU has on the CEEC.
After the collapse of the Soviet Union, the EU has signed a number of
Europe Agreements, or association agreements, with the CEEC. The gist of
these agreements is that most industrial products originating in the associ-

ated countries can enter the EU free of tariffs and quantitative restrictions (with the exception of certain ECSC steel products and certain textile and clothing products). In agriculture, the Europe Agreements consolidate preferences granted under the Generalized System of Preferences that are meant to favour countries with low per capita income and low manufactured exports relative to the EU. As a result, the CEECs redirected their trade towards Europe to such an extent that they have become important trade partners of the EU. In 1996, the CEECs accounted for 8.5 per cent of the extra-EU imports in goods and 11.1 per cent of the extra-EU exports in goods (Eurostat, 1998, p. 1). The important question is: what have been the effects for the CEECs in terms of trade patterns and development?

Consider agriculture first. As seen in chapter 4, section 1, under colonialism, the countries of the centre are net importers of agricultural goods and raw materials from, and net exporters of industrial goods to, the dominated countries. This model corresponds to a situation in which overproduction characterizes only the industrial sectors and not the agricultural one. The situation examined here, on the other hand, is new in that it is characterized by EU structural agricultural surpluses as well, as table 6.5 shows.

Table 6.5   EU trade with CEECs in food, beverages and tobacco (ECU bn)

	1991	1992	1993	1994	1995	1996
Imports from CEECs	2.2	2.2	2.1	2.3	2.6	2.7
Exports to CEECs	1.7	2.3	3.2	3.4	4.2	4.7
Balance	−0.5	+0.1	+1.1	+1.1	+1.6	+2.0

Source: Eurostat, 1996, 1998.

In the 1991–6 period, the EU has changed from a net importer (ECU −0.5bn in 1991) to a net exporter (ECU +2bn in 1996) of agricultural and food products. This is due to a slightly increased volume of EU imports from the CEEC as against an almost tripled volume of EU exports to the CEEC. One cannot but wonder 'whether the Association Agreements contribute to improve the CEEC food and agricultural trade, or whether they merely protect the CAP' (Bojnec, 1996, p. 452). The CEEC's agricultural sector seems to have joined the industrial one as functioning as a market absorbing EU's agricultural products. On the other hand, the classical colonial pattern (greater imports than exports by the EU for raw materials) emerges for mineral fuels, lubricants and related materials (table 6.6).

Let us now consider manufactured goods. As table 6.7 shows, trade in this sector has almost quadrupled in the same period and the EU surplus in this sector has become structural (from ECU 3.0bn in 1991 to ECU 19.2bn in 1996), thus supporting the thesis of the overproduction of commodities in the developed countries (the EU).

The result of this first 'post-communist' decade is a structural balance of trade deficit with the EU. The three macroscopic examples are Poland

Table 6.6 EU trade with CEECs in crude materials, including mineral fuels, ECU bn

	1991	1992	1993	1994	1995	1996
Imports from CEECs	2.4	3.1	3.4	4.0	5.7	5.5
Exports to CEECs	1.0	1.4	1.7	1.7	3.0	3.4
Balance	− 1.4	− 1.7	− 1.7	− 2.3	− 2.7	− 2.1

Source: Eurostat, 1996, 1998.

(from ECU +604m in 1988 to ECU − 1.7bn in 1994 to − 7.6bn in 1996), Romania (from ECU +1.6bn in 1988 to ECU − 134m in 1994 to − 800m in 1996) and Hungary (from ECU − 196m in 1988 to ECU − 1.2bn in 1994 and 1996). In 1996, the Czech Republic had a 4.2bn trade balance deficit, the largest after Poland's.[11] A disaggregation of table 6.7 by sectors is revealing (see table 6.8).[12]

Table 6.7 EU trade with CEECs in manufactured products (ECU bn)

	1991	1992	1993	1994	1995	1996
Imports from CEECs	11.3	16.7	20.7	27.1	38.1	40.7
Exports to CEECs	14.3	20.1	27.3	34.1	50.1	59.9
Balance	+3.0	+3.4	+6.6	+7.0	+12.0	+19.2

Source: Eurostat, 1996, 1998.

Table 6.8 shows that the positive trade balances result from a negative (but decreasing) trade balance in miscellaneous manufactured goods which is more than counterbalanced by a greater (and increasing) positive balance in chemical products and machinery and transport equipment (high-technology goods[13]). While the CEECs increase their exports of high-technology products, their imports increase even more so that their negative trade balance in these goods has grown from 0.5bn + 4.9bn = 5.4bn in 1991 to 4.8bn + 14.7bn = 19.5bn in 1996. Moreover, the CEECs penetration

Table 6.8 EU trade with CEECs in manufactured goods by sectors (ECU bn)

| | Chemicals | | Miscellaneous manu. articles | | Machinery and transport equipment | |
	1991	1996	1991	1996	1991	1996
Imports	1.5	3.3	7.4	24.0	2.3	13.4
Exports	2.0	8.1	5.1	23.7	7.2	28.1
Balance	+0.5	+4.8	− 2.3	− 0.3	+4.9	+14.7

Source: Eurostat, 1996, 1998.

of the EU market is due in a growing measure to outward processing trade (OPT). This is the processing by companies in Central and Eastern Europe of intermediate inputs for EU enterprise.[14] Export figures from the CEECs to the EU are thus an inflated measure of these countries' export competitiveness.

Besides trading in goods, the EU and the CEECs trade in services as well. Here too the CEECs have taken an important place in EU exports and imports. In 1995, 4.5 per cent of the exports and 4.9 of the imports of the total extra-EU trade in services were accounted for by the CEECs (Eurostat, 1998, p. 6). As for the major players, table 6.9 shows only the two major importers and exporters. The other EU states follow far behind and are not shown. Data refer to 1995. For sake of comparison, figures within parenthesis refer to 1993.

Table 6.9 EU trade balance in services with CEECs (ECU bn)

	Exports		Imports		Balance	
Germany	(1.3)	1.9	(2.5)	3.3	(−1.2)	−1.4
Austria	(2.5)	2.9	(1.0)	1.4	(+1.5)	+1.5
EU 15	(7.2)	8.1	(6.7)	8.5	(+0.5)	−0.4

Source: Eurostat, 1998.

In the 1993–5 period, the overall trade balance has gone from a small surplus to a small deficit. The larger exporter of services was Austria, which had a positive balance of 1.5bn. The largest importer was Germany with a negative balance of 1.4bn. If exports and imports of services are broken down by items, the three major voices are transportation, travel and other business services.

Finally, the EU invests in the CEECs. The figures are telling. In 1955, the outflow of foreign direct investments (FDIs) from the EU into the CEECs amounted to ECU 5.6bn, representing 12.6 per cent of the extra-EU outflows. The CEECs have become an important outlet for CEEC foreign investments. On the other hand, the inflow of FDIs from the CEECs into the EU was insignificant, ECU 0.1bn, or 0.04 per cent of the total extra-EU inflows. The imperialist pattern could not be clearer. The countries most interested in investing in the CEEC were Germany (ECU 2.1bn), France (1.0bn), the Netherlands (0.9bn) and Austria (0.5bn). These five countries made up about 82 per cent of the EU outflows to the CEEC (Eurostat, 1998, p. 8).

The dominant role played by Germany emerges in this context as well. First, the primary EU trading partner of the CEECs is Germany. Its 2.1bn FDI in the CEECs represent more than 38 per cent of the total EU FDI in those countries. This is a major reason for Germany's interest in the expansion of the EU to the east. Second, with Agenda 2000 the Commission proposed in 1997 to start negotiations with six of the eleven countries asking to join the EU. The fact that three of these six, the Czech Republic,

Hungary and Poland, border directly with Germany and that Slovenia borders with Germany's extension, Austria, indicates the weight Germany has also on the new accessions, given its interest in not being the EU border nation to the East.[15]

Up to now, the current account deficits have been at least partly compensated by capital inflows. The problem with this is that foreign capital may stop coming in for a host of different reasons. This would create considerable disruptions and hardships, as the examples of the Mexican crisis (see Carchedi, 1997) and of the Asian crisis have shown. Moreover, part of this inflow is due to privatization receipts and thus not recurrent. The CEECs are subordinated to the EU not only in terms of trade flows (large trade deficits expose the CEECs to the dictate of the EU and of international organizations like the IMF and the World Bank) but also in terms of capital flows.

In short, the data above indicate the dominant weight of German interests and leadership in the process of extension to the East. This process is based on a colonial relationship with the CEECs as far as raw materials are concerned (excluding agricultural and food products) and on a dependent development relationship with regards to agricultural goods, manufactured goods and foreign direct investments. As far as trade in goods is concerned, the trade between the EU and the CEECs is centred upon manufactured goods and is characterized by a net and growing negative balance of trade for the CEECs. These countries operate in technologically less advanced sectors and with technologically less advanced production methods. This is a sure recipe for unequal exchange and thus for the reproduction of the economic dependence. This seems to exclude a path towards joining the core of the EU countries. The question, then, is which of the CEECs will be able to reinforce the tendency towards dependent development and which will undergo a process of de-industrialization (or will never be able to start such a process), thus falling into (or remaining in) some sort of colonial domination.

Contrary to the thesis submitted here, that the economic malaise of the CEECs is due to their integration in the world imperialist system, official economics holds that this malaise is caused by their insufficient integration in the world capitalist system. Two arguments emerge consistently. First, the CEECs have gained in productivity and modernization, as can be seen from their increased penetration of EU markets. However, the CEECs' increased exports to the EU are not due to this cause. Rather, they are the result of a redirection of CEEC exports towards the EU instead of towards the former CMEA countries. This redirection of trade has been made possible both by the lowering of Cold War trade barriers in 1990–1, as part of the Association Agreements between the EC and the CEECs, and by the disappearance of the CMEA. Before the collapse of the Soviet Union, the lack of penetration of the CEECs' manufactured goods into the EC was due not to low quality, poor marketing, and so on, that is, to the legacy of 'communism', but to the EC's politically motivated protectionism (Gowan, 1995, p. 21).

The second argument focuses on 'shock therapy'. The supporters of the integration of the CEECs into the EU submit that foreign trade is of great importance for the CEECs both because of the export possibilities to the huge EU market and because of the accession to cheap EU inputs. The smaller the country, the greater the advantage it derives from entering the EU market and thus the greater the impact of foreign trade on its economy. A sound economic policy, it is held, requires a strong currency. Through it, technologically advanced means of production can be cheaply imported, given that new technologies are of essential importance to exit the CEECs' state of backwardness. On the other hand, a strong currency has negative effects on exports. These effects must be countered by low prices, and this requires low inflation which, within the neo-liberalist creed, is synonymous with a policy of wage containment. In short, the essence of the thesis is that the CEECs will have to compete not through competitive devaluation but through highly efficient, 'high value added', production and low inflation, that is, low wages. This is the restructuring the EU as well as other international organizations (like the IMF and the World Bank) require.[16] This implies that a large sector of the economy, that which is not internationally competitive, will have to disappear. Inevitably, closures and high unemployment rates will follow. But this, it is held, is only the first phase, the 'shock therapy'. As a new internationally competitive economic structure emerges in the CEECs, employment will grow and with it economic welfare. This is the alpha and the omega of the shock therapy that should usher the CEECs into the golden age of capitalism.

More specifically, the 'shock therapy' forecasts (1) the initial disappearance of the less efficient (state monopolistic) enterprises (2) their replacement, due to technology transfers, by (privately owned, free competition) technologically advanced ones, and (3) a recovery fuelled by the export of these technologically advanced ('high value added') products which translates into levels of living higher than those in the former centrally planned economies.[17]

(1) As to the first point, the CEECs' economies have indeed been devastated and scores of enterprises (especially in the consumer goods sector) have ceased to exist. In Hungary, for example, the two major consumer electronics producers declared bankruptcy in 1991 and 1992 and the major iron and steel producers were on the verge of disappearing (Gowan, 1995, pp. 24 and 31). However, closures and bankruptcies have been due not so much to insufficient competitiveness once the CEECs had been opened to international competition. On the contrary, evidence shows that the CEECs were reasonably competitive. Following the lowering of EU trade barriers for CEEC imports in 1990–1, 'taking 1989 as 100, Poland's exports to the EC rose to 208.2 in current US dollars in 1992, Czechoslovakia's jumped to 250, and Hungary's to 178.6.' (Gowan, 1995, p. 21). Rather, the causes of the enterprises' high mortality rate are different.

First, the Western countries insisted on the breaking down of the CMEA and thus on the disappearance of regional trade and production linkages. This could not but cause great disruption. Second, the replacement of these production and trade linkages within the CMEA by linkages with the EU has floundered against the measures on trade liberalization incorporated in the Europe Agreements with the CEECs and in other agreements with former Soviet republics. These are strongly asymmetrical in favour of the EU. For example, the Europe Agreements focus only on tariff barriers; non-tariff barriers as well as tariff barriers on EU textiles and agricultural products are excluded. Third, the international financial institutions insisted, under threat of withholding loans, on reducing government deficits and on public spending cuts. This precipitated a major credit crunch just at the time of the most severe slump since the Second World War. The consequences could not but be disastrous. The EU countries, of course, would never apply the same measures to their economies even in times of much less severe economic distress.

(2) As for the second point, the emergence of a new industrial structure able to compete with that in the West, the above has shown an opposite trend. To begin with, the measures taken within the frame of the shock therapy were aimed at reducing the CEECs' capacity to compete with the EU rather than encouraging their retooling and modernization. The following makes this point clear:

- Spending for educational infrastructures and for R&D is continuously reduced following the requirements of the international financial institutions either for higher educational and medical treatment fees or for budget cuts (which inevitably result in the erosion of such expenditures).
- Concerning FDIs, the shock therapy theorists deem them essential for the technological upgrading of the CEECs and for the export-led recovery that these countries are supposed to achieve. This presupposes that FDIs set up new and technologically upgraded production facilities rather than buying existing plants in order to catch existing markets. But reality is just the opposite.
- As for privatization, which is supposed to bring economic rationality into an irrational, state-led, system, it is again useful to separate myths from reality. To begin with, even though the flow of FDI to the CEECs for the purchase of privatized companies has been relatively small, the number of enterprises that have been bought is large (55,000 by the end of 1993). This is due to the fact that privatized firms have been sold to foreign capital for next to nothing. This is a consequence of the economic slump within which these assets have been sold as well as of the ban on restructuring them before privatization. The ideology of privatization holds that restructuring should be carried out by private capitalists rather than by the state since it is the former who are the carriers of the system's economic rationality. In reality, by selling potentially profitable enterprises before restructuring, private capitals can buy them for prices far below their real value. In addition, big foreign capital has consistently required local governments to confer on them the monopolistic power of local markets, contrary to what shock therapy theorists would like the real world to be. Finally, the local holders of capital who have been able

to purchase privatized enterprises are mainly former corrupt government officials, currency speculators and plain crooks, hardly an example of carriers of capitalism's economic rationality (at least in neo-liberalist thinking).

(3) Finally, as for the claim that capitalism brings higher standards of living, even a glance at the daily press reveals how savage has been the attack to the welfare of the masses in the CEECs and the former Soviet Union. Higher mortality rates, health crises, poverty and malnutrition have all dramatically increased. The IMF has estimated that even in Poland, the West's showcase, 'living standards will not return to their 1989 levels until the year 2010 at the earliest' (Gowan, 1995, p. 55). Maybe. But the experience of other dominated countries indicates that this might just another wrong prediction based on the wrong theory. And even if the export-led revival of (some of) the CEECs does indeed materialize, it will be another example of dependent (and thus limited) development.

Since the level of technological development of those CEECs which will achieve a measure of growth and industrialization will be consistently less advanced than that in the leading EU countries, a constant loss of value will characterize the sale of the former countries' commodities on the international markets. Through this structural loss of value, their capital accumulation will be thwarted, to the advantage of capital accumulation in the developed centre. Therefore, both their exports to, and their imports from, the leading EU countries will be conditional upon the level of saturation of the market of, and thus upon the economic cycle in, those countries. They will have to earn enough hard currency to be able to import those EU commodities which cannot be absorbed by the EU markets. Their relative backwardness will demand low wages. The loss of purchasing power and thus of consumption capacity of the CEECs' masses, far from being a passing phenomenon, will become a structural feature of their having embraced the capitalist system on terms dictated by the 'developed' countries. The unemployment resulting from the application of the model imposed by the international financial institutions on behalf of the leading powers will cause ebbs and flows of their labourers from and to the leading EU countries according to the needs of capital accumulation in those countries. The export-led model that the EU tries to impose upon the CEECs is just a rationalization of their having to fulfil this new role in the international economy.

Reality is thus very far from the idyllic picture in which, owing to comparative advantages, all nations are supposed to gain from dismantling tariffs and non-tariff barriers to trade. Obstacles to trade are in principle removed only if this serves the interests of multinational corporations. However, the process through which, and the measure in which, the multinationals are advantaged is far from being unilinear and straight-forward. The multinationals must represent their interests through their national governments as well as through the various international insti-tutions, like the EU. National governments must represent not only the great corporations' interests but also those of smaller capitals and of other conflicting classes and groups. International institutions have the same function within a broader setting, that is, they balance the interests of the different national sectors, classes and fractions of classes. It is the power relations – themselves an indirect expression of the different nations' economic power – between these actors which decide which obstacles to trade are removed and which are not (or newly introduced). But, aside from this complex game, in which the nature of the different interests is often altered beyond recognition by official ideology, one thing stands out clearly. Nowadays, one third of international trade is accounted for by trade between different plants within the same 100 international enterprises and another third between different international enterprises. Or, two-thirds of international trade is carried out by 100 multinationals. Within the constraints imposed by the representation of conflicting interests, freedom of trade is the freedom 100 multinationals have to play according to their own rules (Strange, 1998, p. 13).

6.3 The European Union and the Common Defence Policy

Before the introduction of the EMU, the EU had not posed a real threat to US imperialism. While some European nations (capitals) had managed to become powerful competitors of US capital in some sectors, the US economy as a whole had been vitally challenged in its world dominant role neither by any single EU country nor by the EU as a whole. The first such challenge has occurred with the introduction of the EMU and thus of the Euro. There are basically two reasons for this. First, it has been shown that the technological leaders and thus the dominant imperialist countries appropriate part of the surplus value produced by the technological laggards. This has been called unequal exchange. The mechanism is through the objectively determined appreciation of the currencies of the former and depreciation of the currencies of the latter. This increments the capital accumulation of the technological leaders at the cost of the technological laggards.

The second advantage of being the dominant imperialist country is that its currency becomes the world currency. That country appropriates international value simply by printing (within limits) non-convertible paper money. This is the role of the US dollar. But this privilege could be threatened by the Euro. Obviously, the US is quite keen to check this from happening for as long as possible. The point is that, to become a veritable rival of the US dollar, it is not sufficient for the Euro to be the currency of a powerful economic bloc (the EU). Something more is needed. First, this currency has to be managed as if it were a world currency (see chapter 4, section 3). And, second, it has to be backed by sufficient military strength. In fact, similarly to the dollar, the Euro will be accepted as a world currency only if backed by the military power needed to conquer and subject to EU imperialism those countries with an economic or geo-political import for the Union or for its individual member states (e.g. to 'protect' EU investments or to impose an economic policy functional for the colonial robbery or dependent development of those countries). While the EU as a whole has the economic strength to challenge the US and attempts to manage the Euro as if it were a world currency, it lacks a military power comparable to its economic might. The US disposes of this power; the EU does not. It is precisely on the military level that the US tries to contain the emergence of the Euro as a challenger of the dollar. The question then is: why doesn't the EU develop its own military arm? The answer lies in the deeply contradictory process of emergence of a European military might. Let us review some of its salient features.[18]

The point that, in order to impose its trade and (under)development policies, the EU needs a military arm has been expressed in more official terminology time and again. For example, in a five-point statement following an agreement on the Common Defence Policy reached on 4 December 1998 in Saint-Malo, Britain and France asserted that

> the European Union needs to be in a position to play its full role on the international stage.... To this end, the Union must have the capacity for autonomous action, backed up by credible military forces, the means to decide to use them and a readiness to do so, in order to respond to international crises. (*The New York Times*, 5 December 1998)

The difficulty for the EU is that, while one nation is predominant in economic power (Germany), the same cannot be said of military power. On a military plane, not only is there no clear-cut predominance of one nation over the others; also, each member state still has its own military means to advance its own interests. This is an important factor accounting for European weakness in the military sphere.

This has been the case from the very beginning, that is, from the first defence treaty after the Second World War. In 1948, the Brussels Treaty was signed establishing the *Western European Union* (WEU). Its members were Belgium, France, Luxembourg, the Netherlands and the United Kingdom. Its purpose was collaboration in economic, social and cultural matters and collective self-defence: in the event of a member state becoming the object of a military attack, the other members would have to 'afford the Party so attacked all the military and other aid and assistance in their power' (article 5). Also, in 'recognizing the undesirability of duplicating the military staffs of NATO', the WEU pledged to rely 'on the appropriate military authorities of NATO for information and advice on military matters' (article 4). The WEU, thus, was born as the European pillar of NATO and as the extension of that military structure aimed at the defence of Western imperialism.

This was not sufficient for France, which has traditionally been the supporter of a European defence project (relatively) independent from US hegemony. In the 1950–4 period, attention in France focused on a new project, the *European Defence Community* (EDC), which was advocated by the

Pleven Plan (whose author was Jean Monnet). The proposal provided for a European army under NATO run by a European Minister of Defence and the Council of Ministers, with a joint commander, common budget and common arms procurement. All participant member states, except Germany, could keep their national forces apart from the European army for colonial and other purposes. It was a proposal to rearm Germany (a need dictated by the Cold War) without re-establishing a German army.

This scheme was contrasted by De Gaulle's vision of 'an integrated European army retaining a multiplicity of national commands' (Howorth, 1997, p. 13). In spite of these differences, both plans shared a common feature: the belief that 'Europe could not be Europe without its own army' (Howorth, 1997, p. 12). In the event, the attempt to set up the EDC foundered on 31 August 1954 after the rejection by the French Parliament. Consequently, Germany joined the WEU in 1954 and NATO in 1955.[19] As for De Gaulle's superpower ambitions, they were aborted given that they were not shared by other NATO European states.

Owing to the failure to set up the EDC, the WEU got a new impetus on the basis of a modified treaty that was signed in Brussels in 1954. In spite of minor modifications, the 1954 Treaty called again for collaboration in self-defence (article 5) which had to rely on NATO for information and advice (article 4). Like its predecessor, then, the 1954 Treaty was only a pale version of the EDC and sanctioned the *de facto* NATO, and thus US, hegemony. The WEU led a dormant existence until the early 1980s, when interest in it reawoke partly as a response to the 'Euromissiles' crisis sparked by NATO's December 1979 decision to deploy intermediate nuclear force (INF) weapons in Europe. However, as long as the 'Soviet threat' was present, the short-term fear of weakening NATO by strengthening the WEU weighed more than the long-term advantage of having a more independent European military arm. With the fall of the Berlin Wall, then, one should have expected a smaller role for NATO and a greater role for the WEU. Yet, as we shall see shortly, this has not been the case.

The declaration of the WEU member states at the Maastricht Summit of 1991 reads: 'The objective is to build up WEU in stages as the defence component of the European Union. To this end, WEU is prepared, at the request of the European Union, to elaborate and implement decisions and actions of the Union which have defence implications.' The Petersberg declaration of 1992 extends the scope of the operations to 'humanitarian and rescue tasks; peacemaking tasks; tasks of combat forces in crisis management, including peacemaking'. This indicates a considerably wider scope for the WEU than simply defence. Intervention (that is, aggression) anywhere in the world can thus be legitimated as 'humanitarian and rescue tasks; peacemaking tasks; tasks of combat forces in crisis management, including peacemaking,' whenever such intervention is perceived as being in the interest of the EU. NATO's 1999 'humanitarian' aggression against Yugoslavia shows that this is a very real and even likely possibility.

However, as the Maastricht declaration adds, 'The objective is to develop WEU as a means to strengthen the European pillar of the Atlantic Alliance. . . . WEU will act in conformity with the positions adopted in the Atlantic Alliance.' The WEU is developing its act, but within the limits of a persisting *de facto* subordination to NATO and thus to the US.[20] It is within these limits that the US favours a strengthening of the WEU. In the immediate future, the EU remains a second-rate imperialist power. But this need not remain the case in the longer term. Power relations might become more favourable to the EU. This new state of affairs might be a harbinger of a new world conflict.

Two factors help to explain this persisting weakness. The first is the division within the WEU itself, that is, among its member states, concerning the role of the WEU and its relation to NATO. The key aspect of this divergence of opinion is British reticence to develop an autonomous European military power. The UK has always been for military cooperation but against military integration.[21] There are historical and ideological reasons for this, such as Britain's fear of losing its national sovereignty or Britain's 'choice, made at the end of the Second World War, to try to retain a status as close as possible to that of a great power by finding a genuine great power to influence' (Chuter, 1997, p. 114). However, these and other similar factors should be explained in terms of conscious economic policies and interests. Thus, attachment to the notion of national sovereignty, and thus fear of losing it, is a residue of an historical phase when Britain was a great imperial power. This is an example of how ideologies can survive the economic situation that determined them. The reason this ideology has survived the imperial age is that it defended, and still defends, the interests of the weakest sectors of British capital. These are those which stand to lose the most from ever-stricter forms of European economic integration and which use the argument of a loss of national sovereignty as an ideological weapon against joining (before 1973) or deepening (after that date) the scope of European economic integration.

As for Britain's attempt to retain the status of a great power, we have seen in chapter 1 that Britain had very specific economic interests first in not joining the EEC and than in joining it in 1973. While, originally, it thought it could gain the most from a free trade area, shortly after the formation of EFTA it realized that both trade flows and capital concentration and centralization demanded accession to the EEC. However, Britain wanted and still wants to restrict the scope of economic integration because full integration would be in the interests neither of the less advanced sectors of its industrial capital nor of its financial capital. Concerning British financial capital, consider the EMU. Within the EMU the pound would be absorbed into the Euro, that is, into a currency managed according the criteria reflecting, even though in a mediated way, the interests of German oligopoly capital (see chapter 4, section 3) and London would have to play a subordinate role both economically in general and more specifically in financial markets. Now, an independent European military force would be a strong factor pushing towards some sort of a (federalist) European state and thus towards a full economic integration of the UK within the EU. This explains Britain's opposition to making of the

WEU an incisive military force.[22] However, as we shall see in a moment, the momentum given by the EMU to the process of integration might render this policy obsolete.

The negotiations preceding the 1997 Amsterdam Treaty (the Intergovernmental Conference), which tackled the question of the WEU, can be seen in this light. The UK was in favour of keeping the WEU under, and as an autonomous arm of, NATO, while Germany and France wanted to bring the WEU under the second pillar of the EU, the Common Foreign and Security Policy (CFSP). This difference reveals the wish of the UK to resist the movement towards a (federalist) European state, something which is more favoured by Germany and France. Moreover, the European Parliament was against retaining the three pillars and would have liked to bring the CFSP (as well as Justice and Home Affairs) under the EC. This, it was held, would have stimulated the formation of a common foreign policy, which at present is practically non-existent (as the recent failure to intervene in ex-Yugoslavia shows). At the same time, this would have increased the democratic content of EU foreign policy. The outcome of the Amsterdam Treaty has been that the WEU has not been integrated into the EU, contrary to the wishes of France and Germany, due to Britain's opposition. It is, however, doubtful whether this policy will be sustainable in the long run (see below).

The second reason for the weakness of the WEU is superior US military might. Rather than imposing its will directly, the US manifests its military superiority through NATO. NATO was founded in 1949, officially to contain Soviet expansionism but actually to contribute, through its military power, to the destruction of the Soviet Union so as to gain unchallenged global sway. In 1991, with the fall and dissolution of the Soviet Union, NATO (and the US behind it) saw its military weight increase even more. There are at least three recent instances in which the US has revealed its military superiority over the WEU through NATO.

The first is related to the dismemberment of former Yugoslavia. While both the US and the European Community (especially Germany) have gained from the break-up and *de facto* re-colonization of Yugoslavia, the US did not particularly favour unilateral secession but Germany did, as a way 'to pursue economic dominance in the whole Mitteleuropa' (Chossudovsky, 1997, p. 252). However, the US has retained its absolute military superiority *vis-à-vis* the WEU through the implementation of the Dayton Accord. In fact, it was agreed that the WEU countries could carry out military operations decided within the framework of the WEU and the Organization for Security and Cooperation in Europe (OSCE)[23] by using NATO infrastructures (possibly without the participation of the US). As official statements put it, the basis has been laid for the development of the European Security and Defence Identity (ESDI).[24] But it is clear that Europe's military independence remains fictitious, given that it is NATO which provides the operational structure and which maintains its watching brief over those developments. In terms of power relations, the US can control, and has a right of veto over, any military EU initiative.

The second way in which the US shows its military might over the WEU derives from the recent agreement between NATO and Russia to start cooperation in the political and military spheres. In May 1997, the 'Founding Act on Mutual Relations, Cooperation and Security between NATO and the Russian Federation' was signed. This is not a binding treaty (something Russia had hoped for) but simply a commitment between heads of state and of government. Russia and NATO will sit on a permanent joint committee but NATO will take decisions on its own in case of emergency and crisis situations. Clearly, Russia has accepted a position of subordination relative to NATO. This reduces the influence of the OSCE, which both Russia and many European states would like to see strengthened. The reason, obviously, is that the US has greater influence within NATO than within the OSCE.[25]

Finally, the third way that US military superiority, and WEU dependence, is revealed is NATO's policy towards the CEECs, on the one hand, and the Arab countries, on the other. Concerning NATO's expansion to the East, Poland, Czechoslovakia and Hungary have already become NATO members; other CEECs will follow suit. The specific aim of this policy is to extend the US sphere of influence from the military to the economic, thus countering the EU's (and especially Germany's) economic ties with these countries. The means through which this is being accomplished is military procurements. In fact, NATO membership implies that the new member states renew their armaments to make them compatible with those used by NATO. For example, the new member countries have already begun acquiring F-16 fighter-bombers to replace the Soviet Mig. A new, colossal, business is thus being opened for the American military-industrial complex, which already controls half of the world trade in armaments. Moreover, once these weapons have been acquired, more will have to be spent on maintenance, spare parts and further replacements. Given that these countries lack the funds for such huge expenditures, they will have to resort to US credit, thus becoming economically dependent upon the US (Dinucci, 1998, p. 26). The same will hold for Russia, as soon as its huge, 'obsolete' weaponry has to be replaced.

As for the Arab countries, US policies are aimed at oil reserves in the Gulf. Even though the US is the second oil producer after Saudi Arabia, it has reserves which, at the present pace of consumption, are estimated to last only ten years. Iraq's reserves too will last ten years while Saudi Arabia's can last eighty years. But this is not the only factor. About 57 per cent of Middle East oil exports goes to the Asian countries (of which 25 per cent to Japan only) and 25 per cent to Western Europe. Control of these reserves, thus, is of fundamental strategic importance for the US to retain economic and military leadership over all countries, including its allies (Dinucci, 1998, p. 27). This explains NATO's policies in the Middle East, including its having replaced 'communism' with 'Arab fundamentalism' as the new menace to world peace and democracy.

As a result of these developments, NATO's political connotation has undergone a change. While, up to the end of the 1980s, its basic function was perceived as being one of 'defence' against the 'communist threat', with the fall of the Soviet Union NATO's new image is that of providing global 'security' for the 'international community', including protection against 'Arab fundamentalism'. This includes the prevention of wars between states, the reinstitution of democratic governments that have been overthrown, and the facilitation of the downfall of 'undemocratic governments'. Of course, NATO itself decides which wars should be prevented, which governments are democratic, and which wars should be waged (if need be, disregarding international law). NATO is now being projected in the world's collective consciousness as the guarantor of world democracy, peace, order and human rights. It has emerged stronger than ever since the 1990s. This, together with the WEU's inner weakness, are the two elements hindering any projects, like the WEU and the OSCE, aiming at building a centre of military power alternative to that dominated by the US.

The EU's military weakness is a powerful brake on its potential to become a true superpower whose military might match and further propel its economic strength. However, an important factor making for this weakness, that is, the reluctance of the UK to proceed towards greater political and military integration, is being eroded by economic forces and might come to an end sooner than one might expect. For example, the awareness is growing that no single European stock market (including London) is sufficiently large to compete with other, much greater, stock exchanges. The following makes this point crystal clear:

> The stock markets of the 11 euro-countries and Britain were valued at some $5.5 trillion at the end of last year [that is, 1997], half as big as the entire US market and more than twice the size of the Japanese market. . . . But the potentials for growth are huge. The European economy is slightly larger than America's . . . and EU governments are likely to privatize thousands of companies worth as much as $300 billion in coming years. (Buerkle, 1998)

Consolidation is thus mandatory. It is not by chance that London has sought an alliance with Frankfurt (the financial heart of German capital and, not by chance, the site of the European Central Bank) as a first step towards developing a single system for trading the stocks of the largest 300 European companies. Eventually, the other European exchanges will have to join them in what will become a single European equity trading system. Its advantages will be greater liquidity, possibly lower interest rates, lower transaction costs and the elimination of exchange-rate risks for investors. The reward will be in terms of commissions and charges. With the introduction of the Euro, investments will be facilitated, as fund managers will be able to compare corporate earnings statements of enterprises in different countries in terms of just one currency. It is worth noting that the chief executive of the London Stock Exchange declared that London 'would even switch to quoting stocks in Euros if a majority of its members supported such a change' (Buerkle, 1998). This would be an important factor pushing for the introduction of the Euro in the UK. For the same reasons, the UK will sooner or later have to join the EMU. At this point its attitude towards a common military force might change. This, inasmuch as it would result in an integrated and relatively autonomous military capability, would make of the EU a much more influential 'international actor'.

Another important factor making for the strengthening of the WEU is, paradoxically, the strength of NATO and of the US. The limited military capability of the EU has become even more obvious after NATO's 'humanitarian' intervention in Yugoslavia, in 1999. NATO itself has pushed for a greater role of Europe in 'crisis management'. The WEU would in any case remain subordinated to NATO and an extended role for the WEU would shift some of the burden of military operations from the US (NATO) to the EU (WEU). This explains the wish expressed by the Summit of Cologne in June 1999 to integrate the WEU into the EU (*Europa van Morgen*, 1999; European Council, Cologne, 3–4 June 1999, Conclusions of the Presidency, Appendix III, point 5). This only a short time after the Amsterdam Treaty had not managed to achieve this integration.

The strengthening of the WEU is taking place right when its absurd consequences are becoming increasingly obvious. Let us take just one example. In 1994, Italy's military expenditure (ME) was 2 per cent of GNP. This is more than US$20bn. This would seem to be a relatively modest sum. But, first, an alternative use of it would achieve miracles. For instance, it will be mentioned in chapter 8 that universal access to primary education at the world level would cost between US$7bn and US$8bn, a little more than one third of what Italy alone spends on weapons. Second, ME is 2 per cent of GNP but 4 per cent of central government expenditure (CGE). If the Italian Government would spend annually 4 per cent of its CGE for means of consumption or education and health services or housing to be distributed to the needy, real wages (in terms of use values) would jump up. Third, arms sales gobble up substantial resources of the acquiring countries. One of the features of the post-1989 world is that ME in the US, Europe and Russia has decreased while it has increased by 15–20 per cent per year in the past few years in many dominated (developing) countries. Arms sales are a dead weight for those countries' development. It might be objected that it is they who ask for arms. But, first, it is their corrupt elites which require those weapons (often for purposes of internal repression) and, second, this does not exempt the imperialist centre from the responsibility for selling instruments of death. Moreover, most conflicts in the developing world are either a consequence of the centre's colonial past or are directly, if covertly, caused by it.[26] Finally, while the use of most other goods increases human well-being directly or indirectly, the use of weapons achieves the contrary. One machine gun costs little, but it can cause a disproportionally greater economic destruction and immense human suffering not quantifiable in money.[27]

What has been said about one country is magnified at the EU and world level (see table 6.10).

The hypocrisy of the EU is revealed by the fact that 'Last year [i.e. 1997]

Table 6.10   ME, ME/GNP and ME/CGE, 1995

	ME US$ bn	ME/GNP	ME/CGE
World	864	2.8	9.9
Western Europe	300	2.9	7.3

Source: US Arms Control and Disarmament Agency, 1996, table 1.

the European Parliament proposed to stop development aid to ACP-countries spending more than 1 per cent of Gross National Product on defence' (Broek, 1998, p. 3) while the EU itself spends 2.9 per cent.

Not only the alternative use of these funds but also the reduction of the damage caused by the use of arms would achieve miracles for the world's collective labourer and for humanity at large. However, it is pure fantasy to imagine that such a conversion of military industry could be achieved under capitalism. Capitalism generates contradictions and wars and needs the military industry and thus the military.[28] Under capitalism, conversion is acceptable but only if profitable, irrespective of human well-being. The recent experience of the ex-Soviet Union is exemplary. Its military industry cannot be converted due to Russia's deep economic crises, that is, to the lack of the market for the civilian goods which could be produced instead of weapons (Menshikov, 1998).

Unfortunately, to the strength of the expansionary drive of both US and EU imperialism there corresponds the weakness of the European working class, which has yet to recover from the series of débâcles starting from the defeat of the mass social movements of the 1970s. The enthusiastic participation of European social democracies in the 1999 war against Yugoslavia is only history's last brushstroke to an abysmal picture. It is the interrelations of these factors which allow us to speak of a new phase in capitalist development, more specifically of inter-imperialist transatlantic relations, at the start of the new millennium. This new phase is fraught with grave dangers and could be the harbinger of a new world conflict.

The Common Agricultural Policy

7.1 Main Landmarks: Green Rates and Appropriation of Value[1]

Nowadays, agriculture plays a relative small direct role in the income-generating activities of the EU. It accounts for less than 3 per cent of its GDP and for 6 per cent of its employed civilian working population (over 8 million persons). These averages hide wide national and regional differences. Agriculture's share of employment is 22 per cent in Greece and 18 per cent in Portugal but around 3 per cent or less in Belgium, Germany, Luxembourg and the UK (European Commission, 1994a, p. 17). Yet agriculture remains an important sector of the EU economy for at least two reasons: first, it represents a significant share of employment in rural areas; and second, while it contributes only a modest share of EU exports, it is the second largest agricultural exporter after the US.

Shortly after its inception, the Common Market instituted a Common Agricultural Policy (CAP). Agricultural spending under the CAP is very largely financed from the EU budget. Agriculturally derived revenues are provided by levies on imported agricultural products and also from producer levies. This kind of revenue grew from below ECU 1 billion per year in the early 1970s to over 4 billion in 1991 and 1992, but following the 1992 CAP reform (see below) has now fallen to 1.5 billion. Given that CAP expenditures are much greater than these revenues, the EU budget must provide for additional finances. The combined resources flow into the European Agricultural Guidance and Guarantee Fund (EAGGF). The Guidance section finances structural reforms and the Guarantee section finances price support. This is shown in table 7.1.

Table 7.1 EAGGF (ECU bn)

	1973 (EC9)	1980 (EC9)	1985 (EC10)	1986 (EC12)	1992 (EC12)	1996 (EC15)
Guarantee	3.6	11.3	19.7	22.1	31.2	40.8
Guidance	0.01	0.3	0.7	0.8	2.8	3.7
Total EU budget	4.7	16.5	28.8	35.8	60.3	85.1
Guarantee as % of EU budget	77	68	68	62	52	48

Source: Tracy, 1996, p. 13, table 1.3.

Two points emerge from table 7.1. First, income transfers for price support dwarf those for structural reforms. Second, the Guarantee section increases over the years in absolute terms but decreases as a proportion of the total Community's budget, from 77 per cent in 1973 to 48 per cent to 1996.

To understand these figures, we must go back to 1958 and to the reasons for the inclusion of agriculture in the EEC's common policy. It is usually pointed out that the 1958 Rome Treaty was a delicate balance between the contrasting national interests of the contracting parties. More specifically, the following points are usually emphasized. First, while Germany would have profited from free trade in industrial goods because of its higher industrial efficiency, France would have profited from free trade in agricultural goods due to its more productive agricultural sector. To level their respective competitive positions, free trade in both categories of goods had to be introduced. Second, in 1958 agriculture was a low-productivity, low-income occupation which employed 20 per cent of the working population. Governments had to aim at maintaining a certain level of stable prices while at the same stimulating production and productivity growth. Finally, memories of the famines of the Second World War played a great role in creating the perception that Europe had to become self-sufficient in food production.

Here too a different reading, based on class analysis, helps to reveal the nature of the project. First, the introduction of agriculture in the common economic policy had nothing to do with reasons of equity but was a necessary step for the achievement of an integrated economy.[2] Second, the wish to provide a minimum income for European farmers was certainly not motivated by reasons of social justice. Rather, the farming community formed a formidable lobby upon which rested the power of the European governing parties, especially the Christian Democratic and other conservative parties. A certain measure of guaranteed income (price support) for farmers was a very sensitive and important political issue in a political and ideological climate dominated by the Cold War. Stable (rather than falling) agricultural prices would have helped release agricultural labour power in an orderly fashion. Finally, the real aim of self-sufficiency in food production was not so much the prevention of famines (an objective valid in exceptional circumstances, like a war). Rather, an adequate supply of food, while in itself not a feature of imperialism, was and is an absolute precondition for an imperialist policy.

These interests shaped the aims of the CAP as set out in article 39 of the EC Treaty. They are: (a) to increase agricultural productivity; (b) to ensure a fair standard of living for farmers; (c) to stabilize markets; (d) to provide certainty of supplies; (e) to ensure supplies to consumers at reasonable prices. But the Rome Treaty gave little indication as to how to achieve these aims. It was only in 1962, when the market organization for cereals was introduced, that the CAP got started. Several periods can be distinguished.

7.1.1 The Original System: 1962–68

Given that the original six member states had their own currencies and exchange rates, uniformity of prices within the EEC was subject to two requirements. First, prices had to be expressed in a common denominator. This was the *Agricultural Unit of Account* (AUA), which was introduced in 1962 (*Official Journal of the European Communities*, 1962).[3] The AUA was not a currency but an accounting device. It was defined in terms of gold and its value was fixed at 0.88867088 grams of fine gold, which was also the value of the US dollar. Given the convertibility of the dollar into gold, this meant that the value of one AUA was set at US$1.

But AUA agricultural prices had to be converted into national currencies prices. The second requirement was that the exchange rates used for this conversion had to be stable, or competitive (dis)advantages would result from conversion rates fluctuations. These were called green exchange rates, or *green rates* for short.[4] Given the stability of the exchange rates relative to the dollar, it was decided for convenience to convert AUA agricultural prices into national currencies prices through the market rates, that is, to equate market and green rates. Strictly speaking, it was possible for market and green rates to diverge, but these differences were minimal. 'Under the then existing rules of the International Monetary Fund, countries with declared parities were obliged to limit the margins of fluctuation between their currencies and the $US to + or − 1 per cent of the par value. The exchange rates ... were to all intents and purpose fixed' and kept within the fluctuation limits by Central Banks' interventions (Irving and Fearn, 1975, p. 3). For the purposes of this work it can be assumed that the market and green rates coincided, as illustrated in table 7.2. For example, if the AUA price of one ton of wheat was set at AUA 100, prices in French francs and German marks would have been FF 493.707 and DM 400.

The AUA prices to which the green rates were applied were those fixed by the Community, that is, the target prices, the threshold prices and the support prices. This can be exemplified by considering the price support system for cereals, barley and maize (other agricultural products had similar systems). This is exemplified in figure 7.1.[5]

To begin with, the Community (basically, the Council of Ministers) fixed a *target price* for each category of good (durum wheat, common wheat, barley, rye and maize). This was the market price farmers should have received in the German town of Duisburg. Since Duisburg was the centre of the Community's principal deficit area, that is, where market prices would have been higher, the target price formed the upper end of the

Table 7.2 Green and market rates: initial situation, 1962

	France	Germany
Market rate	AUA 1 = FF 4.93707	AUA 1 = DM 4
Green rate	AUA 1 = FF 4.93707	AUA 1 = DM 4

Figure 7.1   The original price support system for cereals, barley and maize

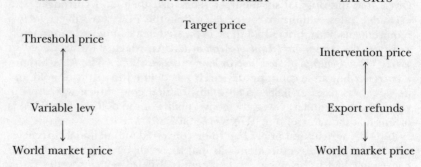

IMPORTS   INTERNAL MARKET   EXPORTS

Target price

Threshold price   Intervention price

Variable levy   Export refunds

World market price   World market price

price band within which market prices could fluctuate. The lower end was set by *intervention price*, that is, the market price in the area of greatest surplus, the French town Ormes. The intervention price was lower than the target price by the cost of transport between Duisburg and Ormes plus a marketing margin. If farmers were not able to sell (part of) their produce at a price higher than the intervention price, the intervention stores would buy the surplus at that price. If demand was such that the market price was higher than the intervention price, farmers could sell on the market rather than bringing their produce to the intervention office.

Usually, market prices tended towards intervention prices because of the EC's surpluses. But for some products (maize and hard wheat) market prices could tend towards target prices if the Community was less than self-sufficient. It was also possible for market prices to be lower than the intervention prices if farmers preferred to sell their produce on the market rather than waiting for payments from the intervention agency, or for fear of having to remove their products at their own expense from the intervention stores in case of rejection of their produce by the intervention agency on grounds of insufficient quality. The surplus stored in the intervention offices could be sold on the world market at the world market price. Since usually this was lower than the internal market price, traders received an export subsidy equal to the difference between the internal and the world market prices. The world price could also be higher than the internal market price. In this case, variable levies were applied to exports and subsidies to imports.

Given that usually the world market price was lower than the target price, a variable import levy was added to the world price so as to bring the price at which wheat entered the Community up to the level of the target price. This was the *threshold price*. This was derived from the target price by allowing for transport costs from Rotterdam (the main EC's grain import port) to Duisburg. If the threshold price was higher than the internal market price, imports stopped (this is the case depicted in figure 7.1). In the opposite case, imports followed. As the European Commission (1994a) points out,

Other forms of supportive interventions were available, such as the British system of deficiencies payments, but these would have involved large payments from the small Community budget ... whereas market support promised import levy revenue which could be used to offset, and perhaps cover, CAP expenditures. (p. 63)

This system was highly protectionist. The US was against it from the very beginning, given the greater efficiency of US agriculture and its orientation towards foreign markets. But, 'since the US supported European integration for other, mostly non-economic reasons, they had to swallow the closing of the EEC's agricultural markets' (Rieger, 1996, p. 106).

7.1.2 The Agrimonetary System, 1969–71

The original CAP system was suitable for a situation of (relative) stability of exchange rates. But towards the end of the 1960s, monetary turbulences and volatility in exchange rates began to emerge. This had important repercussions on agricultural prices and was the origin of the agrimonetary system which was launched in 1969 after the French franc was devalued and Germany revalued the mark.[6] Consider first the devaluation of the franc from US\$1 = FF 4.93707 to US\$1 = FF 5.55419. Suppose one tonne of wheat cost AUA 100 = US\$100. If the green rate had followed the market rate, French farmers would have received AUA 100 = US\$ 100 = FF 555.419 instead of FF 493.707. This would have caused a rise in agricultural prices and incomes and possibly an inflationary movement. To avoid this, France was allowed to retain its old green rate for intervention prices, that is US\$1 = FF 4.93707 (see table 7.3).

But now French traders could buy a tonne of wheat for FF 493.707 from French farmers (assuming that market price and intervention price coincided), transport it to Germany, and sell it to the German intervention agency for DM 400. These could be exchanged at the market rate for FF 555.419, that is, at a profit equal to $555.419 - 493.707 =$ FF 61.712 (DM 45 if German traders had engaged in this operation). Wheat exports from France to Germany increased due purely to these exchange rate fluctuations. To correct this competitive disadvantage, an export levy on French agricultural exports to Germany was charged. A French trader wanting to sell a tonne of wheat would have received FF 493.707 in France and DM 400 = FF 555.419 in Germany. But this positive difference was annulled by a levy of an equal amount that the trader had to pay in order to export to Germany.[7] Similarly, French traders could buy a tonne of wheat either in

Table 7.3   Green and market rates: devaluation of the franc

	France	Germany
Market rate	AUA 1 = FF 5.55419	AUA 1 = DM 4
Green rate	AUA 1 = FF 4.93707	AUA 1 = DM 4

France for FF 493.707 or in Germany for DM 400. To purchase DM 400 on the foreign exchange market they needed FF 555.419. Imports suffered. An import subsidy was granted on French imports from Germany.

The opposite held for the revaluation of the DM from $1 = DM 4 to $1 = DM 3.66. A change in the green rate to $100 = DM 366 would have provoked a fall in German agricultural prices and thus incomes, something Germany wanted to avoid for political reasons. Germany was allowed to retain its old green rate, that is, $1 = DM 4 (see table 7.4).

Table 7.4   Green and market rates: revaluation of the mark

	France	Germany
Market rate	AUA 1 = FF 5.55419	AUA 1 = DM 3.66
Green rate	AUA 1 = FF 4.93707	AUA 1 = DM 4

But now German traders could have bought a tonne of wheat from French farmers for FF 493.707 that cost them on the foreign exchange market DM 355. This wheat was transported to Germany, where it was sold to the German intervention office for DM 400. They would have realized a profit equal to DM 400–DM 355 = DM 45 (aside from transport and other costs). Since imports were favoured, an import levy was charged on French wheat imports into Germany. Similarly, German traders could sell a tonne of wheat either to the German intervention office for DM 400 or in France for FF 493.707. These, at the market rate, were exchanged for DM 355. German exports were disadvantaged. Thus, a subsidy was granted on German wheat exports to France.

The levies and subsidies which were imposed or granted as a result of devaluations and revaluations were called *monetary compensatory amounts* (MCAs). Thus, in case of devaluation (France), negative MCAs, the granting of compensatory amounts on imports and the charging of compensatory amounts on exports, were applied. In case of revaluation (Germany), positive MCAs, that is, the charging of compensatory amounts on imports and the granting of compensatory amounts on exports, were applied. MCAs were called positive because they compensated for green rates higher than market rates and negative because they compensated for green rates lower than market rates.

Also, in the absence of compensations, internal trade distortions could have arisen as a result of trade with non-member countries following exchange rate adjustments. Thus, a revaluing country was charged an MCA on imports and granted an MCA on exports (*Official Journal*, 1971). The opposite held for devaluing countries.

In addition, in the absence of MCAs, trade distortions would have been caused by export refunds and import levies (see European Parliament, 1992, pp. 11–12). Suppose the DM revalued from $1 = DM 4 to $1 = DM 3.66 with an unchanged green rate equal to $1 = DM 4 (see table 7.5). If traders exported from France, the export refund was FF 493.707 (the

Table 7.5 Revaluation of the mark with unchanged green rates

	France	Germany
Market rate	AUA 1 = FF 493.707	AUA 1 = DM 3.66
Green rate	AUA 1 = FF 493.707	AUA 1 = DM 4

French intervention price) minus the world market price. These FF 493.707 would have exchanged on the foreign exchange market for DM 366. If traders exported from Germany, they received an export refund equal to DM 400 (the German intervention price) minus the world market price. This greater export refund fostered community exports from Germany. MCAs were applied.

Suppose now France devalued from $1 = FF 493.707 to $1 = FF 555.419 while its green rate remained unchanged. Assume that the threshold price and the intervention coincided. This is shown in table 7.6. Now traders could import into France, thus paying a levy equal to FF 493.707 minus the world market price, or into Germany, thus paying a levy equal to DM 400 minus the world market price. But for these DM 400 they had to pay FF 555.419. This fostered Community imports into France. MCAs were applied in this case as well. It is important to notice that the MCAs discussed in this section were fixed.

By 1973 this system had become 'highly complex', as the Council acknowledged (*Official Journal*, 1973). Also, MCAs were alien to a common internal market and were specifically prohibited by article 9 of the EC Treaty, according to which the Community shall 'involve ... the prohibition between Member States of customs duties on imports and exports and of all charges having equivalent effect'. Nevertheless, the MCAs were introduced, that is, farm prices were equalized,[8] because this was the answer to the 'German problem' (Weinstock, 1975, pp. 120–1), that is, to the need to avoid a sure fall in German farmers' incomes. Negative MCAs, on the other hand, were far less important for weaker currency countries because their absence would have meant a sure rise in farm incomes (a politically non-objectionable outcome) which would not necessarily have been followed by inflation.[9] The agrimonetary system, a flagrant violation of the EEC principles, both reflected and fostered from the very beginning the interests of Germany, that is, of the German conservative ruling classes.

Table 7.6 Devaluation of the franc with unchanged green rates

	France	Germany
Market rate	AUA 100 = FF 555.419	AUA 100 = DM 400
Green rate	AUA 100 = FF 493.707	AUA 100 = DM 400

7.1.3 The Agrimonetary System, 1971–79

Towards the end of the 1960s the long period of economic growth in the Western world was coming to a close. Increasing quantities of capital unable to find sufficiently profitable outlets in the real sphere were flowing into the financial markets, where higher rates of profit were possible. The shifts of these speculative masses of financial capital began undermining the ability of the Central Banks to maintain their central rates through intervention (see Carchedi, 1991, ch. 5). In May 1971, West Germany was forced to cease to observe the margins of fluctuations prescribed by the IMF rules and floated the DM. In August of the same year, the convertibility of the dollar into gold was suspended and the Benelux countries and Italy floated their currencies. This created for the countries involved a disparity between the market rates and the green rates, which had remained fixed at their old pre-float levels. To counter the effects of these disparities (see above), MCAs were introduced, only now they were variable in nature, given the variability of the market rates. Thus, MCAs kept being calculated with reference to the US dollar.

The instability of the international exchange system continued in 1972. As a result, in that year the US dollar was devalued by raising the price of gold from \$35 to \$38 per ounce. Also, a new system was introduced. On the one hand, the bands of fluctuation around the dollar were increased from ± 1 per cent to ± 2.25 per cent. The rates around which these fluctuations could take place were called *central rates relative to the US dollar*. On the other, the EEC Council of Finance Ministers decided to restrict the margins of fluctuations between member states currencies to ± 1.125 about their central rates. This arrangement was called '*the snake in the tunnel*', the snake being the narrower band of fluctuations of the EEC countries relative to one another and the tunnel being the wider bands of fluctuations of the EEC countries relative to the US dollar.

In 1973 the dollar was further devalued and Belgium, Denmark, France, Germany, Luxembourg and the Netherlands decided not to keep their currencies within the ± 2.25 per cent band relative to the dollar. Rather, they would maintain a ± 2.25 per cent band around their own central rates defined in terms of Special Drawing Rights (SDRs), a 'basket' of world currencies. This became known as the '*joint float*'. These technical changes were an expression of the decreasing dominance of the US and thus of the dollar (as revealed by the dollar's devaluations). On the one hand, the definition of central rates shifted from the US dollar to SDRs and, on the other, some European countries' central rates began to float relative to each other rather than to the US dollar.

As for the CAP, this meant frequent changes in the MCAs. The system had become exceedingly cumbersome. It was thus decided to introduce fixed MCAs at least for those member states that participated in the joint float: West Germany, the Netherlands, Belgium, Luxembourg and Denmark. Fixed MCAs required a fixed relation between market rates and the green rates (which had remained unchanged). Given that the former were floating, the latter had to float too. This was achieved by defining the AUA as an average of the member countries' central rates relative to the SDRs. Then, if a country within the joint float changed its central rate, it had also to change its green rate in order to keep the same fixed MCAs (the example of the Netherlands in September 1973). If the green rate remained the same, the fixed MCAs changed too (the example of Germany in June 1973). As for the free floaters, the UK, Ireland and Italy, their MCAs remained variable.

The basic drawback of this system was two-fold. It was extremely complex and it did not reflect the changed economic relations between Europe and the United States. European central rates were still related to the dollar, through the SDRs. But the changed relations between the two blocs as well as the increasing integration within Europe called for a European currency to which the national currencies could be fastened, thus reducing revaluations and devaluations.

7.1.4 The EMS, the ECU and the MCAs (1979–84)

This currency was introduced in 1979 as an integral part of the European Monetary System (EMS)[10] and was called the ECU. This has been dealt with in chapter 4. For the purposes of the CAP, the introduction of the ECU was supposed to have several advantages. First, the ECU would provide a stable reference basis for exchange rate fluctuations. By tying the national currencies to it, the former would achieve stability, thus avoiding both devaluations and revaluations. Second, it would avoid the politically intractable problem of having to choose one of the national currencies as the anchor for the others. Third, it would rule out the possibility of using the US dollar for this purpose, also a politically important feature. And, last but not least, the ECU was seen as the precursor of a single European currency, the only definite solution to exchange rate fluctuations and all the negative consequences implied by them. From 1979 on, MCAs were computed relative to the difference between central rates relative to the ECU and green rates. Initially, this system had a stabilizing effect on exchange rates, since all member countries tried not to alter their central rates, but eventually, as seen in chapter 4, stability of exchange rates proved to be illusory.

7.1.5 The Switch-over Mechanism, 1984–92

In 1984 the Council decided to phase out the positive MCAs and to avert new positive MCAs. As far as the phasing out of the old MCAs is concerned, farmers would be compensated in the event of agricultural price reductions in the strong countries (especially Germany) following the revaluation of the green rates. As for new positive MCAs, the switch-over mechanism was introduced. Basically, whenever a strong-currency country (Germany) revalued its central rate, instead of it imposing new positive MCAs, the existing negative MCAs on weak-currency countries were raised. Technically, this was achieved by introducing *green central rates*. These were equal to central rates multiplied by a so-called 'switch-over factor'. The reason for this was that at that time 'increases in ECU prices were being severely restricted' (European Parliament, 1992, p. 42). It was then opted for an increase in the central rates for agricultural products.

Since agricultural prices were expressed in ECUs, and since green central rates were higher than central rates, the adaptation of green rates to the green central rates resulted in higher agricultural prices in national currencies in all member states except Germany (whose lower agricultural prices due to revaluation had been compensated by its higher green central rate and thus by higher DM prices). Hypothetically, suppose Germany revalued from ECU 1 = DM 4 to ECU 1 = DM 3.5. Then, a tonne of wheat = ECU 100 would earn a German farmer DM 350 instead of DM 400, a politically undesirable effect. In this case, a switch-over factor was applied such that the green central rate was 1 tonne of wheat = DM 400. The green rate did not fall to ECU 1 = DM 3.5 but remained ECU 1 = DM 4. German farmers' incomes did not fall. But then the green rates in other member countries had to be increased by the same percentage. Prices in national currencies in these countries rose. At the same time, the difference between the central rates of the other member states and the new (higher) green rates increased. This called for an increase in the existing negative MCAs for these countries to counter the effects of trade distortions.

This system, thus, achieved a disguised increase in agricultural prices.

> As far as the Community of Ten is concerned, common prices in ECU's have recorded a fall since 1983/4, although, as a result of adjustments to the green rates, they have displayed significant annual increases in national currencies ... France, Ireland, and Italy obtained, during the period in question, nominal increases in prices in their own currencies in excess of 4 per cent per year. (European Parliament, 1992, p. 43)

Officially, the reason for introducing the switch-over mechanism was that it would have been easier to dismantle negative MCAs (given that this would have increased agricultural prices, a politically acceptable result) than positive MCAs (for the opposite reason). Consequently, to begin with, no new positive MCAs were to be imposed (European Parliament, 1992, p. 15). This called for the increase of the weaker countries' negative MCAs. As opposed to the offical reasons, the real point is that the adoption of this system fostered the economic interests of the strongest country, Germany. A politically undesirable effect of DM revaluation (lower agricultural prices in Germany) was achieved at the expense of other nations' price levels, that is, by causing inflationary movements in these nations. In the 1984–8 period, German revaluations caused common agricultural prices to rise by 13.7 per cent (European Parliament, 1992, p. 42). In other words, price increases of other member states' agricultural goods were caused by Germany's industrial power and reflected Germany's interest in maintaining the stability of its own agricultural prices.

7.1.6 The 1992 (MacSharry) Reform

During the 1970s and 1980s it became increasingly difficult to finance this system. As production and productivity increased, the Community became a net exporter of many agricultural products. By 1990/1 the EU had become self-sufficient in all its main food commodities except oils and fats and fresh fruit. Thus, on the one hand, both intervention costs and export subsidies became increasingly onerous and, on the other hand, the import levy, which originally accounted for one third of CAP expenses, became increasingly less important.[11] This led to the introduction of the 1992 reform, which rested on three pillars. First, there was a reduction of intervention prices of about 33 per cent for cereals and 15 per cent for beef. Second, lower prices were to be compensated by direct income payments. The shift from price to direct income support was seen as non-trade distorting. And third, for cereals, compensations were made conditional upon farmers agreeing to reduce their arable land by 15 per cent (the set-aside system). This condition applied only to large-scale producers, that is, those with production levels exceeding 92 tonnes of cereals equivalents. This aimed at encouraging farmers to cut their surpluses. The reform proposals were much less drastic for animal products. These are still elements of the present system, to be discussed shortly.

Brouwer and van Berkum (1996, p. 28) have evaluated the first two years of the 1992 reforms for cereals. In 1994/5, production decreased to around 160 million tonnes, that is, to between 6 per cent and 7 per cent less than the average of the three years prior to the reform. At the same time productivity has increased by 5 per cent to 7 per cent, due to the setting aside of less productive land. Production has also shifted from barley to wheat, due to the latter's higher productivity. This increased output, together with a reduction in the intervention price (see above), might result in a shift of cereals from human consumption to animal feed. This is food degradation, to be discussed in section 7.2.

7.1.7 The Single Market and the New Monetary Turbulences, 1992–93

The single market, which was completed in 1992, aimed at dismantling all levies and subsidies on trade between member states. Given that the MCAs were levied at the national borders, they had to go. The new system, without MCAs, was thought up by the Commission during a period of relative calm on the international monetary markets. Due to this lack of volatility, it was thought that the EC currencies were tied by practically fixed exchange rates. Therefore, it was thought possible once more to tie the green rates to the market exchange rates. For the weak-currency countries, in the event that the difference between these two rates became too big, the green rates would have been adjusted automatically to the market exchange rate, without the intervention of the Council. This adjustment could have taken place very quickly, after three days. For the strong-currency countries (those with the 2.25 per cent band within the

ERM), changes in the green rates would have been possible only in case of a realignment of the central parities.

The monetary turbulences in the autumn of 1992 changed the scenario completely. Given the considerable fluctuations in practically all countries' exchange rates, the Council revised drastically the Commission's proposal. In short, in addition to the system just sketched, the switch-over mechanism was retained. This meant that every time central rates were adjusted because of the revaluation of the Deutschmark (the strongest currency within the EMS), the switch-over factor would have had to be raised in order to raise the green central rates. This led to an increasing budgetary burden for the EU, given that higher green central rates meant a greater quantity of ECUs to be used for intervention. This system was ended in 1995.

7.1.8 The Present System

The present system of market price support retains some elements of the original system but in a modified form, due mainly to the replacement of the ECU by the Euro.

• Variable import levies, which force external producers to sell inside the EU at above the threshold price, are adjusted as often as daily according to the world market price level. The world market price is the price at Rotterdam. Following the Uruguay Round (see chapter 6), levies are to be replaced by tariffs.
• Export refunds, also variable according to world market conditions, compensate EU exporters for the difference between internal EU prices (usually somewhat below the threshold price) and the lower world price. They are applied identically throughout the EU. Before 1 January 1999, both export refunds and import levies were calculated on the basis of common ECU prices and world prices converted into ECUs. As of 1 January 1999, the Euro has replaced the ECU for the calculation of export refunds, and import levies and world prices are converted into Euros (*Official Journal*, 1998b, article 2, paras 1 and 2).
• Before the introduction of the Euro, intervention prices (at which the EU purchases farm products when oversupply pushes market prices below the intervention level) were fixed in ECUs and converted into national currencies through the green rates. With the advent of the Euro, intervention prices are fixed in Euros (*Official Journal*, 1998b, article 2, paras 1 and 2) and converted into the national currencies of the EMU countries at the irrevocably fixed exchange rates between the Euro and the national currencies (*Official Journal*, 1998b, article 10, para. 3).
• Non-EMU member states may grant compensatory aid to farmers in case of appreciable revaluation (*Official Journal*, 1998b, article 4, paragraph 1). Half of the monetary compensation must be paid by the Community and the other half may be paid by the national government (which, however, is not obliged to do so) (*Official Journal*, 1998b, article 6).[12]

- Reductions in the intervention prices are offset by compensatory payments to farmers on condition that they set aside a certain percentage on which they cultivate their arable crops. This condition does not apply to small producers, defined as farmers who produce up to 92 tonnes of cereals, who receive compensatory payments on all areas sown to arable crops. Set-aside areas may not be used for the production of either human or animal food. However, other uses are allowed.

An assessment of the CAP in its present form will be carried out in the next section. Here suffice to mention a few of the drawbacks mentioned by its own supporters. First, owing to the numerous modifications to the original price support and the introduction of experimental and *ad hoc* schemes, the administration of the CAP has become increasingly complex and fraud-ridden. Second, in spite of all these efforts, differences in farm incomes across the EU remain. And third, the financing of the CAP has become too costly and future accessions will raise the costs even more. Moreover, as the Community reached self-sufficiency, national and community-wide farm lobbies lost some of their power to impose an agricultural protectionist policy, as shown by the content of farm reforms. Nevertheless, these lobbies are still a formidable force which no politician can afford to ignore. This explains why agriculture was excluded from both the Kennedy and the Tokyo Round but not any more from the Uruguay Round. These internal factors were compounded by other external reasons. Particularly important was the relation between the EC and the US, which had always been keen to include this sector in the GATT talks.

With regard to the CAP, as a result of the Uruguay Round (see chapter 6, section 1.4), it was decided that within six years: (a) border protection measures other than customs duties (mainly, variable import levies) should be converted into tariffs and that both tariffs and customs duties should be reduced by 36 per cent; (b) other nations should be allowed to export to the EC between 3 per cent (at the beginning of the implementation period) and 5 per cent (at the end of that period) of the EC's own consumption; (c) direct export subsidies spending should be reduced by 36 per cent and subsidized export volumes by 20 per cent; and (d) internal market support should be reduced by 20 per cent (but many exceptions were agreed upon).

It was also agreed that further negotiations would be started in 1999. These negotiations would not be a new general round of trade negotiations but a review of the Uruguay Round. Preparations were started by the WTO in December 1999. Since the least developed countries have no delegates at the WTO, their interests (both in the agricultural and in other fields) are bound to be under-represented.

7.2 Agricultural Prices, Protectionism and World Hunger

The previous section has reviewed the CAP's main features and developments. Official, and very often apologetic, literature emphasizes some
major achievements. Let us assess them.

7.2.1 International Prices and Food Appropriation

The first claim is that the CAP has caused a downward pressure on
agricultural prices, thus greatly stimulating production and consumption
of food. It is pointed out that in the last twenty years the percentage of
household expenditure on foodstuffs has fallen from 28 per cent to 20 per
cent (European Commission, 1996b, p. 7).[13] The two drawbacks usually
admitted are the system's great complexity and the production of surpluses.
But it is also mentioned that price support is being simplified and that,
after the 1992 reforms, these surpluses have been greatly reduced. In 1995
agricultural stocks were 28,000 tonnes, less than a week's production, wheat
stocks had dropped from 25 million tonnes in 1990 to 5 million tonnes,
and beef stocks had fallen to less than 5 per cent of production (European
Commission, 1996b, p. 10). This first subsection will argue the following
two points. First, the formation of international agricultural prices hides
the appropriation of international value by the imperialist centre (and thus
by the EU) from the dominated countries. This manifests itself as world
hunger irrespective of whether prices fall or not. Second, declining agricultural prices have negative effects on the incomes of the poor countries.
This worsens world hunger.

To prove the first point, the results reached in chapter 4 will be relied
upon. Different organic compositions of capital (the relation between
constant and variable capital) are assumed both between sectors (given
that each sector has by definition different and non-comparable production
processes) and within sectors (given that enterprises compete by introducing different production processes). Therefore, different techniques both
between and within sectors produce different quantities of new value and
thus of surplus value per unit of capital invested. In this subsection the
focus will be on the relation between the imperialist centre and the
dominated countries under the assumption that the centre produces both
means of production and means of consumption (more specifically, food
items) while the dominated countries produce only food items. The
question then is: how do the system's objective laws of movement redistrib-
ute the value contained in these means of production and food items, and
what are the consequences for food appropriation, that is, world hunger?
Let us first specify which laws of movement are referred to.

A first cause of redistribution of (surplus) value is given by the exchange
of commodities produced in different sectors, that is, of different use
values. As seen in the previous chapters, given the different organic
compositions of capital (OCC), the low OCC sectors lose value to the high

OCC sectors. To find out the quantity appropriated/lost, we will assume that all capitals in different sectors realize *the same rate of profit*. This procedure is justified by the observation of a real movement, that is, the movement of capitals from the sectors with low profit rates to sectors with high profit rates. The different profit rates constitute a modification of this tendential redistribution of (surplus) value. This is unequal exchange because this appropriation of value (whether tendential or actual) arises when the products of different sectors exchange against each other. The assumption is that all commodities in one sector cede value to (or gain value from) commodities in another sector in equal amounts. This is so because of the implicit assumption of no technological differentiation within sectors. Let us now drop this assumption.

A second cause of redistribution of value is given by the exchange of the same type of commodities (the same use values) produced with different techniques (OCC) for other commodities. Here, to find out the quantity of (surplus) value appropriated/lost due to different productivity levels, the assumption is that the commodities sell for *the same price*. Again, this procedure is warranted by the observation of a real movement, that is, price competition which forces all the products of the same sector (the same use values) to be sold for the same price. Again, this is a tendential situation. The existence of different prices for the same commodities is only a deviation from this tendential price level. These commodities do not appropriate value from each other (given that products within the same sector do not exchange for each other). Rather, they appropriate value (in different quantities) from other sectors when they are sold, that is, exchanged for commodities of other sectors due to different technological levels.

Thus, the laws of movement which allow us to inquire into the redistribution of value are the tendency towards the equalization of profit rates across sectors and the equalization of prices within sectors. We can now tackle the question posed above, namely what are the consequences of these two laws of movement for international food appropriation and world hunger? Consider first one country (A) in the imperialist centre producing and exporting means of production (MP) and another country (B) in the dominated bloc producing and exporting means of consumption (MC), more specifically food. Country B produces 200,000MC of which 100,000 are supposed to be sufficient for internal consumption (we disregard here for sake of simplicity the subdivision of these 100,000MC between wages and profits) and the other 100,000 are available for export (i.e. exchange for the 100MP produced by A). As we know, value quantities can be read also as money quantities. Consider table 7.7.

The average rate of profit is $p = 30$ per cent. Country B loses 10V, that is, $200,000 \times 10/140 = 14,286MC$. These are its decreased consumption. Suppose now that country A improves its productivity, thus producing less value (110V instead of 120V) but more MP (110MP instead of 100MP). This is shown in table 7.8.

Now, the average rate of profit is 25 per cent. Country B loses 15$V =$ $200,000 \times 15/140 = 21,429$. Its consumption decreases by that much (this

Table 7.7   Loss of food by B due to the equalization of
A's and B's profit rates

A $80c + 20v + 20s = 120V$ $100MP$
B $60c + 40v + 40s = 140V$ $200,000MC$ of which
100,000 for internal consumption
100,000 for export

is a further drop in consumption by $7,143MC$ relative to the situation
before A's productivity increase). Country B could try to import less *MP*
thus giving up less *MC*. But, on the one hand, B needs to buy as many *MP*
as possible in order either to industrialize or to try to catch up with A. On
the other, A (hit by the profitability problem and thus by the realization
problem) needs to impose upon B the purchase of as many *MP* as possible
either through coercion or through less obvious imperialist means (loans
by international organizations, etc.). The more country A increases its
productivity, relative to its previous level, in the internationally tradable
MP, the more B must cede *MC*, the more is hunger bound to emerge in B.

Table 7.8   Loss of food by B due to A's increased
productivity in the capital goods sector

A $90c + 10v + 10s = 110V$ $110MP$
B $60c + 40v + 40s = 140V$ $200,000MC$ of which
100,000 for internal consumption
100,000 for export

Let us now consider, as for example in table 7.9, the agricultural sectors
of two countries, one of which (A) is situated in the imperialist centre and
the other (B) in the dominated bloc.

Here there is equalization not of the profit rates but of prices. The total
value available for redistribution is $120 + 140 = 260$. The total quantity of
commodities is 350. The tendential unit price is $260V/350MC = 0.7429$.
Thus A realizes $0.7429 \times 200 = 148.5$, that is, a rate of profit equal to 48.5
per cent while B realizes $0.7429 \times 150 = 111.5$, a rate of profit of 11.5 per
cent. If A and B sell their products at the same price, A appropriates more
value from other sectors (countries) while B loses value to other sectors
(countries). If other countries' (sectors') value is embodied in *MP*, A gets
more *MP* than B for each *MC*. This hampers B's economic growth and thus

Table 7.9   Loss of food by B due to A's greater
productivity in the consumption goods sector

A $80c + 20v + 20s = 120V$ $200MC$ $p = 48.5$ per cent
B $60c + 40v + 40s = 140V$ $150MC$ $p = 11.5$ per cent

indirectly B's production of *MC.* A's possibility of purchasing the commodities produced by other sectors (countries) has increased at the cost of B. A further increase in A's productivity would further accentuate this difference.

If the outcomes of the analyses exemplified in tables 7.8 and 7.9 are combined, it can be seen that B suffers from an increased productivity in A. Country B must counteract both the loss of food (*MC*) as a result of country A's increased productivity in the *MP* sector and the loss of *MP* as a result of Country A's increased productivity in the *MC* sector. World hunger is thus implicit in the redistribution of international value inherent in capitalism's price forming mechanism. Lower prices for, and unchanged export levels of, country B's products cannot but worsen the problem.

One way to achieve this increased sale of agricultural commodities is for B to increase the cultivable areas upon which to grow those food items that are demanded by the centre. Concerning the EU, imports of food by the EU from the dominated countries imply the use of these countries' soil for EU food consumption. Conversely, exports of food by the EU to the dominated countries imply the use of EU soil for the dominated countries. Consider the trade in grain, rice, potatoes, sugar and vegetables (EU products) and in citrus fruits, bananas, soy beans, tapioca, molasses, coffee beans, cocoa beans, sunflower seeds, palm oil, cotton, tea, tobacco, groundnuts and natural rubber (dominated countries' products). It has been estimated that the EU uses 228,000 km² of the dominated countries' soil for the production of food consumed in the EU and that the dominated countries use 97,000 km² of EU soil for the production of food consumed in the dominated countries (Friends of the Earth Europe, 1995, table 3.13 of Supplement). The EU uses a net area of 130,000 km² of the dominated countries' soil (the size of Greece) for the production of food for its own consumption.[14] This soil could be (and mostly was previously) used for food production in the dominated countries.

The second point to be made in this subsection is that, besides the appropriation of food through unequal exchange, taxpayers-financed export subsidies and the dumping of European surpluses has undermined prices on the world market. On the one hand, this has denied the food producers (especially small farmers) of the dominated bloc a market for their produce. This has had a three-fold negative effect. First, it has worsened those countries' balance of payments problems by claiming a substantial part of scarce hard currency for food imports. Second, it has created a food-import dependency for many countries of the dominated bloc. Third, it has caused an incredible concentration of food production and distribution in just a few corporate hands. 'Seventy per cent of world grain trade is carried out by just six companies' (PANOS, 1997, p. 63). Trade liberalization measures following the Uruguay Round will certainly strengthen this trend by forcing producers in the dominated bloc also to reduce their protective tariffs. This will force even more small producers out of business, thus increasing concentration, unemployment and destitution.

On the other hand, lower world prices have facilitated purchase of food by countries dependent on imports of food. Often, this has not benefited the poor and the destitute of the dominated countries but 'meant cheap food could be provided for their politically volatile urban centres' (Middleton et al., 1993, p. 129). Moreover, export subsidies reductions agreed under the Uruguay Round will increase world food prices and thus affect negatively the food import bills of low-income food-deficit countries. Estimates vary. According to the UN's Food and Agricultural Organization (FAO), food imports for these countries will be 55 per cent higher in 2000 than they were in 1987–8. As far as small farmers are concerned, once they have been forced off the land by lower market prices and their place has been taken by large corporations, there is no land for them to go back to if prices rise again. It is the large farms and corporations that profit from these higher prices. As for those peasant farmers who are still tilling their land, while they might benefit from higher prices, they 'will face competition from the massively subsidized producers in the USA and the EC' (Middleton et al., 1993, p. 130), with the effects mentioned above.

The above allows us to puncture four well-established tenets of orthodox economic ideology, for which lower prices are supposed to restore the equilibrium between demand and the increased supply of agricultural goods following productivity increases, thus ensuring greater consumption for Europe's masses. First, as the previous chapters have shown, the capitalist system neither is in nor tends towards market equilibrium and, even if the equality between demand and supply were to be reached, the disequilibrium inherent in the inevitability of crisis would emerge and upset the previously reached market equilibrium. Second, lower prices are the result of technological innovations, unemployment and thus reduced purchasing power (rather than of a greater quantity of use values offered on the market). Thus, lower prices are at least partially matched by, because they are a consequence of, the lower disposable income resulting from technological innovations within capitalist production relations (unemployment). Third, as we have seen, a sizeable part of this increased quantity of agricultural articles available for consumption is appropriated from the dominated bloc through unequal exchange. And, fourth, lower prices drive small farmers off the land, thus fostering concentration in larger and more efficient farm holdings. Let us assess the consequences of this process.

7.2.2 Losers and Winners

The second claim made by the supporters of the CAP is that it has fostered the rationalization of agriculture, that is, the leaning towards bigger farm sizes. This is certainly the case. Capitalism generates naturally a tendency towards concentration and centralization. However, the question that should be posed is: how has the CAP fostered agricultural concentration and centralization, and who has profited from this process of capitalist rationalization?

First, inasmuch as the CAP raises the intervention prices, it favours the more productive farms, that is, usually the larger farmers, due to their larger output per unit of capital invested. Inasmuch as it lowers prices, it hits the low-productivity farmers more than the more efficient ones, due to the former's reduced profit margins and thus due to the meagre finances they can draw upon in case of economic difficulties. Thus, positive price movements favour larger producers more than smaller ones and negative price movements hit smaller producers more than larger ones.

A second way the CAP has fostered concentration and centralization has been through income transfers. 'One estimate (CEC, July 1991) is that 80% of the CAP spending goes to only 20% of farmers, overwhelmingly the bigger and richer ones. This is partly the result of tying spending to production and of biasing it towards "northern" products'[15] (European Commission, 1994a, p. 27). Consequently, there has been a decline in the number of small farms (1 to 10 ha) and of middle-sized farms (10 to 50 ha) accompanied by a growth in the number of large farms (larger than 50 ha), as show by table 7.10. These latter account now for a high proportion of output. However, the structure of European agriculture is still far from the sizes and productivity levels required to face up to US competition without any protectionist walls.

As a result, '75 per cent of all European agricultural produce now comes from 25 per cent of its farms' (Middleton et. al., 1993, p. 127). These figures do not diverge substantially from those for the US, where, as a result of concentration of agricultural holdings, '84 per cent of the agricultural support payments – $8.5 billion – went to the top 30 per cent of farms in 1991, ranked by gross income' (Roodman, 1997, p. 139). Consequently, income disparities within agriculture have increased as small farms have gained relatively little from price support. Moreover, while price support has avoided a drastic reduction of farm incomes, agricultural share in national incomes has been falling, and 'the transfer of manpower from agriculture to other sectors, though substantial, was in most countries

Table 7.10 Number of holdings by size (in 1,000s)

	Total	<1 ha	1–5 ha	5–10 ha	10–20 ha	20–50 ha	>50 ha
EC 10							
1970	7,667		3,087	1,244	1,115	850	201
1975	7,100	703	2,728	1,044	938	867	325
1977	6,802		2,632	1,012	895	865	330
1979	6,820	1,362	2,494	923	847	852	338
1983	6,515	1,338	2,342	866	762	830	355
1985	6,359	1,321	2,275	826	751	816	367
1987	5,005		2,312	813	719	780	373
EC 12							
1987	6,920		3,411	1,163	936	946	473

Source: European Commission, 1994a, p. 53.

barely sufficient to avoid further widening of the gap in incomes per head
between agriculture and the rest of the economy' (Tracy, 1993, p. 162).

7.2.3 A Value Theory of Europe's Agricultural Protectionism

Let us summarize the results reached in section 7.2.1 above concerning the
connection between value, prices and world hunger. Contrary to a commonly held opinion, hunger in the dominated countries does not find its
ultimate cause in skewed consumption relations, in the fact that one bloc
consumes too little food because the other bloc consumes too much food.
Striking inequalities in terms of food consumption among countries (and
among classes within countries) are certainly a feature of capitalism. They
are one of the many forms of appearance of equally striking inequalities in
power relations. But these power relations can only be explained in terms
of the objective laws generated by capitalist production relations. Once
these laws are revealed, the insane logic of capitalism becomes apparent:

- It dictates that the majority of the world population consumes too few
  commodities (too little food) because the imperialist bloc produces too
  little surplus value, that is, because it produces too many commodities
  relative to the purchasing power in the centre.
- The need to realize higher quantities of surplus value (profits) and thus
  to find the necessary purchasing power pushes capitals in the centre
  towards export markets.
- The redistribution of surplus value inherent in the international prices
  arising from this process of international competition imposes upon the
  dominated bloc the exchange of an increasing quantity of their commodities (food) for each commodity produced by the imperialist bloc.
- Physically, this means fewer food items for the (masses of the) dominated
  bloc and thus world hunger.
- Falling world prices cannot but worsen this outcome.
- As far as the EU is concerned, the story is simple: there is a direct
  relationship between greater consumption in the EU and unequal
  exchange, even though the latter is not the only source of the former.

This perverse mechanism does not necessarily need protectionism. Protectionist policies, however, accentuate the international appropriation of
value. Price support mechanisms such as the CAP are based on the transfer
of value from other sectors of European societies to the agricultural one.
This transfer of value reduces the profit rates in those sectors of the
European economies thus putting pressure on them to increase their
productivity and thus the value appropriated through unequal exchange.
As explained above, this increases world hunger. If, as in the CAP, price
support mechanisms result in agricultural surpluses, *protectionist policies create
both food surpluses in the centre and hunger in the dominated countries.* This is
why surpluses in some countries can exist alongside hunger in other
countries.

Even orthodox economics can see that the roots of this evil are in a skewed distribution. But what orthodox economics cannot see is that this skewed distribution is a necessary manifestation of capitalist production and thus distribution relations. What this means is simply that, due to technological innovations, a decreased production of value becomes empirically manifest both as increased unemployment and as increased production of use values. This descreased value is then redistributed through the tendential equalization both of the rates of profit among sectors and of prices within sectors. This redistribution becomes empirically manifest as skewed income distribution. Capitalist production relations generate necessarily capitalist distribution relations. To try to eradicate the latter without overthrowing the former is a dangerous illusion artfully perpetuated by orthodoxy.

The question is not primarily a moral one, the unwillingness of the 'rich countries' to give their surpluses to the 'poor countries'. From a capitalist point of view, this is perfectly rational, even though profoundly immoral from the point of view of the satisfaction of basic human needs. If the system works thanks to the appropriation of value (in the form of food staples), it makes no sense for this system to give back what it had to take away. A different policy would imply that the EU would support its farmers in order for them to produce for the dominated countries. The costs of such a policy would be financed through the appropriation of surplus value by state institutions from the capitalist class or from the working class. The former case would worsen the crisis of profitability, the latter the crisis of realization. But these are exactly the evils that unequal exchange and thus the appropriation of surplus value (in the form of food as well) are meant to relieve. The same reasons prevent the system from distributing the surpluses to the needy in the EU. Such a policy would decrease the demand for those products, thus increasing intervention costs. Therefore, only a minimal part of agricultural surpluses can be disposed of in this way.[16] One figure helps to put the question in its proper perspective. In the nine years since 1987, almost ECU 1bn worth of foodstuffs was distributed to the poor of the EU (European Commission, 1996b, p. 9). This is less than 2.5 per cent of the Guarantee section of the EAGGF (more than ECU 40 billion) for only one year, 1996.

The profound immorality of poverty, hunger and starvation alongside opulence and waste is the outcome neither of a malfunctioning in the system nor of moral callousness. Rather, it is the expression of the way the system works. This situation is worsened by the above-mentioned attempts to reduce the size of agricultural surpluses. In what follows, the focus will be on the two major ways to reduce this surplus: the set-aside system and on food destruction and degradation.

Concerning the set aside system, it has been mentioned that agricultural surpluses have been reduced thanks to this system, that is, at the cost of paying farmers in order not to produce (see European Commission, 1994a; Marsh, 1977, cited in Swann, 1995, ch. 8). The extent of the land set aside is actually the obverse of what the surplus would have been without that system. It is an indication of a potential surplus. As such it does not solve surplus production (underproduction of surplus value) but it hides it. Even if agricultural surpluses in the EU were to disappear, the dumping of food on the world market, the set-aside system, and food degradation and destruction would be a clear indication of the existence of potential surpluses, of surpluses that exist but are not allowed to become manifest.

Some basic facts might help put this question in its proper perspective. On the one hand, 'in 1994/95 (EU-12), out of a total "base area" of 49mn. ha., . . . "commercial" producers had 33 mn. of which they set aside 6 mn.; "small farmers" had 12 mn. ha.', and therefore were exempt from the set-aside requirement (Tracy, 1996, p. 20). This means that 12.25 per cent of useful acreage is purposely not cultivated.[17] The US, of course, has a set-aside programme too. This was introduced in 1970 and went through some changes up to the 1985 Food Security Act (FSA), under which 'price supports were to be progressively reduced and acreage reduction was made condition for support' (Tracy, 1996, p. 52). Table 7.11 indicates the magnitude of the set-aside in the US.

Another disturbing feature of the present system is food destruction. Statistics on food destruction are hard to come by, due to the conjunctural nature and to the sensitivity of this phenomenon. Yet anecdotal and journalistic evidence suggests that this is a common practice by member states. More systematic is food degradation. This concept is not self-evident. Here a distinction will be made between physical degradation and economic degradation. Physical degradation refers to transforming food fit for human consumption into something different or to reducing its nutritional content, given a situation of hunger or malnutrition. Economic degradation refers to the use of labour to operate the above-mentioned transformation if this labour, instead of adding value to the product, transforms it into something which would have required less value to begin with. This is an example of value destroying labour (see Carchedi, 1991a, ch. 5).

Table 7.11   US acreage reductions

	% acreage reduction	
	Wheat	Maize
1987	27.5	20
1988	27.5	20
1989	10	10
1990	5	10
1991	15	7.5
1992	5	5
1993	0	10
1994	0	0
1995	0	7.5

Source: Tracy, 1996, p. 54.

Take meat first. Fresh meat is first-quality meat. But if surplus meat is frozen, it becomes automatically second-quality meat. If there is no loss of nutritional content, there is no physical degradation. If the freezing of meat is necessary for future consumption or for transportation and thus for the realization (use) of this particular product in a different place, there is no economic degradation either. The case is different for milk, butter and wine. Surplus milk can be turned into milk powder. Inasmuch as this is used for human consumption, there is no degradation. On the contrary, just as in the case for meat, this might be a necessary transformation to make milk available in distant places and at a later time. But if milk powder is used, as it is, for chicken and pork feed, then there is both physical and economic degradation. Alternatively, milk can be turned into butter. Again, there is no degradation here. But if butter is turned into fat unsuitable for human consumption, then there is degradation. Or, take the case of wine. If it is evaporated so that only its alcoholic content is left and if this is used in the chemical industry, then there has been degradation. As for cereals, 'Today, chickens, sheep, pigs, and cattle eat 57 per cent of the European Union's grain output. . . . Another 7 per cent gets exported. Thus people in the European Union are producing three times as much grain as they eat' (Roodman, 1997, p. 140). Up to 1974 the Community used to pay denaturing premiums. For wheat this meant to use dye or fish oil to ensure it could not be used as human food. For example, in 1972 denaturing premiums amounted to 7.7 million ECUs (Harris et al., 1983, table 4.2, p. 64).

Thus, on the one hand, we have set-aside and degradation. On the other, 'One in seven of the world's inhabitants, or 800 million people, are still chronically undernourished. One third of the world's children are malnourished. Most of the hungry are in the developing countries; 37 per cent of the population in Africa, 20 per cent in Asia and 13 per cent in Latin America.' Yet, 'aid to developing country agriculture has fallen from $10 billion in 1982 to $7.2 billion in 1992 (in constant 1985 US$)' (PANOS, 1997, p. 64). This indicates 'in the FAO's words, "a decreasing political will to address the problem" of world hunger'. Further, 'global demand for food is projected to rise by up to fifty per cent in the next fifteen to twenty-five years as a result of population growth and rising incomes', while 'world food production grew 3 per cent annually in the 1960s, 2.4 per cent in the 1970s and 1.6 per cent in the last ten years between 1985 and 1995. FAO predicts the figure will be 1.8 per cent up to 2010' (PANOS, 1997, p. 64). Finally, 'stocks of wheat are at a twenty-year low, while those of maize are at a fifty-year low. The shortages have pushed up world market prices by 30–50 per cent, adding an estimated US$3 billion to the food bills of "low income food-deficit countries"' (PANOS, 1997, p. 64).

While some analysts believe that the declining growth rate of world food production shows that the limits to growth are being reached, others believe that there is plenty of scope for further improvements 'by extending existing techniques into areas which have not so far adopted them, and through greater efficiency in water use' (PANOS, 1997, p. 64). According to the FAO, the falling growth rate of food production is due not so much to technical-natural factors but to slow population growth, saturation of demand in the developed countries, and insufficient purchasing power in the dominated countries. This admission is revealing.

As argued above, the saturation of demand in the centre is not biological (this would be the case if everybody were totally satisfied in their food needs) but economic, that is, the lack of purchasing power is due to the tendency the system has towards recurrent crises. It is therefore not accidental that decreasing demand set in in the 1970s, when the long wave of economic depression hit the Western developed world. Similarly, insufficient purchasing power in the dominated countries is the result of the pumping of value out of the dominated countries and into the imperialist centre.

> Terms of trade for agricultural commodities, which form the bulk of many developing countries exports, declined drastically in the 1970s and in the 1980s. Developing countries' share of world agricultural exports fell from 40 per cent in the early 1960s to 27 per cent in 1993, while the EU's share rose from 20 per cent to 45 per cent in the same period. (PANOS, 1997, p. 70)

The burden of the long-term crisis originating in the developed countries, that is, in their technological innovations and higher efficiency within the context of capitalist production relations, is borne by the masses of the dominated countries in terms of poverty, deprivation and hunger.

7.3 The Common Agricultural Policy and the Environment

In assessing the CAP, one point has not been dealt with: its environmental impact. This topic deserves special and separate treatment.

7.3.1 The Declarations of Intent

In article 39 of the Rome Treaty, which lists the aims of the CAP, there is no reference to the environment. However, this flaw is remedied by the Maastricht Treaty. Article 3(k) specifies that 'the activities of the Community shall include . . . a policy in the sphere of the environment'. This means that all Community policies must respect the objectives of the environmental policy. In fact, article 130r(2) recites: 'Environmental protection requirements must be integrated into the definition and implementation of other Community policies.' Therefore, this holds for agricultural policies as well. Against this background, let us deal with the Community environmental policy before inquiring into its relation with the CAP.

The aims of the Community environmental policy are set out in article 130r(1). They are (a) preserving, protecting and improving the quality of the environment, (b) protecting human health, (c) prudent and rational utilization of natural resources and (d) promoting measures at international level to deal with regional or worldwide environmental problems. The pursuance of these aims is based on five principles.

The first is *sustainability*. Verhoeve et. al., (1992, pp. 14–15) point out two deficiencies in this regard. First, the notion of sustainability is not defined. Second, the Treaty on European Union (TEU) is unclear as to what should be sustainable. It does not seem to make any distinction between 'sustainable economic and social progress', 'sustainable economic and social development of the developing countries', and 'sustainable and non-inflationary growth respecting the environment'. Progress, development and growth seem to be interchangeable in the Treaty's terminology, whereas in common usage growth has a more limited scope than development. It is uncertain whether this lack of definitional clarity has any effect on the Community's concrete environmental policies. What is important is that article 2 of the EC Treaty refers to 'sustainable and non-inflationary growth respecting the environment', that is, that environmental protection and sustainability have become an integral part (at least, in theory) of economic policies (Verhoeve et. al., 1992). It follows that the second principle is that of the *integration* of environmental policies into other, and especially into economic, policies.

Third, article 130r(2) lays down that environmental policies should aim at a *high level of protection*. This could be interpreted as the highest level among the member states. However, the same article adds immediately: 'taking into account the diversity of situations in the various regions of the Community'. This seems to limit the force of the principle and, given that different countries have different environmental standards, opens the way to the possibility of adopting average or even low standards. The fourth principle is the *precautionary principle*, according to which appropriate action has to be taken to avert environmental threats.

Finally, there is the *polluter-pays principle* (PPP for short), which, given its popularity, deserves a more detailed examination. This principle is unexceptionable concerning delinquent behaviour. However, if it is, as it usually is, interpreted as 'those responsible for causing pollution are required to bear the costs of pollution prevention and control measures', then 'strong policy statements are usually not backed up by actions' (Tobey and Smets, 1996, pp. 64–5). For example, 'detailed case studies of environmental protection measures in agriculture in six European countries (Belgium, Denmark, France, Germany, the Netherlands and the United Kingdom) [found] that the costs of environmental protection in the agricultural sector are insignificant relevant to production costs' (Tobey and Smets, 1996, p. 68). Also, 'pollution abatement expenditures relative to production costs are small even in pollution-intensive industries' (Tobey and Smets, 1996, p. 69).

But the most important point is that the PPP is made irrelevant by actual agricultural practices. As Roodman (1997) so cogently puts it, 'it makes little sense for societies to begin making the polluter pay . . . unless we first stop paying the polluter' (p. 134). Agricultural assistance encourages reduced crop diversity, the over-production of crops that are highly erosive, the cultivation of marginal lands that tend to be more subject to soil erosion and moisture deficiencies, and the conversion of wetland and forestland to agricultural production. High and stable prices for agricultural commodities also influence tillage practices, the use of fertilizers and pesticides, the amount of excess manure and the intensity of land use. (Tobey and Smets, 1996, p. 82)[18]

Thus, 'Studies in the United States and Europe have found clear associations between the level of subsidies in a region and the amount of farm chemicals used' (Roodman, 1997, p. 141).

If agricultural subsidies are largely responsible for environmental damage, the insignificant size of environmental protection and pollution abatement costs relative to those subsidies cannot but lead to a very sober appraisal of the PPP's practical impact. Roodman's (1997) advice makes good sense:

> In agriculture, just dropping the top-grossing farms from the subsidy rolls would cut budgetary costs dramatically, boost small farms, and reduce the artificial incentive for environmentally destructive farming. Basing the remaining subsidies on income rather than output – in effect, converting them to welfare payments – would improve effectiveness even more. (p. 142)

These recommendations contrast with the neo-classical approach to pollution reduction. For example, Tobey and Smets (1996) draw a simple diagram in which the vertical axis indicates dollars and the horizontal axis indicates pollution emission. This diagram displays an upwards sloping Marginal Social Damage (MSD) curve and the farm's downwards sloping marginal abatement costs (MAC) curve, which 'represents the incremental environmental costs of the farm's polluting emissions' (p. 81). The intersection of the two curves is the equilibrium point, that is, the desired level of environmental quality.

This is a good example of the inadequacy of neo-classical models. In what follows, only the MSD curve will be analysed.[19] First, given the interconnectedness among the practically infinite number of nature's component elements, there is no way one can know both the shape and the quantitative coordinates of the MSD curve. Therefore, it is impossible to quantify the MSD curve in monetary terms. Even less likely is that a farmer might attain that knowledge. Second, even if the farmer did know the MSD curve, s/he would not care about it and the point on the MAC curve at which s/he would stop polluting would be unrelated to the MSD curve. There is no reason why the farmer should stop polluting at the intersection point between the MSD and MAC curves. This 'equilibrium' point is meaningless. Therefore, the diagram cannot explain the farmer's actual behaviour (a necessary prerequisite, given that the PPP aims at being an instrument of economic policy). Finally, even if one wants to disregard the above, that intersection point would be the individual farmer's 'equilibrium' point. But there is no reason to assume that this would also be the point at which nature's reproduction is in equilibrium. The market mechanism can put a price tag on natural resources but this has nothing to do with environmental sustainability and nature's preservation.

As for the procedural aspects, the Single European Act required unanimous agreement by the Council and did not increase the role of the Parliament, which remained purely consultative. The TEU has changed this into the principle of qualified majority and has extended the power of the Parliament both to the cooperation and to the co-decision procedures. However, article 130s of the Treaty is unclear as to when each of these procedures should be adopted. Paragraph 1 of this article states that the objectives of the environmental policy (see above) should be achieved in accordance with article 189c, that is, following the cooperation procedure. But according to paragraph 3 of the same article, 'in other areas,[20] general action programmes setting out priority objectives to be attained shall be adopted by the Council acting in accordance with the procedure referred to in article 189b', that is, the co-decision procedure. In spite of this lack of clarity, as a general rule, it can be said that 'the co-operation procedure has become the standard means for adopting environmental legislation' (Verhoeve, et. al., 1992, p. 31). The Court of Justice can impose a fine on a member state which has not complied with its obligations. This, of course, holds also for environmental questions.

In short, formally, the TEU strengthens the EU environmental policy by laying down that economic growth must be sustainable, by aiming at a high level of protection, by introducing the principle of qualified majority voting in the Council and that of co-decision between the Parliament and the Council for certain environmental proposals. On the other hand, these positive features are significantly restricted by the lack of clarity surrounding the notion of sustainability, by the qualifications attached to high environmental protection, and by the obscure drafting concerning the applicability of the co-decision and cooperation procedures.

7.3.2 The Cohesion Fund

The major instrument for EU environmental policy is the Cohesion Fund. It was set up in 1993 and endowed with ECU 16bn over a seven-year period. Its aim is 'to provide a financial contribution in the fields of environment and trans-European networks in the area of transport infrastructure' (EC, art. 130d). It finances between 80 per cent and 85 per cent of the public expenditure on a project, a much higher proportion than that of the Structural Funds (to be examined in chapter 8). Its resources are meagre. In 1999 they amounted to about Euro 3bn, that is, 3.5 per cent of the budget (European Commission, 1999, p. 9).

The chronological contemporaneity with the Maastricht Treaty and the official launching of the EMU is no coincidence. It was recognized that compliance with the Maastricht criteria, and the concomitant budgetary restraints, could be an obstacle to a policy of public investments needed to foster economic and social convergence between the member states, that is, transport infrastructures. At the same time, the negative effects of these measures could not be denied and the provision was made that these moneys could be used to repair the environmental damage inherent in these measures. The Cohesion Fund finances projects in areas 'where any reduction in public investment because of strict budgetary discipline would be extremely damaging' (European Commission, 1994a, p. 5). The reason why a new fund was set up instead of strengthening the Structural Funds is two-fold. On the one hand, the Cohesion Fund focuses on transport infrastructure and its environmental effects, while no sector is excluded for the Structural Funds. On the other, the Cohesion Fund makes financial assistance available to member countries whose GDP is 90 per cent or less than the Community's average, while this restriction does not hold for the Structural Funds.

An improved transport network is an indirect but important condition for higher efficiency both in production and in distribution on a European level. The projects financed by the Fund are meant to be complementary with other EU projects, particularly those concerning the trans-European networks. While in principle all economic actors will have equal opportunities to use these improved networks, in reality a better transport infrastructure will favour those enterprises which, due to their higher efficiency, can profitably reach farther markets both within the EU and in neighbouring countries. Moreover, an improved motorway network will benefit a handful of European vehicle manufacturers (oligopolies). There is a relationship between a widening of the motorway system, a thinning of the public transport system and an increase in the production and use of motor vehicles. Given the pollution and environmental degradation caused by the motor vehicle industries, there would seem to be an inherent contradiction between the Fund's two areas of intervention. In reality the Fund's environmental projects can best be seen as an attempt to repair somewhat the damages engendered by the trans-European networks.

It should be stressed that the Fund's financing of environmental projects (and of infrastructural projects) is

> conditional on the beneficiary Member State making a real effort not to run up an 'excessive' public deficit. If a country refuses to bring its public finances under control within the time-limit set by the Council of the Union, assistance from the Fund may be suspended. (European Commission, 1994a, p. 6)

This is in a nutshell the EU philosophy of environmental policies: they are accepted on condition that they pose no real obstacles to those economic, financial and budgetary policies which, to begin with, are the cause of those environmental problems. This is a sobering thought for all those who see in the implementation of environmental policies both an opportunity to clean up our natural habitat and the possibility to stimulate economic growth through the implementation of those policies by private enterprises.

The subordination of environmental concerns to the requirements of economic growth is inherent not only in the environmental philosophy of the EU but also in the vary nature of the capitalist economic system itself.

7.3.3 Towards the Greening of the Common Agricultural Policy?

Let us now look at the actual situation. If by agricultural areas it is meant arable land, area under permanent crops and permanent meadow and pasture, the land use in the EU is as indicated in table 7.12.

Table 7.12 Land use in the EU, 1990 (%)

Agriculture	59
Woods	24
Built-up areas	8*
Fully protected	0.4
Other areas	8
Water surface	1

* Of this 8%, 34% is roads and railways.
Source: Friends of the Earth Europe, 1995, p. 51.

It is evident that the size of the fully protected areas is insignificant. On the other hand, if we consider the total size of agricultural land, the following figures reveal the extent of the damage which has already been done. For the whole of Europe, including the former USSR, 23 per cent of total agricultural land, that is, 2,188,000 km^2, is degraded, that is, unfit for agriculture because of erosion and/or pollution. This is subdivided as shown in table 7.13.

If moderately, severely and extremely degraded areas are combined in one category, almost 20 per cent of European agricultural land is more than lightly degraded. This ranks second only to Central America and

Table 7.13 Degrees of degradation of agricultural land, 1991

Extremely degraded (completely lost for agricultural purposes)	31,000 km^2*
Severely degraded (major engineering work will be required to reclaim these soils and restore their full productivity)	107,000 km^2
Moderately degraded (action is needed if irreversible damage is to be prevented)	1,444,000 km^2
Lightly degraded (can be completely regenerated if their management is changed)	606,000 km^2

* The size of Belgium
Source: Friends of the Earth Europe, 1995, p. 52.

Mexico (24.1 per cent). All other regions of the world, including the world average (10.5 per cent), have a lower percentage of moderately, severely and extremely degraded areas relative to their total. North America's percentage is 4.4 (Middleton et al., 1993, p. 114).

Agriculture plays a substantial role in the pollution of the environment and especially of ground water and thus of agricultural land itself. 'Flushing huge amounts of water through agricultural lands has caused waterlogging and salinization' (Roodman, 1997, p. 144). Or,

> The main problems are caused by the leaching of soluble fertilizers (particularly nitrate) and pesticides as well as the introduction of phosphate into the ecosphere by erosion. Furthermore, we have to take into account the usually underestimated air-borne pollution. 85% of the nitrogèn input from the air is being caused by agricultural ammonia emission. (Friends of the Earth Europe, 1995, p. 57)

The emission of nitrogen and phosphorus has devastating effects on the North Sea, 'causing epidemic growth of algae and resulting in oxygen shortage, mass-dying of fish and even intoxication of fish and thus the human food chain' (Friends of the Earth Europe, 1995, p. 57). Moreover, 'due to overly high nitrate concentrations, inland water [is] partly no longer a possible source for drinking water. Too much nitrate has as well been detected in ground water fed wells' (Friends of the Earth Europe, 1995, p. 57).

The European Commission comes to broadly similar conclusions:

> the search for higher production, stimulated by price support, is having negative consequences for the quality of natural resources. Unwanted effects include pollution from such inputs as nitrate fertilizers, aesthetic damage caused by practices such as field enlargement and intensive stocking, and highly artificial methods of livestock husbandry. Simple market support cannot deal satisfactorily with these problems and may even contribute to them despite environmental and animal-welfare regulations

while set-aside schemes are incapable of addressing the complexity of the issue (European Commission, 1994a, p. 29). It follows that, just as there is a relationship between CAP surpluses and hunger in the world, there is also a relationship between CAP surpluses and increasing environmental deterioration. The CAP subsidized system fosters concentration in large farm holdings which can compete internationally only through intensive, that is, polluting, production methods. Small farmers, to compete and survive, are dragged along.

Agriculture plays an important role also in soil degradation, as shown by table 7.14, which refers to both Europe and the former USSR.

If overgrazing and deforestation are seen as an effect of unsustainable agriculture, then this latter is responsible, directly or indirectly, for 91 per cent of soil degradation. Agriculture is in a strict sense responsible for soil

Table 7.14   Causes of soil degradation (%)

Industry	9
Agriculture	29
Overgrazing	23
Deforestation	39

Source: Friends of the Earth Europe, 1995, p. 62.

degradation because of 'detrimental land use practices as the unsuitable application of fertilizers, monocultures or the reduction in fallow periods, as well as to the cultivation of slopes and mountain sides without suitable precautions' (Friends of the Earth Europe, 1995, p. 62). As for industrial practices, they contribute to soil degradation through the accumulation of waste material as a result of industrial concentration (Friends of the Earth Europe, 1995, p. 62).

Further, agriculture has also become a major threat to forestry through the ammonia contained in agricultural inputs. This, added to other types of airborne pollution deriving from traffic, power plants and industry, as well as to modern practices in forestry management (monoculture of fast-growing trees; the introduction of non-indigenous species such as eucalyptus which endanger the water balance because of high water requirements; clear felling, etc.) have lead to deforestation:[21] one quarter of all European forests have been hit by 25 per cent defoliation. But perhaps even more alarming is the threat to biological diversity. There 'are at least ten insect species associated with each plant species, a wide variety of soil organisms, macro and micro, as well as birds and other higher animals' (Friends of the Earth Europe, 1995, p. 72). As a result, in an afforested area a great deal of genetic diversity is lost relative to natural forests. The above-mentioned factors plus the building up of natural areas endanger the ability of forests to adapt to future stresses. 'And these stresses are foreseeable: ozone depletion will cause increased UV-B radiation, nitrogen input from traffic and agriculture is twenty times above capacity levels, and climate change will increase temperature and evaporation', change rainfall patterns, and pro-long periods of drought (Friends of the Earth Europe, 1995, pp. 72–3).

In short, the deterioration of the European environment caused by agricultural policies includes water, soil and air quality, biodiversity, land-scape and natural habitats. Moreover, a further important aspect which is only mentioned here is that intense production methods rely on the use of chemicals in plant production and on the use of hormones in animal production. Owing to increased public concern over the environmental and health consequences of these methods, the CAP has mobilized four categories of policy measures.[22]

(1) *Price support measures.* Basically, this means lower agricultural prices. The assumption is that this (a) will reduce output, and thus also plant pro-tection inputs and fertilizers, and (b) will encourage 'more extensive farming systems' which will reduce 'the negative environmental consequences of

farming activities' (Brouwer and van Berkum, 1996, p. 6). These conclusions are based on static assumptions which disregard the competitive
and dynamic nature of capitalist production. Lower output prices cause
more intensive competition rather than reduced supply. Increased competition is based basically on higher productivity and thus on more (rather
than on less) intensive farming systems. This means an increased, rather
than a decreased, use of agrochemicals. If lower prices decrease output,
they decrease the output of small producers by forcing them out of
business. But, owing to more intensive production methods, both the
productivity and total output of the larger farms will be increased and with
them also the use of agrochemicals. Moreover, 'farmers may change their
cropping plant towards products which require more intensive production
methods and higher dosages of agrochemicals (e.g. fruit, vegetables,
potatoes)' (Brouwer and van Berkum, 1996, p. 149). Finally, these measures
do not apply to products for which price support is negligible, as in
intensive livestock, which causes acute animal manure problems.

(2) *Structural policies.* These policies revolve around two major hinges.
The first is a special support scheme for the less-favoured agricultural areas
(LFAs). These are mountain areas, areas in danger of depopulation, or
areas affected by specific handicaps. Conditions for granting compensatory
allowances to farmers in these areas might include practices aimed at the
conservation of the countryside and at safeguarding the environment.
However, such 'conditions are set in national LFA schemes only to a very
limited extent, making the apparent benefits of this scheme for nature
conservation rather small' (Brouwer and van Berkum, 1996, p. 151). The
second hinge is the 1988 reform of the Structural Funds which integrated
the Guidance section of the EAGGF with the European Social Fund and
the European Regional Development Fund. Projects aiming at speeding up
the development of laggard regions, at encouraging rural development,
and at accelerating the adjustment of agricultural structures can be co-
financed by the Structural Funds. The 'ex-post and ex-ante evaluation with
special regard to the environmental impact of the programmes is central
in the approach' (Brouwer and van Berkum, 1996, p. 59). Here too, the
evaluation is sobering. Programmes financed by the Structural Funds
during the 1989–93 period 'focussed on stimulating economic activity
(including agriculture) rather than on safeguarding the environment'
(Brouver and van Berkum, 1996, p. 59).

(3) *Accompanying measures.* These aim at stimulating the adjustment of
the agricultural structure by measures other than structural ones. A first
scheme (Regulation 2080/92) aims at spurring afforestation as an alternative use of agricultural land. However, in 1996 only a small fraction of the
1.5 million hectares designated for afforestation in the 1993–9 period had
been actually added to forestry areas. 'The main reason is the rather low
compensation for planting costs, maintenance and income losses. Furthermore, the regulation and its compensation levels compete with measures
... for keeping an open landscape' (Brouwer and van Berkum, 1996,
p. 152). A second scheme aims at stimulating farmers aged over 55 to retire

in order to encourage the adjustment of agricultural areas. The scheme has an environmental requirement in that farming land transferred to other farmers as a result of early retirement has to be used in a way which serves the environment. This policy has been successful in terms of early retirements in France, Greece, Spain and Italy. In Germany its impact has been insignificant, while Luxembourg, the Netherlands and the United Kingdom have not developed such schemes.

(4) *Other policy measures.* These concern basically organic agriculture. The two most important EU regulations are 2092 of 1991 and 2078 of 1992.[23] Regulation 2092 (*Official Journal*, 1991) aims at safeguarding consumers against products falsely claiming to have been produced using organic methods or without the use of synthetic chemicals. This regulation defines organic production as that which maintains or increases fertility and biological activity by (a) cultivation of legumes, green manures or deep-rooting plants in an appropriate multiannual rotation programme and (b) incorporation in the soil of organic material, composted or not. Moreover, pests, diseases and weeds must be controlled by a combination of a choice of appropriate species and varieties, appropriate rotation programme, mechanical cultivation procedures, protection of natural enemies of pests and flame weeding. All stages of production and marketing should be subject to inspection. This regulation, thus, does not actively facilitate organic production but only protects this sector against unfair competition from cheaper, because non-organically produced, labels.

The second regulation, No. 2078 (*Official Journal*, 1992), takes a more active line. It openly states that the requirements of environmental protection are an integral part of the Common Agricultural Policy and aims at compensating farmers for any income losses caused by reductions in output and/or increases in costs as a result of biological farming and for the part they play in improving the environment. It institutes a Community aid scheme financed partly by member states and partly by the Guarantee section of the EAGGF. It specifies the nature and the amounts of the annual premium to be paid to farmers who undertake, among other things, (a) to reduce substantially their use of fertilizers and/or plant protection products, or to keep to the reductions already made, or to introduce or continue with organic farming methods; (b) to use other farming practices compatible with the requirements of protection of the environment and natural resources; and (c) to set aside farmland for at least twenty years with a view to its use for purposes connected with the environment, in particular for the establishment of biotype reserves or natural parks or for the protection of hydrological systems.

Available data do not yet allow an assessment of these regulations. The fact that, in 1993, the area under organic cultivation was only 0.3 per cent of the EU12 total agricultural area (Brouwer and van Berkum, 1996, p. 153) cannot be used to assess negatively the efficacy of two regulations issued only one year and two years earlier. It can, however, be safely predicted that the impact of these regulations has been extremely modest, given that financial assistance for them over the five-year period ending in 1997 was estimated in 1996 to 'represent well less than one per cent of total agricultural assistance' (Tobey and Smets, 1996, p. 79). Very likely, biological farming will gain a greater role only if consumer demand increases in spite of higher prices. But, whatever beneficial effects biological farming can have on the environment, they will be more than counterbalanced by other 'market oriented or structural' EU policies (Venneman and Gerritsen, 1994, p. 118), like the trans-European networks. The development of transport as well as the greater use of energy following from this policy will have serious consequences for the European environment. The Cohesion Fund contributes to this contradictory policy (see above).

To sum up, EU agricultural policy measures seem to give little hope. But it is often submitted that environmental degradation of agricultural land can be alleviated also through less specifically agricultural measures. The most commonly mentioned are marketable emission permits and the eco-tax. Both can be regarded as concrete applications of the PPP.

(1) *Marketable emission permits.* These are issued by a national authority and allow the owners to discharge a certain quantity of waste. The purchasers pay a certain price and can either use their permits or sell them. In this way, a market for permits is established. The reasoning is that those who need these permit more will be willing to pay a higher price, thus leading to a rational allocation of these permits. However, there are at least three criticisms which can be raised against this scheme. First, even within the theoretical frame (the neo-classical theory) within which this proposal is advanced, the rationality of market distribution depends on a large number of purchasers and sellers in a market in which initial endowments are disregarded. This is obviously not the case here. Put differently, those who purchase these permits are not necessarily those who need them most but those who can afford to pay a higher price. Second, even if permits were rationally distributed (in terms of demand and supply), the distribution of pollution arising from them would not necessarily be the less damaging for the environment. And third, the intractable question arises concerning not only the quantification of, but also whether it is at all morally acceptable to attach a price tag to, the right to destroy life species and to endanger the reproduction of our natural habitat. The price of emission permits should be infinite and attention should be turned to alternative, non-polluting and environmentally friendly production systems.

(2) *Eco-taxes.* These aim at punishing unsustainable uses of natural resources while providing at the same time new opportunities for jobs. The idea is based on a transfer of income from environmentally undesirable activities to the state (or to European institutions) and from there to those sectors which are environmentally desirable. It is also usually stressed that tax neutrality should be guaranteed so that a certain amount of environmental taxes should be offset by an equal amount of tax reductions for the desirable sectors, including environmental protection activities. The issue is too complex to be dealt with in satisfactory detail here. Only a few remarks will have to suffice. Nowadays, the greatest source of environmental pollu-

tion is the car. Its negative effects could be countered by discouraging both its production and its consumption (use). The former case is easily disposed of. If taxes, subsidies or any other form of state interference stood in the way, auto producers would move to other regions or countries whose governments did not pose those obstacles to their activity. A limited application of eco-taxes is possible but only inasmuch as it does not significantly alter the cost/price system upon which profitability within the context of international competition is based. This type of eco-tax might work only if equally applied on a world scale – a clearly unrealistic hypothesis.

But the greatest source of pollution derives from the use, rather than the production, of cars. If one disregards the specific capitalist social relations both of production and of consumption, it would seem plausible to discourage the use of cars and to encourage alternative (public) systems of transportation. But once those relations are taken into account, it becomes clear that the shift from private to public transportation systems implies a reduction in the production of automobiles and thus a major societal change affecting not only millions of jobs in the auto industry, but also the oil industry, road construction, and so on. There have been powerful economic interests behind 'auto-mobility' from the very beginning, basically the auto-oil lobby. These same interests are as powerful nowadays as at the beginning of the car era. The change to public transportation would necessitate a major shift in inter-capitalist economic and political power relations, something which no government or European institution either wants or is able to carry out. It is for this reason that an eco-tax discouraging the use of cars cannot alter significantly the private transportation system and thus the ecological damage caused by it. The same holds for technological fixes such as catalytic convertors and noise barriers on highways. Inasmuch as these and other similar 'remedies' are meant to improve capitalism's abysmal ecological record by correcting the 'imperfect' functioning of the market, no significant improvement can be expected. Such measures are socially and ecologically relevant only if placed within the context of a wider project of societal change.

Another example of the limits of technical solutions which are not part of a wider and radical approach to both hunger and environmental destruction is provided by the green revolution. Originally, genetically engineered varieties of cereals promised large yield increases and seemed to keep that promise. However, upon closer inspection, it was seen that these new varieties are more vulnerable to a large number of pests and diseases. This led to an increase in the use of fertilizers and pesticides. Moreover, only rich farmers could afford these fertilizers and pesticides (which are of course produced in the developed world) so that poor farmers became poorer and rich farmers richer. The same applies to the access to water, given that the new seeds depend on careful irrigation. This too is financially accessible only to richer and greater farms. Also, the greater farms introduce new, labour-saving machinery, thus increasing unemployment. And finally, the poor derived no gain from increased yields since they lacked the necessary purchasing power.

To conclude, in a report published in 1992, the European Parliament evaluated the Common Agricultural Policy as follows:

> the system has become increasingly complex and the changes made [over the years] have gradually deprived it of any transparency . . . very few people, with the exception of specialists in the Commission, in the administration of the member states and in the private sector, understand it entirely. (European Parliament, 1992, pp. 50–1)

It is true that considerable patience and dedication are needed in order to penetrate the technical aspects of this system. But it is equally true that an understanding of these features is a necessary condition if one aims at uncovering the power relations and the economic interests which have shaped the European agricultural policy. In its turn, knowledge of these relations and interests is an indispensable prerequisite in order to reveal the relation between this policy, on the one hand, and hunger and environmental degradation, on the other.

The market-oriented economic and fiscal measures, aimed at reducing the effects of the CAP on pollution and hunger, ignore that these negative outcomes are an expression of a complex web of socio-economic relations and that the technical measures proposed are only an expression of these relations. It is these latter, including market relations, which must be changed if both pollution and hunger are to be permanently eradicated. Market-oriented measures provide at most temporary and partial solutions, thus leaving the essence of the problem untouched. Familiarity with the CAP, then, should cease to be the exclusive domain of 'very few people'. Given that it affects not only our natural habitat but also the physical survival of millions around the world, a proper understanding of this policy should be extended to the largest possible number of people as a first step towards its radical reform and the democratization of its decision-making process.

Social Policies

8.1 Destitution Amidst Wealth

Speaking, in June 1997, on poverty in Europe at a news conference with Chancellor Helmut Kohl of Germany, President Jacques Chirac of France said, 'Something isn't right here.' Neither he, nor other European politicians, nor for that matter the economic profession, has yet to provide an answer as to what that 'something' precisely is. The preceding chapters have argued that it is the capitalist nature itself of the EU and its own concomitant economic policies which generate cyclical unemployment as well as poverty, environmental destruction and all the other social problems discussed in the preceding chapters. This is not a feature specific to the European Union. Rather, these as well as other social plights spring directly from the capitalist system of production and appropriation of value and surplus value. A few figures will exemplify the apocalyptic dimensions reached by these problems.

The 1998 and 1999 *Human Development Reports* show in vivid details what this means.

> Globally, the 20% of the world's people in the highest-income countries account for 86% of total private consumption expenditures – the poorest 20% a minuscule 1.3%.... Well over a billion people are deprived of the basic consumption needs. Of the 4.4 billion people in developing countries nearly three-fifths lack basic sanitation. Almost a third have no access to clean water. A quarter do not have adequate housing. A fifth have no access to modern health services. A fifth of children do not attend school to grade five. About a fifth do not have enough dietary energy and proteins.... Worldwide, 2 billion people are anemic, including 55 million in industrial countries. (United Nations Development Programme [UNDP], 1998, p. 2)

In 1996, worldwide unemployment affected one billion people, nearly one third of the global workforce (International Labour Organisation, 1996). 'About 17 million people in developing countries die each year from such curable infectious and parasitic diseases as diarrhea, measles, malaria and tuberculosis' (UNDP, 1998, p. 50).

These problems are not confined to the dependent countries (the so-called 'underdeveloped' or 'developing' countries). In the OECD countries,

more than 100 million people are-income poor. . . . At least 37 million people
are without a job. . . . Unemployment among youth (age 15–24) has reached
staggering heights, with 32% of young women and 22% of young men in
France unemployed, 39% and 30 per cent in Italy and 49% and 36% in
Spain. . . . Nearly 200 million people are not expected to survive to age
60. . . . More than 100 million are homeless, a shockingly high number amid
the affluence. (UNDP, 1998, p. 27)

In industrial countries, too, human poverty and exclusion are hidden among
statistics of success, revealing enormous disparities within countries . . . one
person in eight of the richest countries in the world is affected by some
aspect of human poverty: long-term unemployment, a life shorter than 60
years, an income below the national poverty line or a lack of the literacy
needed to cope in society. (UNDP 1999, p. 28)

The differences between the imperialist centre and the dominated bloc
are mind-boggling.

Per capita private consumption expenditure is $15,910 (1995 prices) in
industrial countries (excluding Eastern Europe and the CIS) but $275 in
South Asia and $340 in Sub-Saharan Africa. . . . Industrial countries, with
15% of the world population, account for 76% of global consumption
expenditure. (UNDP, 1999, p. 50)

Also, 'the top fifth of the world's people in the richest countries enjoy 82%
of the expanding export trade and 68% of foreign direct investments – the
bottom fifth, barely more than 1%' (UNDP, 1999, p. 31). And 'AIDS is now
a poor people's epidemic, with 95% of all HIV-infected people in developing countries' (UNDP, 1999, p. 42).

Perhaps the necessarily unequal development in a capitalist world and
the consequent plight of the great majority of its inhabitants is most vividly
and disturbingly summarized by the following figures: in 1997, the 225
richest people had 'a combined wealth of over $1 trillion, equal to the
annual income of the poorest 47% of the world's people (2.5 billion)'
(UNDP, 1998, p. 30). 'The assets of the 3 richest people are more than the
combined GNP of all least developed countries' (UNDP, 1999, p. 38). The
obscenity behind such figures is brought to the fore even more vividly if it
is considered that

It is estimated that the additional cost of achieving and maintaining universal
access to basic education for all, basic health care for all, reproductive health
care for women, adequate food for all and safe water and sanitation for all is
roughly $40 billion a year. This is less than 4% of the combined wealth of
the 225 richest people in the world. (UNDP, 1998, p. 30)

To ensure universal access to primary education $7–8bn would be sufficient
(UNDP, 1999, p. 38). Notice that $40 billion are also '0.1 per cent of world

income, barely more than a rounding error' (UNDP 1999, p. 37). Donor countries allocate only 2.5 per cent of their total GNP to development cooperation, and even these crumbs are given to foster the donor countries' own interests, as explained in chapter 6.

Faced by this gigantic failure, the economics profession can only come up with one monotonous prescription: more capitalist 'development' will bring generalized cornucopia to all those who have 'not yet' profited by it. The previous chapters have shown the theoretical fallacy of this thesis, which is substantiated by the following figures. 'No fewer than 100 countries – all developing or in transition – have experienced serious economic decline over the past three decades. As a result per capita income in these 100 countries is lower than it was 10, 15, 20, even 30 years ago' (UNDP, 1998, p. 37). 'In 1960 the 20% of the world's people in the richest countries had 30 times the income of the poorest 20% – in 1999, 74 times as much. This continues the trend of nearly two centuries' (UNDP, 1999, p. 36). 'The distance between the richest and poorest country was about 3 to 1 in 1820, 11 to 1 in 1913, 35 to 1 in 1950, 44 to 1 in 1973 and 72 to 1 in 1992. More amazing is that the British in 1820 had an income about 6 times that of the Ethiopians in 1992!' (UNDP, 1999, p. 38).

The same causes behind this abysmal human degradation are also the origin of a galloping environmental degradation. But, here too, it is the rich countries which cause, and the poor countries which bear the consequences of, this degradation.

Some 60% of carbon dioxide emissions come from the industrial countries. But . . . the impact will fall largely on the developing countries. Bangladesh, for example, will lose huge areas of land if global warming leads to rising sea levels. . . . There could also be a serious threat to the very existence of the Maldive Islands. . . . Poor countries cannot afford to build extensive walls – and poor people cannot afford to pay for increasingly scarce water and productive agricultural land. (UNDP, 1998, p. 57)

All over the world, poor people generally live nearest to dirty factories, busy roads and waste dumps. (UNDP, 1998, p. 66)

And, as if all this were not enough, poor countries can become dumping grounds for industrial-country waste (UNDP, 1998, p. 73).

Europe does not fare any better as far as skewed income distribution goes. In May 1977, 17 per cent of the EU population, or 57 million Europeans, lived in poor households (a measure of poverty and deprivation), with Portugal scoring worst (29 per cent) and Denmark scoring best (9 per cent). Income inequality is increasing due to precarious jobs for wage earners at one end of the revenue scale and capital gains and tax evasion at the other end. Even the most prosperous country, Germany, does not escape the economic malaise and mounting disparities. Nearly half a million jobs were lost from October 1996 to October 1997, the number of welfare recipients increased by 9.1 per cent in 1995, and in

Frankfurt, the home of the ECB, one in five residents has fallen below the poverty threshold. On the other hand, in 1993, when German unemployment was rising, the number of millionaire households increased by 24 per cent. In 1994 about 10 per cent of the population held about 50 per cent of the country's assets (Vinocour, 1997a, 1997b).

As for France, between 14 and 20 per cent of national wealth is in the hands of 1 per cent of the population. At the same time, soup kitchens, which had served 31 million meals in 1992–3, served 61 million in 1996–7. 'From 1993 to 1996, the number of households receiving the basic welfare subsistence payment ... grew by 27 per cent. Between 1989 and 1994, revenues for top earners grew by 17 per cent while that of the bottom half of the households grew by only 3 per cent.' As for the United Kingdom, a survey by Income Data Services shows that 'heads of major companies had average earnings last year [1996] of £570,000 ... a rise of 11.5 per cent, or more than double the national individual revenue increase' (Vinocour, 1997a). The reasons for these enormous and mounting disparities within the EU are

> evident. At the lower end of the income scale, part-time jobs, short-term contracts, and changing requirements in jobs qualifications have combined with general downsizing to push towards poverty large numbers of people with limited qualifications. ... At the higher end, more Europeans [become] relatively rich. (Vinocour, 1997a)

A commonly submitted thesis is that technological innovations (TIs) bring about more skilled and qualified jobs and better working conditions. Reality is less glamorous. TI, while possibly leading to more enjoyable jobs for very limited privileged strata of the working class, also lead to new forms of labour's subordination to capital. For example, the computer is a great step forward in human productivity. It also greatly increases labour's control by capital. But even more dangerous are the great strides forwards of genetic engineering. This, on the one hand, alleviates human suffering but, on the other, is already creating new forms of life which reflect the capitalist division of labour and are functional for profit making. One aspect of capital's dream is that of moulding life itself in its own likeness.[1]

But new forms of labour's oppression should not hide the fact that the old forms are alive and well. The predicament which the mixture of TIs, neo-liberalist policies and the weakness of the Left have brought to Europe's labour has been quantified by the Dublin-based European Foundation for the Improvement of Living and Working Conditions (1997). Computers have become an important feature of work (38 per cent of workers use computers). Has this brought about an improvement in labour's working conditions? While EU levels of unemployment reach an average of 11.5 per cent, half of Europe's employed workers work for more that forty hours a week and almost a quarter more than forty-five hours. On the other hand, the proportion of part-time workers is high: 14 per cent work less than thirty hours per week and most of them are women.

Working hours are also characterized by their dispersion (52 per cent of workers work at least one Saturday per month; 29 per cent at least one Sunday; and 21 per cent at night, at least occasionally) and by their irregularity (33 per cent have irregular hours and 13 per cent do shift work).

The proportion of workers affected by stressful physical environments (noise, polluted air, heat, cold, vibrations) and having to carry heavy loads is almost a third, while 40 per cent have to work in painful and tiring positions. These high proportions were basically the same in 1996 as they were in 1991, at the time of a similar survey carried out by the same Foundation. On the other hand, the pace of work had increased sharply between 1991 and 1996. In 1996 more than half of workers were exposed to high speed and tight deadlines. Health problems increase with hours worked. About 30 per cent of the workers questioned believed that their work affected their health. Backache, stress and muscular pain in arms and legs are the most common work-related health problems. Re-skilling is a myth. Thirty-seven per cent of workers must perform short repetitive tasks, for 45 per cent there is no system of task rotation, and the work of 57 per cent involves repetitive hand or arm movement. No wonder that almost a quarter of all workers claim to have been absent from work for work-related health reasons in the past twelve months. Absenteeism increases significantly with the arduousness of work (multiplied by three for painful or tiring positions and by two for repetitive movements). Finally, violence at work is a major problem. Twelve million workers are subjected to psychological violence, six million to physical violence, and three million to sexual harassment.[2]

In short, this is capital's Europe, not labour's Europe. How has the European Union tried to alleviate this predicament? To answer this question is to discuss the Union's social policy.

8.2 The Union's Social Policy

Social policy has been one of the EC objectives from its very beginning, even though originally it played a very subordinate role. The basic stages in the development of the EU social policy are: the Rome Treaty, which founded the European Social Fund; the Single European Act, which introduced qualified majority voting in some social areas; the 1989 Strasbourg Summit, which adopted the Social Charter, or the Community Charter of Fundamental Social Rights of Workers; and a new Action Programme for the 1995-7 period, presented by the Commission in April 1995.

Let us consider these stages in some detail. Article 117 of the EEC Treaty recognizes the need both to improve and to harmonize the working conditions and standard of living for workers. Article 118 identifies the following areas of cooperation in the social field: (a) employment; (b) labour law and working conditions; (c) vocational training; (d) social security; (e) prevention of occupational hazards; (f) occupational hygiene;

and (g) the right of association and collective bargaining between employers and workers. These intentions are weakened by article 118a, according to which the Council's directives imposing minimum requirements should not 'hold back the creation and development of small and medium-sized undertakings'. Article 119 upholds the principle of equal pay for equal work for men and women. Finally, articles 123 to 125 establish the European Social Fund. Its purpose is to facilitate workers' employment, increase their geographical and occupational mobility, and foster vocational training and retraining.

These aims reflect the social context of the first years of EU social policy. The 1950s and 1960s were a period of vigorous economic development. Under these circumstances, economic growth was held back by relative labour shortages, relative labour immobility and lack of qualified personnel. Moreover, it was assumed that the relatively backward member states would catch up with the more advanced ones and that this process would lead to both economic and social convergence. Relatively underdeveloped countries would gain sufficient economic means to reduce their social disparities with the more advanced countries without any substantial EC intervention. European capital did not need any sizeable supra-national social policy at that time because those disparities were not perceived as being a threat to the European (Economic) Community. Perhaps even more importantly, these were years of political and ideological domination of capital over labour. This explains the modest role initially ascribed to the European Social Fund.

Towards the end of the 1960s the EC approach changed. The basic reason was the great wave of workers' militancy and egalitarian aspirations which exploded in the late 1960s and continued up to the mid-1970s. These great social movements modified the power relations between capital and labour in favour of the latter. This, in its turn, forced the EC to replace its low-key approach to social policy with a more interventionist one. In the 1972 Paris Summit it was decided to establish a regional policy (the ERDF, see below) alongside the European Social Fund. Also, the Commission was instructed to draw up a Social Action Programme, which came into effect in 1974. This spurred a flurry of new directives concerning the right of information for workers whose firms were considering redundancies and equal access for women to vocational training and social security.

However, the second half of the mid-1970s saw a downturn in the world economy and a corresponding fall in labour's, women's, students' and other social sectors' militancy. This changed the EC countries' attitude towards social policy. 'The richer states were unwilling to pay for EC policies which would mainly benefit the poorer states, and the poorer states were unwilling to agree to EC policies that they were unable to pay for themselves' (Purdy and Devine, 1994, p. 288). Therefore, by the time these directives 'were implemented, the economic and political context had changed radically, and in the end the high hopes which had been vested in the Social Action Programme were largely disappointed' (Purdey and Devine, 1994, p. 287).

But this situation was bound to change. In the 1980s EU social policy gained renewed attention, but now for a different reason. In 1984, Jacques Delors was elected president of the Commission. Delors is usually given the credit for having revitalized social policy as if this were just a matter of personal preferences. In reality, he interpreted the concern of Europe's more dynamic capital for mounting unemployment and the associated economic and social problems which could arise from it. This new turn in EU social policy occurred under the aegis of capital, that is, under conditions of capital's strength and labour's weakness. Therefore, EU social policy was bound to have a different class content.

This revived interest in social policy resulted first in the Community Charter of the Fundamental Social Rights of Workers, which was signed by all member states except the United Kingdom. This was 'purely declaratory and had no legal force' (Purdy and Devine, 1994, p. 283). The Community Charter formed the basis of the Social Chapter of the Maastricht Treaty. At the insistence of the UK, the Social Chapter was not incorporated in the Treaty but was adopted as Protocol No. 14. Consequently, if the UK does not want to participate in matters covered by the Social Chapter, decisions are taken by the other member states and are binding only for them. The Social Chapter mentions only three of the aims of article 117, that is, employment, labour law and working conditions, and social security, but adds to them the 'dialogue between management and labour' and 'the development of human resources with a view to lasting employment'. Here too we can see how capital's preoccupations shape the EC's perception.

In times of high unemployment and social tensions, emphasis tends to be placed not only on the creation of jobs, the 'highest priority' according to the 1994 Commission's White Paper (European Commission, 1994b), but also on both the development of human resources and social dialogue as a means to reduce social confrontation. Therefore, in the field of labour relations, the focus shifts from the right of association and collective bargaining in the late 1960s and early 1970s to the dialogue between management and labour in the 1990s. Social dialogue is institutionalized in the Maastricht Treaty, article 118b, which stipulates that the 'Commission shall endeavour to develop the dialogue between management and labour at European level'. The dialogue between management and labour is also one of the major features of the 1995–7 Action Programme, together with objectives such as promoting employment and vocational training, facilitating inter-member states labour mobility, establishing minimum requirements, combating racism, and so on.

To endow the Union with that greater legislative power which it needs to deal flexibly with the above-mentioned social problems, the Social Chapter empowers member states to decide by majority voting on matters such as health and safety in the workplace, working conditions, information and consultation of employees, equal employment opportunities for men and women, and integration of the unemployed into working life. These are relatively unimportant areas for capital. Unanimity is required for more critical matters such as social security, the protection of workers upon termination of an employment contract, or the employment conditions of citizens from other member states. Other areas, the really vital ones for capital, such as pay, freedom of association, the right to strike and the right to impose lock-outs, remain an exclusive matter for the member states. Clearly, the Union is excluded from influencing the most significant aspects of capital/labour relations and can decide by majority voting only on the less substantial of these aspects. Even disregarding the overpowering influence capital has on the design and implementation of the Union's laws (see chapter 1.4), this limited legislative scope is a clear indication of the restricted scope the Union grants social policies. Let us now consider which instruments the Union has developed to carry them out.

8.3 The Poverty of Redistribution

Social policies are synonymous with redistribution policies. To this end, the Union needs to appropriate resources. The vehicle through which resources are appropriated and then redistributed (spent) is the budget.[3] The first point to be mentioned is that the budget is characterized both by the prohibition on borrowing and by its limited size. The Rome Treaty establishes the principle of balanced budget. As Bladen-Hovell and Symons (1994) point out, 'subsequent amendments have only served to relax the restriction on borrowing for a limited range of specific purposes – to support the balance of payments and to promote investment within the EC' (p. 368). This is a considerable limit on the scale of the Union's activities. This restriction is further exacerbated by the size of the budget, which accounts for some 1.2 per cent of the Union's GDP as opposed to a much higher average for the member states. Consider the actual size of the budget. The EU expenditures are given in table 8.1.[4]

Agriculture is still the greatest expenditure item. The Guarantee section of the European Agricultural Guidance and Guarantee Fund (EAGGF) (see chapter 7) still accounts for 47.8 per cent of the Union's financial

Table 8.1 Estimated expenditures, 1998 (ECU m) and 1999 (Euro m)

	1998		1999	
EAGGF	40,937	(49.0)	40,940	(47.8)
Structural operations	28,595	(34.2)	30,658	(35.9)
Research and development	2,999	(3.6)	2,999	(3.5)
External action	4,508	(5.4)	4,275	(5.0)
Other	6,490	(7.8)	6,685	(7.8)
Total	83,529	(100.0)	85,557	(100.0)

Note: Figures in parentheses are percentages.

Source: European Commission, 1998, pp. 8–12; European Commission, 1999, pp. 8–12.

commitments in 1999, down from 59 per cent in 1988. Structural operations, that is, the European social policy, have risen from 18.5 per cent in 1988 to close to 36 per cent in 1999. This item encompasses the European Social Fund (ESF), the European Regional Development Fund (ERDF), the Guidance section of the EAGGF, the Financial Instrument for Fisheries Guidance and the Cohesion Fund. The Union's research policy is aimed at complementing that of the individual member states (see chapter 4). It focuses on a small number of clearly defined sectors, such as information and communication technology, industrial technologies, bio-technologies, energy, environment and health. External action encompasses funds for the economic restructuring of the CEEC, for non-member Mediterranean countries participating in the large Euro-Mediterranean area, for cooperation with Latin American and Asian countries, for the new independent states of the former Soviet Union, and for food and humanitarian aid. In addition, there is a myriad of other policies which are funded through the budget.

Let us now consider the revenue side. The original system of contributions relied upon *direct contributions* from member states, each country contributing different percentages according to its size. This agreement was codified by article 200 of the Rome Treaty. France, West Germany and Italy paid the larger contributions, Belgium and the Netherlands paid less, and Luxembourg paid very little. The contributions varied also relative to the different categories of expenditure, such as the EAGGF, ESF and the ERDF. The principle informing this system was that actual payments should reflect differences in ability to pay. Moreover, France and West Germany contributed relatively more to the EDF – France because of the weight its former colonies had in the Community's aid burden, and West Germany because of the economic advantages it was expected to reap from its access to those territories.

But the Rome Treaty provided also for a different system of contributions. Article 201 envisaged the gradual replacement of direct contributions by the Community's *own resources*, that is, resources of the Community by right. Consequently, in 1970 a system of own resources was introduced. The Six agreed that own resources should come from the proceeds of the common external tariff (first resource), from agricultural import levies (second resource), and from value added tax, or VAT (third resource). Member states could retain 10 per cent of the common external tariff and of agricultural levies for collection costs and had to pay the rest to Brussels. As for VAT, member states had to pay up to 1 per cent of it to the Community.

As the 1970s progressed, this system came under strain. On the one hand, the revenues from the first and second resource fell due to the gradual dismantling of tariffs resulting from the GATT negotiations (see chapter 6) and from the fact that the EC was becoming increasingly self-sufficient in agricultural production. On the other hand, VAT revenues stagnated due to the decreasing share of consumer expenditure in the member states' GNPs. This at a time when the EC's spending needs were increasing. Therefore, it was agreed at the Fountainebleau Summit of 1984 that the VAT rate should be raised to 1.4 per cent. As it became apparent that this measure too was not sufficient, it was decided in 1988 to introduce a fourth resource calculated in relation to the GNP of each member state. The uniform rate of the fourth resource is determined each year. For example, in 1992 it was 0.17 per cent of each member state's GNP. The growth of the own resources was limited to 1.2 per cent of the EU's aggregate GNP in 1996, rising to 1.27 per cent in 1999. The EU is now totally dependent on the system of own resources. The estimated revenues for 1998 and 1999 are given in table 8.2. (The figures for the actual revenues are not yet available at the time of writing.)

Table 8.2   Estimated revenues, 1998 (ECU m) and 1999 (Euro m)

	1998		1999	
Agricultural duties and sugar levies	1,671	(2.0)	1,921	(2.2)
Customs duties	11,144	(13.3)	11,894	(13.9)
VAT	34,135	(40.9)	30,374	(35.5)
Fourth resource	35,908	(43.0)	39,260	(45.9)
Surpluses available from previous year	44	(0.0)	1,478	(1.7)
Miscellaneous	628	(0.8)	631	(0.7)
Total	83,529	(100.0)	85,558	(100.0)

Note: Figures in parentheses are percentages.

Source: European Commission, 1998, p. 23 and European Commission, 1999, p. 23.

Let us now focus on the budget as a redistributive tool. First, a breakdown of contributions from, and payments to, countries shows that in 1994 Germany and the UK were the biggest net contributors (ECU 13bn and ECU 5bn respectively), followed by France, the Netherlands and Italy, and that Spain, Greece, Portugal and Ireland were the biggest net receivers (Court of Auditors, 1995, pp. 10, 17).[5] The reason why the bigger countries are net contributors has nothing to do with their greater 'sense of responsibility'. Rather, after what has been said in the preceding chapters, it should be clear that the advantage of their being net contributors is that of keeping a system going which allows their most advanced capital to appropriate international surplus value. But, of course, this does not preclude their governments from complaining about this 'unfair treatment'.

Second, the previous chapters have argued that redistribution cannot permanently cancel those social problems which have their roots in the mode of production. But redistribution policies can and do make a difference in the working class's conditions of life. What, then, is the Union's record in this respect? It has already been mentioned that, given the principle of budget balance, the means to be redistributed through the budget are severely limited. Moreover, about half of these funds are spent to support farmers (see table 8.1 above) and profit mainly big agricultural enterprises (see chapter 7). Therefore, what is distributed to Europe's collective labour is only a fraction of a little more than 1 per cent of the Union's GNP. A conclusion follows inescapably: redistribution policies not only are greatly limited but also profit capital more than labour. Labour gets the crumbs back after having provided the whole meal.

Let us now consider the budget's main channels of redistribution. They are the European Social Fund and the European Regional Development Fund.

8.4 Employment Policies

The instrument explicitly aimed at combating unemployment in its different aspects (long-term unemployment, youth unemployment, etc.) is the European Social Fund (ESF). This Fund is aimed at fostering 'investment in human resources, the fight against unemployment and the working of the labour market' (European Commission, 1994b, p. 26). 'By way of example, the ESF could co-finance pre-training, counseling, upgrading of basic skills, community employment or work experience, job search assistance, and support for promoting geographical and career mobility' (European Commission, 1995, p. 6).[6] Since money talks more than words, let us gauge the EU commitment to employment polices by relating the Euros allotted to the ESF both to the EU budget and to the EU GNP. In 1999, still in the midst of a long period of high unemployment, the ESF was allotted Euro 9.6bn out of total payment appropriations of Euro 85.6bn. This is a meager 8.2 per cent of the EU budget and a non-existent 0.08 per cent of its GNP.

However, the ESF is not the only source of moneys meant to foster employment. Since 1989, the four structural funds, that is, the EAGGF guidance (see chapter 7), the ESF, the FIFG[7] and the ERDF (see further down), have been given six common objectives. Objective 1 aims at promoting the development and structural adjustment of regions whose development is lagging behind, that is, regions with a per capita GDP lower than 75 per cent of the EU average. They comprise the Mediterranean South, Ireland and the former East Germany. These regions comprise 22 per cent of the total EU population. The goal of objective 2 is the conversion of regions seriously affected by industrial decline. Objective 3 concerns combating long-term unemployment and facilitating the integration into working life of young people and the unemployed. The intent of objective 4 is to facilitate the adaptation of workers to industrial changes and changes in production systems. Objective 5 is split into objective 5A, that is, the adjustment of agricultural structures deriving from the reform of the CAP, and objective 5B, that is, the promotion of the development of rural areas. Finally, the purpose of objective 6 is the promotion of the development of regions with an extremely low population density. The 1999 figures are as shown in table 8.3.

Table 8.3 Structural funds by objective, 1999 (Euro m)

Objective	EAGGF guidance	FIFG	ERDF	ESF	Total
1	2,573	473	11,580	5,378	20,004
2			2,942	673	3,615
3				2,190	2,190
4				914	914
5a	1,539	333			1,872
5b	1,008		1,013	388	2,359
6	53	2	119	68	242
Total	5,173	808	15,654	9,611	31,196

Source: European Commission, 1999, p. 19.

Given the aims of these six objectives, only objectives 3 and 4 can be considered to foster exclusively employment opportunities. They are allocated a meager Euro 3,104 million, that is, less than 10 per cent of total allocations. The aims of the other four objectives (90 per cent of total allocations) are such that both capital and labour profit from the structural funds. It is impossible to know in what measure the collective labourer gains from them. But even if the whole of the Euro 3.1bn were to benefit only labour, the extremely modest size of this sum reveals that the commitment to job creation policies is little more than verbal and cannot but have an extremely limited impact on employment creation.

But even if much greater sums were to be allocated to this aim, the cyclical occurrence of unemployment would be inevitable. Contrary to the neo-classical thesis, so-called 'market failures' (like unemployment, social differences, etc.) are the necessary outcome of capitalist accumulation and competition, and ultimately capitalist production relations. Capitalism neither is in nor tends towards equilibrium (see chapter 3). Redistribution policies aim at correcting some of these inequalities, inasmuch as these inequalities are perceived as being too sharp and potentially destabilizing. Ameliorations for labourers are not excluded but, inasmuch as they are not imposed by substantial social movements, are brought about only if functional for the interests of Europe's advanced capitals.

These interests shape not only EU social policy but also the notion of solidarity informing that policy, thus weakening that very notion upon which the collective labourer's strategy should be based (see 8.6 below). In its 1994 White Paper, the Commission states the need 'to build a new solidarity based on using productivity gains to create new jobs rather than increase incomes of those in employment' (European Commission, 1994b, p. 18). This, of course, is no new solidarity, it is the old-fashioned wage ceiling which is accepted by labourers in the hope that the correspondingly increased profits not only will be reinvested but also will be reinvested in the real rather than in the speculative sector and in labour-intensive rather than in capital-intensive production methods. Pending a guarantee that these conditions will be satisfied (and they are largely not satisfied in times of economic crises), the only certainty is lower wages.

The Commission also shows its 'solidarity' with the labourers of the dominated bloc:

> The EU recognizes that other regions may need to compete on the basis of lower labour costs, based on lower wages, longer hours and more difficult conditions, but it is not in the interests of international cooperation that the exploitation of workers should become an instrument of international competition. (European Commission, 1994b, p. 60)

This is little more than a call for the technologically less developed countries to give up competition on the basis of lower wages, which is the basic way those countries (capitals) can compete internationally. The Commission 'new solidarity' is the old-fashioned refrain which conjugates lower wages at home with higher wages outside the EU.

8.5 Regional Policies

Economic disparities exist both between and within states. They are 'not only substantial; they also show remarkable persistence over long periods of time. Poor regions tend to stay poor and rich regions tend to stay rich' (Armstrong et al., 1994, p. 174). Or, as Steinle argues,

> In general, top regions are stagnating relative to others ... in the less developed, mostly peripheral regions of Europe, there are no signs of catching up, with a few exceptions.... By contrast, there is plenty of movement in the regions mid-field. A vast number of regions are falling behind; others show clear signs of catching up. (quoted in Camagni, 1992, p. 351)[8]

Table 8.4 indicates the extent the problem had reached in 1990.

The European Regional Development Fund (ERDF) targets the reduction of regional disparities. Let us look again at the figures. The 1999

Table 8.4 Regional unemployment, 1990 (%)

Country	National average	Regional maximum	Regional minimum
Germany	5.2	10.4	3.0
Spain	16.1	24.1	12.4
Portugal	5.1	12.4	2.8
UK	6.3	15.7	3.9
Italy	10.2	21.7	3.4

Source: Armstrong et al., 1994, p. 173.

budget commits Euro 15.6bn for the ERDF. This is 18 per cent of the budget and 0.2 per cent of EU GNP. These figures, while approximately double those of the ESF, are far from being impressive. But the ERDF is not the only instrument of regional policy. While Euro 15.6bn were allocated to this fund in 1999, objectives 1, 2, 5 and 6, for a total of Euro 28.1bn, aim at fostering regional development (see table 8.3 above). This is 33 per cent of the budget and 90 per cent of the allocations for the structural funds. This money can benefit both capital and labour, as opposed to 10 per cent of these allocations which supposedly benefit only labour. Having put the figures in their proper class perspective, the question arises as to whether much bigger funds could bring about a more balanced regional development, irrespective of whom they benefit. Again, the answer is negative.

Regional studies have shown time and again, and observation supports these findings, that technologically advanced and economically powerful firms tend to concentrate in certain regions which then become high-growth areas. An extension of the analysis submitted in the preceding chapters to the regional case shows that high-growth regions appropriate resources from low-growth regions and that this results in the creation and maintenance of regional economic backwardness alongside economic growth. If the backward regions relate to the leading ones as 'colonies', they supply the latter with cheap labour power as well as possibly with cheap raw materials and means of subsistence. If they relate as 'dependent development' regions, they can also undergo substantial rates of accumulation while at the same time remaining dependent upon (surrendering surplus value to) the high-growth regions. But this comparison between different nations, on the one hand, and different regions within nations, on the other, does not carry the analysis far enough. For example, backward capitals (regions) reproduce their backwardness because they lose value through a mechanism and a level of exchange rates reflecting the interest of the more technologically advanced capitals (regions). That value cannot be reinvested in those regions, and underdevelopment is reproduced. This point is particularly relevant for regional (under)development in the European Union. Let us elaborate briefly on this.

We have seen that, as a general rule, technological leaders (nations) tend to revalue and technological laggards (nations) tend to devalue. This implies a transfer of value from the latter to the former. Similarly, backward regions must compete in the international market on the basis of over-valued exchange rates relative to their productivity level. In fact, national exchange rates are determined (if not exclusively, at least principally) by the trade flows of the great multinationals, that is, by the usually most efficient capital units. This holds in the case of flexible exchange rates. But this is the case also for fixed exchange rates, whose level is greatly influenced by the unofficial but very concrete political relations between the national governments (through the monetary authorities) and private and public economic interests. Inevitably, in these informal negotiations the great multinationals and the most efficient and export-oriented producers will have a greater say. The exchange rate level, then, will reflect these latter's interests rather than those of the less efficient enterprises clustered in that country's less developed regions.[9] If these regions were independent countries, they would devalue. Since they are not, they have to accept an exchange rate penalizing their external trade. Put differently, their *virtual exchange rate* is overvalued. Or, their *virtual trade balance* is in constant deficit (Camagni, 1992). In this indirect way, the advanced regions force the backward ones to lose value to foreign (rather than to national) competitors and thus to reproduce their situation of underdevelopment.

This negative process is magnified by the creation of the EMU. Chapter 4 above has argued that, in the decision-making process within the ECB, it is the economic weight of the most advanced capitals and countries, to begin with Germany and its oligopolies, which weight the most in the determination of the Euro's exchange rate level. This level will tend to be overvalued, as far as the less developed countries and regions are concerned, and this will multiply the negative impact upon them. The catching-up race will become even more biased. This by the way shows how reality belies the theory of comparative advantages. Once a head start has been gained, a cumulative process is set in motion which reinforces, rather than diminishes, regional (and other) differences. Of course, some underdeveloped regions can undergo development and some advanced regions can fall back in a state of backwardness. But this changes the map of underdevelopment without erasing it. The outcome of this process is well put by Camagni (1992):

> inefficient areas (in all possible sectors) are forced out of the competitive arena. . . . Their fate is desertification – in the case of high labour mobility – or huge unemployment and enlargement of the black, informal or even criminal economy – in the case of lower labour mobility. (p. 362)

These are only some of the mechanisms through which regional disparities are created and reproduced. However, beyond a certain level, regional divergences can become a hindrance to capitalist development. To add only two examples to the one mentioned above, infrastructures might become insufficient for the delivery of products, or for an efficient communication. Or, purchasing power in the backward regions might fall to a level insufficient to absorb production and might generate regional social tensions. If this is the case, and if the economic conjuncture allows it, national as well as regional policies are introduced. These take a variety of forms, like government grants and subsidies and other financial incentives to the private sector in regions with a high concentration of declining industries; public investments (sometimes compulsively located in the poorer regions, as in the case of state-owned industries in the Italian Mezzogiorno); regional employment programmes; training programmes;

the construction of infrastructures; measures aimed at increasing labour mobility (migration) from high unemployment regions, and so on. It is within this frame that EU regional policies can be best understood.

These general considerations should be placed within the context of the business cycle. As Armstrong et al. (1994) report, the European states have gone through three periods. In the first period, only two of the future EC member states had a regional policy: the UK and Italy (with its *Cassa per il Mezzogiorno*). In the second phase, from the 1950s to the early 1970s, most European states followed the Italian and British example and instituted some form of regional policy. The reason was both the high level of social tension, requiring greater structural investments in backward regions, and the availability of the economic means as a result of the vigorous economic growth characterizing that period. In the third phase, from the mid-1970s on, regional policies have been de-emphasized in the face of budget cuts resulting from the long wave of economic downturn. However, this third phase sees at the same time an increase in the EC's efforts in this area.

This poses an interesting question: why has the EC regional policy been strengthened in a period of diminishing state involvement and increasing emphasis on budget restraints? Several reasons can be adduced. A first factor is the accession to the EC of the southern countries, which, while in great need of a more balanced regional development, lack the financial means to implement the required policies. The EC's greater emphasis on regional development policies reflects these countries' political pressure. Second, there is the effect of German reunification. Some 80 per cent of the ERDF is earmarked for the regions defined as 'objective 1', which comprise not only the Mediterranean South and Ireland, but also, and most importantly for obvious ideological reasons, East Germany. Germany's political clout is obviously not foreign to the EC's greater emphasis on regional transfers.

However, the transfer of income meant to reduce regional differences might be counteracted by leakage from the less developed regions to the more advanced ones. Laggard regions might lack the capital goods sector. This means that a considerable share of the income multiplier effect deriving from government expenditures benefits the advanced regions.[10] According to D'Antonio's estimates, 'the total net income multiplier of investment projects activated by the new law 64/1986 for the Mezzogiorno, equal to 1.79, is estimated to be split in the two areas of Mezzogiorno and Centre–North in the proportion 55% to 45%' (quoted in Camagni, 1992, p. 373). This reduces the impact of public intervention in backward areas and tends to reproduce the relation of technological dependency and economic backwardness.

In short, regional disparities become an area of concern for the Community only inasmuch as the dominant interests (those of the oligopolies) within it might suffer significantly from such disparities. They, like more generally all redistribution policies, can at most alleviate the consequences of capital accumulation and exploitation. If in the recent past they have seemed to have achieved substantial improvements in the living conditions of the European people it is only because of the joint effects of a long-term phase of economic growth and of the massive transfer of value from the dependent countries to the imperialist centre.

8.6 Immigration Policies

In discussing immigration policies, usually two positions emerge. Some hold that (forced) repatriation of foreign (i.e. allochthonous) labourers would both liberate more jobs for national (that is, autochthonous) labourers and drive their wages upwards, thus providing the purchasing power needed for economic growth. This argument ignores that this measure, while possibly making it easier for (some) autochthonous workers to find a job, is a redistribution of existing jobs rather then the creation of new jobs. The purchasing power gained by the autochthonous workers is lost by the allochthonous ones. Once the 'positive' effect for the autochthonous workers (higher wages and lower unemployment) is over, more unemployment would follow due to the inner dynamics of the capitalist economy. Except that, at this point, not only would there be no foreign workers left to blame but also labour's fighting power would have been greatly weakened since labour would have accepted capital's view that unemployment and crises are caused by a 'too high labour supply' and thus by too low wages and purchasing power, that is, by labour (which either is too abundant or consumes too little) rather than by capital.

Others, in an attempt to counter the thesis for forced repatriation, argue that immigration, by lowering wages, increases profitability and investment, thus spurring growth and employment.

For this thesis it is high wages which are the cause of crises. Here too it is not capital itself which generates crises but labour, that is, its insufficient supply. Both accounts rest on different strands of orthodox economics and both are intuitively appealing, given that the dogmas of orthodox economics have been hammered into the heads the broad layers of society. Nevertheless, they are both wrong. Crises and thus unemployment are caused neither by too high nor by too low wages.

As chapter 3 has argued, crises are ultimately caused by capital itself, that is, by its constant drive to introduce more efficient technologies while at the same time expelling the labour force. While high wages decrease actual profitability, low wage rates increase it only potentially because they at the same time decrease the masses' purchasing power. It is only if and when that purchasing power can be increased (through, for example, exports) that potential profits can become actually realized profits. But then one exports one's own difficulties abroad. Moreover, once these profits have been realized, their investment in productive (of value) activities depends not so much on the individual entrepreneur's ability or willingness to do so but on the phase of the business cycle. The level of wages neither causes nor can indefinitely hold back crises.

Consider, first, economic expansion. Initially, lower wage rates (possibly due to the abundance of labour following the previous crisis or to immigration) increase potential profitability. At the same time, employment and thus the (surplus) value produced rise. Aggregate purchasing power rises too. Inasmuch as this rise in total purchasing power (total value and surplus value produced) offsets its fall due to lower wage rates, profitability rises without realization difficulties. The period of economic growth is lengthened. However, eventually, wage rates start to rise (possibly due to the drying up of the labour supply). This decreases profitability but at the same time increase the masses' purchasing power. Profitability falls even in the absence of realization difficulties. In order to hold back the fall in profitability, enterprises start accelerating the rhythm of technological innovations. This favours the technological leaders but causes a fall in aggregate profitability, growth and employment. Wages come under attack. Thus, in this phase, higher wage rates accelerate the emergence of crises while low wage rates retard (but cannot avoid) it.

Consider now the downturn. Lower wage rates (possibly due to greater unemployment) reduce the masses' purchasing power but increase potential profitability. With falling employment, purchasing power is reduced even more and potential profits cannot be realized. Actual profitability falls on this account. Depression and crises are worsened. If wage rates are increased in order to increase purchasing power, actual profits fall. Inasmuch as this increase in purchasing power neutralizes the fall in purchasing power due to rising unemployment, there are no realization difficulties and yet profitability falls. Here too depression and crises are worsened. Thus, both lower and higher wage rates exacerbate the downward phase. The difference is that with higher wage rates depression and crises worsen even if purchasing power is not lacking (something which is perceived by a strand of orthodox economics as evidence that wage rates must be cut), while with lower wage rates this worsening manifests itself as a lack of purchasing power (so that the other strand of orthodox economics calls for higher wage rates).

In short, the level of wage rates can only modify the shape of the cycle, by delaying or quickening the emergence of crises (in the ascending phase) or by worsening them in one way or another (in the descending phase). But the level of wage rates neither is the cause of crises nor is it their remedy. This conclusion is significant for foreign labour. If, in neo-classical fashion, lower wages were the way out of crises (via high profitability, investments, growth and employment), it would make sense to expel foreign labour (in order to reduce the cost of, i.e. the resources going to, the working class, such as old age pensions, educational and health facilities, etc.) while at the same time clamping down on wage rates. If, in Keynesian fashion, higher wages were the way out of crises (via greater purchasing power and demand stimulation), it would make sense to expel foreign labour (in order to decrease labour supply and increase the negotiating power of the autochthonous workers) while increasing wage rates. In both cases, one would have found the economic rationale for the expulsion of foreign labour and thus for the contradictory objective interests between the two sectors of European labour.

If, on the contrary, crises cannot be exited by manipulating wage rates, the expulsion of foreign labour would only modify the shape of the cycle, through its effect on wage rates, without providing a way out of the crisis. This latter would continue hitting both sectors of the working class. The argument for the contradictory economic interests between allochthonous and autochthonous workers is a myth based on orthodox economic analysis. Acceptance of orthodox economics' dogmas cannot but lead to the acceptance of the notion that the autochthonous and allochthonous sectors of European labour have contradictory interests. This goes a long way in explaining labour's startling inability to develop its own strategy.

If this is the case, the essence of what should be labour's strategy can be discerned. If repatriation is not (part of) the solution, that is, if there are no objective contradictions between the autochthonous and the allochthonous sectors of the collective labourer, these sectors' strategy should focus not on taking away existing jobs from each other but on fighting for more jobs within the context of new economic relations based on international solidarity. It is by opposing repatriation, and by developing arguments against it, that labour can find the objective reasons for a policy based on international solidarity as being its own policy. Moral arguments, important as they are, are not sufficient. For Europe's labour, repatriation of allochthonous workers is both economically useless and ideologically self-defeating. Moreover, solidarity requires egalitarianism and this in its turn requires self-management. International solidarity, egalitarianism and self-management are thus the three pillars of labour's strategy, the only winning card labour can play. These themes will be picked up again in the next chapter.

Before dwelling on this point in more detail, let us consider some of the problems specific to foreign labour within the EU and concomitant strategies.

A first specific problem concerns the EU's *democratic deficit*. As seen in chapter 1, section 4 above, labour's possibility of influencing European laws is far less than (the already restricted) similar powers within the member states. This deficit is accentuated for *EU immigrants*. Article 8 of the Treaty on European Union (TEU) states that every person holding the nationality of a member state is a citizen of the Union. This confers the right to move and reside freely within the territory of the member states,[11] the right to vote and to stand in municipal and European Parliament elections, the right to diplomatic protection and representation, the right to petition the European Parliament, and the right to apply to the Ombudsman. However, the exercise of these rights is severely limited (a) by the immigrants' scarce knowledge both of the existence of these rights and of the host country's language and institutions and (b) by their partly justified fear of using, or uneasiness in making use of, those facilities.

These difficulties are compounded for non-EU immigrants. The TEU excludes from the above-mentioned limited rights the nine million legally resident Third World citizens within the EU, not to mention illegal immigrants. These have been called the EU's sixteenth member state. Moreover, the TEU makes citizenship of the Union dependent upon holding a member state's nationality. It therefore makes the enjoyment of these limited rights dependent upon national legislations which are basically aimed at excluding immigrants from nationality.

Exclusion from labour's organizations and more generally from civil and political rights forces foreign workers into illegality. This makes them an easy prey for unscrupulous entrepreneurs who can use them to blackmail and weaken the negotiating power of the legally resident and autochthonous workers.[12] Labour should demand EU citizenship for all legal immigrants as well as quick and transparent procedures for the legalization of illegal immigrants. These demands should be framed within a perspective stressing egalitarianism, solidarity and self-management.

A second specific problem concerns the immigrants' *right to entry* into the EU. A closed-door policy does not mean that immigration has stopped. What it means is that legal immigration has drastically fallen while illegal immigration continues due both to the push from the desperate masses of the dominated countries and to the pull of those EU enterprises which can survive only thanks to higher than normal rates of surplus value. This holds for all EU countries even if in different degrees. Traditional countries of emigration, like Greece, Portugal, Spain and Italy, have turned into immigration as well as emigration countries. Italy and Spain were estimated in 1995 to host over one million workers each from non-member states and Greece over 500,000 illegal immigrants (Geddes, 1995, p. 201).

If autochthonous labour perceives (new) foreign workers as capital does, as competitors for jobs, instead of a potential help in the struggle of autochthonous labour against capital, labour's power will be weakened. If, however, labour considers allochthonous workers as its own members to be integrated into the struggle for jobs and higher wages within a socialist perspective, then not only will the socialist project be furthered in each member state, not only will labour be free from capital's blackmail, but also this policy will have contributed to international solidarity, thus reinforcing the socialist project in the host country. Labour should foster an open-door policy aimed at integrating immigrants in its project of socialist development. This policy implies a wider one, stressing the need to eliminate the causes of forced migration from non-EU countries through, for example, massive aid programmes fostering socialist economic growth in those countries. The concrete shape an open-door policy will take will depend on the concrete conditions under which it is fought for. All that can be said here is that it might have to be regulated in order to allow the host country to create the necessary facilities for this policy to be run according to socialist organizational principles.

A third specific problem concerns the *criminalization of immigration in the EU.* Article 7 of the Schengen Agreement mentions in one breath the need to protect the member states 'against illegal immigration and against activities which might endanger security' (*Tractatenblad van het Koninkrijk der Neder-*

landen, No. 102, 1985). Following the same approach, the TEU deals with asylum, internal migration and immigration from third countries, in article K.1, the *same* article which deals with combating drug addiction and trafficking, fraud on an international scale, terrorism, and other serious forms of international crime. Moreover, the TEU, while forbidding discrimination on grounds of nationality (for member states' nationals) in article 6 and on grounds of sex in article 119, does not forbid discrimination on ethnic or racial grounds. Even the Social Charter declares in its preamble that 'it is important to combat every form of discrimination' but mentions explicitly only 'discrimination on grounds of sex, colour, race, opinions and beliefs', thus forgetting ethnic discrimination (European Commission, 1990). The results of this approach are disastrous.

First, extensive policy measures and instruments have been and are being developed in order to deal with immigration (both legal and illegal) and asylum seekers from non-EU countries. The most noticeable is the *Schengen System.*[13] The *Schengen Agreement* was signed on 14 June 1985. By it, Belgium, France, Germany, Luxembourg and the Netherlands agreed to remove gradually their common frontier controls and introduce freedom of movement for all nationals of the signatory member states, other member states and third countries. At the same time, the Agreement aimed at coordinating the fight against crime. The Agreement was an intergovernmental pact which neither required parliamentary involvement nor laid down the arrangements and guarantees for implementation. This latter was the task of the *Schengen Convention,* signed by the same five states on 19 June 1990, which was subject to parliamentary ratification. The Convention also amends the relevant national laws.[14]

An important part of the system of control set out in Schengen is the Schengen Information System (SIS), as codified in articles 92 to 119 of the Schengen Convention. The SIS is centred upon feeding information into, and retrieving information from, a central computer (the 'technical support function') located in Strasbourg. The purpose of this is to collect all information needed to strengthen internal control concerning not only, for example, stolen cars and passports, but also personal data for each citizen of the Union committing an offence and for unwanted foreigners. Article 94 of the Schengen Convention accepts the recommendation of the Council of Europe (Convention of 28 January 1981 for the Protection of Individuals with regard to Automatic Processing of Personal Data) and therefore prohibits the collection of data on religious conviction, political affiliation, race and sexual predisposition. However, these safeguards are greatly weakened by the recommendation itself, which allows for the collection of these data if necessary for the purposes of the inquiry (Bunyan, 1993, p. 26). At the same time, control on non-EU immigrants is sharpened, 'fueled perhaps by the increasing severity of certain national policies towards immigrants, which in turn may be being pushed by the recent rising levels of xenophobia, if not by extreme nationalism' (Convey and Kupiszewski, 1995, pp. 942–3).

While the danger exists that autochthonous workers might accept

heightened barriers for non-EU citizens in exchange for their own greater
freedom of movement (the aim indicated by article 7 of the Schengen
Agreement is the abolition of internal frontiers and their displacement to
the external frontiers), the point is that both this greater freedom of
internal migration and the increasing restraints upon non-EU citizens from
entering the EU are shaped by capital's, rather than by labour's, needs.
Capital needs the labourers' freedom of movement and of residence but at
the same time it needs to control and check forms of mobility which might
not be functional for capital's own needs. Basically, it is capital which
defines who is an illegal immigrant. This is not only the drug dealer and
similar delinquents but also those immigrants who cannot be used (any
more) by capital. In short, capital needs free mobility of people as labour
power and thus only inasmuch as the movement of labour power back and
forth across national frontiers is convenient for capital itself rather than for
(autochthonous and allochthonous) labour.

Checking, controlling and preventing illegal immigration is a costly
affair. The costs of these repressive measures have not been estimated but
they might well exceed whatever expenses the Union might want to bear
in order to host immigrants (and it is on these costs that arguments against
an open-door policy rest). But even if these expenses were minimal (which
is far from being the case), the fact that control and repression have been
chosen instead of reception and care is a clear indicator that these
measures reflect the freedom that capital needs, not the freedom that
labour (especially 'illegal' immigrants) needs.

Moreover, as Geddes remarks, if immigration is construed as a criminal
problem, then not only are anti-immigration policies legitimated at national
and supranational level but also groups advocating racist ideologies are
drawn closer to mainstream political debate (Geddes, 1995, pp. 207–8).
This might be a factor explaining why the EU has developed no legal
provisions at the supranational level to counter racism and xenophobia. As
for the member states, they have developed only a very limited capacity to
deal with these phenomena. In 1995, 'Of the seven treaties identified by
the Commission . . . as most applicable to combat racism and xenophobia'
only three had been ratified by all member states (Geddes, 1995, p. 199).
Also, 'legislative redress for victims of racial discrimination depends on
national provisions' (Geddes, 1995, p. 211). In 1995, of the fifteen member
states, only four (the UK, the Netherlands, France and Belgium) had
developed comprehensive anti-racist laws. But even these countries show a
lax attitude towards racist violence and propaganda.

Immigration and asylum policies show that, if and when a new European
state emerges from this complex process, it will have features which no
democratically minded European citizen will welcome:

Taken together with the policies on immigration and asylum . . ., the culture
of secrecy . . . and the backdrop of rising racism and fascism, the European
state institutionalizes the 'cordon sanitaire' at its external borders and sets
up draconian mechanisms for internal control which will affect the whole

community. It has all the hallmarks of an authoritarian state in which power resides in the hands of officials with no democratic or legal mechanisms to call them to account. (Bunyan, 1993, p. 33)

Labour should demand the de-criminalization of immigration and asylum, the dismantling of the Schengen Agreement and other repressive apparatuses, and the reformulation (through a truly democratic process of decision making) of entry criteria.

In accepting capital's logic and policies, European autochthonous labour might win a short-term tactical victory but will certainly lose the strategic battle. Europe's labour should press for greater representative and participatory power for allochthonous workers as a means for labour *as a whole* to achieve greater representative and participatory power. Existing barriers to entry should be lifted and criteria for admission should be formulated as a means to gain more, rather than less, power for labour. Foreign workers should be seen as entitled to the same rights as those enjoyed by autochthonous workers. This and other policies should be framed within a perspective stressing solidarity and equality between these two sectors of labour as elements of a democratic system based on people's self-management. In short, labour's strategy should be based on the consciousness that there is no such a thing as foreign labour.

9

Epilogue

The previous chapter has painted a bleak picture of the policies borne by the European Union. Are there alternatives to unemployment, destitution, oppression, environmental degradation and all the evils afflicting not only Europe but also the quasi-totality of humanity? A first choice, by far the most diffuse in these years of rampant neo-liberalism, would be that of accepting capital's rules of the game in the hope that the inner 'rationality' of this system will lead to the best of all possible worlds. 'Responsible restraint' is being exercised by most trade unions and social-democratic governments in wage and other demands as the foundation of a policy of cooperation with capital at times called 'new realism' or 'industrial democracy'. But the thesis that lower wages lead to higher growth and employment is based on a number of fallacies. First, as seen above, lower wages do translate into higher potential profits but ultimately their realization crashes against the barrier of labourers' decreased purchasing power. Second, even if lower wages do result in higher actual profits, the latter might not be reinvested in productive and growth-generating activities. In periods of economic downturns and crises, a more likely outlet is financial and speculative investments. And, finally, even in the case of productive investments, capital might be spent in more efficient means of production so that the impact on employment might be minimal or null. The neo-classical argument that wage reductions are the means to achieve higher growth and employment, of which budget cuts are an important feature within the context of the EMU, does not hold water.

Given that the neo-liberalist medicine has had its chance and has failed, some argue that it is time for the pendulum to swing back again to Keynesian policies, that is, to resort to expansionary monetary, fiscal and budgetary policies and to public works. This, it is argued by their proponents, would alleviate the difficulties of realization, thus giving a new impulse to production and employment. These fallacies too have been exposed in the previous chapters. Inasmuch as income is redistributed from capital to labour, inventories fall. The question, however, is, where does the money (i.e., the monetary form of value) come from? Inasmuch as it comes from labour, and thus ultimately from lower real wages, potential profits rise but their realization is hindered. Inasmuch as it comes from capital, more is sold but profits fall. The effect on aggregate levels of production and employment is not automatic. If this redistribution is within acceptable limits (to capital), that is, if capital is willing and able to accept lower profit rates, growth and employment might not fall. This is the implicit assumption behind moderately radical trade unionism. But if these polices are too radical, growth and employment will fall. Moreover, incisive redistribution policies are objectively possible only if both the economy is in an ascending phase and the collective labourer manages to impose such policies. This is not the present conjuncture.

Finally, some argue for the need to go further than redistribution measures, without necessarily denying their usefulness. For example, Corporate Europe Observatory (1997, ch. 6.1, p. 3) focuses on the need to 'regain democratic control over finance and capital'. It has been shown above that capital must grow or perish and that this growth is tumultuous and anarchic. This holds even more for financial and speculative capital. Capital can be controlled only within (narrow) limits, but this does not change its nature and thus its negative influence on society and nature. A really democratic control of capital implies its supersession. Alternatively, the *Human Development Report* acknowledges the limits of capitalism (United Nations Development Programme, 1998, pp. 14, 86, 104, 105, etc.), such as the diversion of resources from the Third World (and from those in the Third World who most need them) to the production of luxuries and useless commodities in the imperialist countries. It argues for a change in consumption patterns, for a different type of commodities produced, and for the promotion of technological innovations in the dominated countries (pp. 87, 91, 96). But all this ignores that a different distribution of the world's income as well a different set of use values produced do not affect the exploitative and irrational nature of this economic system. As for technological innovations, this work has argued that more of them within capitalist production relations (whether in the imperialist or in the dominated countries) is the ultimate source of crises with all their deleterious consequences.

If the essence of a social system resides in its social relations, and if no improvement of the capitalist system can ever lead to the liberation of the world collective labourer from its dire predicament, new social (and to begin with, economic) relations should be created which are the exact opposite of the capitalist ones. If the latter are based upon the division between owners and non-owners of the means of production, on inequality, and on competition, the former should be based on (international) solidarity, egalitarianism and self-determination. Each of these three terms implies the other two. Equality implies the abolition of the difference between owners and non-owners of the means of production, that is, the collective labourer's self-determination; it also implies solidarity, given that competition cannot but lead to inequality. Equally, solidarity implies lack of privileges (equality), which in its turn implies self-determination. And self-determination implies the disappearance of the difference between owners and non-owners of the means of production, which in its turn implies equality and solidarity.

The above does not deny but endorses and encourages the struggle for economic (as well as other) reforms. In this it does not differ from (radical) social-democratic schemes. The difference is that within those schemes the struggle for those reforms (no matter how radical) is carried out from the perspective of capital (and thus within capitalist production, distribution and consumption relations), thus severing those reforms from the strife for a different society.[1] The reduction of workloads, the creation of new jobs possibly through public works, the imposition of legal and other types of restraints on capital, a guaranteed minimum income, the shift in the type of commodities produced to less ecologically damaging products, and so on, will be turned, as shown by past experiences, into so many conditions for the reproduction of capitalism unless these measures are instances and concretizations of a new vision stressing solidarity, egalitarianism and self-determination in all spheres of society as something to be implemented, as far as possible, already now. This means that the struggle for social reforms and amelioration of the living and working conditions of labourers does not necessarily imply embracing Keynesian and orthodox economic analysis. On the contrary, as chapter 3 has shown, there is a basic incompatibility between Keynesian and value theory. Any attempt to reach a synthesis of these two approaches can only be internally contradictory and can only lead to inherently weak political programmes.

No doubt, some readers will raise well-known objections. Perhaps the argument most often heard is: 'Well, what would you put in its place?' As Seabrook (1990) aptly puts it, 'This conundrum should more properly be thrown back at the advocates of the system themselves; what are they proposing to put in place of the exhausted earth, the depleted resources, the contaminated water and vitiated air?' (p. 188). What they are proposing, we may answer, is more of the same and thus more crises, unemployment, poverty, ecological destruction and all the features which have been associated with the present social system from its inception onwards. What this work proposes is a society based on the three above-mentioned, radically alternative, principles. A realistic prefiguration, not a blueprint, of such a society, has been sketched in Carchedi (1999a). The realism of this prefiguration is based on an analysis of what has already realized itself, of what is potentially present but not yet realized, of the recurrent aspirations of the labour movement and of other social movements, and of these movements' (up to now) failed attempts to create a new society. Here, only one example will be given shortly, that concerning another type of technical division of labour.

Then there is the 'cynical argument' according to which an egalitarian and altruistic mentality is against human nature. This work has shown that this mentality has its roots in an historically specific production process (and thus production relations), the capitalist one. Moreover, simple observation tells us that an egalitarian and altruistic mentality does exist even under capitalism, for example among friends or between parents and children or in any circumstance in which some sacrifice themselves for the good of the collectivity. Also, even a superficial acquaintance with social anthropology shows that there have been types of societies which were based on cooperation. A few excerpts from Margaret Mead's celebrated investigation of the Arapesh of New Guinea, carried out in 1931–3, will suffice:

> Each man plants not one garden, but several, each one in co-operation with a different group of his relatives. In one of those gardens he is host, in the others he is guest. (Mead, 1962, p. 37)

The same lack of individualism characterizes hunting as well:

> In hunting, too, a man does not hunt alone. . . . The man, be he host or guest, who sees the game first claims it, and the only tact that is necessary here is the tact of not seeing game very much more often than other people do. (p. 39)

Similarly for the distribution of food:

> The ideal distribution of food is for each person to eat food grown by another, eat game killed by another, eat pork from pigs that not only are not his own but have been fed by people at such a distance that their very names are unknown. . . . The lowest man in the community . . . is the man who eats his own kill. (p. 45)

Finally, faced by the impossibility of holding on to the 'cynical argument', critics usually retreat to the 'technical impossibility argument': cooperation and altruism might be feasible in those primitive and small societies but are not feasible in our modern and complex societies, as the failure of 'communism' has shown. The 'technical impossibility' argument will be summarily answered here. As for the collapse of the Soviet system, it can be shown that its cause was not technical but social, that is, that that system was not based on solidarity, egalitarianism and self-determination. The Soviet system was a spurious system, drifting more and more towards a purely capitalist system. It was this spurious nature which made it vulnerable to classic capitalism's onslaught (Carchedi, 1993).

Let us then deal briefly with the division of labour and with its supposed incompatibility with a society based on solidarity, egalitarianism and self-determination. A commonly heard objection to this thesis is that modern techniques and the division of labour they require are too complicated for such an alternative organization of the labour process. This critique disregards the fact that the fragmentation and de-qualification of positions is socially, rather than technically, determined. At one end of the spectrum there are those jobs which require only a few weeks or months to be learned mostly through on-the-job training, such as in office work, operating telex and dictaphone, word processing, the keeping of archives, and so on. Rotations of tasks such as these among employees are checked by their effects on profitability and not because of any insurmountable technical obstacles. At the other end of the spectrum there are those jobs which require great expertise and specialized skills. The time required for the acquisition of this expertise and these skills, however, could be considerably shortened. But, much more important, the time won by society by abolishing the production of weapons and wasteful products, the sales effort, the repressive state apparatus, and on on, would be more than enough to offer everybody the chance, if they so wanted, to graduate several times in their lifetime in different fields.

An important contribution can be made by the sociological literature on job redesign, once its ideological message is discarded, that is, once it is recognized that job redesign (a) is spurred by the contradictions inherent in capitalist production relations (e.g. by absenteeism, poor product quality, etc.) rather than by genuine interest for better labour conditions (something which does not exclude a genuine altruistic motivation in some job redesign experts), (b) is the task of experts who either ignore or appropriate the collective labourer's knowledge rather than being the task of the labourers themselves, (c) is a once-and-for all proposition (i.e. either there is a tangible improvement from the point of view of capital or the experiment is abandoned) rather than being based on the labourers' engaging in a continuous process, of thinking about, and changing when needed, the organization of their own labour process and (d) is a re-composition of positions such that increased job satisfaction and content of positions (e.g. more variety of tasks) are but a way to motivate labourers to increase productivity and/or endure a higher intensity of labour and/or accept greater capital control. Job redesign schemes which do not increase productivity and/or the intensity of labour and/or control by capital are not taken into consideration in spite of the fact that they might result in vast improvements in labour conditions.

But these counter-arguments, important as they are, do not yet touch upon the core of the problem. All labour processes, including planning, production, distribution, allocation and social consumption, are based on some sort of technical division of labour. If the ultimate aim of a truly human society is to make it possible for each and every one to develop to the maximum feasible extent his or her potentialities, then all labour processes should be organized in a way consonant with this aim. In other words, it is the labourers taking part in that process who should collectively define the clusters of tasks, that is, the positions, which ensure all participants their maximum development and self-realization. However, some of these tasks are desirable, others are not; some offer more possibilities for inner development, others fewer; some prepare people for the social process of decision making, others do not; and so on. Each position, then, should be roughly equal in terms of (a) desirability, (b) possibility for self-development and (c) possibility of partaking in the social process of decision making. It is in this sense that positions should be *balanced*.[2] It is also in this sense that positions should be flexible, adaptable to the needs of the labourers themselves. They should be changed whenever a new hierarchy of preferences arises, whenever new labourers join in, and so on.

This does not mean that everybody working in a certain labour process has to, or even can if s/he wants, perform all tasks (e.g. not all labourers in an airport have to be pilots, not even in turns). But it does mean that, first, given the balanced nature of positions, everybody has an equal share of both positive and negative aspects in that labour process; second, the balancing is done by the labourers themselves; and, third, voluntary internal mobility (i.e. among the different positions of a labour process) and external mobility (i.e. from one labour process to another, and therefore from one position to another) ensures that each individual is exposed to the maximum of possibilities for self-development (in sociological terms there is no vertical mobility, only horizontal mobility among balanced positions). Thus, an alternative technical division of labour is based not only on a system of balanced and thus continuously changing positions but also on the labourers' rotation among these positions. A similar balancing should be made also among labour processes.[3]

Under capitalism, the technical division of labour is tendentially based on the fragmentation of positions, on the separation of mental from material labour, on routine and alienation and thus on de-qualification. An alternative technical division of labour tends towards the re-composition of positions (they should encompass the largest possible number of tasks), towards the combination within each position of both material and mental labour, towards minimum routine, and thus towards the maximum development of each individual's potentialities, that is, on re-qualification. Re-qualification under capitalism holds only for certain positions and maintains both the function of capital (the work of control and surveillance) and the division between material and mental labour; an alternative re-qualification should aim at an equal enrichment of all positions in which both the function of capital and the division between agents performing only material and agents performing only mental labour have been abolished.

Under capitalism new technologies lead to unemployment and economic crises. Under an alternative economic system production is adjusted to the needs of the producers (and thus of the consumers). No unemployment follows technological innovations, only more free time, and thus no economic crises. The notion of productivity changes too and becomes incommensurable with the capitalist notion of productivity. On the one hand, the destruction of nature, capitalist waste, and unemployment of both people and means of labour disappear. On the other hand, emphasis is not so much on increased production as on the full development of all labourers. Conflicts concerning the balancing of positions, rotation, and so on, do not disappear but are solved collectively, by the participants themselves, on the basis of egalitarianism and solidarity, and through a process informed by the notion that each individual's well-being is the condition for all other individuals' well being.

This discussion on the possibility of a technical division of labour consonant with a radically alternative society shows that the road to a new society is not impossible. However, it is enormously difficult and the difficulties are compounded at the European and world level. Yet, the development of capitalism itself fosters the objective conditions from which a radically alternative consciousness can emerge. Ecological problems, a product of capitalism, are increasingly affecting the whole globe. A class analysis of the causes of environmental disasters – acid rain, global warming, holes in the ozone layer, loss of biodiversity, and all the natural disasters caused by them – can help create a world-wide class consciousness and thus consciousness that international solidarity is needed in order to escape catastrophe. Biotechnology can be another avenue to an alternative collective consciousness. Serious health hazards and, even more, the possibility of moulding life according to the imperatives of profit making can also contribute to a radical critique of the capitalist system and thus to the awareness that it should be substituted by a different one. Consumers' defence groups, groups and movements fighting against the exploitation of women, children and ethnic minorities, anti-militarism, even the spread of HIV/AIDS (which hits disproportionally more the poor of the world) can all be starting points and inspirations for the spreading of the consciousness that national and even local problems are actually localized forms of more general problems rooted in capitalist development.

A few groups and movements have been mentioned above which could be the humus from which an alternative generalized consciousness could emerge. This should not be taken as if trade union and industrial struggles have become irrelevant. On the contrary, they retain their centrality, due to the centrality of capitalist production relations for the reproduction of the capitalist system. Only, they are not necessarily the catalysts of a broad alternative movement. A promising development is social movement unionism. This is based on three elements. First, union demands should not be contrary to the interests of the social texture surrounding them. Second, union members should be activated when shaping those demands. This requires a restructuring of the union along non-bureaucratic lines, given that the members' passivity is the result of their exclusion due to bureaucratic and authoritarian structures. Third, while most struggles are local or national, the perspective and the strategy should be international. The final aim is that of developing a coordinated strategy in order to counter capital's relocations as a way to pressure labour. Recent successful examples are the Canadian Auto Workers' 1996 collective bargaining programme, which, after twenty-one days of strike, culminated in the seizure of a plant from which General Motors was attempting to remove material in order to resume production elsewhere. This seizure, far from alienating the general public, actually won its support (Moody, 1997, p. 61). Another example is that of the very successful 1997 UPS (United Parcel Service) strike, which was supported both by the AFL/CIO and by the public at large (*Notizie Internazionali*, 1997, pp. 6–11).

This strategy is a tremendous improvement on the trade unionism based on the ideology of social partnership. It should be fitted into a strategy based on the following three principles. First, the consequences of crises should be borne by those who cause them, that is, by capital, and not by labour. Therefore, similarly to the policies advocated by social-democratic forces, labour should demand an income redistribution in its own favour.

Second, if this provokes capital's blackmail, that is, casting off of labour, closures, capital flight, and so on, labour should not be intimidated but should be ready to take over that enterprise and run it itself. The chances of this strategy succeeding are greater the greater is their popular support. Third, and most importantly, labour-run enterprises should begin to function according to the three above-mentioned principles, that is, on the basis of solidarity (within the enterprise and as much as possible in its relation to the outer world), egalitarianism (again, both internally and as much as possible externally) and self-determination (that is, the collective ownership of the enterprise). The difficulties inherent in this project are immense but, short of a major contemporaneous radical change on a world scale (or at least in its imperialist core), there seems to be no alternative to this strategy.

It is the exposure to social relations based on solidarity, egalitarianism and self-determination which can propel labour beyond purely defensive visions and policies and which can generate those radically different insights and life experiences upon which a new society can be based. *The most important question as we enter the third millennium is whether this consciousness has any chance of emerging in the foreseeable future.* Given the virulence of present capitalist ideology (especially in its neo-liberalist version), it is possible that a major disaster might have to occur first, such as a period of generalized fascist-like rule following a major economic crisis, a third world war, a global ecological catastrophe directly endangering human survival, or widespread tampering with human nature following the 'advances' in genetic manipulation. These are not doomsday prophecies but possible outcomes, real possibilities, because already contained in present-day reality. But opposite outcomes, forms of social life in which the full development of each individual is the condition for the full development of all, are equally possible and might follow not such global disasters but the generalized awareness of their increasingly possible occurrence and the concomitant struggle to avoid them. This work hopes to contribute to the spreading of such an awareness.

Some will argue that right now such a strategy has no chance of succeeding and that one should resign oneself to the status quo without dreaming of utopias. But it is one thing to gauge which demands are realistic given the power relations between capital and labour at any given moment. It is another is to renounce *a priori* any demands challenging the inhuman nature of this society. As for utopias, the hope for another Europe gleaming through this work is indeed a utopia, but a realizable one. After all, isn't progress the realization of utopias?

Notes

1. History, Institutions and Enlargements

1. For an assessment of these two approaches, see Bieling and Steinhilber, 1997.
2. For example, the European Commission could be seen as the embryo of a new fraction of the European capitalist class creating its own conditions of existence and expanded reproduction, that is, the bureaucratic apparatus giving it power. The Commission has to do this by mediating the interests of the member states (see below in this chapter) within the context of the domination of the EU member states by one of them, Germany, that is, by German oligopoly capital (see chapter 4). One condition for the Community to express its own fraction of the European ruling class is financial autonomy. But the Commission is still dependent upon the contributions of the member states, which, moreover, are relatively small, some 1.2 per cent of the Community's GDP (see chapter 7). This corresponds to the minimum surrender of national sovereignty compatible with the performance of those activities needed by 'European' capital, that is, those capital units arising from the interpenetration of national capitals. There is, however, one realm in which the Community's institutions act as if they were the expression of a supranational European state, the ideological.
3. The US had an interest of its own in, and contributed to, the economic reconstruction of Europe, which it saw as a precondition for Europe to play the role of the anti-communist bastion.
4. This has been a constant of French policy, starting in 1951, when the European Coal and Steel Community was conceived as a means towards Franco-German reconciliation, up to 1992, when an important motivation in negotiating the Treaty on European Union (the Maastricht Treaty) was to contain Germany's economic predominance after the 1990 reunification.
5. The *European Economic Community* (EEC), founded in 1958, became the *European Community* (EC) in 1965, when it was merged with the European Coal and Steel Community (ECSC) and Euratom, and this became the *European Union* (EU) in 1992. (See below).
6. Even nowadays Europe's role in forming the dependent countries' elites is far smaller than that of the US. European universities host 50,000 Asian students as opposed to the 215,000 Asian students admitted to US universities.
7. Beyen, the Dutch foreign minister who first proposed the Common Market, 'was not an elected politician but a former executive for Philips and director of Unilever parachuted from the IMF straight into the Dutch cabinet' (Anderson, 1997, p. 63), and Monnet, the 'father' of European integration, was an international banker by profession.
8. With the exception that, in line with France's wishes, the Council's secretary-general shall exercise the function of high representative for the CFSP (article J.8)
9. So much for the 'priority' given by the TEU to employment policies.
10. In 1975, after the Labour Party was returned to power, the UK renegotiated the terms of entry. On some issues it got a better deal but, equally important, on some other issues it realized that its fears had been groundless. (See Swann, 1995, pp. 39–42.)
11. They are Turkey, Cyprus, Malta, Switzerland, Hungary, Poland, Romania, Slovakia, Latvia, Estonia, Lithuania, Bulgaria, Czech Republic, Slovenia, Croatia (*Europa van Morgen*, 1996). After the elections of November 1996, the new Labour government in

Malta shelved plans to join the EU. However, Malta reactivated its application for membership in October 1998.

12. This is an acronym for 'Poland, Hungary: Assistance for Restructuring Economies'.

13. While policy-making power resides with the EU, implementation has been claimed by the Commission to be with the target governments. However, this is far from being the case,

> since 'almost none' of the leading personnel in these management units are nationals of the recipient countries: they are from Western Europe, appointed by EC bodies and work under the supervision of the Commission and of EC/EU delegations in the recipient countries. (Gowan, 1995, pp. 35–6)

Even the Court of Auditors has been unable to trace how this money has been really spent.

14. These Agreements had been preceded by trade concessions from the beginning of the 1990s

> which took the form of expanding the Generalized System of Preferences (GSP) to east European countries as well as a suspension of non-specific, and the abolition of specific, quantitative restrictions applied exclusively against state-trading countries. . . . Subsequently, bilateral agreements on trade and commercial and economic cooperation were concluded. . . . These Agreements paved the way for the Europe Agreements. (Economic Commission for Europe, 1995, p. 111).

15. The European Council should not be confused with the Council of Europe, an organization set up in 1949 to which adhere forty European states. The Council of Europe is organizationally separate from the institutions of the European Union. It monitors democracy and human rights. Thus the reader should keep in mind that the Council of Europe is different from both the European Council (the European Summit) and the Council of Ministers (which comprises the ministers of the EU member states).

16. But the ministries of the member states are equally responsible as the Commission for the administration of the policies and for the carrying out of the laws.

17. This often goes hand in hand with the EU's Structural Funds and Cohesion Fund.

18. This is a very important committee.

> It is in permanent session, and coordinates the preparatory work for Council meetings, determining the priorities and urgency of the items on the Ministers' agenda when they meet in the Council. It can also reach agreement on technical points, with the Ministers merely rubber-stamping measures adopted unanimously by the Permanent representatives. (Borchardt, 1994, p. 45)

19. However, the European Parliament approves the EU budget each year according to a modified procedure (see chapter 7) which allows it to reject the budget.

20. What follows leans heavily upon Corporate Europe Observatory, 1997.

21. Alongside the ERT, there is also the *Union of Industrial and Employers' Confederation of Europe* (UNICE). While the ERT influences the general criteria informing European legislation, UNICE reacts to specific pieces of legislation and makes sure that they are tailored to business's interests.

22. For example, EuropaBio lobbies the bio-technology sector during high-level meetings with EU institutions. It is very influential in the Commission but fortunately less so with the Parliament. Or, as Susan George (1999) reports,

> presided over by the chairman of Barclays Bank, the European Service Leaders' Group (ESLG) is concerned with 21 sectors. As a service to the ESLG [during the next WTO negotiations] the Brussels commission has set up an electronic system enabling European negotiators to consult the business community quickly.

23. The same cannot be said of other lobby groups which reject the neo-liberal project.

24. As Gianni Ferrara (1996) points out, one would look in vain for the word 'equality' in the several European Treaties.

2. The Ideology of Economic Integration

1. Presumably, this result would not change in case of international capital immobility due to the possibility for Portuguese producers to undersell their English competitors. This case, however, is not contemplated by Ricardo.

2. Ricardo's theory allows us to find only the upper and lower limits of international prices, rather than the prices themselves. (See Carchedi, 1991a, pp. 218–19.) Even more advantageous would be if Portugal specialized in both products, thus producing two units of clothing and two units of wine for a total cost of $80 + 80 + 90 + 90 = 340$. But this presupposes capital mobility.

3. It could be argued that both table 2.1 and table 2.2 are based on labour, the former because it quantifies the hours needed to produce a certain commodity, the latter because the commodities are the outcome of the application of $1R$, of which labour is a component. The point, however, is that as long as the focus is on physical, and thus on qualitatively different, objects, the labour needed to make them is also qualitatively different and thus incommensurable. This type of labour differentiates products rather then being the common denominator which makes their quantitative comparison (i.e. their exchange in definite proportions) possible. This theme will be introduced in section 2.3.2 and further pursued in the rest of this work.

4. Definition of factor abundance in terms of factor retributions would only lead to tautology. Let the rate of interest (r) be the price of capital and the wage rate (w) be the price of labour. Then, K would be defined as being more abundant in country 1 than in country 2 if r/w is bigger in country 2 than in country 1. But why is r/w bigger in country 2 than in country 1? Because capital is more abundant in country 1 than in country 2.

5. The real return on K is not the interest rate but the rate of profit. The interest rate is one of the determinants of the rate of profit. What is (tendentially) equalized, then, is the rates of profit, under the assumption of capital mobility. This may or may not imply an equalization of the rate of interest.

6. Explanations of the Leontieff paradox abound. However, the fact which has not been stressed is that the theory assumes equal technologies. But the most important way to compete within sectors is through technological innovations. Thus, the hypothesis would have had to be that the technologically advanced nations export high-tech goods. This is indeed the hypothesis to be submitted later in this work.

7. This is the cardinalist approach, which assumes that utilities can be given finite quantities. As orthodox theory concedes, no way has been found of quantifying utilities. Therefore, orthodox theory has shifted to the ordinalist approach, according to which it is sufficient to rank preferences relative to each other without having to assign them definite numbers. The ordinalist approach is subject to the same criticism as the cardinalist approach.

8. The argument that the supply and demand curves are only ideal types and that abnormal behaviour can be explained as deviations from these ideal types (Walras, 1977, p. 71) is impotent against the above-mentioned criticism. If the norm cannot be substantiated, 'explanations' of actual behaviour as a deviation from the norm no longer hold.

9. For the majority of the world's population, their purchasing power ranges from severely limited to non-existent.

10. There is a notion of disequilibrium in orthodox economics. This is the case if notional demand and effective demand do not coincide, that is, if, owing to income constraints, what the purchasers/sellers want to purchase/sell does not coincide with what they can actually purchase/sell. Aside from the fact that this discrepancy is the case for almost the totality of the world's population, disequilibrium here relates to a psychological dimension, basically dissatisfaction. The following chapters will show that demand and supply can coincide (i.e. the markets clear), whatever the definition of demand, and yet the system can and will generate crises and all that goes with it. Thus, the approach to be submitted below is not a *dis*equilibrium approach (since it would imply the theoretical validity of the notion of equilibrium) but stresses *non*-equilibrium, the theoretical irrelevance of that notion for economic analysis.

11. What follows is of course an extremely simplified rendition. It is no less, however, than what is offered by introductory books on economic integration.

12. It has become standard procedure to express the conditions of equilibrium in terms of inequalities. Given the character of this work, this topic will not be further pursued here. Only one remark might be in order. One variant of GET is given by a multi-period model in which each good is considered to be a different good at different moments in time. This move may be interpreted as introducing time in a static model. But this is far from being the case. In this case, the existence of a general equilibrium situation depends upon the existence of equilibrium prices in all markets at all times. This implies that all decisions regarding present and future goods are taken by all economic agents at the beginning of the first period. In the following periods the economic agents would only carry out the decisions taken initially. Clearly, this method, rather than introducing time and thus change in any period, extends atemporality to time itself.

13. This and similar cases are discussed here only for the sake of completeness, given that no economic theory has been based on this notion.

3. A Value Theory of European Economic Integration

1. For neo-classical economics, a commodity's use value *is* its value. We have seen why this position is untenable.

2. This holds for the value produced, or contained in commodities. This is quantitatively different, as we shall see shortly, from the value which is realized through their sale. If commodities realize the average value (a common price), then those which have been produced with less (more) than average intensity of labour realize more (less) value than the value contained in them.

3. The assumption is that the commodity enters the next production process right away. It could remain idle for some time, but this changes neither the problem nor the solution.

4. Since the same commodity is both the output of $t0-t1$ and the input of $t1-t2$, the value it realizes at $t1$ as output of $t0-t1$ must be the same as the value it contains, also at $t1$, as input of $t1-t2$.

5. This is contrary to the claim, held by some, that value (and especially the value contained in commodities) cannot be measured in labour hours but only in money terms. For a critique of this position, see Carchedi and de Haan, 1996; Giussani, n.d.

6. Focus on the temporal succession of production and distribution periods is essential to avoid confusion between value contained and value realized. Given $t0-t1$, the value contained in a commodity, say x, produced during $t0-t1$ is *not* the value it realizes at $t1$ (see below). But the value realized by x at $t1$ as an output of $t0-t1$ becomes its value contained (obviously, also at $t1$) as an input of $t1-t2$.

7. When a labourer starts working, s/he advances his/her wage to the capitalist because s/he gets paid at the end of the first month (week) of his/her labour contract. With that payment, s/he advances again his/her wage for the second period, and so on.

8. Carchedi (1991a, ch. 2) submits a theory of knowledge as a capitalist commodity. The basic elements are as follows. A mental transformation is defined as the transformation of one type of knowledge, K, into a different type of knowledge, K^*. A mental transformation thus encompasses both production and transmission of knowledge. All mental transformations which either actually or potentially result in the knowledge needed to produce, transform or prevent the deterioration of material use values is productive labour. Mental transformations are said to be actually needed for a certain process if they are actually part of that process. They are said to be potentially needed for that process if, while not being part of that process, nothing prevents them from being used in a future labour process. For example, the 'transmission of communi-cations, letters, telegrams, etc.' (Marx, 1967b, p. 52) concerning the organiza of a production process is a mental transformation needed for that production process. It is then productive labour. Teaching in a privately owned school is also productive labour because it can, even though it will not necessarily, be used for productive purposes. It follows that all mental transformations which are actually needed (a) for unproductive labour, (b) for the work of control and surveillance and (c) for the destruction of use

values cannot be productive labour.

All labour processes need the transformation both of material goods (material transformation) and of knowledge (mental transformation). Once mental transformations become a separate activity, it is possible to distinguish between material labour (in which the material transformations are dominant, as seen by the material nature of the outcome) and mental labour (in which the mental transformations are dominant, as seen by the non-material nature of the outcome, i.e. knowledge).

9. Therefore, money is the form of manifestation of value but is not value, unless it is a commodity not functioning as money, basically gold and silver. But, in this case, it has a value as a commodity, not as money.

10. It is more precise to say that they participate in the creation of use values because the other use value creating element is labour as concrete labour.

11. Some functions might encompass both aspects of the managerial function. This, however, does not invalidate the analytical distinction. It is upon this distinction that a theory of the new middle classes can be built. (See Carchedi, 1977.)

12. There is a certain level of inventories (wanted inventories) which fulfils a buffer function. This amounts to defining D (demand) = S (supply) at a certain level of unsold commodities.

13. This section deals with the ultimate cause of economic crises. Section 3.2 deals with the form of manifestation of crises, the cycle. It discusses anti-cyclical measures as well. Section 3.3 extends this analysis to the international dimension with particular accent on monetary crises. Finally, chapter 8, section 6 returns to the cycle, but this time from the perspective of whether wage policies have any effect on the cycle.

14. For a proper understanding of this and the following tables, three points should be kept in mind. First, the assumption that the two sectors realize different rates of profit implies capital immobility. This is unrealistic. Capital mobility implies the tendential equalization of the rates of profit, that is, the tendential formation of an average rate of profit. In the example above, ARP = 100/300 = 33.33 per cent. Thus some capitals would move from sector I to sector II until the two rates of profit are equalized. This aspect is not dealt with here because the focus is on the production and realization of value as a result of TI *ceteris paribus*, that is, irrespective of the effects on the production and realization of value due to capital movements.

Second, these are not reproduction tables, that is, we disregard the requirement that the value produced in sector I and incorporated in MP must be equal to the value invested in MP by all capitalists in both sectors. Equally, the value produced by sector II and incorporated in MC must be equal to the value available to both capitalists and labourers in both sectors and spent on those MC. Since cI is produced and consumed within sector I and $vIIa + sIIa + vIIb + sIIb$ are produced and consumed in sector II, the condition for simple reproduction is $cIIa + cIIb = vI + sI$. The quantitative aspect of this condition is disregarded here because, as already mentioned, the focus is on the effects TIs have on the production and realization of value. If table 3.1 had been meant to be a reproduction scheme, sector I would have had to invest, say, $80v$ and $60v$ so that it would have produced $60s$. Then, $cIIa + cIIb = 60 + 60 = vI + sI = 60 + 60$.

Third, comparisons within productivities are possible only within sectors, that is, only between producers of the same commodities. Such a comparison is not possible among sectors. Thus, in table 3.1 the fact that sector I has a productivity of $100MP/100(c + v)$ = 1 and that sector II has also a productivity of $200MC/200(c + v) = 1$ is purely accidental.

15. Notice that if labour gets $140M$ and capital gets the same amount as profits, only $120M$ is left to the capitalist for the purchase of the means of production in the next cycle. However, the capitalists need a value of $200V$, or $200M$. This discrepancy is not corrected here because, as said in the previous note, these are not reproduction schemes.

16. If wages were paid at the beginning of $t0–t1$, that is, at $t0$, the value of labour power would be $100V$ at $t0$ and $140V$ at $t1$ as the beginning of $t1–t2$. However, wages are paid at the end of each period (they are advanced by the labourers to the capitalists). Thus, at $t1$ as the end of $t0–t1$ wages are $100V$ even if the value of labour power has changed at $t1$ as the beginning of $t1–t2$ to $140V$. The new value of labour power is paid only at t 2 as the end-point of $t1–t2$, that is, payment is postponed by one period.

17. The quantity of money falls with the quantity of value produced. In reality, of course, this need not be the case in each specific instance. However, this assumption is justified for the reasons to be mentioned in the next note.

18. We can now understand why in table 3.2 M falls with the fall in V. To understand this we must make explicit at least the rudiments of the value theory of money. There are two basic tenets to this theory. First, the quantity of money in circulation is determined by the quantity of value produced and circulating. Second, given a constant monetary expression of value (the ratio between the quantity of money in circulation and the quantity of value produced and circulating), the two quantities move in the same direction. Let us see why. If V increases, it must be because v and/or c and/or s have increased. The capitalists need more money to finance these extra investments ($c + v$) and/or to realize the extra surplus value. If V decreases, it might be because of two reasons. Either such a decrease is caused by a contraction of the volume of investments and/or surplus value, and in this case M falls (e.g. money is hoarded). Or, given a certain rate of surplus value, TIs have been introduced so that more c and less v have been invested, as in table 3.2, and thus less s has been produced. The money needed for the means of production rises but that needed for the purchase of labour power (and thus of the means of consumption) falls. The effects on the quantity of money depend on whether one of the two terms (c and v) rises (drops) more than the other. In table 3.2, c and v are in percentage terms, so that the increases in c compensates the decrease in v. However, s has fallen too so that V has decreased. Here, less money is needed to realize less surplus value.

It will immediately be objected that a sustained decrease in the value produced can be and is usually met by the monetary authorities by increasing the quantity of (paper, inconvertible) money. This is one of the principal counter-cyclical measures. In this case, a decreased production and circulation of value (unemployment, closures, lower capacity utilization) would be met by an increased quantity of money in circulation (inflation). This seems to invalidate the direct relation between money and value quantities submitted above. But this greater quantity of money implies a change in the monetary expression of value, that is, a change in the terms of comparison. The direct quantitative relation between money and value quantities presupposes an unchanged unit of measure, a given monetary expression of value, over time. An index of deflation applied to the new (higher) monetary expression of value would reveal the drop in the money quantity following a drop in the value quantity.

The above should not be confused with the *quantity theory of money*. In its classic and simplest version, this theory holds that, given a certain velocity of circulation of money and a certain level of output, money prices *as tags attached to use values* are determined by the quantity of money in circulation. Money is the independent variable and money prices the dependent variable. If the former grows (falls), the latter rise (fall). For the *value theory of money* submitted here, prices *as expressions of value*, and thus value, determine first money prices and then the quantity of money. This is a logical, not a chronological, sequence. More specifically, each commodity has a value contained whose quantity is its value price. Since value can realize itself only as money, the moment those commodities enter into circulation, they get a money price (which, through both the tendential equalization of the rates of profit and the effects of demand and supply, implies that the value contained in a commodity differs from the value it realizes). The sum total of these prices gives the quantity of money in circulation.

It is true that, *empirically*, an increase (decrease) in the quantity of money increases (decreases) money prices, *ceteris paribus*. But this does not *explain* the quantity of money. The difference between the two theories lies in the conceptual apparatus and thus in the possibility of explaining the quantity of money, rather than taking it for granted, that is, determined exogenously. First, the quantity of money is determined by the economic system, rather than by the monetary authorities as something external to that system. Second, this quantity is explained through the use of value categories and thus through a logical sequence of events going from value prices, to money prices, to the quantity of money. Changes in the quantity of money inflate or deflate the price structure but cannot explain it and thus cannot explain the quantity of money itself. To explain the quantity of money, one needs to start from money prices as modified expressions of value prices. It is only after this has been done that one can inquire into its variations. These can be caused either by changes at the level of the production and distribution of value or by inflationary or deflationary movements (which, as mentioned two paragraphs above, are also ultimately determined by changes at the production level).

Thus, the assertion that 'Marx ... anticipated modern Keynesian endogenists, [and argued] ... that the quantity of money in circulation is determined by economic activity, and not the other way around' (Henwood, 1997, p. 220), can be agreed upon only if by economic activity is meant the production and circulation not only of use values (as in orthodox theories, including Keynes), but also and above all of (exchange) value. While Henwood does not reject the notion of value, regrettably this dimension is absent in his treatment of money and credit. It is thus hard to see how he differs from Keynesianism on this score. Another Keynesian tinge can be found in Henwood's exaggerated trust in credit extension as a modern way (as opposed to Marx's times) to avoid crises (p. 221). Credit extension by central banks does hold back and postpone both financial and real crises, but cannot avoid them. Asia, Brazil and Russia are only three of the most recent cases in point.

The fact that in the post-war years the US and the other countries of the imperialist centre have avoided major financial débâcles (as well recounted by Henwood) is not the merit of credit extension in itself. Rather, credit extension and the bailing out of quasi-bankrupt financial institutions is just another example of a massive redistribution of value (from the taxpayers to the financial world) which is possible only in the imperialist centre. In these countries, it is possible to lessen the labourers' lower purchasing power implied in this redistribution of value because of a partial redistribution to the labourers of the value appropriated from the dominated countries. But this option is of course open only to the imperialist core. It is this appropriation, that is, imperialist policies, rather than the credit system (Keynesian policies) which explains the centre's success (up to now, at least) in holding back major economic and financial disasters. Keynesian polices can work in the centre only inasmuch as they cannot work in the dominated bloc.

19. It could be argued that the system could be insulated from realization difficulties in sector II (which absorbs the masses' purchasing power) if capitalists invested more and more in the sector producing means of production needed to produce means of production, Ipp. Investment in Ipc (the sector producing means of production to produce means of consumption) would only postpone technological unemployment and the fall in the masses' purchasing power. The labourers expelled by Ipc and II could be absorbed by Ipp. High productivity in sector II would ensure sufficient means of consumption both for the whole of the labour force and for the capitalists. But this option would work only if capitalists could be forced to invest increasingly in Ipp. But capitals must be free to invest where the rate of profit is highest. There is no theoretical reason to assume that the rate of profit in Ipp would be higher than in Ipc and in II. On the contrary, the huge scale of investments which would be necessary in Ipp to absorb all the labour power expelled in the whole economy (including Ipp itself) due to TI would increasingly depress the rate of profit in this sector. Capital would keep investing in both Ipc and in II.

20. The following is often quoted: 'The ultimate reason for all real crises always remains the poverty and restricted consumption of the masses as opposed to the drive of capitalist production to develop the productive forces as though only the absolute consuming power of society constituted their limit' (Marx, 1967c, p. 484). This has been interpreted as if the lack of purchasing power were the ultimate cause of crises. However, as this quotation makes clear, the ultimate cause of crises is *both* the lack of purchasing power *and* the development of the productive forces, that is, technological innovations. The original *MEGA* text is even more explicit: 'The ultimate reason for all real crises always remains the poverty of the masses on the one side and, on the other, the drive of capitalist production to develop the productive forces as though only the absolute consuming power of society constituted their limit' (Marx, 1992, p. 540). If both TI and the lack of purchasing power are the ultimate cause of crises, what is the

connection between these two aspects of this complex process? An unprejudiced reading of Marx shows that TIs cause a decrease of the value produced and thus of the value which can be realized. This manifests itself as a lack of purchasing power. Thus, the ultimate cause of crises is TI and the decreased production of value it engenders. It is only if one of its forms of manifestation is considered, purchasing power, that the lack of purchasing power become part of the ultimate cause.

The reason why Marx focuses on the lack of purchasing power as (part of) the ultimate cause of crises is that he wishes to oppose the view that crises are caused by 'a disproportion of production in various branches of the economy, and as a result of the disproportion between the consumption of the capitalists and their accumulation' (Marx, 1967c, p. 484). But, Marx observes, 'the replacement of the capital invested in production depends largely upon the consuming power' both of the capitalists and of the workers. Marx's focus on purchasing power should be seen within this polemical context.

21. Actually, all modal capitals, as we shall see in section 3.3.
22. As long as one focuses only on a commodity's use value, exchange cannot be explained. In fact, use values are different by definition. If they exchange for each other, they must have something in common, something which abstracts from their specific features and thus from their being the product of concrete, specific labour. This common feature can only be their being the result of the expenditure of abstract labour, that is, their having value.
23. Underconsumption theories in terms of use values run aground on this objection. (See Carchedi, 1999b.)
24. Some orthodox economists sense the contradiction between use values and exchange value, that is, the contradiction inherent in the introduction of TI within the capitalist production relations, but their perception is limited to 'too many goods . . . chasing too little demand'. This 'overcapacity problem' follows from 'fierce cost-price competition [which] leads companies to take measures – cutting labor costs, modernizing production [i.e. introducing TI], trading jobs to get access to hot markets – that both erode the worldwide consumption base and creates extra output' (Greider, 1997).
25. Thus, ARP can fall also during recovery, towards its end. As we shall see, it rises at the beginning of the recovery (when its conditions have been created by the preceding crisis) or (irrespective of the phase of the cycle) because of the emergence of new, labour-intensive sectors (e.g. software).
26. Initially, it is possible that employers might not want to lay off trained, trusty (etc.) workers in the hope that economic difficulties might be temporary. This is disguised unemployment. But sooner or later unemployment will appear.
27. Mandel (1970) lists the principal factors decelerating expansion, that is,

> the drop in the investment rate as the result of growing excess capacity, the fall in the average rate of profit, and the inability to make up in the long run for the growing gap between productive potential and effective demand by a steadily expanding inflation of credit. (p. 10)

To these, the growth in the organic composition of capital, that is, of constant capital relative to variable capital per unit of capital, could be added. But these are all aspects of the ultimate cause of crisis, the decreasing production of (surplus) value as a result of technological innovations within the context of capitalist production relations. This becomes visible as an increase in the rate of profit of the technological leaders but as a fall in the rate of profit of the laggards and thus in the ARP. Investments decrease. Owing to bankruptcies of those capital units with lower organic composition and to the investments of the technological leaders, the organic composition of the economy grows but purchasing power falls (i.e. excess capacity increases). Inflation can provide only temporary relief because (a) if wages rise less than the price of wage goods, potential profits increase. However, inasmuch as purchasing power is not transferred to other classes or commodities sold abroad, the realization of those profits in sector II becomes increasingly difficult. (b) If wages rise more than the price of wage goods, purchasing power in sector II increases but profits fall.
28. The money needed for this new cycle of revival has a double origin. The money needed

for the initial investments is money already existing as reserves and savings accumulated during the previous crisis. It corresponds to already produced but not yet realized commodities (means of production, means of consumption and luxuries) as well as to the labour power which has been laid off and is waiting to be employed again. The creation of extra money is required by the creation of extra surplus value, once all reserves have been used and if unit prices are to remain constant.

29. For a detailed critique of the underconsumptionist thesis, see Carchedi, 1999b.

30. As Marx (1967) observes, a builder must buy a large plot of ground, build many houses on it and thus

embark on an enterprise which exceeds his resources twenty to fifty times. The funds are procured through mortgaging and the money is placed at the disposal of the contractor as the buildings proceed. Then, if a crisis comes along and interrupts the payment of the advance instalments, the entire enterprise generally collapses. At best, the houses remain unfinished until better times arrive; at the worst they are sold at auction for half their cost. (p. 234)

This is not destruction but redistribution of value.

31. In this case, their constant capital is devalued and the rate of profit increased.

32. 'Interruptions, disturbances of the process of social production, in consequence for instance of crises, have therefore very different effects on labour-products of a discrete nature and on those that require for their production a prolonged connected period. In the one case all that happens is that to-day's production of a certain quantity of yarn, coal, etc. is not followed by to-morrow's new production of yarn, coal, etc. Not so in the case of ships, buildings, railways, etc. Here it is not only the day's work but an entire connected act of production that is interrupted. If the job is not continued, the means of production and labour already consumed in its production are wasted. Even if it is resumed, a deterioration has inevitably set in the meantime' (Marx, 1967b, p. 230).

33. See also Moseley, 1986, 1988a, 1988b, 1989a, 1989b, 1989c, for computations of the US profit rate based on the recasting of official data into value categories. Moseley's results broadly agree with what is submitted here.

34. If poverty is so great in the underdeveloped countries, why do the more advanced countries not engage in a massive programme of food aid? The reason is that this aid is food bought by the government and given to the poor countries. This money must be raised through taxes. If it is the capitalists who are taxed, profits are reduced. If it is the labourers who are taxed, real wages are reduced. Any sizeable scale of food aid would then be checked by political opposition. One way to avoid this obstacle is by having the labourers themselves and the population at large donate food 'spontaneously' through the organization of pop concerts and other activities stirred by the mass media, and so on.

35. The derivation is as follows: $p' = s/(c + v) = (s/v)/[(c + v)/v] = s'/[(c/v) + (v/v)] = s'/(q + 1)$.

36. The rate of profit remains constant in sector II but rises in sector I. The ARP rises.

37. For a detailed discussion, see Carchedi, 1991a, ch. 5.

38. In the US, at a time when 'many industrial sectors are burdened by dangerous levels of overcapacity ... household debt has reached an astonishing 91 percent of disposable personal income, compared with 65 percent in 1980' (Greider, 1997).

39. This is the essence of the critique of the multiplier (see above and Carchedi, 1991a, ch. 5).

40. Notice that an increase in the quantity of money does not neccessarily cause inflation. First, it can meet the increased production of material use values, thus keeping unit prices unchanged. Second, it can be used for the purchase of unsold products, including idle resources. And third, it can be used for imports. But these arguments remain within the boundaries of orthodox economics that relate the quantity of money to the quantity of use values. If, on the other hand, one conceives of inflation as an increase in the quantity of money greater than the increase in the value produced, then the rate of inflation is much greater than that given by official statistics. In fact, in periods of economic depression and crises, while the quantity of value produced falls

(due to unemployment), the quantity of money is increased in order to stimulate demand.

41. According to orthodoxy, budget debts generate inflation through the higher employment and thus the higher wages originated by state spending. But, as mentioned above, higher wages could be compensated by lower profits, so that no inflation need follow. The thesis that state borrowing creates inflation through higher wages is an implicit rationalization of capital's interests.

42. This topic cannot be dealt with here in any detail. (See, on this point, Carchedi, 1991a, ch. 5.)

43. However, official data on profit rates can be used if properly filtered. See figures 3.1, 3.2 and 3.3 above. See also Moseley, 1986, 1988a, 1988b, 1989a, 1989b, 1989c, for computations of the US profit rate based on the recasting of official data into value categories. Moseley's results broadly agree with what is submitted here. Also, unemployment figures are notorious for underestimating the real size of unemployment.

44. The method for deriving value quantities from their monetary expressions has been expounded above in this chapter. (See Carchedi and de Haan, 1996.)

45. The term 'price of production' implies that we consider (as a first step) only the production side in the determination of prices. Demand will be considered shortly.

46. Allowance should be made for the fact that a part of the output is kept on a regular basis as inventories, so that the $D = S$ assumption applies to the net output of inventories.

47. Table 3.5 can be extended into table 3.6 because table 3.6 has been previously compressed (simplified) in table 3.5. For reasons of exposition, it has been chosen to start with a discussion of table 3.5 first.

48. Another way to put this point is that the concept of ARP does not refer to the value that would be produced and thus realized in the future if only the high productivity capitals would remain. Or, the question is not which capitals would realize the average of that future value. Rather, it refers to the question as to which capitals would realize now the ARP given the present value produced. This cannot be otherwise because we want to determine present, not future, prices.

49. To repeat, the difference between this notion of $D = S$ and the neo-classical one is that this notion stresses that market equilibrium, far from leading to the equilibrium between production, distribution and consumption, leads towards crises and unemployment.

50. For nine important aspects of this model, see Carchedi, 1991a, section 3.4.5.

51. Of course, funds can be kept in foreign currencies, but this case is disregarded here because it does not affect the argument.

52. Depreciation and appreciation refer to a system of flexible exchange rates, while devaluation and revaluation refer to a system of fixed exchange rates. In what follows, flexible exchange rates will be assumed unless otherwise stated.

53. This is the direct quotation. In the British convention, or indirect quotation, the rate of exchange is defined as the rate at which foreign currencies are converted into one unit of national currency. There is no space here for an analysis of the formation of rates of exchange. Suffice it to mention that, just as the market prices tend towards the production prices, that is, the prices at which the average productivity capitals tendentially realize the average rate of profit, in the same way, given sufficient international capital mobility, the international market prices tend towards international prices of production, that is, those prices at which all average productivity producers on a global scale tendentially realize the international average rate of profit. (See Carchedi, 1991a, ch. 7, and Carchedi, 1991b.) The same works introduce the concept of *tendential rate of exchange*, that is, the rate which converts the international prices of production expressed in international currency into national prices of production expressed in national currency so that all average productivity capitals tendentially realize that quantity of international value expressed in their national currencies corresponding to the average rate of profit. The actual rates of exchange tend towards the tendential one. This theory relates exchange rates to productivity and thus to trade. Speculative movements are ultimately determined by these fundamental factors, as the following sections will argue.

54. Take the case of German exports, x, and a rate of exchange of DM 1 = \$1. Suppose $1x$

= DM 1 = \$1. After appreciation, 1 unit = DM 1 = \$2. By exporting $1x$, German exporters gain \$2 instead of \$1.

55. Take now the case of German importers of American goods, y. Suppose $1y$ = \$1 = DM 1. After appreciation, $1y$ = \$1 = DM ½. By importing $1y$, German importers save DM ½.

56. Technological innovation is the essence of capitalist competition within sectors. Therefore, it allows a better penetration of foreign markets than competitive depreciations. For example, the *Financial Times* of 1 November 1995 reports that between 1987 and 1994, Italy's EU market share declined from 13.22 to 12.28 per cent, in spite of the lira's heavy devaluation.

57. I disregard here the advantage for those engaging in import substitution because this falls outside the scope of this work.

58. The implicit assumption in using this terminology is that the underdeveloped countries have not yet reached, but will eventually reach, the level of development of the developed ones. This position is rejected here. But the same terminology can be used as long as it is understood that (a) the dominated bloc is such because it has been and is being underdeveloped by the dominant bloc, and (b) there is no question of all countries reaching the same capacity to compete (let alone the same level of development).

59. Hoarding and savings are disregarded here for the sake of brevity.

60. Thus, the massive US trade deficit represents at the same time a massive appropriation of international value through seigniorage. It is for this reason that the US deficit, while signalling an economic malaise, that is, the relative (as opposed to absolute) decline of US productivity, is at the same time beneficial for the US economy.

61. 'On foreign-exchange markets, the dollar is involved in one way or the other in 85 per cent of the transactions. Often the only way to exchange Mexican pesos for British pounds is to convert pesos into dollars and then into pounds' (*Financial Times*, 9 March 1995).

62. Other strong currencies might be put under pressure to support the dollar, thus losing international purchasing power when the dollar devalues: 'This intervention has already cost the BoJ [Bank of Japan] a small fortune. Since last summer, its foreign exchange reserves – mostly dollars – have risen by \$14bn to more than \$125bn. Since the dollar has fallen by an average 10% over that time, the loss to the BoJ is considerable' *Financial Times*, 9 March 1995).

63. What follows can be used to analyse both the 1994–5 Mexican crisis (see Carchedi, 1997) and the 1997–8 Asian crisis.

64. The absurd rationality of this system becomes manifest as, on the one hand, capital unable to offer employment (because unable to find investment outlets outside the speculative sphere) and, on the other, a swelling reserve army of labour looking for employment. The depth of the crisis is revealed both by unemployment figures (approaching for some countries those of the Great Depression) and by the sheer size of financial capital on the speculative markets.

65. See, for example, Allen, 1994. For a critique, see Carchedi, 1996.

66. This can partly compensate the negative effects of a fall in A's stock exchange.

67. This competitive depreciation might undo A's advantages deriving from its own depreciation.

68. The dilemma for countries experiencing this kind of difficulty is that lower interest rates may stimulate exports but may also provoke capital outflows. In the Asian stock exchange and monetary crisis of 1997–8, the IMF advocated higher rates and financial discipline while the World Bank advocated lower rates and expansionist policies.

69. This saturation should be explained not in terms of overproduction of use values (see Carchedi, 1999b) but in terms of underproduction of surplus value (see section 3.2 above).

70. Radical critics too tend to blame free capital markets without mentioning the value dimension. Thus, Wade and Veneroso (1998) blame the 'international capital markets' (p. 33), Strange (1998) stresses 'reckless over-lending' (p. 120), and Cumings (1998) seems to advocate 'global regulation [and] international macro-economic policies to stabilize the whole' (p. 72) but also stresses the willingness of the US to bring down the Japanese–South Korean development model (based on sheltered economies) after the

fall of 'Communism' (p. 45). As I will argue in a moment, one should inquire into value production to begin with and then analyse its manifestations in the financial and monetary sphere.

71. Thus, speaking at the World Economic Forum in Davos, Switzerland, on 29 January 1999, Deutsche Bank's chief economist in Asia 'saw massive world-wide excess capacity in almost every sector of traded goods'. He also stressed 'a dangerously big exposure by banks in industrialized countries to emerging market creditors and weak political leadership'. (Chote and de Jonquières, 1999).

72. Which of course have consequences for the next period's production of value and surplus value

73. 'As many critics of the Asian model have pointed out, these countries overinvested in some manufacturing sectors and in essentially speculative ventures in real estate, infrastructure and equities, resulting in inefficient investment, assets bubbles, credit excesses and exchange rate overvaluation – the ills that led to the current crisis' (Wade and Veneroso, 1998, p. 31).

74. This explains why even countries with good 'fundamentals' might be subjected to speculative attacks. In 1998, Korea, Thailand, Malaysia and Indonesia had built up huge current account surpluses. But these surpluses had been caused by import falls by 30–40 per cent in the past year rather than by export expansion. Import falls are both the effect of economic malaise and can provoke inflation. On both accounts they spell the danger of currency depreciations (Wade and Veneroso, 1998, p. 15). Even Hong Kong, which in 1998 had low debt, large exchange reserves and a current account surplus, has seen its currency being put under pressure by foreign speculators. 'The hedge funds calculated that, when competitor countries had devalued by 30–40 per cent and more against the US dollar, the Hong Kong dollar would have to be devalued as well' (Wade and Veneroso, 1998, p. 23).

75. For years, the exchange rate of the Argentinean peso against the US dollar has been 1 to 1. In this way, the quantity of pesos in circulation has been set equal to the dollar reserves of the Central Bank. If speculators sell pesos and buy dollars, the Central Bank reduces the quantity of pesos and the interest rate rises. Inflation is defeated but the real economy contracts. Conquering inflation is given such a prominence that in January 1999 a proposal was put forward by Argentina's then president, Carlos Menem, to replace the peso with the US dollar! See chapter 5 below.

76. In 1994 Brazil tied the value of the real to that of the US dollar by allowing the real to depreciate by a maximum of 7.5 per cent against the dollar. In September 1998, contagion spread from Asia and Russia to Brazil. Investors were worried about Brazil's debt level (state debt was US$189bn) and started to pull out their capital. In January, 1999, after massive capital flights had more than halved Brazil's foreign reserves, exchange controls had to be lifted and the real was allowed to fluctuate freely. A $41.5bn bailout package from the IMF and a variety of nations and international agencies was unable to stem the outflow of capital. The real had become the object of speculative attacks because of fear of contagion from the Asian crisis which had surfaced eighteen months earlier. But a country is susceptible to contagion only if it (its economy) is weak. This was the case in Mexico. High interest rates had not only strangled productive capital but also hit exports through the high value of the real. Unemployment had skyrocketed (even if for a few years a new layer of workers with relatively stable and high wages had emerged). Deflationary policies had brought down inflation but could not avert the crisis. These policies, as stressed above, are not the cause of the crisis but only one way in which, in spite of the economic agents' intention to hold back the crisis, the crisis becomes manifest.

77. 'Capital curbs are an idea whose time has returned in the minds of many Asian government officials' (Wade and Veneroso, 1998, p. 27) as well as in that of many Western economists.

4. The Economic and Monetary Union

1. The role of the IMF is that of forcing the dependent countries to compete through lower labour costs (wages) while fostering at the same time a dependent form of industrialization.

2. This does not imply that the colonies' fortune would automatically improve if foreign capital inflows were to stop. Systematic plunder of natural resources makes development (in whatever form) impossible. Moreover, the alternative to capitalist underdevelopment is a different type, a socialist type, of development.

3. These are: (a) aerospace, (b) telecommunications, (c) computer and office machines, (d) electronics, (e) consumer electronics, (f) scientific, medical, optical apparatus, prostheses, (g) machinery, (h) nuclear power, radioactive elements and isotopes (i) chemicals and (j) weapons.

4. Singapore imported a total of 25.8bn, of which 38.0 per cent came from ASE6, 22.7 per cent from the US, 20.3 per cent from Japan and 9.4 per cent from the EU.

5. Singapore exported 23.6bn, of which 34.8 per cent went to ASE6, 26.4 per cent to the US, 17.4 per cent to the EU and 8.2 per cent to Japan.

6. In this table, high-technology sectors are defined as (a) chemicals and chemical products, (b) office machinery and computers, (c) radio, television and communication, (d) motor vehicles, trailers and semi-trailers, (e) machinery and equipment, (f) electrical machinery and (9) medical, precision and optical instruments. This definition is broadly similar to that in note 3 above.

7. Patents are granted, according to a uniform patent system, by the European Patent Organization, which was established in 1973. The European Patent Organization comprises its legislative body, the Administrative Council, and its executive body, the European Patent Office (EPO). The EPO was established in 1977. Its headquarters are located in Munich. It has a staff of around 3,800. In 1997, it granted 39,646 patents and opposed 2,518.

8. The question that is left unanswered is: if the market is rational, how come it can generate irrationality, that is, anti-competitive behaviour? Neo-classical economics has no answer to this question. It explores the way in which obstacles to competition arise, but it does not tackle, let alone answer, the above question. The real reason for the centrality of perfect competition in orthodox theory is purely ideological, in that it rationalizes the capitalist system as the best of all possible worlds. Moreover, as will be seen soon, the ideological function of the notion of perfect competition as the inspirer of competition policy is that of fostering the interests of those firms which are really free to compete, the oligopolies, those same enterprises whose power competition policy claims to fight.

9. A rise in the profit rate of a certain sector due to technological innovation is based on the appropriation of value from (a) all other sectors of the economy as well as from (b) the less efficient capitals in that sector. Moreover, such a rise in a certain sector does not necessarily cause capital inflows if that higher profit rate is still lower than that of the other sectors of the economy. See chapter 3. (For more details on these and related topics, see Carchedi, 1991a, ch. 3.)

10. For the intellectual representatives of big capital, free competition means something quite different from what neo-classical economics means. They interpret this notion quite literally, irrespective of whether the size of their operations does affect prices or objectively excludes smaller capitals from the market.

11. Actually, we witness a double process. On the one hand the aggregation of nation states in the EU is a step towards a United States of Europe but on the other a tendency towards secessionism within the existing nation states, as in the case of northern Italy and Bavaria. This theme cannot be pursued here.

12. For an earlier version of this section, see Carchedi, 1997.

13. 'Following the Smithsonian Accord the margin of fluctuation on either side of the central rate in relation to the dollar was 2.25 per cent, giving a maximum band of 4.5%. This was the tunnel. However, the Council decided that this condition could not apply to intra-Community currencies since if, simultaneously, one currency rose from the bottom to the top of the band while another fell from the top to the bottom, then their

relative fluctuations would be 9%. This would have an unacceptable effect on the CAP pricing system. The Council, therefore, decided to restrict the intra-EEC rate band – the snake – to 2.25%' (Swann, 1995, p. 215).

14. The price of gold was set at the average of the prices, converted into ECUs, recorded daily at the two London fixings during the previous six calendar months. The US dollar was valued at the market rate (against that nation's currency) two working days prior to the value date. Decision (No. 12/79) of the Board of Governors of 13 March 1979, article 2.1.

15. ibid., article 2.3.

16. Council Regulation (EEC) No. 3181/78 of 18 December 1978 relating to the European Monetary System, articles 1 and 2.

17. Big capital organizes the representation of its interests also through its own organizations. For example, concomitant with the introduction of the EMS, the Association for the Monetary Union of Europe was founded. According to its own presentation on the Internet it was founded

> by European industrialists who agreed on the objectives of monetary stability and a single currency for the success of the Single Market. The President of the Association is Étienne Davignon, President of Société Générale de Belgique. The Vice-President is François-Xavier Ortoli, Honorary Chairman of Total, and former President of the European Commission. The Secretary General is Bertrand de Maigret. . . . Companies and banks, which are members of the Association, globally employ nearly 8,000,000 people. Small and medium-sized companies participate in the activities of AMUE through professional organizations such as the Italian Confindustria, the Federations of Dutch, Greek and Swedish Industries, the French Chambers of Commerce, the Belgian, Irish, Finnish and Spanish Employers' Confederations.

18. Consider by way of example the maximum fluctuation of the FF and the HFL relative to each other. Suppose the FF lost value relative to the HFL (i.e. the HFL gained value relative to the FF). Either the FF devalued by a maximum of 15 per cent or the HFL revalued by a maximum of 15 per cent. Politically, there is a difference between Holland revaluing relative to France or France devaluing relative to Holland. France preferred the former option in order to avoid the negative image associated with devaluation. Computationally too these two outcomes are not the same. Then, the average was taken. For example, in 1995, ECU 1 was equal to HFL 2.152 and to FF 6.406 (*Financial Times*, 7 March 1995). Then, HFL 2.152 = FF 6.406. Or, FF 1 = 2.152/6.406 = HFL 0.3359 and HFL 1 = 6.406/2.152 = FF 2.977. If the FF devalued by 15 per cent, it fell to (6.406 + 15 per cent of 6.406) = FF 7.3669 relative to HFL 2.152. This means that if HFL 2.152 = FF 7.3669, HFL 1 = 7.3669/2.152 = FF 3.423. If the HFL was revalued by 15 per cent, it rose to (2.152 − 15 per cent of 2.152) = HFL 1.8292 relative to FF 6.406. This means that HFL 1.8292 = FF 6.406, so that HFL 1 = 6.406/1.8292 = FF 3.5021. If the average is taken, (3.5021 + 3.423)/2 = FF 3.46255. This gave the maximum devaluation of the FF relative to the HFL (i.e. the maximum revaluation of the HFL relative to the FF). Or, given that the cross rate was HFL 1 = FF 2.976, the FF was allowed to devalue relative to the HFL (i.e. the HFL could revalue relative to the FF) up to a maximum of HFL 1 = FF 3.457. Similarly for the case in which the FF was revalued relative to the HFL (i.e. the HFL was devalued relative to the FF).

Actually, the currency whose maximum divergence spread was computed was itself a component part of the ECU. That currency, inasmuch as it was a part of the ECU, could fluctuate around itself, that is, could fluctuate around the ECU only by 100 per cent minus its weight in the ECU. For example, if the mark formed 30.2 per cent of the value of the ECU, it could fluctuate only by 100–30.2, that is, 69.8, around the ECU, that is, against the other currencies forming the ECU. Then, the limit up to which the mark could fluctuate against the value of the ECU expressed in marks, the maximum divergence spread for the mark, was 0.698 × 5 = ±10.47 per cent. It follows that the maximum divergence spread was different for each currency, that is, high (close to 15 per cent) for those currencies with a low weight and low for those currencies with a high weight. The *divergence indicator* showed the extent to which a given currency deviated from its maximum spread. When this indicator reached 75 per cent of the maximum divergence spread (the *divergence threshold*), in this example ±10.47 × 0.75 = ± 7.85 per cent, there was a presumption that that government would take remedial action.

19. Which does not necessarily mean that Germany's rate of surplus value is lower than that of the other less advanced countries.

20. Inflation can be an instrument of class struggle relatively independent of technological differentials, that is, as a means to recoup profitability losses due to high labour combativeness, as in Italy in the late 1960s and early 1970s. This is why Germany is suspicious of governments which cannot 'properly manage' their working classes.

21. This highlights the reason why exchange rates within the ERM could not be stable: this is the member states' unequal development. But there is also a second reason. Investors, when moving out of dollar positions for fear of a fall in its value, sought a safe currency. They usually did not purchase other European currencies but preferred the mark, which was in no (or less) danger of being devalued. This extra demand for the mark affected the exchange rate between the mark and the other European currencies, putting the bilateral bands under strain and possibly forcing realignment. In this way, a large influx of dollars threatened the working of the ERM, whose aim was to avoid realignments.

22. Italy was readmitted to the ERM in August 1996. It had joined the EMS at its inception. From 1979, when the EMS began operating, until 1989, Italy enjoyed wider bands of fluctuation, ±6 per cent as opposed to ±2.25 per cent, the other member countries' bands. In 1989 Italy decided to renounce its wider bands and to reduce them to ±2.25 per cent. The timing was badly chosen. The German interest rates hike which followed reunification caused an outflow of capital from Italy (as well as from other countries) and a decrease of foreign reserves. A higher Italian interest rate was not an option, given the authorities' belief that such a move would have ushered in a recession. Speculators bet that Italy would not have been able to defend those narrow bands and thus that central rate. They won the bet, in spite of Germany's intervention to the tune of DM 44bn to prop up the pound and the lira. Facing a massive outflow on international reserves, Italy withdrew from the EMS in September 1992, thus allowing the lira to fluctuate, that is, to devalue. However, Italian advanced industrial capital, while profiting in the export sector in the short run from this devaluation, had a longer-run interest in remaining in the EMS, because of the reasons submitted in this section and thus because of its interest in Italy joining the EMU if and when it would be formed.

    The UK did not seek readmission because it was not interested in joining the EMU, for reasons to be highlighted in chapter 6, section 3.

23. Within labour, some strata, such as women, children, foreign workers, racial and other minorities, etc., are penalized more than others. This important point cannot be pursued here. (See Gill, 1997.)

24. Formally, access to the EMU was made conditional upon the following criteria: the deficit could not be greater than 3 per cent of GDP; the national debt could not be greater than 60 per cent of GDP; inflation could not be higher than 1.5 per cent of the average of the inflation rates of the three countries with the lowest rates, long-term interest rates could not be higher than 2 per cent of the rates of the three countries with the lowest rates; and the exchange rates must be within the ERM. It has been pointed out repeatedly that, quantitatively, they were arbitrary (why 3 per cent and not any other figure?) and irrational: Japan would not have been allowed membership in the EMU due to its high level of debt. In the event, accession to the EMU was dictated more by political manoeuvring than by adherence to (politically motivated) so-called 'objective' criteria.

    These continue to play a role also after the introductionn of the EMU. On 8 November 1995, the German minister of finance, Theo Waigel, spelled out his proposal for a 'stability pact'. This was approved at the Dublin summit of 13–14 December 1996. Basically, after joining the EMU, member countries have to aim at a budget deficit of 1 per cent in normal times and of no more than 3 per cent in difficult times. Countries failing these requirements will have to pay a deposit (of between 0.2 per cent and 0.5 per cent of GDP), which, if the deficit is not be corrected within two years, will be turned into a fine. There are also escape clauses (*Europa van Morgen*, 1996).

25. This is the meaning of article 3a(3) of the EC Treaty, which lays down the EMU's guiding principles: stable prices, sound public finances and monetary conditions and a sustainable balance of payments.

26. For a lucid analysis, complementary to the present one, of this and related points concerning Britain's membership of the EMU, see Bonefeld and Burnham, 1996.

5. The Geo-politics of the Euro

1. The following, even though of general application, has been written with the condition of Latin America in mind. I wish to thank all the participants in the seminars I gave at the universities of Buenos Aires and of Quilmes as well as at the Confederation of Argentinian Workers (CTA) in April 2000. Their comments and suggestions have been most useful in improving this chapter.

2. 'For much of Latin America, the story of the past decade has been the story of democratization. But recent developments – the semi-coup in Ecuador last month and the 1998 election of an authoritarian leader in Venezuela, escalating guerrilla warfare in Colombia – are causing concern in Washington that the momentum may be shifting' (Lancaster, 2000).

3. The Canadian case is complex. The case has forcefully been made that Quebec's premier, Lucien Bouchard, favours Quebec's independence only in order to enter subsequently into a common currency area with the Mercosur countries, which constitutes the central trading bloc for Quebec. This common currency can only be the American dollar. *The Hidden Face of Lucien Bouchard's Argentina Visit*, by Bruce Katz and René Silva, internet article. It can be requested from the author.

4. Dollarization can refer to the substitution of a local currency by any currency (a nice example of cultural imperialism). However, this chapter will refer to the use of the US dollar.

5. As mentioned above, Ecuador and East Timor should be added to this list.

6. The text by Schuler contains the following note: 'The new $20, $50, and $100 bills cost about twice as much to print because they have more elaborate features to protect against counterfeiting, but they also have longer average lives than the $1 bill.'

7. In an oft-quoted paper, Fischer (1982) measured national seigniorage for groups of countries (he actually measured the seigniorage which would be lost in case of dollarization, which is the same). He did not use absolute figures of high-powered money but the ratio of high-powered money to GNP. He found the average to be about 8 per cent for 1976. He concluded, 'The transition cost [to dollarization] appears to be prohibitive' (p. 305). However, Bogetic (1999) objects that since then the ratio of currency to GDP has fallen. According to his own computation for seven selected Latin American countries, the ratio of currency in circulation to GDP averaged 4.6 per cent in the 1991–7 period (table 5). This figure would have been much lower had it not been for Ecuador, whose ratio is 12.2 per cent. For Argentina the ratio is 3.7 per cent.

8. Paper money's value is given by its purchasing power, but on condition that it can purchase. As long as they remain in the vaults of the central banks, or circulate outside the US, dollars cannot be made to purchase US goods.

9. The Special Drawing Rights have remained a unit of account basically because their use as a world currency is not in the interest of the US.

10. See Hanke and Schuler, 1999, for a review of the way the currency board works. The difference between a currency board and full dollarization is that in the latter the local currency ceases to exist (except, perhaps, for small coins). In this case, monetary policy is a realm of the US only. A monetary union is different from dollarization in that monetary policy is made collectively, even though some member countries may have a bigger say than others.

11. Not necessarily dollar notes. See below.

12. Seigniorage sharing is thus confusingly conceived in the literature as the reimbursement

by the US to the dollarized country of a part of the interests the US does not pay any more, that is, of the interests the dollarized country loses when it converts US securities into dollar notes. If there is no such sharing agreement, the US is said to collect all seigniorage. 'The United States collects all seigniorage on the use of U.S. dollar in Panama, and there is no seigniorage sharing' (Bogetic, 1999).

13. Commentators take it for granted that the conversion rate will be $1 = 1 peso. However, credit money has to be converted as well. In principle, the Argentinian central bank or the treasury can change the denomination of its debt from pesos into dollars. This would require extra dollar notes only for the net debt which is not renewed (and depends therefore on the confidence of the public in the solidity of the treasury). However, the argument that extra dollars will be needed for the conversion might be used in order to justify a lower conversion rate (e.g. $1 = 1.2 pesos) for reasons to be mentioned below.

14. This value appropriation is also called unequal exchange. See above and Carchedi, 1991a, ch. 7.

15. The United States Joint Economic Committee has proposed the following formula if Argentina dollarized fully: ([US$580bn $\times$ 0.05] $-$ US$1bn) $\times$ 0.028 $\times$ 1 = (US$29bn $-$ US$1bn) $\times$ 0.028 $\times$ 1 = US$784m (Bogetic, 1999). This sum should be paid every year. Here, $580bn is the estimated monetary base in the year 2000, 0.05 is the interest rate (5 per cent) of ninety-day Treasury bills as a proxy for the opportunity cost of reserves, $1bn is the net operating costs of the Federal reserves, 0.028 is Argentina's share of total average dollar monetary base, and 1 (or 100 per cent) indicates that the US would have to pay the whole amount. Notice that $784bn does not differ substantially from $750bn.

16. The focus here is on international seigniorage. The loss for the Argentine state is compounded by the loss of national seigniorage.

17. As experiences with US contributions to the UN demonstrate.

18. Bogetic (1999) mentions a proposal by Barro 'that the United States simply transfers to Argentina the U.S. dollar equivalent of its peso currency in circulation, estimated at about U.S.$16 billion'. Schuler's (1999a) objection is that 'Argentina could take the lump-sum payment, then turn around and reintroduce its domestic currency, cheating the U.S. government out of $16 billion.' This is far-fetched. The US could easily impose a clause for the restitution of that sum if Argentina were to de-dollarize and could easily impose the honouring of that clause. The reasons why the US will not choose any such proposal have just been given.

Interestingly enough, while those $16bn are not considered as an appropriation of value by the US from the dollarizing country, if that country de-dollarized, that sum 'would suddenly become available to be spent on US goods and services. This would be represent a multi-billion dollar gift to the economy in question, which is most definitely not appropriate' (Testimony of Dr Michael Gavin, 1999). Obviously, for the US it *is* most definitely appropriate to receive a multi-billion dollar gift from the dollarizing country to the tune of $16bn!

19. From the point of view of the labour theory of value, if Argentina exports goods to the US, it cedes real value in exchange for worthless paper (dollar) notes. Argentina gets back real value if it exchanges those dollar notes for US goods, that is, if it imports from the US. If Argentina does not use those notes to import US goods (because of seigniorage), it has given real value for free to the US. Alternatively, if those dollars are used by Argentina to import from the US, real value is got back and this is to the detriment of the US, that is, it is a reduction of its seigniorage. Yet orthodox economics sees these imports by Argentina as an advantage for the US because it focuses on the difficulties of realizating the value produced in the US and thus on the possibility of realizing that value in Argentina. What from the point of view of labour is a negative factor for the US (loss of seigniorage, i.e. value) is seen as a positive factor from the point of view of capital, as the realization in Argentina of US value.

20. Many commentators stress that dollarization in and of itself is no panacea. To reach its objectives, exports must increase, technological development must reach international levels, foreign capital must be enticed through low tax rates, and so on. But, of course, if a country could do this, there would be no need for dollarization to begin with.

21. This is why the governor of the Mexican Central Bank thinks that dollarization could be 'a potential addition to country risk' (Ortiz, 1999).
22. In Ecuador the fall of nominal wages did not have to wait for official dollarization. Monthly salaries fell from \$150 in August 1998 to \$50 in January 2000 (Acosta and Schuldt, 2000).
23. This concerns dollarization proper. Usually, dollarization is proposed as a part of a neo-liberal package featuring both privatizations and lower real wages through, for example, the scrapping of subsidies, labour flexibility, and so on. In fact, it is argued, without those measures dollarization could not work. In this sense, dollarization is the 'final chapter' of neo-liberalism (Acosta, 2000). The argument that the money accruing to the state from privatizations will be used for infrastructures and/or higher wages spirits away by the touch of a magic wand all the social, economic and political conditions which have led to lack of infrastructures and low wages before dollarization. Moreover, given that the dollarizing country will probably need capital very badly, the receipts from privatization will be much less than the value of the companies privatized.
24. The currency risk of a country is measured by the interest rate differential between national currency contracts and dollar contracts in that country. The country risk is measured by the differential between interest rates on US Treasury debt and the dollar-denominated debt of that country. (Bank of International Settlements, 1999, p. 59.)
25. As long as the country dollarizes, the currency risk is removed by definition. The reason why some commentators prefer to speak of a reduction of that risk is that they do not rule out the possibility for that country to revert to its own currency.
26. In Ecuador the directors of the Central Bank had to be fired and replaced by new directors favourable to dollarization (*El Comercio*, 2000a).
27. In Ecuador, in anticipation of the loss incurred by retailers due to the fixing of the conversion rate and thus to the loss of value of their savings, local businesses did not hesitate to raise their prices (Martone, 2000). According to *El Comercio* (2000d), wages will be 'fixed by the Government' while prices cannot be fixed in a free competition system. As if wages were not the price of labour power! Given that too high a rate of inflation is prejudicial to international competitiveness, most likely governments will intervene to hold inflation down.
28. Not all sectors of the bourgeoisie favour dollarization. For example, in Argentina a sizeable fraction of capital seems to favour a managed devaluation of the peso. They are export capital and financial capital, which, knowing beforehand when devaluation would take place, could sell pesos at a higher rate and re-buy them at a lower rate. Also foreign capital favours a managed devaluation, for example foreign financial capital and foreign productive capital which has bought Argentine firms.
29. Mercosur is a trade area formed in 1991 and including Argentina, Bolivia, Brazil, Chile, Paraguay and Uruguay.
30. Argentina's full dollarization would increase its trade integration with the US at the cost of its integration within Mercosur. The same holds for all other member countries. It would make it impossible for Mercosur to develop its own currency and thus to limit US seigniorage.
31. In the words of Lawrence Summers, 'by acquiring dollars for use in their domestic economies, dollarizing countries would be extending an interest-free loan to the United States' (US Treasury, 1999).
32. While 'seigniorage' sharing is not appealing to the US, lack of it is not appealing to the countries considering full dollarization. 'The prospect of losing seigniorage [in reality, interests on US treasuries] is one factor that explains why official dollarization is rare today despite potential benefits' (Schuler, 1999b, sect. 4).
33. The US prefers to leave this task to the IMF. As soon as the Ecuadorian government's intention to dollarize became public, the IMF sent a team of experts (on 12 January) to 'advise' the government (*El Comercio*, 2000c). On 26 February an IMF delegation arrived at the Ecuadorian Congress discussing the dollarization bill to illustrate its objections to that bill. The session was suspended and the weekend used for last-minute negotiations (*El Comercio*, 2000d).
34. In the words of Lawrence Summers, 'it would not be appropriate' for the US to take this responsibility upon itself (*Latino Beat*, 1999). Sachs and Larrain (1999) prefer

flexible exchange rates with responsible monetary policies, thus showing a lack of appreciation of geo-political and international monetary factors.

35. These interests are worded by Hanke and Schuler (1999, p. 16), for whom Argentina should unilaterally dollarize without entering into a treaty with the US.

36. Not by chance, the decision to dollarize by Ecuador was criticized by Venezuela's President Hugo Chávez Frias, who favours a single South American currency (*El Comercio*, 2000b). As for Argentina, the choice for, or rejection of, dollarization is determined by the broad strategies of the different sectors of classes and, to begin with, of the local bourgeoisie. At present, the interests of those in favour of dollarization are represented by ex-President Carlos Menem. For them, fuller integration with the US, as opposed to Mercosur, has several advantages: the impossibility to de-dollarize; participation in US seigniorage (even though in a subordinate position); the possibility of devaluing the peso one more time (if the rate of conversion is lowered); and a further legitimization of neo-liberal policies. The interests of those against dollarization and in favour of a strengthening of Mercosur are represented by Argentina's current president, Fernando de la Rua.

37. 'Holdings of the dollar monetary base seem to be growing faster abroad than in the United States' (Schuler, 1999a, sect. 8).

38. The Philippines supports the creation of a common ASEAN currency, a regional strategy which, according to the Philippines Trade Secretary, is 'already in its mature stage' (Chipongian, 2000). ASEAN groups the Philippines, Indonesia, Malaysia, Brunei, Thailand, Singapore, Vietnam and Laos. Since Japan and South Korea (not to mention China) are not part of ASEAN, it is doubtful whether this aim is realistic at all.

39. It should be clear that rejection of dollarization implies by no means acceptance of freely floating exchange rates. The controversy between 'dollarizers' and 'floaters' is alien to the approach of this chapter.

40. 'Latin America suffers the worst income disparities of any region in the world (with sub-Saharan Africa running a close second)' (Hakim, 1999).

41. The first draft of this chapter was finished shortly after the decision by Great Britain's Home Secretary to stop former dictator Augusto Pinochet's extradition to Spain and trial for crimes against humanity.

6. Trade, Development and Wars

1. The International Monetary Fund and the World Bank are the two other major institutions serving the interests of the dominant bloc. They have been dealt with, even if summarily, in chapter 4.

2. The above disregards independent producers who sell their products to local entrepreneurs who, in their turn, sell those goods on foreign markets. This case is dealt with in Carchedi, 1991a, pp. 259–61. Here suffice it to mention that the capitalist world system is a system in which the capitalist production and thus distribution relations are dominant. Therefore, if the product of an independent producer is sold on the capitalist market, the labour which has been necessary to make it counts as if it had been expended under capitalist production relations. That product realizes the value determined by capitalist distribution relations.

3. In 1960, 42 of the 50 largest corporations were US and 8 EC. Japan had none. In 1994, the EU and the US had 14 each and Japan 22.

4. For example, India objected, in the words of McDowell (1994), that advances in, and trade liberalization of, information technology served the needs of multinational corporations.

5. Since the countries of the EU are concerned about the health risks inherent in hormone-treated beef, the EU introduced a ban on the importation of such beef (basically from the US). In 1998 the WTO, in the name of free trade, ruled against the EU ban, thus actually exposing European consumers to potential health hazards. This decision was made possible because, while before the WTO a company had to prove that its product was not harmful before it was brought on the market, with the WTO it is the importing country that has to prove that that product is harmful. Since such proof can be provided only after the product has been introduced into the market, in

case of harmful products people must actually get ill or die before measures can be taken. Another example. The US forbids the sale on its own market of shrimps caught in ways that kill endangered sea turtles. Four Asian nations (India, Malaysia, Pakistan and Thailand) using these environmentally damaging methods challenged this law and the WTO, again in the name of free trade, decided in their favour. A third example. The US wants a 'Global Free Logging Agreement'. But the elimination of tariffs on forest products, here too in the name of free trade, will increase logging just 'at a time when the world's native forests are facing extinction' (Working Group on the WTO/ MAI, 1999).

6. This is of course a huge simplification. Its purpose is to refute a country-based, as opposed to a class-based, analysis.

7. In 1955, the EU had stipulated other agreements as well. (1) *The Agreement on the European Economic Area (EEA) between the EU and EFTA.* The EEA provides for the free movement of goods, people and capital. It came into force on 1 January 1994. (2) *Agreements with Mediterranean countries* (Cyprus, Malta and Turkey; since 1 January 1996, Turkey is tied to the EU by a customs union). Besides a common tariff policy, this provides for freedom of movement of industrial goods, common legislation on technical barriers to trade, and implementation of EU competition and intellectual property rules. (3) *Partnership and Co-operation Agreements (PCAs) with the members of the Common-wealth of Independent States (CIS).* They remove quantitative restrictions on imports from the CIS, with the exception of steel and textile products. Both EU direct investments in the CIS and repatriation of funds and dividends into the EU will be unrestricted. (4) *Agreements and arrangements in Asia.* These too are non-preferential CAPs. The Commission underscores the need to accord Asia a higher policy priority. This, of course, refers to Japan. (5) *Arrangements in other regions.* They refer to negotiations underway with Mercosur, whose members are Argentina, Bolivia, Brazil, Chile, Paraguay and Uruguay. The short-term objective is a commercial and economic cooperation agreement; in the longer run the objective is the establishment of an inter-regional association.

8. Needless to say, diversification and industrialization are promoted only if they do not clash with the interests of the donor countries. For example, the Netherlands pays Tanzania Euro 200,000 per year in order to foster that country's dairy industry. At the same time, the amount of subsidies the Netherlands pays its own producers of powdered milk in order to export powdered milk to Tanzania is three times as much (Van der Laan, 1999).

9. In any case, this preferential status might soon come to an end. Take EU imports of bananas from the ACP countries. The WTO has ruled that, given that the most favoured nation clause demands equality of treatment for similar products from different member countries, the other producers of bananas, basically the huge US-owned banana plantations in South America, should access the EU market on the same terms. This spells certain ruin for the small banana producers in the ACP countries.

10. The CEECs include Albania, Bosnia-Herzegovina, Bulgaria, Croatia, the Czech Republic, Estonia, FYROM (former Yugoslav Republic of Macedonia), Hungary, Latvia, Lithuania, Poland, Romania, Slovakia and Slovenia.

11. Data for 1988 and 1994 are from *Economic Bulletin for Europe,* 1995, table 5.3.2, p. 114. Data for 1996 are from Eurostat, 1998, p. 4.

12. In table 6.8, the 1991 data include the category 'manufactured goods classified chiefly by materials' within the category 'miscellaneous manufactured goods'. The 1996 data disaggregate the two categories. Consequently, table 6.8 sums up the two categories in order to obtain the 1996 data on miscellaneous manufactured goods.

13. In 1995, the EU's most important exports to the CEECs included road vehicles, industrial and electrical machinery, medical and pharmaceutical products, office machines and computers, and chemical materials. The CEECs' most important exports to the EU included clothing, iron and steel, furniture, cork and wood, coal, coke and briquettes, and footwear. The pattern of technological dependency is clear.

14. 'The share of outward processing in the total exports of Eastern Europe [Poland, Hungary, Romania, Bulgaria, the Czech Republic and Slovakia] to the EU reached 18.5% in 1994, with textile and clothing accounting for more than 75 per cent of total

OPT [outward processing trade] exports to the Union' (*Economic Bulletin for Europe*, 1995, p. 109).

15. The other two are Cyprus and Estonia.

16. The dependent countries can also compete through devaluations. But this would not stimulate their dependent development that the centre needs.

17. What follows relies heavily on Gowan, 1995.

18. This is one important element explaining the 1999 NATO war against Yugoslavia. But there are other causes as well. Even though this topic cannot properly be dealt with here, a few comments are in order. First, it is said that this war was not caused by inter-imperialist contradictions. The above argues to the contrary: the US tries to prevent the rise of an imperialist competitor. It cannot be ruled out that inter-imperialist contradictions similar to those between the US and the USSR might emerge again, this time between the US and other blocs, including the EU. Second, it is said that, with the fall of the USSR, NATO has changed from a defensive to an offensive organization. A different view will be submitted below. Third, it is said that this was a 'humanitarian' war, to defend the Albanian Kosovars from Serbia's aggression and ethnic cleansing. This assertion is amazing, given the countless examples of both NATO and the US not only ignoring but also actually supporting gross and massive violations of human rights. But even more surprising is the readiness of public opinion to swallow this lie, even though crimes against humanity did happen in that country (both against Kosovars and against Serbs).

There are at least three real reasons, besides the one just mentioned, for NATO's intervention in Yugoslavia. First, the US/NATO wanted to show the rest of the world that the US military machine reigns supreme and that it would be unwise to challenge it. This holds particularly for Russia, just in case the critics of Russia's subordination to Western imperialism might be tempted to reverse the course. Second, both the US and the EU have economic interests in the Balkans, namely a safe corridor for the pipeline needed to transport the oil of the rich Caspian fields to the Mediterranean through Bulgaria, Macedonia and Albania. It is for this reason that the Balkans had to fall within the US and the EU sphere of influence. And third, the US/NATO wanted to create a precedent of an intervention motivated by 'humanitarian' purposes (e.g. the defence of ethnic groups or of human rights) or justified as anti-terrorist measures. Wars against 'villains' such as Cuba (on the basis of supposed violations of human rights or of international terrorism) or even Russia or China (both multi-ethnic countries where ethnic strife can be fomented deliberately through covert actions as well as through propaganda) might find in the destruction of Yugoslavia their test case, justification and rationale (B. Carchedi, 1999).

19. Within the French Parliament, the arguments against the EDC were varied. Some claimed that the EDC would stimulate the arms race, since the Soviet Bloc would perceive it as a new military threat; others were fearful that the EDC would provide fewer checks than would NATO to a new German military power; still others did not want to be put on the same level of importance as two defeated nations and three small countries. But, outside France, sentiments for the EDC were favourable. Not only had the agreement for the EDC been signed by the governments of the Six and ratified by the other five parliaments, but also President Eisenhower was in favour of it. The reason for this stance are probably those made clear by the opinion (widely shared in reactionary circles) of an adviser of the US Navy to the effect that a first-class European tactical and strategic nuclear power would have cost a united Europe 7 per cent of its GNP but would have forced the Soviet Union to spend 30 per cent of its GNP. This would have destroyed the Soviet economy, thus making it impossible to raise its standard of living (Galtung, 1972, p. 214). This opinion, voiced in 1971, was a constant of the Cold War period up to the collapse of the USSR.

20. At present, the WEU has ten full European Members, five Observers, three Associate Members and ten associate partners.

21. An indication of the weakness of the WEU is given by the British readiness to join the WEU but hostility to the EDC.

22. There are of course differences between the major political players. In the 1970s and 1980s, the Conservative Party leaned towards policies in tune with the Community's

restrictive monetary and fiscal policies as *the* way to stimulate the European economies. The Labour Party, on the other hand, leaned more towards import controls, state intervention and subsidies for declining industries (Newman, 1989).

23. The CSCE, or Conference on Security and Cooperation in Europe, was started at the 1974 Helsinki Conference and has subsequently been transformed into the Organization for Security and Cooperation in Europe (OSCE). In 1992 it was decided to develop the role of the OSCE in peacekeeping, early warning and crisis management. NATO has offered to make its resources and experience available to support OSCE tasks. While the OSCE comprises all the countries of Europe, together with the US and Canada, in the WEU the CEECs and the Baltic states have only a status of Associate partners.

24. As Howorth (1999) points out, 'the delightfully equivocal notion of 'identity' is a semantic attempt not to tread on any institutional toes' (p. 10).

25. NATO's greater influence has been strengthened by France's realization that progress towards a stronger WEU has been lacking and by its decision, announced on 5 December 1995, to re-enter (at least partially) NATO. France had left NATO in 1966, knowing that a hegemonic project like that behind a united Europe necessitated a strong, independent military organization.

26. It is certainly not by chance that:

> it is the permanent members of the UN Security Council, namely the US, Russia, Britain, France and China, that are the main arms suppliers. The first three now dominate the global market. . . . With the decline in arms demand in the industrialised countries following the end of the Cold War, arms manufacturers have had to rely more on sales to the developing world and on the opening up of new markets in the emerging economies. (Kempster, 1998, p. 2).

27. > The United Nations estimates that two million children have been killed in armed conflicts in the past decade (most in developing countries) and three times this number seriously injured or permanently disabled. Millions more have had their lives spoiled forever by the effects of war: hunger, disease, uprooting from home, sexual violence and, for some, the trauma of being made to fight. (Kempster, 1998, p. 1)

The same author stresses the inverse relationship between, on the one hand, military spending and, on the other, lack of social investments, the burden of foreign debt (it is estimated that some 20 per cent of the developing world's debt can be attributed to arms procurement) and environmental degradation.

28. The army, in its turn, is a truly dictatorial organization, as revealed by military training, whose aim is to take 'away [soldiers'] individuality and train them to unthinkingly do what they are told to do', that is, to kill (Dumas, 1998, p. 6). Conversion implies at the same time a retraining of the military mind.

7. The Common Agricultural Policy

1. This section has has greatly benefited from several discussions with Professor Gerrit Meester of the University of Amsterdam. However, responsibility is mine alone.

2. Moreover, the analysis of green rates further below will reveal that this system favoured Germany rather than France.

3. 'The unit of account was chosen for a number of [other] reasons: it avoids the need to choose a national currency as a denominator; it emphasizes the fact that the price or amount in question is the same throughout the Community; and, finally, it implies . . . that adjustment is necessary in line with monetary developments, in order to maintain the unity of the market' (European Parliament, 1992, p. 10).

4. Synonyms for green rates are green money, agri-money, official conversion rates for agricultural purposes, and representative rates.

5. See de Bont, 1994; Harris et al., 1983; Irving and Fearn, 1975; Silvis and Mookhoek, 1994.

6. Already in 1968, Council Regulation 653 allowed for a change in the value of the AUA 'automatically, when the parities of the currencies of all Member States move simultaneously and in the same direction', and 'by decision of the Council, if necessary, where there is a change in the parity relationship between the currencies of the Member States' (*Official Journal of the European Communities*, 1968a). Regulation 1134 (*Official Journal of the European Communities*, 1968b) lays down the rule for the implementation of Regulation 653.

7. The levy on a tonne of wheat would have been $(493.707 \times 100/555.419) - 100 = 11.11$ per cent. That is, on a tonne of wheat it would have been FF 555.419×11.11 per cent of $555.419 = 61.70705$. Then, $555.419 - 61.70705 = 493.71$.

8. For example, in terms of table 7.3 above, a French farmer would have received FF 493.707 in France or the same price in Germany after the imposition of the export levy.

9. There is no necessary relationship between devaluation and inflation. Inasmuch as import prices rise and more purchasing power is spent on imports, less purchasing power is spent on internally produced products whose prices fall. It is only if the quantity of money available for the latter goods is increased that inflation follows. In 1992–3, to mention only one example, Italy resorted to sizeable devaluations. Yet inflation was moderate.

10. 'The transition from prices expressed in AUA to prices in Ecus was effected by multiplying all the amounts fixed in AUA – and all green rates – by a coefficient of 1.208953, since the value of the Ecu was lower than that of the earlier AUA' (European Parliament, 1992, p. 13). Notice that in 1975 the EEC introduced a unit of account for purposes of administering the EDF and the EIB. This was a 'basket' of EEC currencies which closely resembled the ECU. (See Irving and Fearn, 1975, pp. 54–6.)

11. Attempts to reduce the agricultural costs of surpluses go back as far as 1968 with the Mansholt plan. This plan aimed at shifting emphasis from market and price support to structural improvement. Bigger farms needed to be created (also through consolidation of small plots) and mechanization would have to raise productivity.

> The Mansholt plan came as a considerable shock. The CAP had barely been established when farmers were confronted with the news that many of them were to be made redundant! Not surprisingly, Dr. Mansholt was given the title of 'the peasant killer'. Clearly, the plan was a political hot potato – so much so that the Council of Ministers gave it the cold shoulder. (Swann, 1995, p. 257)

The relevant fact is that in 1968 the Community was not yet self-sufficient in food production, whereas this had become the case in the early 1990s. At this point, farm lobbies began to lose some of their power.

12. Non-participating member states may opt to pay their farmers in Euros. 'A Member State which opts for this possibility must then take the necessary steps to ensure that in the event of [a revaluation or a devaluation] the recipient does not receive an amount higher than would otherwise have been paid in the national currency.' This provision unnecessarily 'implies the need for greater complexity in the monitoring and control of such expenditure' (*Official Journal of the European Communities*, 1998a).

13. Tracy mentions 16.5 per cent in 1989 (Tracy, 1993, p. 82).

14. These figures refer to EU12. These data are taken from different sources with different years of reference ranging from 1990 to 1993.

15. Support regimes for northern products (livestock and cereals) have been more generous than those for the south (fruits, vegetables and wine).

16. For example, the little packets of butter which were handed out in Britain in 1980 to old age pensioners with their pensions, (see Middleton et al., 1993, p. 127).

17. Set-aside schemes can reduce environmental damage:

> many industrial countries have introduced environmental measures that provide financial incentives ... to limit or stop farming activities on environmentally sensitive land. For example, under the Conservation Reserve Program (CRP) in the United States, farmers have been paid to take out of production some 14.4

million hectares of 'highly erodible' cropland (covering some eight per cent of US cropland). (Tobey and Smets, 1996, p. 75)

The relationship between the CAP and the environment will be analysed in the next section. This point is mentioned here to stress the contradictory effects of set-aside schemes.

18. This is true. But it is equally important to stress that the PPP was introduced by the OECD in 1972 not for environmental but for economic reasons, that is, (a) because of the concern that polluting industries might realize competitive advantages through the subsidization of pollution prevention measures (Tobey and Smets, 1996, p. 74) and (b) at a time when the (very small) negative incidence that the costs of these measures might have on production began to be seen as contributing to the reduction of agricultural surpluses.

19. The shape of the MAC curve rests on the (arbitrary) assumption that if pollution emission is low, any extra dollar spent on pollution abatement reduces pollution by less than if the level of pollution emission is high.

20. It is unclear which areas this article refers to.

21. Southern Europe is significantly affected also by forest fires, which are caused both by agricultural practices (e.g. burning off wooded areas for grazing) and by criminal action.

22. The following categorization is taken from Brouwer and van Berkum, 1996, *passim.*

23. Brouwer and van Berkum include regulation 2078/92 in the accompanying measures, whereas here it is included in other measures.

8. Social Policies

1. The first genetically engineered lamb, named Dolly . . . was born two weeks ago [July 1997]. She was cloned from a fetal cell that had a human gene. . . . Cloning experts say the work is a milestone. Animals with human genes could be used, in theory, to produce hormones or other biological products to treat human disease. They could also be given human genetic diseases and used to test new treatments. And genetically altered animals might also produce organs that could be transplanted into humans with less chance of rejection than now exists. . . . Genetic engineering of human beings is now really on the horizon. (Kolata, 1997)

One can only shiver at the idea of what kind of 'human beings' might emerge from profit-driven laboratories.

2. It should be stressed that the effects of the introduction of TIs within capitalist production relations are neither only positive (as held by mainstream literature) nor only negative. Rather, these effects should be seen in terms of tendencies and counter-tendencies. As I have argued through the years, TIs both create new jobs requiring qualified and skilled labour (but some new jobs might already be unskilled) and at the same time de-qualify and de-skill existing jobs. The former is the tendency and the latter is the counter-tendency because, after a while, the new, qualified and skilled, jobs are subject to de-skilling and de-qualification (Carchedi, 1977, 1983, 1987, 1991, 1992).

3. The financing of trade and aid policy with former colonies, through the European Development Fund (EDF), does not come under the Union budget.

4. The budget distinguishes between appropriations for commitments and appropriations for payments. The former are expected expenditures whose implementation extends over several financial years. The latter relate only to the financial year. The estimated expenditures in table 8.1 refer to appropriations for payments (i.e. only for the year in question). Since revenues raised in the budget are intended to cover appropriations for payments (but not for commitments), the total in table 8.1 is equal to the total of table 8.2 below, which gives the expected revenues. The appropriation for commitments are given in table 8.1(a) and are necessarily bigger than those in table 8.1.

Table 8.1a   Estimated expenditures, 1998 (ECU m) and 1999 (Euro m)

	1998		1999	
EAGGF	40,937	(45.0)	40,949	(42.2)
Structural operations	33,691	(37.0)	39,260	(40.5)
External action	6,039	(6.6)	6,224	(6.4)
Research and technological development	3,491	(3.8)	3,450	(3.6)
Administrative expenditures	4,353	(4.8)	4,502	(4.6)
Other	2,502	(2.8)	2,544	(2.6)
Total	91,013	(100.0)	96,929	(100.0)

Note: figures in parentheses are percentages.

Source: European Commission, 1998, p. 7; and European Commission, 1999, p. 7.

5. Luxembourg was a net receiver in 1994 (0.2bn) but a net contributor in 1995 (0.1bn). There are no figures for Austria, Sweden and Finland because they had not yet joined the EU in 1994.

6. As to the way the ESF works, at the beginning of the programming period, in this case that of 1994–9, member states draw up their plans for the use of the ESF resources and make an application to the Commission. A member state submits a *plan*. Subsequently, the Commission together with the applicant state draws up the *Community Support Framework*. This sets up priorities, the amount of funding and the *operational programmes*. The latter set out the measures for the implementation of the priorities laid down in the Community Support Framework. Finally, in order to speed up procedures, the plan, the Community Support Framework and the operational programmes can be submitted, prior to consultation with the Commission, simultaneously as a *Single Programming Document*. The ESF can fund up to 50 per cent of total costs for some projects and up to 75 per cent of total costs for other projects.

7. The Financial Institute for Fisheries Guidance (FIFG) is mentioned here only for the sake of completeness but its resources are hardly relevant.

8. More generally, 'in the short run, it can be expected that the regions most affected are those dependent upon labour-intensive production, whether in agriculture or industry, i.e. declining industrial areas and rural regions, because of new competition from the East' (Camagni, 1992, p. 310). Also, with reference to Objective 1 regions, 'Even if the group of unfavored regions has shrunk, the dichotomy is still clear: a group of lagging regions is progressively diverging and will probably continue to do so in the next decade' (Camagni, 1992, p. 365).

9. Of course, the representation of such interest through institutional channels is far from being straightforward and unmediated.

10. Remember: the income multiplier does not create new value but explains the realization of already existing value, that is, commodities.

11. Subject, however, 'to the limitations and conditions laid down in this Treaty and by the measures adopted to give it effect'.

12. The higher rate of exploitation for non-EU workers can be either a conscious or an unconscious result of this state policy. In Canada, for example, foreign workers admitted through the Non-Immigrant Employment Authorization Program (NIEAP) are bonded to a specific job with a specific employer and for a specific period of time. This reduces their ability to negotiate their wages and working condition, thus increasing their coercion and exploitation since they have to 'accept whatever conditions they are offered or face deportation' (Sharma, 1997, p. 19). By 1993, 70 per cent of (im)migrant workers was made up of these temporary visa workers. As Sharma argues, 'the re-imposition (or the continuation) of unfree forms of labour power ... should be seen within the context of the attempt by the employers to secure (or increase) their profits and to further weaken the strength of the collective working class' (p. 29).

13. The precursors of Schengen are the Trevi group (set up in 1976 to enable European countries to cooperate on issues of terrorism) and several *ad hoc* groups (e.g. the Ad Hoc Group on Immigration, set up to end abuses by asylum seekers, rather than, as

one would expect, of asylum seekers by governments). The Trevi group 'extended its brief in the mid-1980s to embrace all the policing and security aspects of free movement, including immigration, visas, asylum-seekers, and border controls' (Webber, 1993b, p. 142). Immigration and asylum policies have thus been an aspect of criminal (in)justice ever since the Union began being concerned with these policies (which it always considered to be a matter for individual states to regulate). The Trevi group is supposed to be succeeded by Europol (TEU, article K.1). In its initial stage Europol is intended to be an intelligence-gathering operation. On the EU's immigration policies and asylum policies, one of the most shameful aspects of the process of European integration, see Bunyan, 1993; Webber, 1993a, 1993b. The trend is for all these 'ad hoc groups under the umbrella of intergovernmental cooperation ... to be replaced by permanent institutions under the auspices of the Council of Ministers' (Bunyan, 1993, p. 15).

14. By 1998, the Convention had been implemented by Germany, France, Belgium, Luxembourg, Holland, Spain, Portugal, Italy and Austria. Denmark, Sweden, Norway, Finland and Iceland were scheduled to join too. The United Kingdom and Ireland are not members of the Schengen System. The Schengen Convention has not been incorporated into the TEU, which has opted to retain the intergovernmental system. Article 131 of the Schengen Convention sets up an Executive Committee of ministers for the implementation of the Convention itself. Each of the thirteen Contracting Parties (the fifteen EU member states less Ireland and the UK) has the right to one seat on the Committee. The Committee delegates the day-to-day operations to the Central Negotiating Group and to its working parties. Since the Committee's decisions must be taken by unanimity (article 132), the procedure is rather cumbersome. To overcome this drawback, the Amsterdam Treaty incorporates the Schengen System through the 'Protocol Integrating the Schengen Acquis [i.e. the body of legislation upon which the EU rests] into the framework of the European Union'. Article 1 of the Protocol states that cooperation concerning the Schengen Acquis 'shall be conducted within the institutional and legal framework of the European Union'. Consequently, the Council 'shall substitute itself to the Executive Committee' (article 2). The Schengen Acquis will have to be implemented by all EU member states by 2002. Consequently, the United Kingdom and Ireland might have to join this system by that time.

9. Epilogue

1. This applies also to declarations and analyses such as those of the 70 Dutch economists (Verklaring, 1997) and of the 331 European economists (Open letter, 1997). These positions, while challenging the monetarist orthodoxy, do not challenge the irrationality of the capitalist system.
2. I borrow this notion from Albert and Hahnel, 1991.
3. However, if a balanced structure of positions is impossible because, say, certain tasks are so unattractive that they cannot be balanced with any desirable task available in that labour process, each labourer in turn will have to take his or her fair share of that task. This applies also to labourers of other labour processes filling positions whose positive tasks can only partly be compensated by negative ones. As Albert and Hahnel (1991) put it: 'equity would come on average – over reasonable spans of time' (p. 30). This is another reason why rotation within as well as among labour processes is a necessary feature of an egalitarian technical division of labour.

Bibliography

Accattatis, V. (1996) 'Cittadini Europei o sudditi delle multinazionali?', *Altraeuropa*, Anno 2, No. 5, Ottobre–Dicembre, pp. 7–10.

Acosta, A. (n.d.) 'La Trampa de la Dolarización: Mitos y Realidades para a Reflexion'. Unpublished Paper.

Acosta, A. and Schuldt, J. (2000) 'Dolarización vacuna para la Hiperinflación?' Unpublished Paper.

Albert, M. and Hahnel, R. (1991) *Looking Forward: Participatory Economics for the Twenty First Century*, South End Press, Boston.

Allen, R. E. (1994) *Financial Crises and Recession in the Global Economy*, Edward Elgar, Cheltenham.

Anderson, P. (1997), 'Under the Sign of the Interim', in P. Anderson and P. Gowan (eds), *The Question of Europe*, Verso, London, pp. 51–71.

Anderson, P. and Gowan, P. (eds) (1997), *The Question of Europe*, Verso, London.

Armstrong, H., Taylor, J. and Williams, A. (1994) 'Regional Policy', in M. J. Artis and N. Lee (eds), *The Economics of the European Union*, Oxford University Press, pp. 172–201.

Bank of International Settlements (1999) *69th Annual Report*, Basle, 7 June.

Bergsten, C. F. (1999) 'Dollarization in Emerging-Market Economies and Its Policy Implications for the United States'. Statement before the Joint Hearing of the Subcommittee on Economic Policy and the Subcommittee on International Trade and Finance, Committee on Banking, Housing and Urban Affairs of the US Senate, Institute for International Economics, 22 April.

Bieling, H.-J. and Steinhilber, J. (1997), 'Zur Dynamik der Europäischen Integration: Theorien und Projekte', Z., No. 32, December, pp. 18–30.

Bladen-Hovell, R. and Symons, E. (1994), 'The EC Budget', in M. Artis and N. Lee (eds), *The Economics of the European Union*, Oxford University Press, Oxford, pp. 368–87.

Bogetic, Z. (1999) 'Official or "Full" Dollarization: Current Experiences and Issues', *International Monetary Fund*, 9 June.

Bojnec, S. (1996) 'Integration of Central Europe in the Common Agricultural Policy of the European Union', *The World Economy*, Vol. 14, No. 4, pp. 447–63.

Boisson, J.-M. (1999) 'Le Devenir de L'Euro', *EURO*, No. 46, I, pp. 3–6.

Bonefeld, W. and Burnham, P. (1996) 'Britain and the Politics of the European Exchange Rate Mechanism 1990–92'. *Capital and Class*, No. 60, Autumn, pp. 5–38.

Borchardt, K.-D. (1994) *The ABC of Community Law*, Office for Official Publications of the European Communities, Luxembourg.

Borensztein, E. (1999) Transcript of a speech on 'Dollarization: Fad or Future for Latin America?', *IMF Economic Forum*, 24 June.

Broek, M. (1998) 'Military Spending and Development: The Role of the Peace Movement'. Paper presented at the Conference on 'The Economics of Military Expenditure in Developing and Emerging Economies', Middlesex University, 13–14 March.

Brouwer, F. M. and van Berkum, S. (1996), *Cap and Environment in the European Union*, Wageningen Pers, Wageningen.

Buchanan, J. M. (1962a) 'Politics and the Economic Nexus', in J. M. Buchanan and G. Tullock (eds), *The Calculus of Consent*, University of Michigan Press, Ann Arbor.

Buchanan, J. M. (1962b) 'Individual Rationality in Social Choice', in J. M. Buchanan and G. Tullock (eds), *The Calculus of Consent*, University of Michigan Press, Ann Arbor.

Buckley, S. and Dudley, S. (2000) 'Vice President Takes Power in Ecuador', *International Herald Tribune* (Paris), 24 January.

Buerkle, T. (1998) 'London–Frankfurt Stock Linkup Set', *Internatonal Herald Tribune*, 8 July.

Bulmer, S. (1994) 'History and Institutions of the European Union', in M. Artis and N. Lee (eds), *The Economics of the European Union* Oxford University Press, Oxford.

Bunyan, T. (1993) 'Trevi, Europol, and the European State', in T. Bunyan (ed.), *Statewatching the New Europe*, Russel Press, Nottingham, pp. 15–36.

Camagni, R. P. (1992) 'Development Scenarios and Policy Guidelines for the Lagging Regions in the 1990s, *Regional Studies*, Vol. 26, pp. 361–74.

Carchedi, B. (1999) *Colpirne Uno per Educarne Conto*, AltraEuropa, Milan.

Carchedi, G. (1975) 'On the Economic Identification of the New Middle Class', *Economy and Society*, February, pp. 1–87.

Carchedi, G. (1977) *On the Economic Identification of Social Classes*, Routledge and Kegan Paul, London.

Carchedi, G. (1983) *Problems in Class Analysis: Production, Knowledge and the Function of Capital*, Routledge and Kegan Paul, London.

Carchedi, G. (1987) *Class Analysis and Social Research*, Basil Blackwell, Oxford.

Carchedi, G. (1989) 'Between Class Analysis and Organization Theory: Mental Labour', in S. Clegg (ed.), *Organization Theory and Class Analysis*, Walter de Gruyter, Berlin and New York, pp. 346–61.

Carchedi, G. (1990) 'Classes and Class Analysis', in E. O. Wright (ed.), *The Debate on Class*, Verso, London, pp. 105–25.

Carchedi, G. (1991a) *Frontiers of Political Economy*, Verso, London.

Carchedi, G. (1991b) 'Technological Innovations, Internal Production Prices and Exchange Rates', *Cambridge Journal of Economics*, Vol. 15, No. 1, pp. 45–60.

Carchedi, G. (1992) *The Social Production of Knowledge*, Università degli Studi di Roma 'La Sapienza', Materiale di Discussione No. 13.

Carchedi, G. (1993) 'Technological Transfer and Social Transformation: Reflections on 1989', in G. C. Liodakis (ed.), *Society, Technology and Restructuring of Production*, Athens, pp. 54–87.

Carchedi, G. (1996) 'Financial Crises, Recessions and Value Theory', *Review of International Political Economy*, Autumn, pp. 528–37.

Carchedi, G. (1997) 'The EMU, Monetary Crises and the Single European Currency', *Capital and Class*, No. 63, Autumn, pp. 85–114.

Carchedi, G. (1999a) 'Democracy, the Market, and Egalitarianism', in J. Milios, L. Katseli and P. Pelagidis (eds), *Rethinking Democracy and the Welfare State*, Ellinka Grammata, Athens, pp. 28–49.

Carchedi, G. (1999b) 'A Missed Opportunity: Orthodox versus Marxist Crises Theories', *Historical Materialism*, No. 4, Summer, pp. 33–57.

Carchedi, G. and de Haan, W. (1996) 'The Transformation Procedure: A Non-Equilibrium Approach', in A. Freeman and G. Carchedi (eds), *Marx and Non-Equilibrium Economics*, Edward Elgar, Cheltenham, pp. 136–64.

Chipongian, L. C. (2000) 'Roxas Says Gov't in Favor of ASEAN Common Currency', *The Manila Times*, 20 April.

Chossudovsky, M. (1997) *The Globalization of Poverty: Impacts of IMF and World Bank Reforms*, Zed Books, London and Atlantic Highlands, NJ.

Chote, R. and de Jonquières, G. (1999), 'Outlook: Economists Find Plenty to Worry About', *Financial Times*, 29 January.

Chuter, D. (1997) 'The United Kingdom', in J. Howorth and A. Menon (eds), *The European Union and National Defence Policy*, Routledge, London, pp. 105–20.

Convey, A. and Kupiszewski, M. (1995) 'Keeping up with Schengen: Migration and Policy in the European Union', *Internatonal Migration Review*, Vol. XXIX, No. 4, Winter, pp. 939–63.

Corporate Europe Observatory (1997) *Europe Inc.*, <http://www.xs4all.nl/~ceo>.

Council for Investment and Development (1999) *Economic Indicators* <http://www.businesspanama.com>.

Court of Auditors (1995) 'Annual Report Concerning the Financial Year 1994 Together with the Institutions' Replies', *Official Journal of the European Communities*, Vol. 39, 14 November.

Cumings, B. (1998) 'The Korean Crisis and the End of "Late" Development', *New Left Review*, No. 231. September/October, pp. 43–73.

Davenport, M., Hewitt, A. and Koning, A. (1995) 'Europe's Preferred Partners? How the ACP Countries Should Develop Their Trade', *The ACP–EU Courier*, No. 156, March–April, pp. 63–4.

de Bont, C. J. A. M. (1994) 'Markt – en Prijsbeleid (I): Basisprodukten', in J. de Hoog and H. J. Silvis (eds), *EU-landbouwpolitiek van binnen en van buiten*, Wageningen Pers, Wageningen, pp. 51–64.

Dinucci, M. (1998) 'La Nuova Strategia della Nato', *L'Ernesto*, March–April, pp. 26–8.

Dumas, L. J. (1998) 'The Role of Demilitarization in Promoting Democracy and Prosperity in Africa'. Paper presented the Conference on 'The Economics of Military Expenditure in Developing and Emerging Economies', Middlesex University, 13–14 March.

Economic Commission for Europe (1995) *Economic Bulletin for Europe*, Vol. 47, New York and Geneva.

Economist, The (1997) 'Doing the Splits', 8 March.

El Comercio (2000a) 'El Banco Central Votó a Favor de la Medida: el Congreso respalda', 11 January.

El Comercio (2000b) 'Reacciones a Nivel Internacional', 11 January.

El Comercio (2000c) 'El Nuevo Esquema Bancario', 13 January.

El Comercio (2000d) 'Dolarización, 45 Respuestas', 16 January.

El Comercio (2000e) 'Ley Trole con observaciones del FMI', 27 February.

Elf-Thorffin, C. (2000) 'Improving Financial Co-operation', *The ACP–EU Courier*, European Commission, Brussels, Belgium, No. 181, June–July, pp. 24–5.

Europa van Morgen (1996) No. 16, 23 October, pp. 238–42.

Europa van Morgen (1997) No. 12, 19 June, pp. 173–6.

European Centre of Development Policy Management (1996) *Beyond Lomé IV*, Maastricht.

European Commission (1990) *Community Charter of the Fundamental Social Rights of Workers*, Office for Official Publications of the European Communities, Luxembourg.

European Commission (1994a) *EC Agricultural Policy for the 21st Century, European Economy*, No. 4, Luxembourg.

European Commission (1994b) *European Social Policy*, Office for Official Publications of the European Communities, Luxembourg.

European Commission (1995) *The European Social Fund*, Office for Official Publications of the European Communities, Luxembourg.

European Commission (1996a) *The Budget of the European Union: How is Your Money Spent?*, Office of Official Publications of the European Communities, Luxembourg.

European Commission (1996b) *Hoe Beheert de Europese Unie landbouw en visserij?*, Office of Official Publications of the European Communities, Luxembourg.

European Commission (1998) General Budget of the European Union for the Financial Year 1998, *The Figures*, Brussels and Luxembourg.

European Commission (1999) General Budget of the European Union for the Financial Year 1999, *The Figures*, Brussels and Luxembourg.

European Foundation for the Improvement of Living and Working Conditions (1997) *Working Conditions in the European Union*, Dublin.

European Parliament (1992) Directorate-General for Research, *The Agrimonetary System of the European Economic Community and its prospects after 1992*, Luxembourg.

Eurostat (1996) *Statistics in Focus, External Trade*, No. 7, Luxembourg.

Eurostat (1997) *External and Intra-European Trade, Statistical Yearbook, 1958–1996*, Luxembourg.

Eurostat (1998) *Statistics in Focus, External Trade*, No. 3, Luxembourg.

Falcoff, M. (1999) 'Dollarization for Argentina? For Latin America?', *Latin American Outlook*, April.

Ferrara, G. (1996) 'Europa: quale costituzione?', *Altraeuropa*, Anno 2, No. 5, Ottobre–Dicembra, pp. 11–15.

Finardi, S., Trenti, S. and Violante, S. (1988) *World Transport and Trade*, Saima-Avandero Group, Milan.

Fischer, S. (1982) 'Seigniorage and the Case for a National Money', *Journal of Political Economy*, Vol. 90, No. 2. April, pp. 295–313.

Frank, A. G. (1972) *Lumpenbourgeoisie and Lumpendevelopment*, Monthly Review Press, New York.

Frankel, J. A. (1999) Transcript of a speech on 'Dollarization: Fad or Future for Latin America?', *IMF Economic Forum*, 24 June.

Freeman, A. (1998a) 'Il Terzo Pilastro', *Alternative Europa*, Ottobre–Novembre, pp. 54–9.

Freeman, A. (1998b) 'Diritti di Proprieta Intelletuale e "Libero" Commercio', *Alternative Europa*, Dicembre, pp. 52–6.

Freeman, A. (1999) 'Crisis and the Poverty of Nations: Two Market Products Which Value Explains Better'. Unpublished Paper, University of Greenwich, London.

Friends of the Earth Europe (1995) *Towards Sustainable Europe*, Brussels.

Galtung, J. (1972) *De EEG als Nieuwe Supermacht*, Van Gennep, Amsterdam. (Dutch translation of *The European Community: A Superpower in the Making*.)

Geddes, A. (1995) 'Immigrant and Ethnic Minorities and the EU's "Democratic Deficit"', *Journal of Common Market Studies*, Vol. 33, No. 2, June, pp. 197–217.

George, S. (1999) 'Seattle Prepares for Battle – Trade before Freedom', *Le Monde Diplomatique*, November.

Gill, S. (1997) 'The Global Political Economy and the European Union: EMU and Alternatives to Neo-Liberalism'. Unpublished paper.

Giusanni, P. (n.d.) 'On the Economics of Piero Sraffa'. Unpublished paper.

Gowan, P. (1995) 'Neo-Liberal Theory and Practice for Eastern Europe', *New Left Review*, No. 213, September–October, pp. 3–60.

Greider, W. (1997) 'In the Go-Go Global Economy, a Creeping Sense of "Oh No"', *International Herald Tribune*, 2 October.

Hakim, P. (1999) 'Is Latin American Doomed to Failure?' Abstract adapted from an article appearing in the Winter 1999–2000 issue of *Foreign Policy* magazine.

Hanke, S. H. and Schuler, K. (1999) 'A Dollarization Blueprint for Argentina', *Foreign Policy Briefing*, No. 52, 11 March.

Harris, S., Swinbank, A. and Wilkinson, G. (1983) *The Food and Farm Policies of the European Community*, John Wiley and Sons, Chichester.

Henwood, D. (1997) *Wall Street: How It Works and for Whom*, Verso, London.

Hewitt, A. and Koning, A. (1996) 'Europe's Preferred Partners? How the ACP Countries Should Develop Their Trade', *The ACP–EU Courier*, No. 156, March–April, pp. 63–4.

Hoekman, B. M. and Kostecki, M. M. (1995) *The Political Economy of the World Trading System, from GATT to WTO*, Oxford University Press, Oxford.

Hollman, O. and van der Pijl, K. (1996) 'The Capitalist Class in the European Union', in G. A. Kourvetaris and A. Moschonas (eds), *The Impact of European Integration*, Praeger, Westport, CT, pp. 55–74.

Howorth, J. (1997) 'National Defence and European Security Integration', in J. Howorth and A. Menon (eds), *The European Union and National Defence Policy*, Routledge, London, pp. 10–22.

Ichiyo, M. (1987) *Class Struggle and Technological Innovation in Japan Since 1945*, Notebooks for Study and Research No. 5, International Institute for Research and Education, Amsterdam.

International Labour Organization (1996) *Second Unemployment Report*, November, Geneva.

Irving, R. W. and Fearn, H. A. (1975) *Green Money and the Common Agricultural Policy*, Centre for European Agricultural Studies, Wye College, Ashford, Kent.

Julia, C. H. (2000) 'La Estrategia Ecuador', *Realidad Economica*, No. 170, February–March, pp. 46–57.

Kemp, J. (1992) 'Competition Policy', in F. McDonald and S. Dearden (eds), *European Economic Integration*, Longman, London and New York, pp. 59–81.

Kempster, T. (1998) 'Military Spending and Development: The Role of the Peace Movement'. Paper given at the Conference on 'The Economics of Military Expenditure in Developing and Emerging Economies', Middlesex University, 13–14 March.

Kenen, P. B. (1969) 'The Theory of Optimum Currency Areas: An Eclectic View', in R. A. Mundell and A. K. Swoboda (eds), *Monetary Problems of the International Economy*, University of Chicago Press, Chicago, pp. 41–60.

Kiljunen, K. (1986) 'The International Division of Industral Labour and the Core–Periphery Concept', *CEPAL Review*, Comisión Económica de las Naciones Undias para América Latina y el Caribe, Santiago, Chile, December.

Kolata, G. (1997) 'Dolly's Creators Take Next Step', *International Herald Tribune*, 26–7 July.

Krugman, P. R. and Obstefeld, M. (1994) *International Economics*, Harper-Collins, London.

Lancaster, J. (2000) 'Despite Taking Root, Democracy in Latin America Remains Fragile', *International Herald Tribune*, 1 February.

Latino Beat (1999) 'U.S. Cautions Latin America on "Dollarization"', 16 March.

Linder, M. (1977) *Anti-Samuelson*, Urizen Books.

Louis, J.-V. (1997) 'Le Traité de Amsterdam: Une Occasion perdue?', *Revue du Marché Unique Européen*, No. 2, pp. 5–18.

McKinnon, R. I. (1963) 'Optimum Currency Areas', *American Economic Review*, Vol. LIII, No. 4, September, pp. 717–25.

MA.GA (2000) 'A Quito il dollaro regna sovrano: Il governo dice addio al sucre', *Il Manifesto*, 11 March.

Mandel, E. (1970) *Europe vs. America: Contradictions of Imperialism*, Monthly Review Press, New York.

Marsh, J. (1977) 'Europe's agriculture: reform of the CAP', *International Affairs*, Vol. 53, No. 4, pp. 604–14.

Martone, F. (2000) 'Ecuador dollarizzato e ... blindato', *Il manifesto*, 16 January.

Marx, K. (1967a) *Capital Vol. I*, Progress Publishers, New York.

Marx, K. (1967b) *Capital, Vol. II*, Progress Publishers, New York.

Marx, K. (1967c) *Capital, Vol. III*, Progress Publishers, New York.

Marx, K. (1992) *Ökonomische Manuskripte, 1863–1867, Text, Teil 2*, ed. Manfred Müller et al., Dietz Verlag, Berlin/Internationales Institut für Sozialgeschichte, Amsterdam.

Mead, M. (1962) *Sex and Temperament in Three Primitive Societies*, Dell Publishing Company, New York.

Menshikov, M. (1998) 'Problems of Conversion in Russia'. Paper presented at the Conference on 'The Economics of Military Expenditure in Developing and Emerging Economies', Middlesex University, 13–14 March.

Middleton, N., O'Keefe, P. and Moyo, S. (1993) *The Tears of the Crocodile*, Pluto Press, London.

Mihevc, J. (1995), *The Market Tells Them So*, Zed Books, London and Atlantic Highlands, NJ.

Moody, K. (1997) 'Towards an International Social-Movement Unionism', *New Left Review*, No. 225, September–October, pp. 52–72.

Moreno-Villalaz, J. L. (1999) 'Lessons from the Monetary Experience of Panama: A Dollar Economy with Financial Integration', *Cato Journal*, Vol. 18, No. 3, pp. 421–39.

Moseley, F. (1986) 'The Intensity of Labour and the Productivity Slowdown', *Science and Society*, Vol. I, No. 2, pp. 210–18.

Moseley, F. (1988a) 'The Rate of Surplus Value, the Organic Composition, and the General Estimates', *American Economic Review*, March, pp. 298–303.

Moseley, F. (1988b) 'The Decline of the Rate of Profit in the Postwar US Economy: Regulation and Marxian Explanations'. Paper presented to the 'Conferencio Internacional acerca de la Teoria de la Regulación', Barcelona, June.

Moseley, F. (ed.) (1989a) 'Declining Profitability and the Current Crisis', *International Journal of Political Economy*, Vol. 19, No. 1, Spring.

Moseley, F. (1989b) 'Introduction', in F. Moseley (ed.), 'Declining Profitability and the Current Crisis', *International Journal of Political Economy*, Vol. 19, No. 1, Spring, pp. 3–9.

Moseley, F. (1989c) 'The Decline in the Rate of Profit in the Postwar US Economy', in F. Moseley (ed.), 'Declining Profitability and the Current Crisis', *International Journal of Political Economy*, Vol. 19, No. 1, Spring, pp. 48–68.

Moss, N. (2000) 'Ecuador: Dollarization to Go Ahead', *Financial Times*, 3 February.

Mundell, R. A. (1961) 'A Theory of Optimum Currency Areas', *American Economic Review*, Vol. LI, No. 4, September, pp. 657–64.

Newman, M. (1989), *Britain and the EEC: Effects of Membership*, European Dossiers series, PNL Press, London.

Notizie Internazionali (1997) No. 52, October.

Official Journal of the European Communities (1962) Council Regulation No. 129 on the value of the unit of account and the exchange rates to be applied for the purposes of the Common Agricultural Policy, 30 October.

Official Journal of the European Communities (1968a) Council Regulation No. 653 on conditions for alterations to the value of the unit of account used for the Common Agricultural Policy, 31 May.

Official Journal of the European Communities (1968b) Council Regulation No. 1134 laying down rules for the implementation of Regulation (EEC) No. 653/68 on conditions for alterations to the value of the unit of account used for the Common Agricultural Policy, 1 June.

Official Journal of the European Communities (1971) Council Regulation No. 974 on certain measures of conjunctural policy to be taken in agriculture following the temporary widening of the margin of fluctuation for the currencies of certain member states, 12 May.

Official Journal of the European Communities (1973) Council Regulation No. 1112 amending regulation No. 974/71 on certain measures of conjunctural policy to be taken in agriculture following the temporary widening of the margins of fluctuation for the currencies of certain member states, 30 April.

Official Journal of the European Communities (1991) Council Regulation No. 2092 on organic production of agricultural products and indications referring thereto on agricultural products and foodstuffs, 24 June.

Official Journal of the European Communities (1992) Council Regulation No. 2078 on agricultural production methods compatible with the requirements of the protection of the environment and the maintenance of the countryside, 30 July.

Official Journal of the European Communities (1998a) Opinion No. 8/98 adopted by the Court of Auditors on a proposal for a Council Regulation establishing an agri-monetary system denominated in Euro, 27 November.

Official Journal of the European Communities (1998b) Council Regulation (EC) No. 2799/98 establishing agri-monetary arrangements for the Euro, 24 December.

Open letter from European economists to the heads of government of the 15 member states of the European Union (1997) Electronic version, 12 June.

Ortiz, G. (1999) Transcript of a speech on 'Dollarization: Fad or Future for Latin America?', *IMF Economic Forum*, 24 June.

PANOS (1997) 'Third World: Feast or Famine? Food Security in the New Millennium', *Race and Class*, Vol. 38, No. 3, pp. 63–72.

Paterson, H. (2000) 'E. Timor Adopts Dollar as Currency', *Los Angeles Times*, 24 January.

Purdy, D. and Devine, P. (1994) 'Social Policy', in M. Artis and N. Lee (eds), *The Economics of the European Union*, Oxford University Press, Oxford, pp. 269–94.

Ricardo, D. (1966) *On the Principles of Political Economy and Taxation*, Cambridge University Press, Cambridge.

Rieger, E. (1996) 'The Common Agricultural Policy: External and Internal Dimensions', in H. Wallace and W. Wallace (eds), *Policy-making in the European Union*, Oxford University Press, Oxford, pp. 96–123.

Robinson, J. (1962) *Economic Philosophy*, Penguin, Harmondsworth.

Roodman, D. M. (1997) 'Reforming Subsidies', in L. R. Brown, C. Flavin and H. French (eds), *The State of the World 1997*, W. W. Norton and Company, New York and London.

Rother, L. (2000) 'Ecuador Prepares for Indian Protests', *New York Times*, 16 January.

Sachs, J. and Larrain, F. (1999) 'Why Dollarization is More Straitjacket Than Salvation', *Foreign Policy*, Fall, pp. 80–92.

Schuler, K. (1999a) *Encouraging Official Dollarization in Emerging Markets.* Joint Economic Committee Staff Report April.

Schuler, K. (1999b) *Basics of Dollarization.* Joint Economic Committee Staff Report, July.

Seabrook, J. (1990) *The Myth of the Market*, Green Books, Bideford, Devon.

Sharma, N. R. (1997) 'Birds of Prey or Birds of Passage: The Movement of Capital and the Migration of Labour', *Labour, Capital and Society*, Vol. 30, No. 1, April, pp. 8–38.

Silvis, H. J. and Mookhoek, M. L. (1994) 'Gemeemschappelik markt – en prijsbeleid bij veranderende wisselkoersen, in J. de Hoog and H. J. Silvis (eds), *EU-landbouwpolitiek van binnen en van buiten*, Wageningen Pers, Wageningen, pp. 76–86.

Simon, H. (1976) 'From Substantive to Procedural Rationality', in F. Hahn and M. Hollis (eds), *Philosophy and Economic Theory*, Oxford University Press, Oxford, pp. 65–86.

Simon, H. (1979) 'Rational Decision Making in Business Organization', *The American Economic Review*, Vol. 69, No. 4, September, pp. 493–513.

Stein, R. (1999) *Issues Regarding Dollarization*, Subcommittee on Economic Policy, US Senate Banking, Housing and Urban Affairs Committee.

Strange, S. (1998) 'The New Dollar Debt', *New Left Review*, No. 23, July–August, pp. 91–115.

Swann, D. (1994) *The Economics of the Common Market* (7th edn), Penguin, Harmondsworth.

Swann, D. (1995) *The Economics of the Common Market* (8th edn), Penguin, Harmondsworth.

Testimony of Senator Jim Bunning (1999) Hearing on Official Dollarization in Emerging-Market Countries, Subcommittee on Economic Policy and International Trade and Finance, Opening Statement, 22 April.

Testimony of Prof. Guillermo A. Calvo (1999) Joint Hearing of the Subcommittees on Economic Policy and International Trade and Finance, Washington, DC, 22 April.

Testimony of Dr Michael Gavin (1999) Hearing on Official Dollarization in Latin America, Subcommittee on Economic Policy and International Trade and Finance, 15 July.

Testimony of Senator Chuck Hagel (1999) Hearing on Official Dollarization in Emerging-Market Countries, Subcommittee on Economic Policy and International Trade and Finance, Opening Statement, 22 April.

Testimony of Dr David Malpass (1999) Hearing on Official Dollarization in Emerging-Market Countries, Subcommittee on Economic Policy and International Trade and Finance, 15 July.

Testimony of Dr Liliana Rojas-Suarez (1999) Hearing on Official Dollarization in Latin America, Subcommittee on Economic Policy and International Trade and Finance, 15 July.

Tobey, J. A. and Smets, H. (1996) 'The Polluter-Pays Principle in the Context of Agriculture and the Environment', *The World Economy*, Vol. 19, No. 1, pp. 63–87.

Tracy, M. (1993) *Food and Agriculture in a Market Economy*, APS – Agricultural Policy Studies, La Hutte, Belgium.

Tracy, M. (1996) *Agricultural Policy in the European Union*, APS – Agricultural Policy Studies, La Hutte, Belgium.

Tsoukalis, L. (1993) *The New European Economy: The Politics and Economics of Integration* (2nd edn), Oxford University Press, Oxford.

United Nations Development Programme (1998) *Human Development Report*, Oxford University Press, Oxford.

United Nations Development Programme (1999) *Human Development Report*, Oxford University Press, Oxford.

US Arms Control and Disarmament Agency (1996) *World Military Expenditures and Arms Transfers (WMEAT) 1996*, Washington, DC.

US Federal Reserve (1994) Board of Governors of the Federal Reserve System, *The Federal Reserve System: Purposes and Functions*, Washington, DC.

US Federal Reserve (2000) Federal Reserve Statistical Releases, H3 Historical

Data, *Aggregate Reserves of Depository Institutions Not Adjusted for Changes in Reserve Requirements and Not Seasonally Adjusted*, Washington, DC, 27 January <http://www.bog.frb.fed.us/releases/h3/hist/h3hist2>.

US Treasury (1999) Office of Public Affairs, Speech by Deputy Treasury Secretary Lawrence H. Summers at the Senate Banking Committee Subcommittee on Economic Policy and Subcommittee on International Trade and Finance, *Treasury News*, 22 April.

Van der Laan, L. (1999) 'Liberalisering Handel Helpt Zwakkeren', *De Volkskrant*, 24 November.

Venneman, J. G. B. and Gerritsen, J. (1994) 'EU-Mileubelied en landbow', in J. de Hoog and H. J. Silvis (eds), *EU-landbouwpolitiek van bingen en van buiten*, Wageningen Pers, Wageningen, pp. 114–22.

Verhoeve, B., Graham, B. and Wilkinson, D. (1992) *Maastricht and the Environment*, Institute for European Environmental Policy, Arnhem.

Verklaring van zeventing Nederlandse economen inzake de Economische en Monetaire Unie (1997) *De Volkskrant*, 13 February.

Vinocour, J. (1997a) 'Poverty Grows Quietly Along with Wealth', *International Herald Trbune*, 15 October.

Vinocour, J. (1997b) 'Secret Wealth Undermines the Social Model', *International Herald Tribune*, 16 October.

Wade, R. and Veneroso, F. (1998) 'The Gathering World Slump and the Battle Over Capital Controls', *New Left Review*, No. 231, September–October, pp. 13–42.

Walras, L. (1977) *Elements of Pure Economics*, A. M. Kelley, Fairfield, ME.

Webber, F. (1993a) 'The New Europe: Immigration and Asylum', in T. Bunyan (ed.), *Statewatching the New Europe*, Russel Press, Nottingham, pp. 130–41.

Webber, F. (1993b) 'European Conventions on Immigration and Asylum', in T. Bunyan (ed.), *Statewatching the New Europe*, Russel Press, Nottingham, pp. 142–53.

Weinstock, U. (1975) 'Vom "Grünen Dollar" zur Gemeinschaftswährung – die Bedeutung der Rechnungseinheiten für die europäische Integration', in W. von Urff (ed.), *Der Agrarsektor im Integrationsprozeß*, Nomas Verlagsgesellschaft, Baden Baden, pp. 115–46.

Working Group on the WTO/MAI (1999), *A Citizen's Guide to the World Trade Organization*, Inkworks, electronic version, July.

World Bank (1993) 'Poverty and Income Distribution in Latin America', *HRO Dissemination Notes*, No. 3, 29 March.

Young, D. and Metcalfe, S. (1994) 'Competition Policy', in M. Artis and N. Lee (eds), *The Economics of the European Union*, Oxford University Press, Oxford, pp. 119–38.

Ypersele, J. (1985), *The European Monetary System*, The European Perspectives series, Commission of the European Communities, Brussels.

Index